NOSATSU JUNKIE

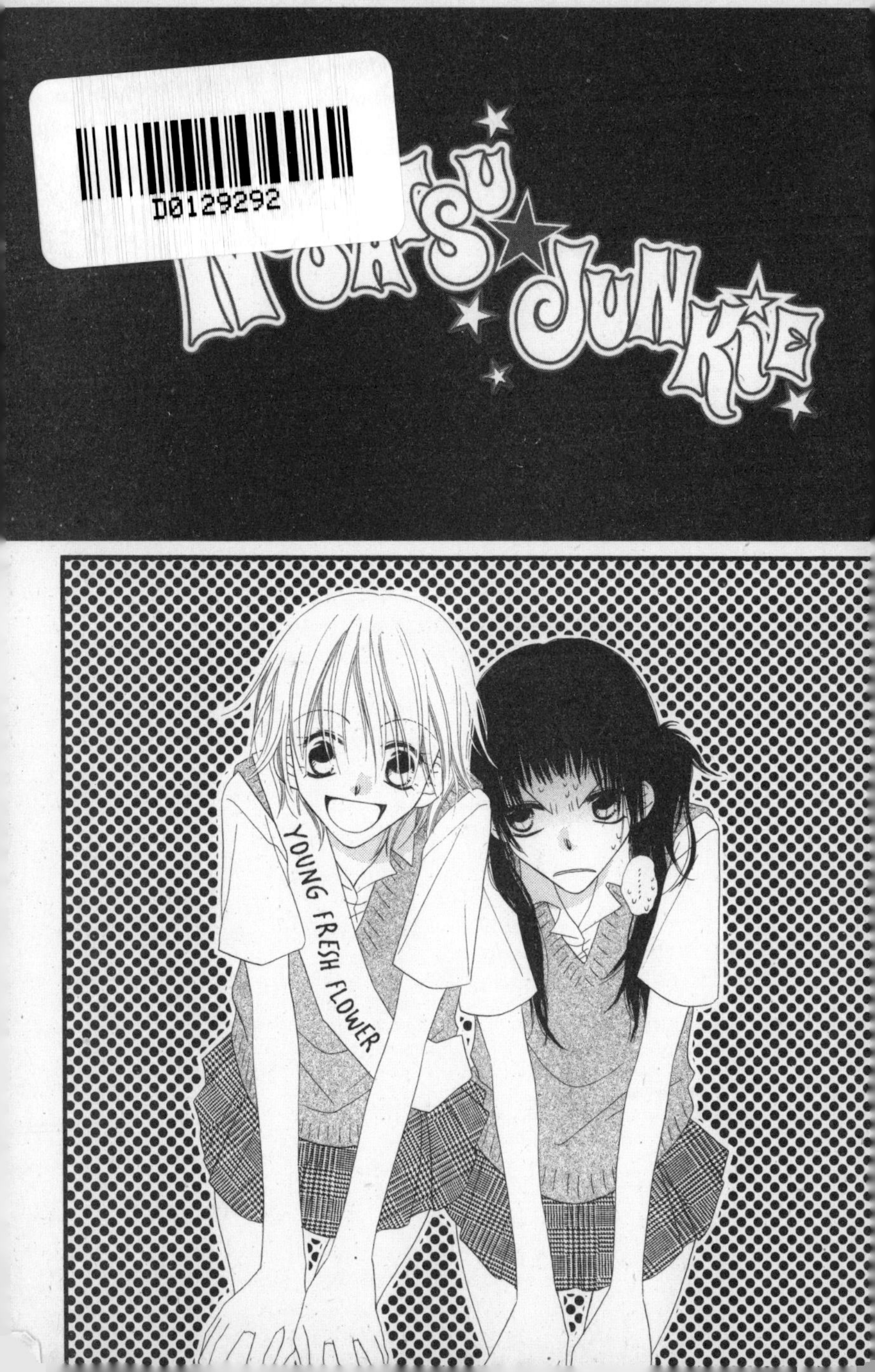
YOUNG FRESH FLOWER

Nosatsu Junkie vol.1
Created by Ryoko Fukuyama

Translation - Alethea Nibley
English Adaptation - Lorelei Laird
Retouch and Lettering - Jennifer Carbajal
Graphic Designer - Jose Macasocol, Jr.

Editor - Carol Fox
Digital Imaging Manager - Chris Buford
Pre-Production Supervisor - Erika Terriquez
Art Director - Anne Marie Horne
Production Manager - Elisabeth Brizzi
Managing Editor - Vy Nguyen
VP of Production - Ron Klamert
Editor-in-Chief - Rob Tokar
Publisher - Mike Kiley
President and C.O.O. - John Parker
C.E.O. and Chief Creative Officer - Stuart Levy

A  Manga

TOKYOPOP Inc.
5900 Wilshire Blvd. Suite 2000
Los Angeles, CA 90036

E-mail: info@TOKYOPOP.com
Come visit us online at www.TOKYOPOP.com

ISBN: 1-59816-654-9

First TOKYOPOP printing: December 2006
10 9 8 7 6 5 4 3 2 1
Printed in the USA

NOSATSU JUNKIE

VOLUME 1

BY
RYOKO FUKUYAMA

TOKYOPOP®

HAMBURG // LONDON // LOS ANGELES // TOKYO

NOSATSU JUNKIE

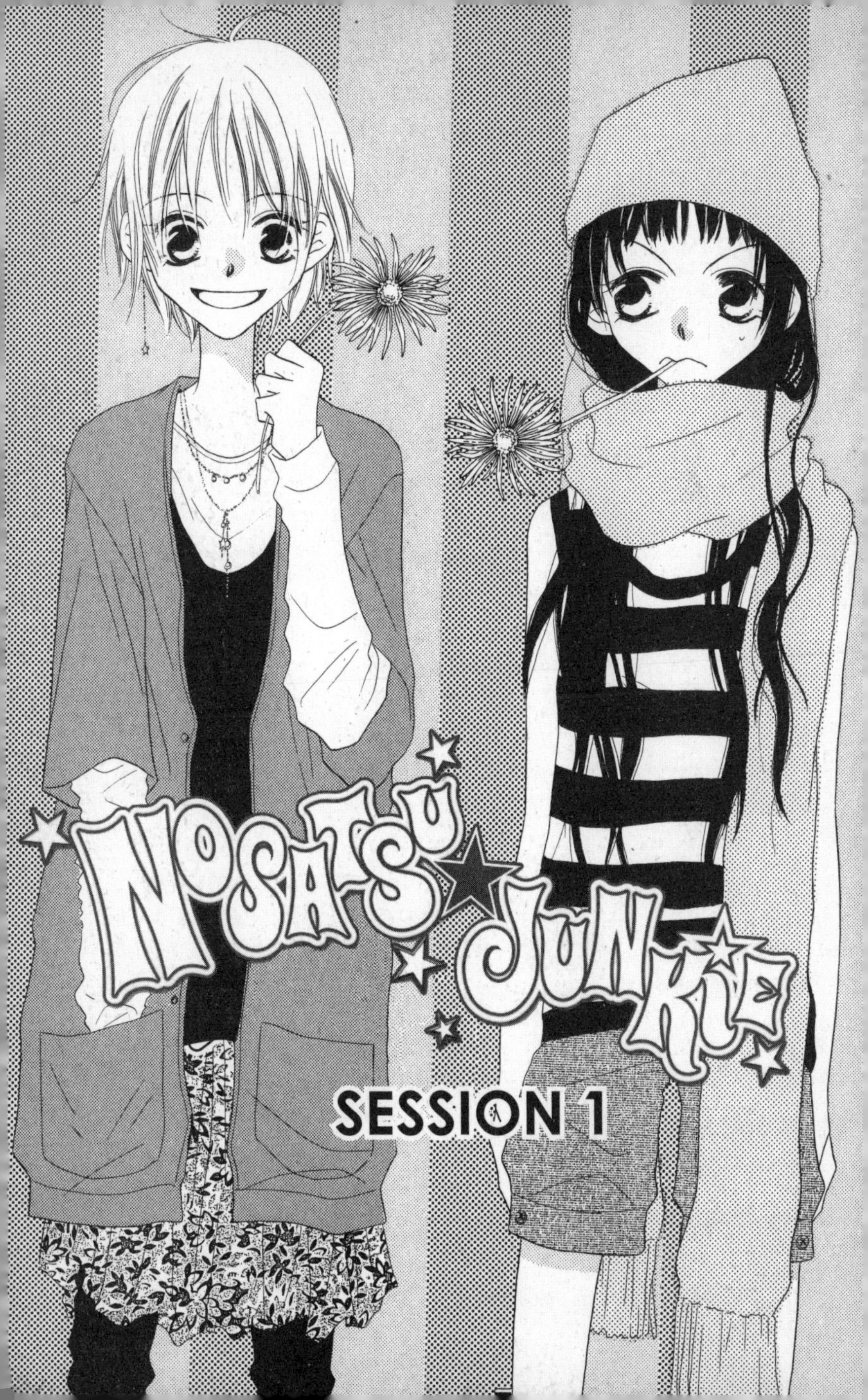
NOSATSU★JUNKIE
SESSION 1

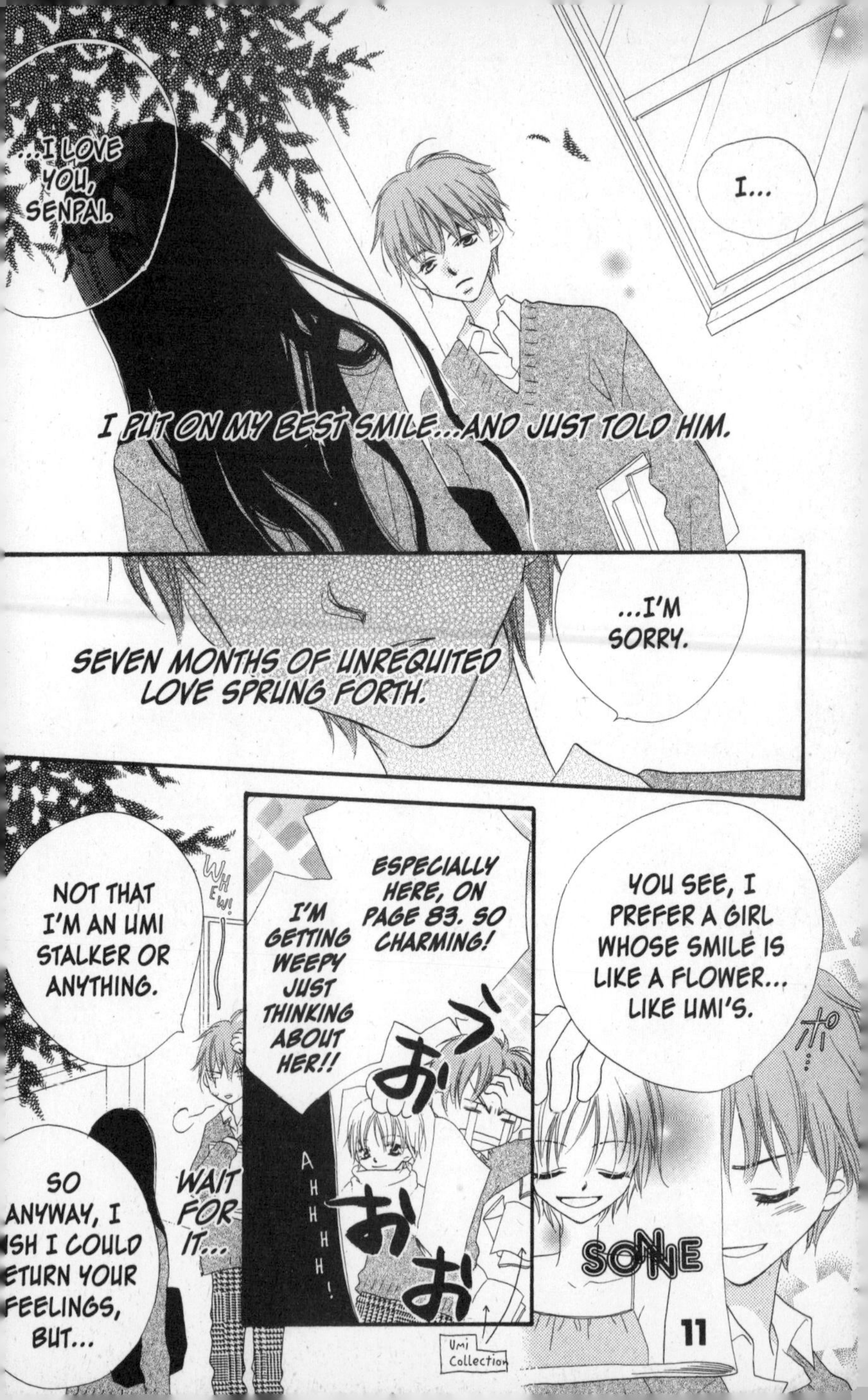
I...
...I LOVE YOU, SENPAI.
I PUT ON MY BEST SMILE...AND JUST TOLD HIM.
...I'M SORRY.
SEVEN MONTHS OF UNREQUITED LOVE SPRUNG FORTH.
YOU SEE, I PREFER A GIRL WHOSE SMILE IS LIKE A FLOWER... LIKE UMI'S.
ポ…
ESPECIALLY HERE, ON PAGE 83. SO CHARMING!
I'M GETTING WEEPY JUST THINKING ABOUT HER!!
うおおお
AHHHH!
Umi Collection
NOT THAT I'M AN UMI STALKER OR ANYTHING.
WHEW!
WAIT FOR IT...
SO ANYWAY, I ISH I COULD ETURN YOUR FEELINGS, BUT...

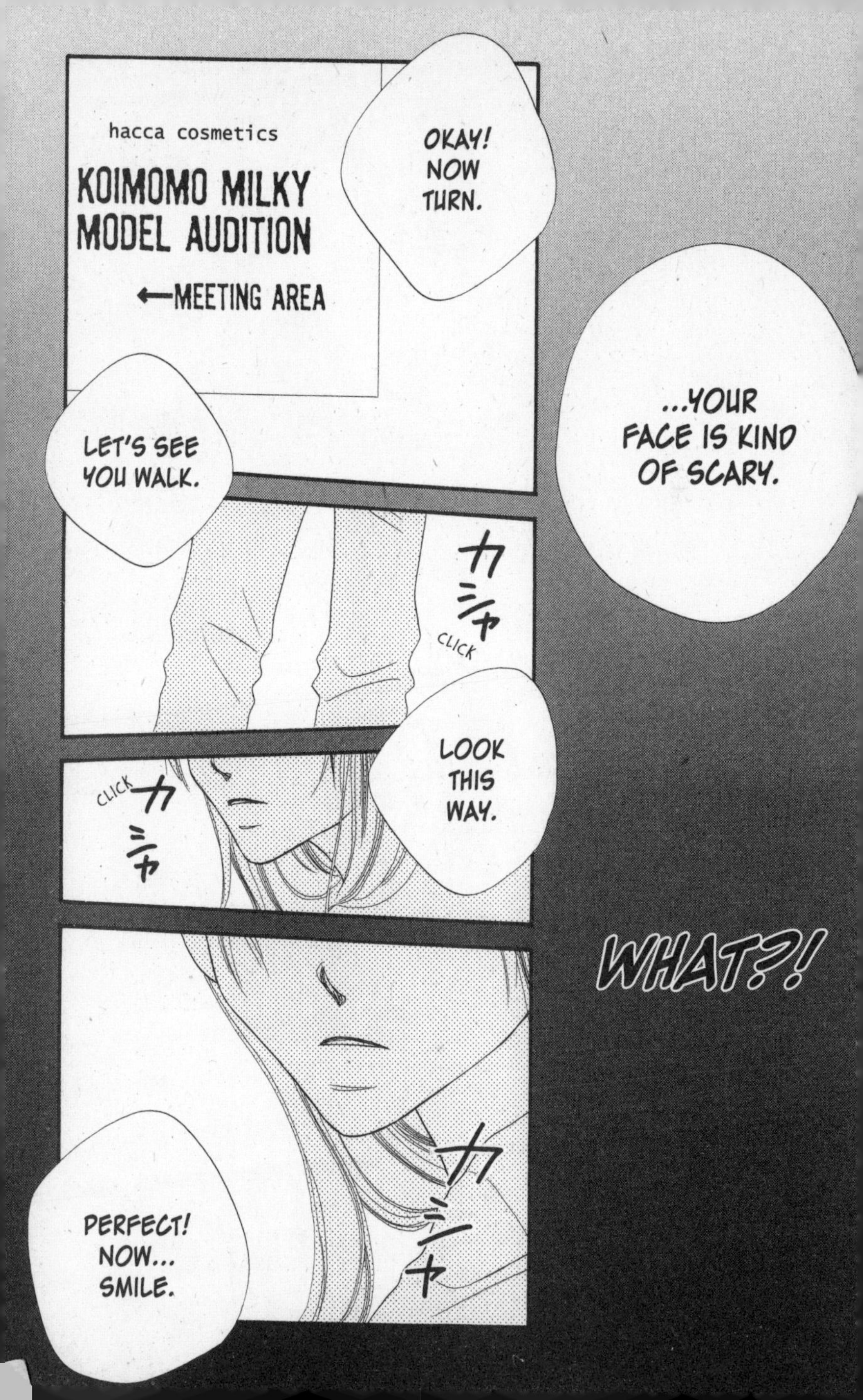
OKAY! NOW TURN.
hacca cosmetics
KOIMOMO MILKY MODEL AUDITION
←MEETING AREA
LET'S SEE YOU WALK.
カシャ
CLICK
LOOK THIS WAY.
カシャ
CLICK
カシャ
PERFECT! NOW... SMILE.
...YOUR FACE IS KIND OF SCARY.
WHAT?!

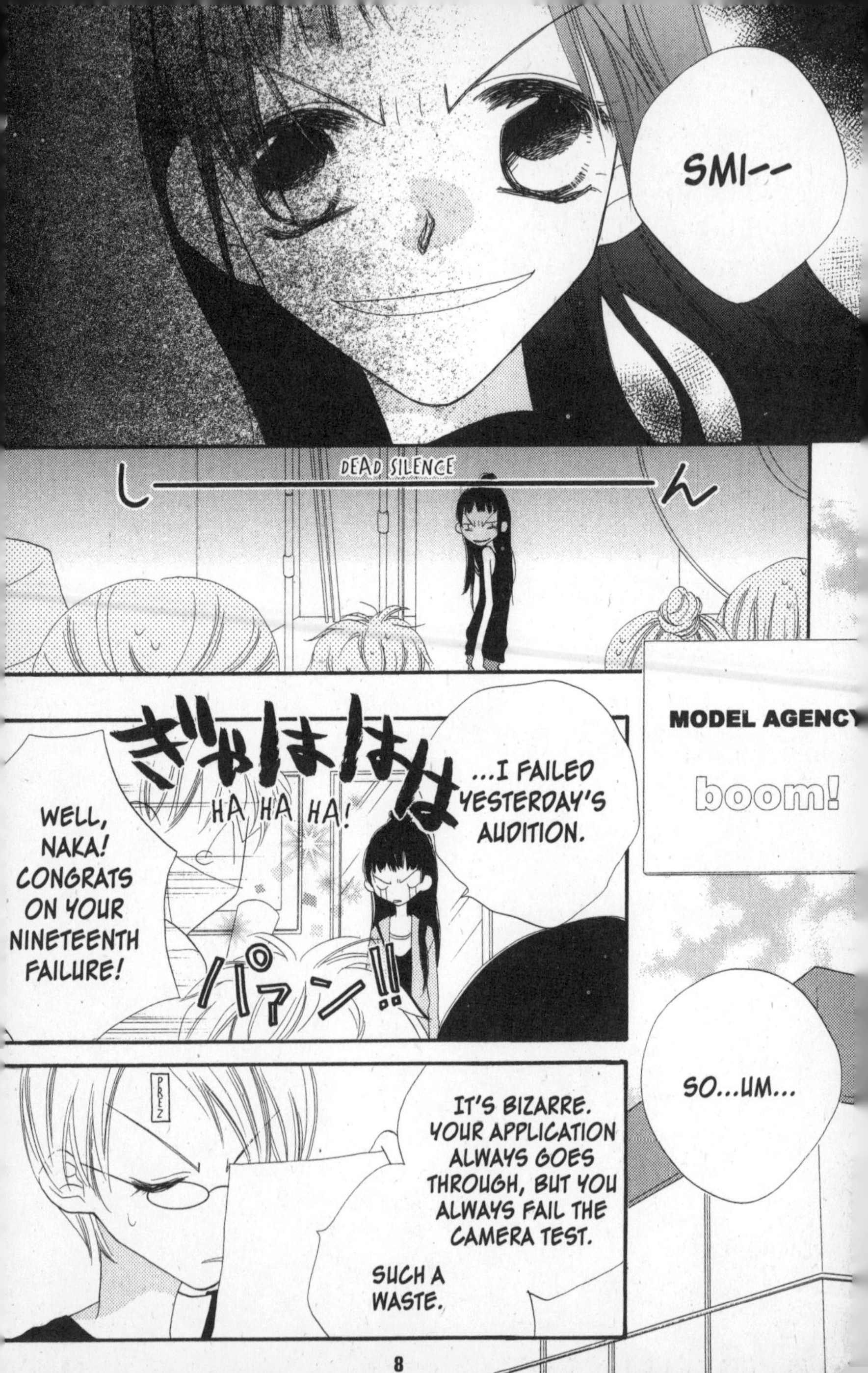

SMI--
DEAD SILENCE
しーーーーん
MODEL AGENCY
boom!
SO...UM...
...I FAILED YESTERDAY'S AUDITION.
ぎゃははは
HA HA HA!
WELL, NAKA! CONGRATS ON YOUR NINETEENTH FAILURE!
パァーン!!
PREZ
IT'S BIZARRE. YOUR APPLICATION ALWAYS GOES THROUGH, BUT YOU ALWAYS FAIL THE CAMERA TEST.
SUCH A WASTE.

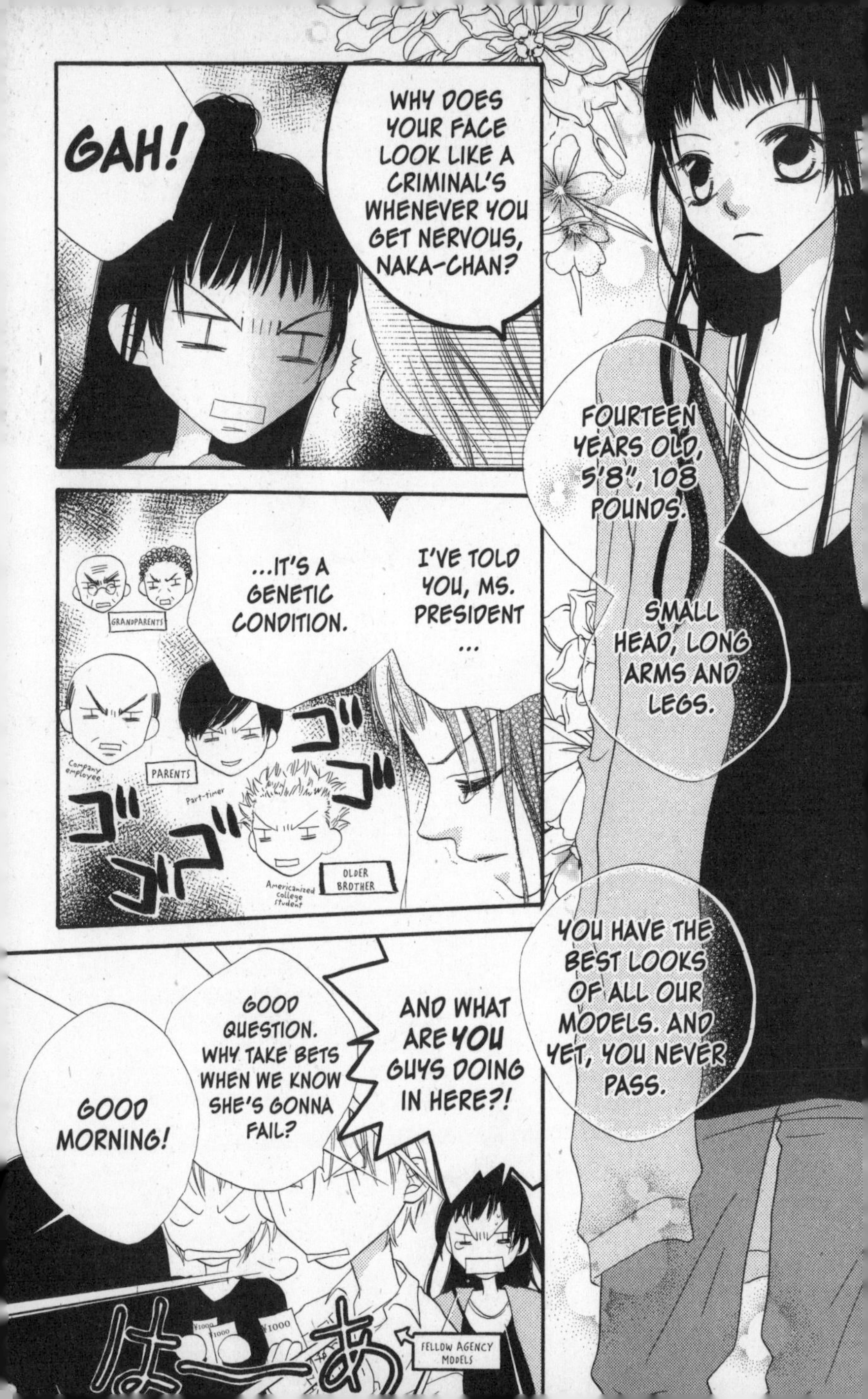
FOURTEEN YEARS OLD, 5'8", 108 POUNDS.
SMALL HEAD, LONG ARMS AND LEGS.
YOU HAVE THE BEST LOOKS OF ALL OUR MODELS. AND YET, YOU NEVER PASS.
WHY DOES YOUR FACE LOOK LIKE A CRIMINAL'S WHENEVER YOU GET NERVOUS, NAKA-CHAN?
GAH!
I'VE TOLD YOU, MS. PRESIDENT ...
...IT'S A GENETIC CONDITION.
GRANDPARENTS
Company employee
PARENTS
Part-timer
OLDER BROTHER
Americanized college student
ゴゴゴゴ
AND WHAT ARE YOU GUYS DOING IN HERE?!
GOOD QUESTION. WHY TAKE BETS WHEN WE KNOW SHE'S GONNA FAIL?
GOOD MORNING!
¥1000
FELLOW AGENCY MODELS
はーあ

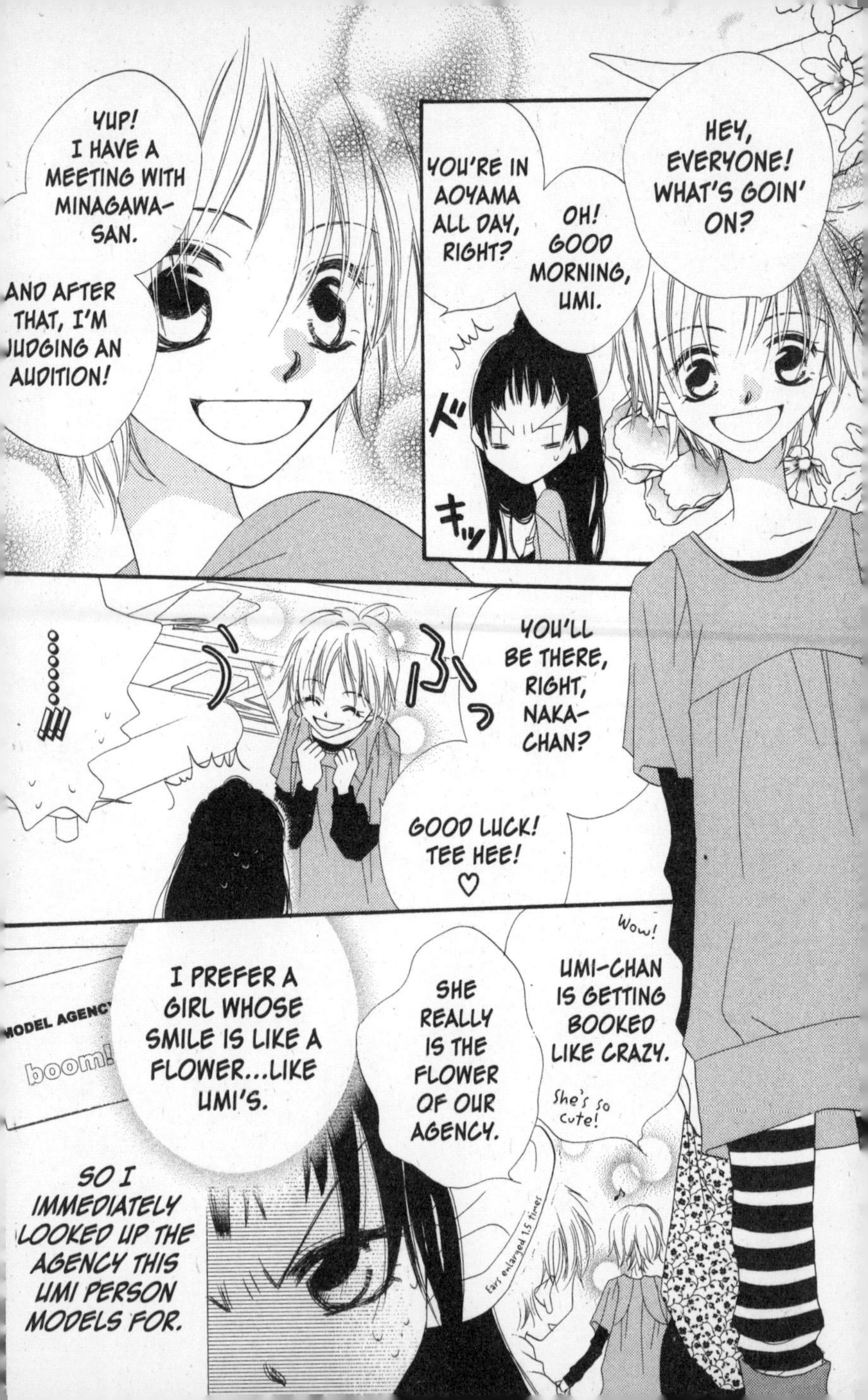
HEY, EVERYONE! WHAT'S GOIN' ON?
OH! GOOD MORNING, UMI.
ドキッ
YOU'RE IN AOYAMA ALL DAY, RIGHT?
YUP! I HAVE A MEETING WITH MINAGAWA-SAN.
AND AFTER THAT, I'M JUDGING AN AUDITION!
YOU'LL BE THERE, RIGHT, NAKA-CHAN?
GOOD LUCK! TEE HEE! ♡
うふっ
OOOOOOO...!!!
Wow!
UMI-CHAN IS GETTING BOOKED LIKE CRAZY.
She's so cute!
SHE REALLY IS THE FLOWER OF OUR AGENCY.
I PREFER A GIRL WHOSE SMILE IS LIKE A FLOWER...LIKE UMI'S.
MODEL AGENCY
boom!
Ears enlarged 1.5 times
SO I IMMEDIATELY LOOKED UP THE AGENCY THIS UMI PERSON MODELS FOR.

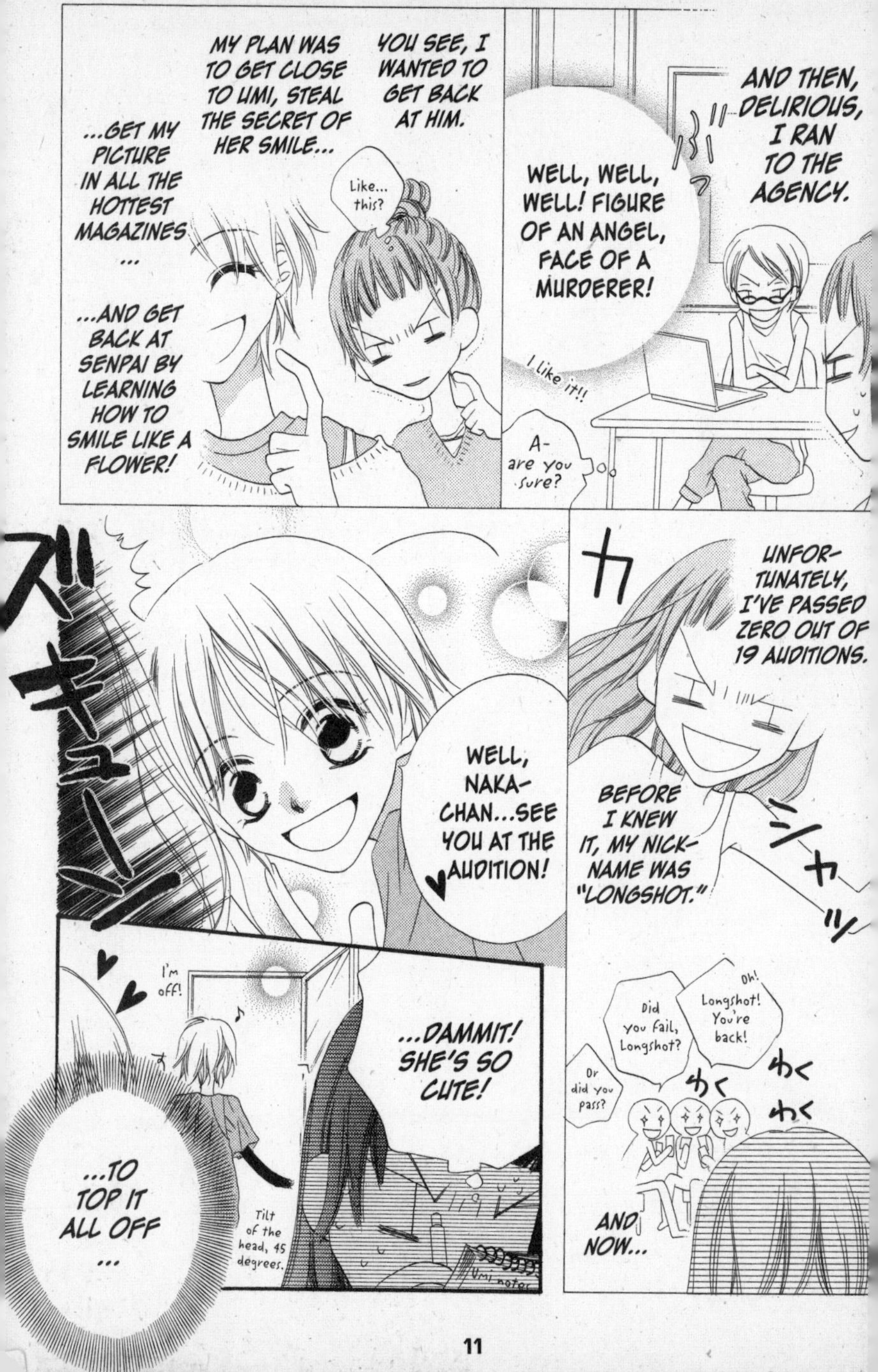
AND THEN, DELIRIOUS, I RAN TO THE AGENCY.
WELL, WELL, WELL! FIGURE OF AN ANGEL, FACE OF A MURDERER!
I like it!!
A- are you sure?
YOU SEE, I WANTED TO GET BACK AT HIM.
MY PLAN WAS TO GET CLOSE TO UMI, STEAL THE SECRET OF HER SMILE...
Like... this?
...GET MY PICTURE IN ALL THE HOTTEST MAGAZINES...
...AND GET BACK AT SENPAI BY LEARNING HOW TO SMILE LIKE A FLOWER!
UNFORTUNATELY, I'VE PASSED ZERO OUT OF 19 AUDITIONS.
BEFORE I KNEW IT, MY NICKNAME WAS "LONGSHOT."
Oh! Longshot! You're back!
Did you fail, Longshot?
Or did you pass?
わく わく
AND NOW...
WELL, NAKA-CHAN...SEE YOU AT THE AUDITION!
I'm off!
...DAMMIT! SHE'S SO CUTE!
Tilt of the head, 45 degrees.
Umi notes
...TO TOP IT ALL OFF...

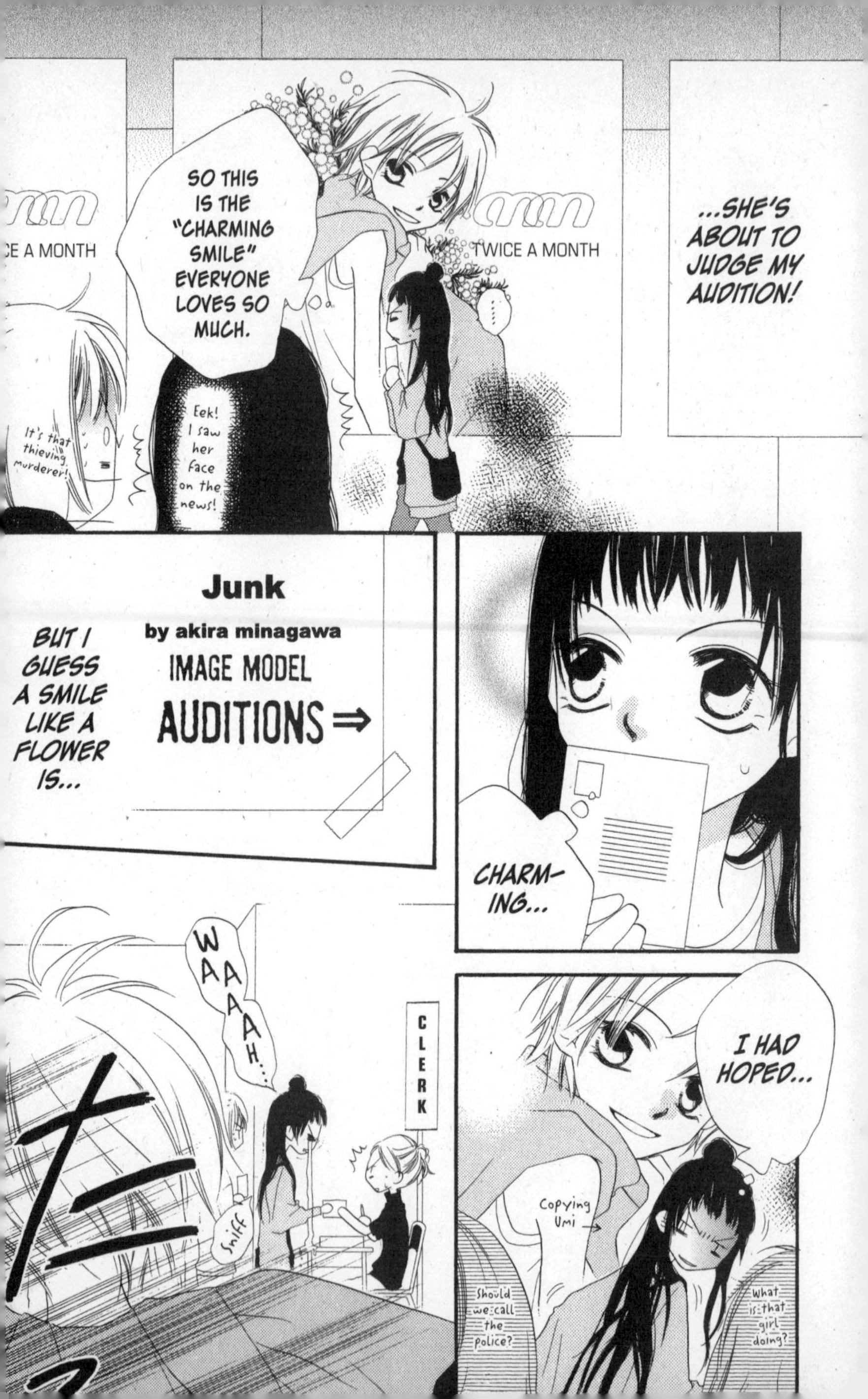

...SHE'S ABOUT TO JUDGE MY AUDITION!
TWICE A MONTH
...
SO THIS IS THE "CHARMING SMILE" EVERYONE LOVES SO MUCH.
CE A MONTH
Eek! I saw her face on the news!
It's that thieving murderer!
CHARM-ING...
Junk
by akira minagawa
IMAGE MODEL
AUDITIONS ⇒
BUT I GUESS A SMILE LIKE A FLOWER IS...
I HAD HOPED...
Copying Umi →
What is that girl doing?
Should we call the police?
WAAAAH...
CLERK
Sniff

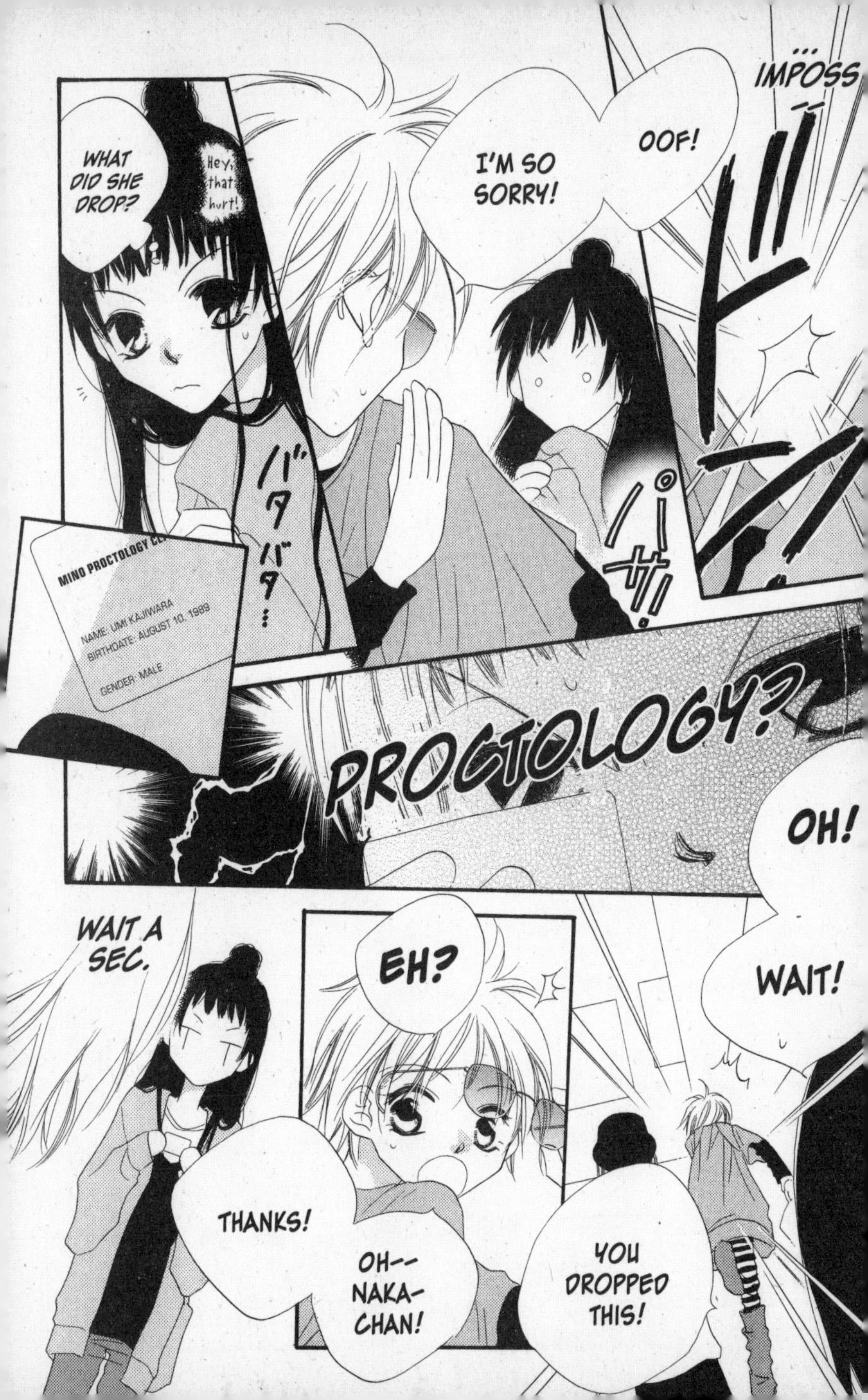
...IMPOSS--
ドーン
OOF!
I'M SO SORRY!
パサ!
WHAT DID SHE DROP?
Hey, that hurt!
バタバタ…
MINO PROCTOLOGY CL
NAME: UMI KAJIWARA
BIRTHDATE: AUGUST 10, 1989
GENDER: MALE
PROCTOLOGY?
OH!
WAIT!
YOU DROPPED THIS!
EH?
OH-- NAKA-CHAN!
THANKS!
WAIT A SEC.

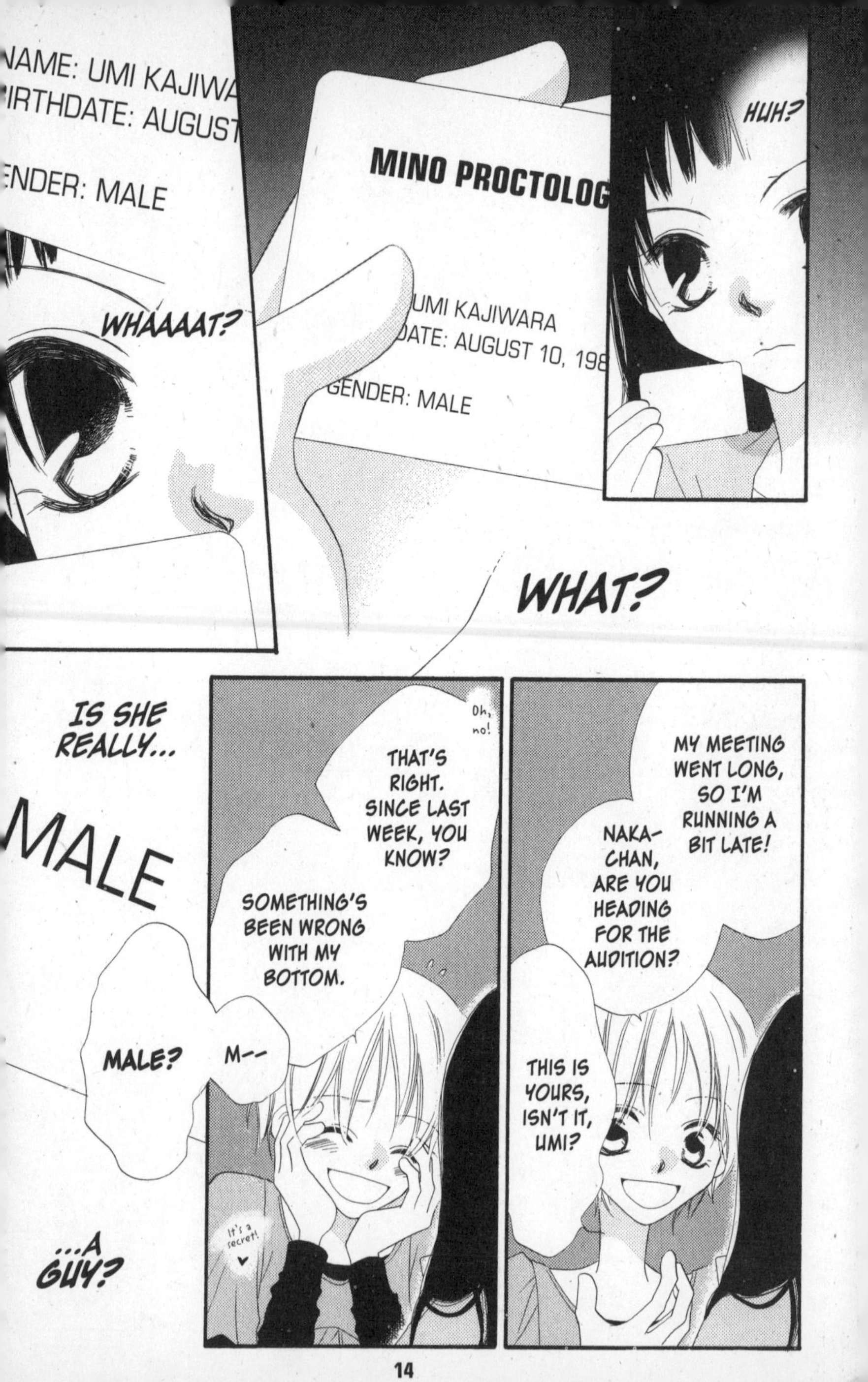
HUH?
MINO PROCTOLOG
UMI KAJIWARA
DATE: AUGUST 10, 198
GENDER: MALE
NAME: UMI KAJIWA
IRTHDATE: AUGUST
ENDER: MALE
WHAAAAT?
WHAT?
MY MEETING WENT LONG, SO I'M RUNNING A BIT LATE!
NAKA-CHAN, ARE YOU HEADING FOR THE AUDITION?
THIS IS YOURS, ISN'T IT, UMI?
Oh, no!
THAT'S RIGHT. SINCE LAST WEEK, YOU KNOW?
SOMETHING'S BEEN WRONG WITH MY BOTTOM.
It's a secret! ♥
M--
IS SHE REALLY...
MALE
MALE?
...A GUY?

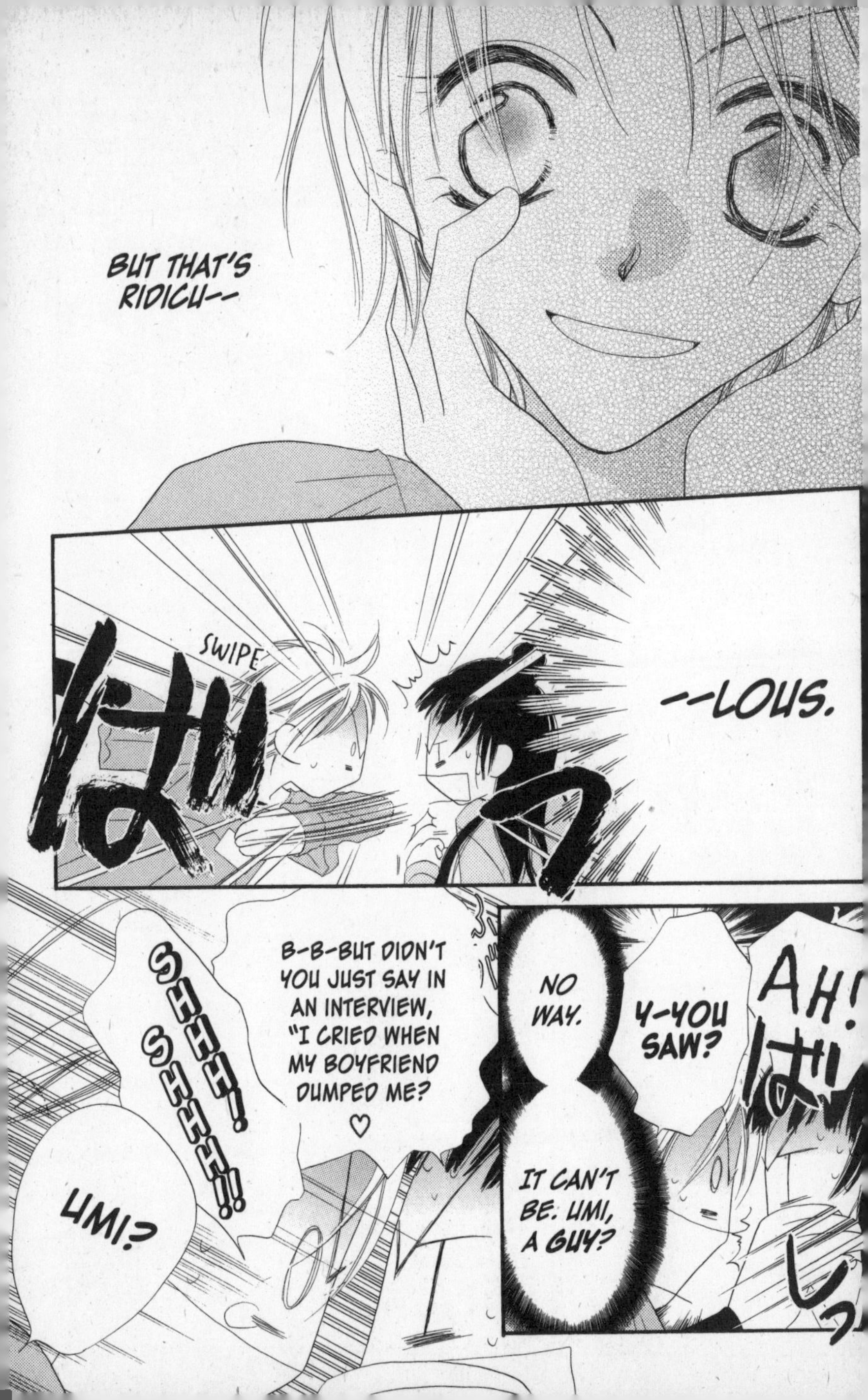
BUT THAT'S RIDICU--
SWIPE
はっ
--LOUS.
AH!
Y-YOU SAW?
NO WAY.
IT CAN'T BE. UMI, A GUY?
B-B-BUT DIDN'T YOU JUST SAY IN AN INTERVIEW, "I CRIED WHEN MY BOYFRIEND DUMPED ME? ♡
SHHHH! SHHHH!!
UMI?

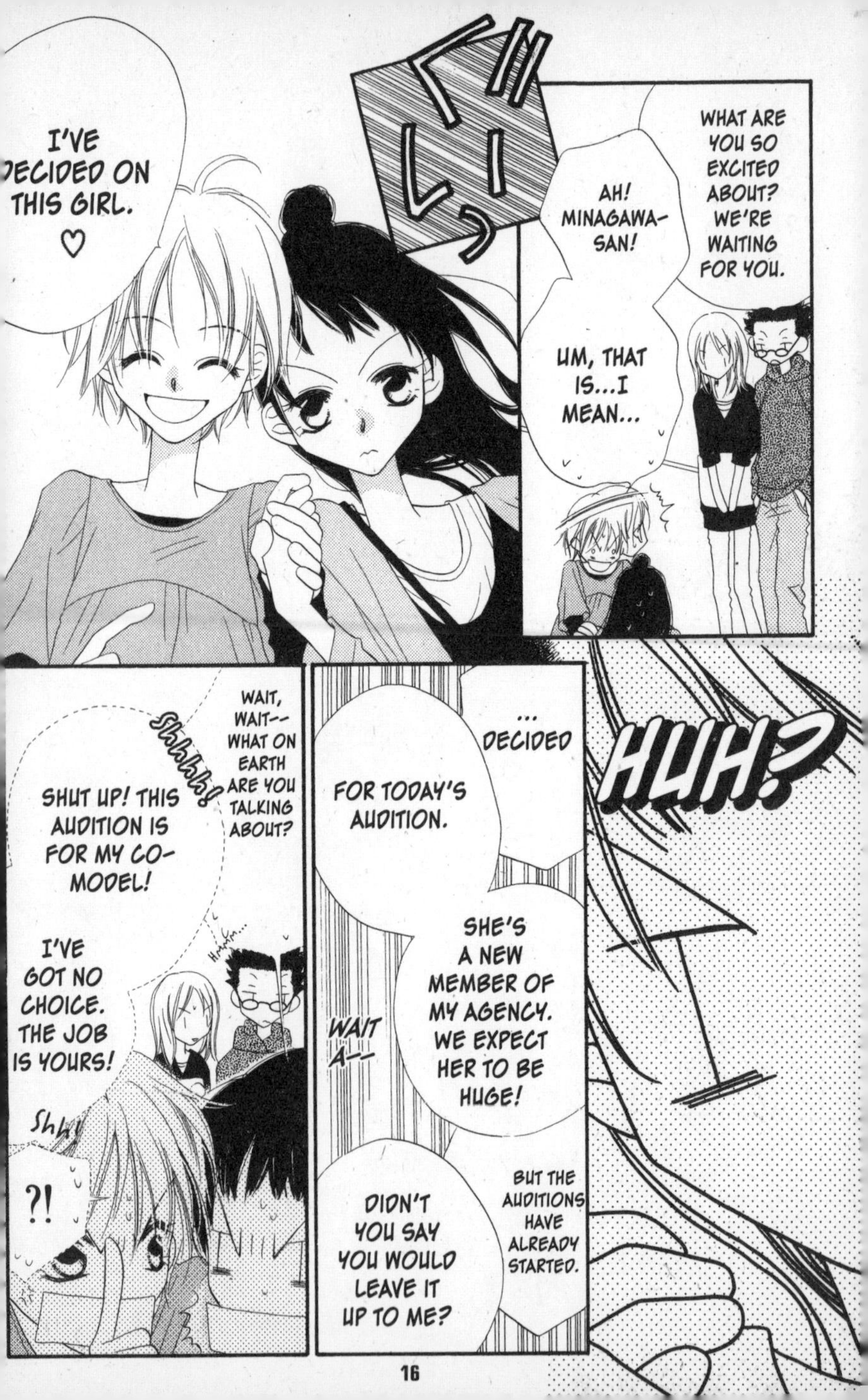
WHAT ARE YOU SO EXCITED ABOUT? WE'RE WAITING FOR YOU.
AH! MINAGAWA-SAN!
UM, THAT IS...I MEAN...
I'VE DECIDED ON THIS GIRL. ♡
HUH?
...DECIDED
FOR TODAY'S AUDITION.
SHE'S A NEW MEMBER OF MY AGENCY. WE EXPECT HER TO BE HUGE!
WAIT A--
BUT THE AUDITIONS HAVE ALREADY STARTED.
DIDN'T YOU SAY YOU WOULD LEAVE IT UP TO ME?
WAIT, WAIT--WHAT ON EARTH ARE YOU TALKING ABOUT?
Shhhhh!
SHUT UP! THIS AUDITION IS FOR MY CO-MODEL!
Hmmm...
I'VE GOT NO CHOICE. THE JOB IS YOURS!
Shh
?!

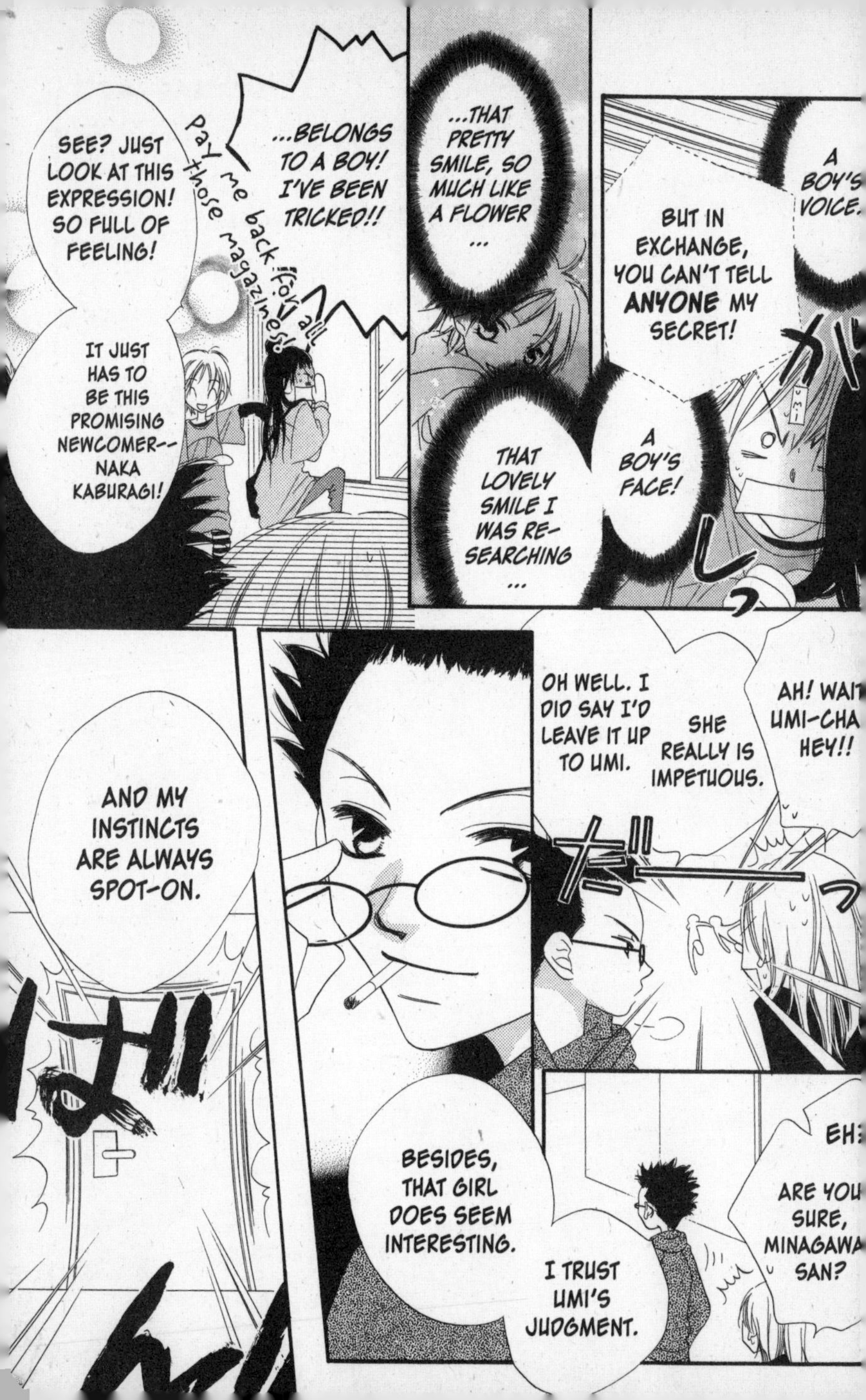
A BOY'S VOICE.
BUT IN EXCHANGE, YOU CAN'T TELL ANYONE MY SECRET!
A BOY'S FACE!
...THAT PRETTY SMILE, SO MUCH LIKE A FLOWER ...
THAT LOVELY SMILE I WAS RE-SEARCHING ...
...BELONGS TO A BOY! I'VE BEEN TRICKED!!
Pay me back for all those magazines!!
SEE? JUST LOOK AT THIS EXPRESSION! SO FULL OF FEELING!
IT JUST HAS TO BE THIS PROMISING NEWCOMER--NAKA KABURAGI!
AH! WAIT UMI-CHA HEY!!
SHE REALLY IS IMPETUOUS.
OH WELL. I DID SAY I'D LEAVE IT UP TO UMI.
EH
ARE YOU SURE, MINAGAWA SAN?
I TRUST UMI'S JUDGMENT.
BESIDES, THAT GIRL DOES SEEM INTERESTING.
AND MY INSTINCTS ARE ALWAYS SPOT-ON.

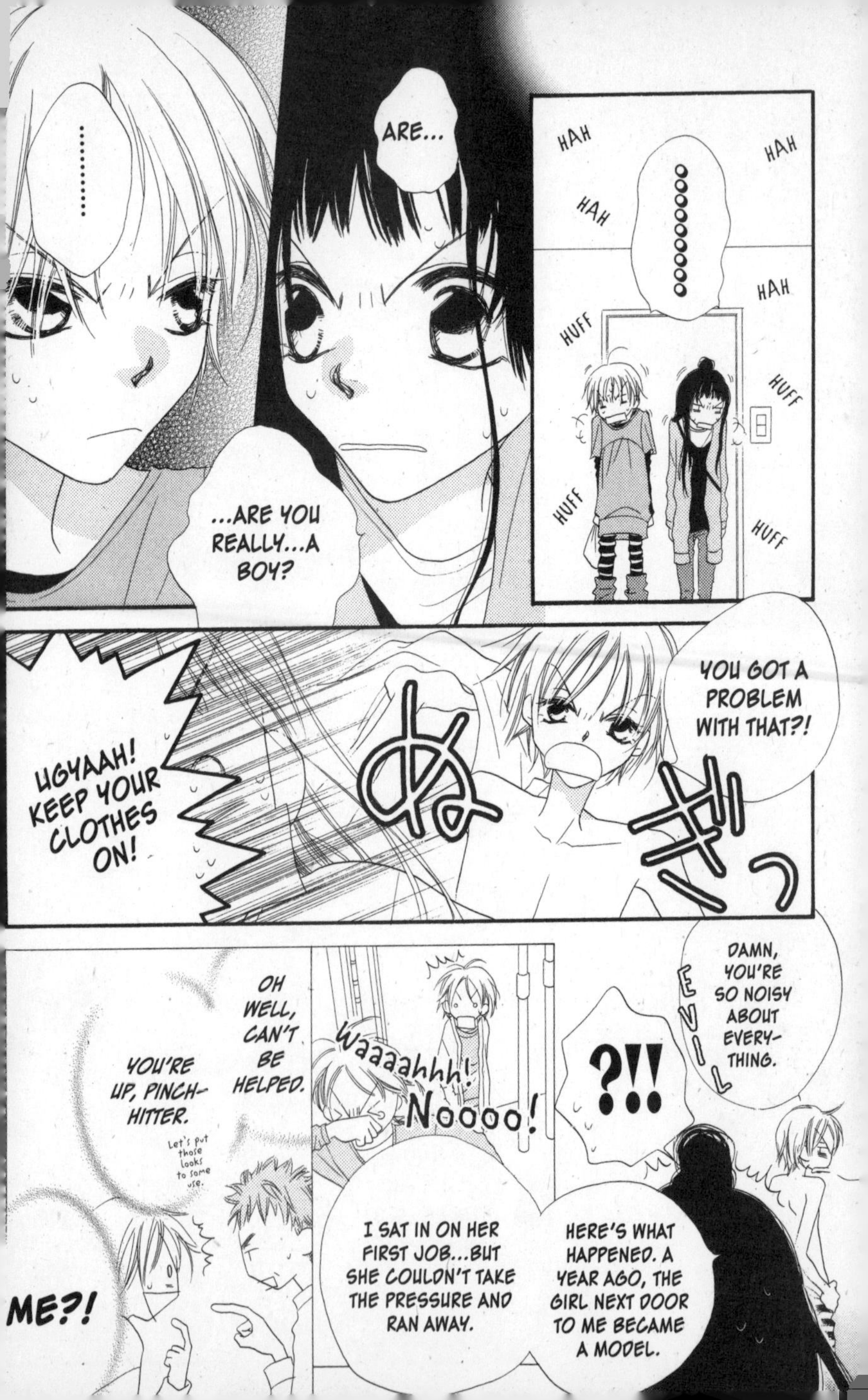
HAH
HAH
HAH
HAH
....
HUFF
HUFF
HUFF
HUFF
ARE...
....
...ARE YOU REALLY...A BOY?
YOU GOT A PROBLEM WITH THAT?!
ぬぎっ
UGYAAH! KEEP YOUR CLOTHES ON!
DAMN, YOU'RE SO NOISY ABOUT EVERY-THING.
EVIL
?!!
HERE'S WHAT HAPPENED. A YEAR AGO, THE GIRL NEXT DOOR TO ME BECAME A MODEL.
I SAT IN ON HER FIRST JOB...BUT SHE COULDN'T TAKE THE PRESSURE AND RAN AWAY.
Waaaahhh! Noooo!
OH WELL, CAN'T BE HELPED.
YOU'RE UP, PINCH-HITTER.
Let's put those looks to some use.
ME?!

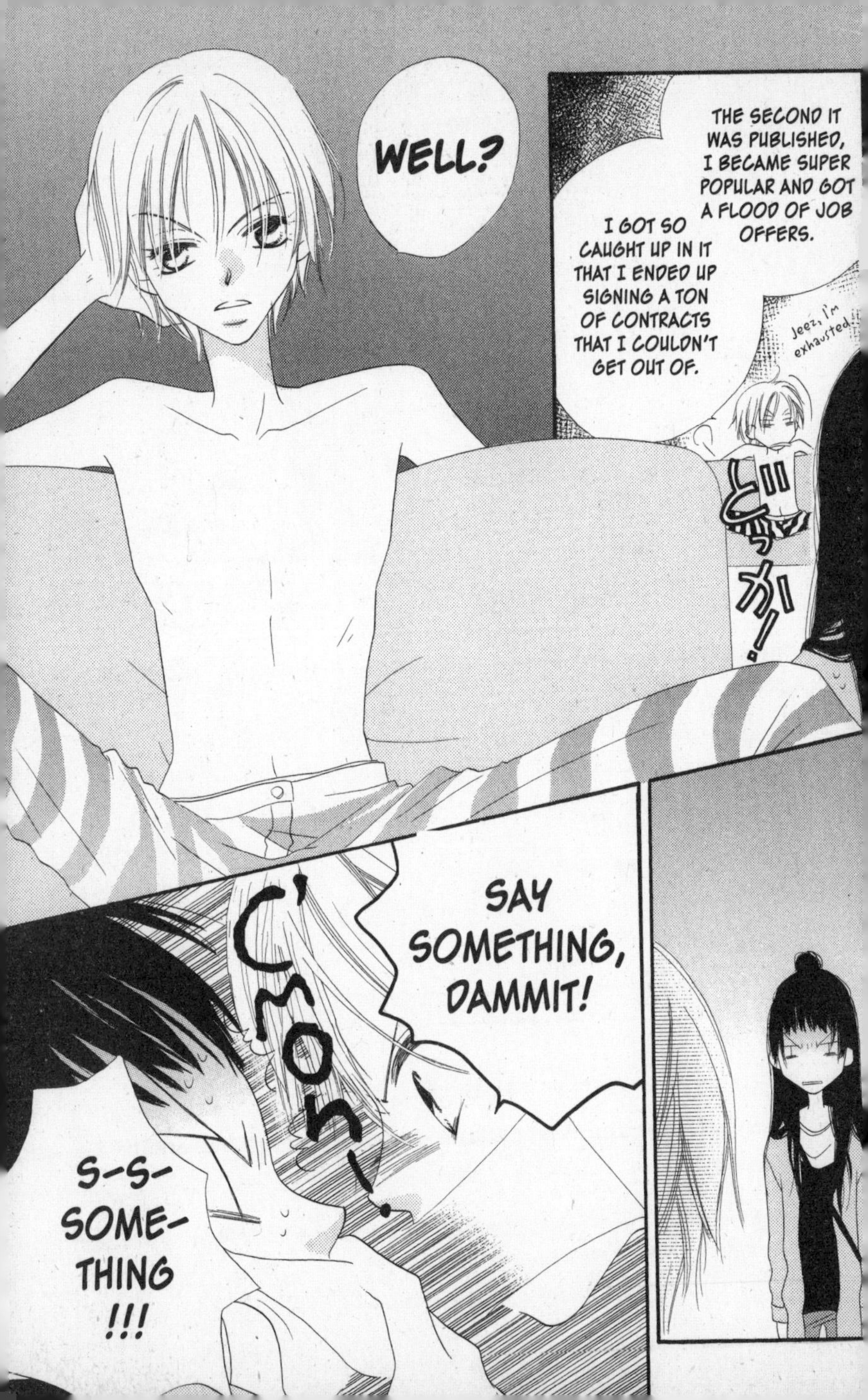
THE SECOND IT WAS PUBLISHED, I BECAME SUPER POPULAR AND GOT A FLOOD OF JOB OFFERS.
I GOT SO CAUGHT UP IN IT THAT I ENDED UP SIGNING A TON OF CONTRACTS THAT I COULDN'T GET OUT OF.
Jeez, I'm exhausted
WELL?
SAY SOMETHING, DAMMIT!
C'mon!
S-S-SOME-THING!!!

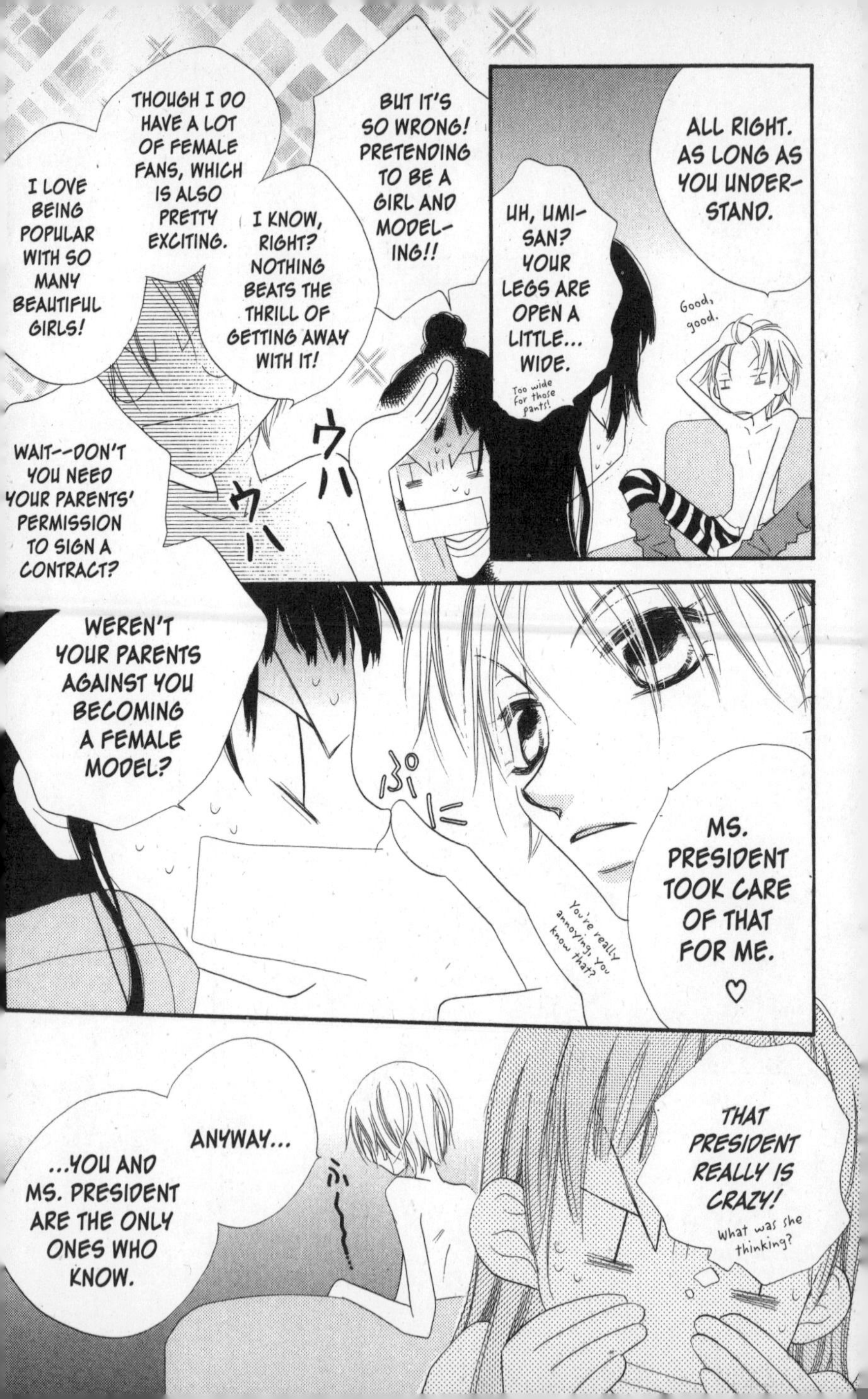
ALL RIGHT. AS LONG AS YOU UNDERSTAND.
Good, good.
UH, UMI-SAN? YOUR LEGS ARE OPEN A LITTLE... WIDE.
Too wide for those pants!
BUT IT'S SO WRONG! PRETENDING TO BE A GIRL AND MODELING!!
I KNOW, RIGHT? NOTHING BEATS THE THRILL OF GETTING AWAY WITH IT!
THOUGH I DO HAVE A LOT OF FEMALE FANS, WHICH IS ALSO PRETTY EXCITING.
ウハ ウハ
I LOVE BEING POPULAR WITH SO MANY BEAUTIFUL GIRLS!
WAIT--DON'T YOU NEED YOUR PARENTS' PERMISSION TO SIGN A CONTRACT?
WEREN'T YOUR PARENTS AGAINST YOU BECOMING A FEMALE MODEL?
MS. PRESIDENT TOOK CARE OF THAT FOR ME. ♡
You're really annoying, you know that?
ぷに
THAT PRESIDENT REALLY IS CRAZY!
What was she thinking?
ANYWAY...
ふ〜
...YOU AND MS. PRESIDENT ARE THE ONLY ONES WHO KNOW.

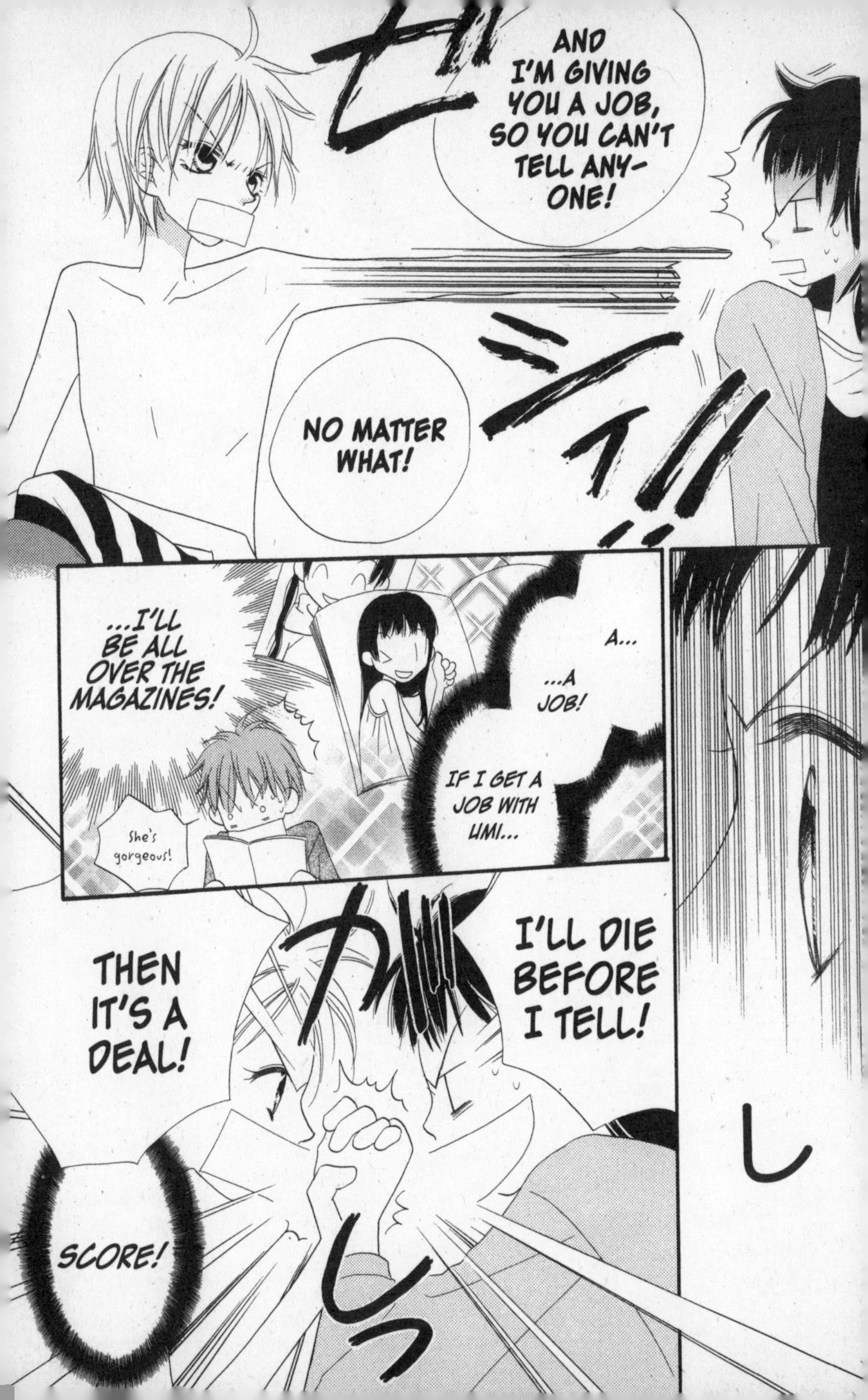
AND I'M GIVING YOU A JOB, SO YOU CAN'T TELL ANY-ONE!
NO MATTER WHAT!
A...
...A JOB!
IF I GET A JOB WITH UMI...
...I'LL BE ALL OVER THE MAGAZINES!
She's gorgeous!
I'LL DIE BEFORE I TELL!
THEN IT'S A DEAL!
SCORE!

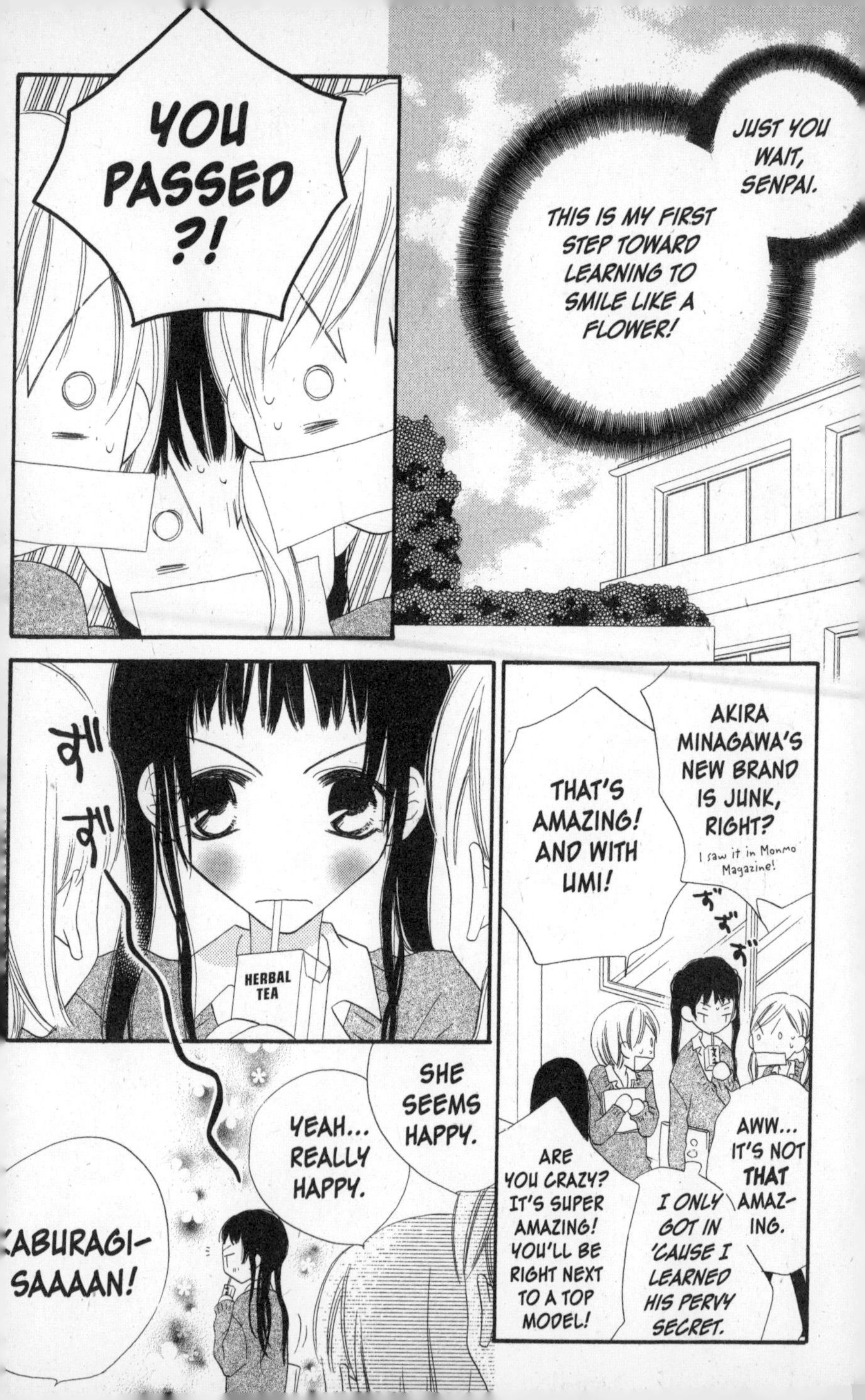
JUST YOU WAIT, SENPAI.
THIS IS MY FIRST STEP TOWARD LEARNING TO SMILE LIKE A FLOWER!
YOU PASSED ?!
AKIRA MINAGAWA'S NEW BRAND IS JUNK, RIGHT?
I saw it in Monmo Magazine!
THAT'S AMAZING! AND WITH UMI!
ずずず
AWW... IT'S NOT THAT AMAZ-ING.
I ONLY GOT IN 'CAUSE I LEARNED HIS PERVY SECRET.
ARE YOU CRAZY? IT'S SUPER AMAZING! YOU'LL BE RIGHT NEXT TO A TOP MODEL!
ずずず
HERBAL TEA
SHE SEEMS HAPPY.
YEAH... REALLY HAPPY.
KABURAGI-SAAAAN!

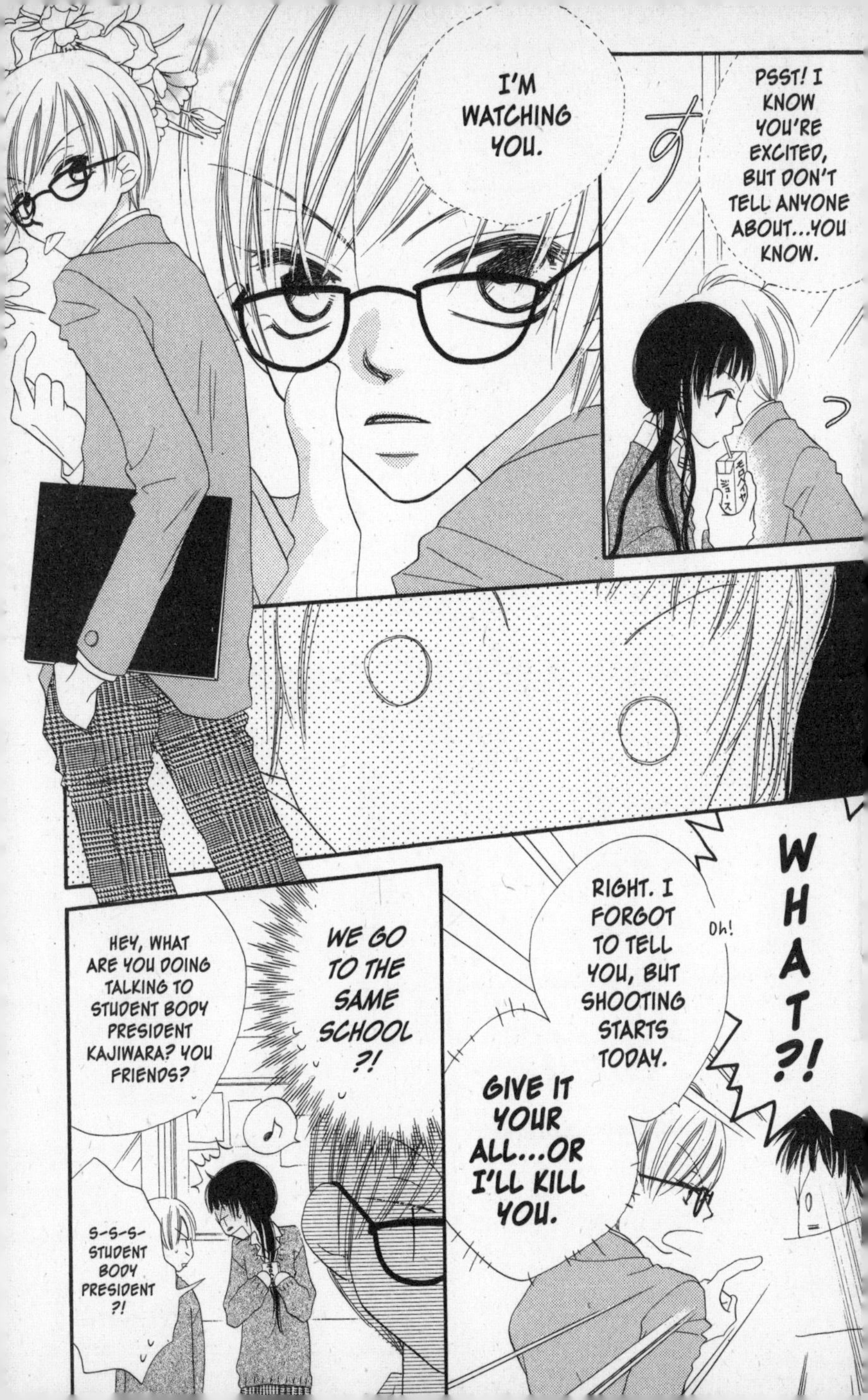
PSST! I KNOW YOU'RE EXCITED, BUT DON'T TELL ANYONE ABOUT...YOU KNOW.
I'M WATCHING YOU.
WHAT?!
Oh!
RIGHT. I FORGOT TO TELL YOU, BUT SHOOTING STARTS TODAY.
GIVE IT YOUR ALL...OR I'LL KILL YOU.
WE GO TO THE SAME SCHOOL?!
HEY, WHAT ARE YOU DOING TALKING TO STUDENT BODY PRESIDENT KAJIWARA? YOU FRIENDS?
S-S-S-STUDENT BODY PRESIDENT?!

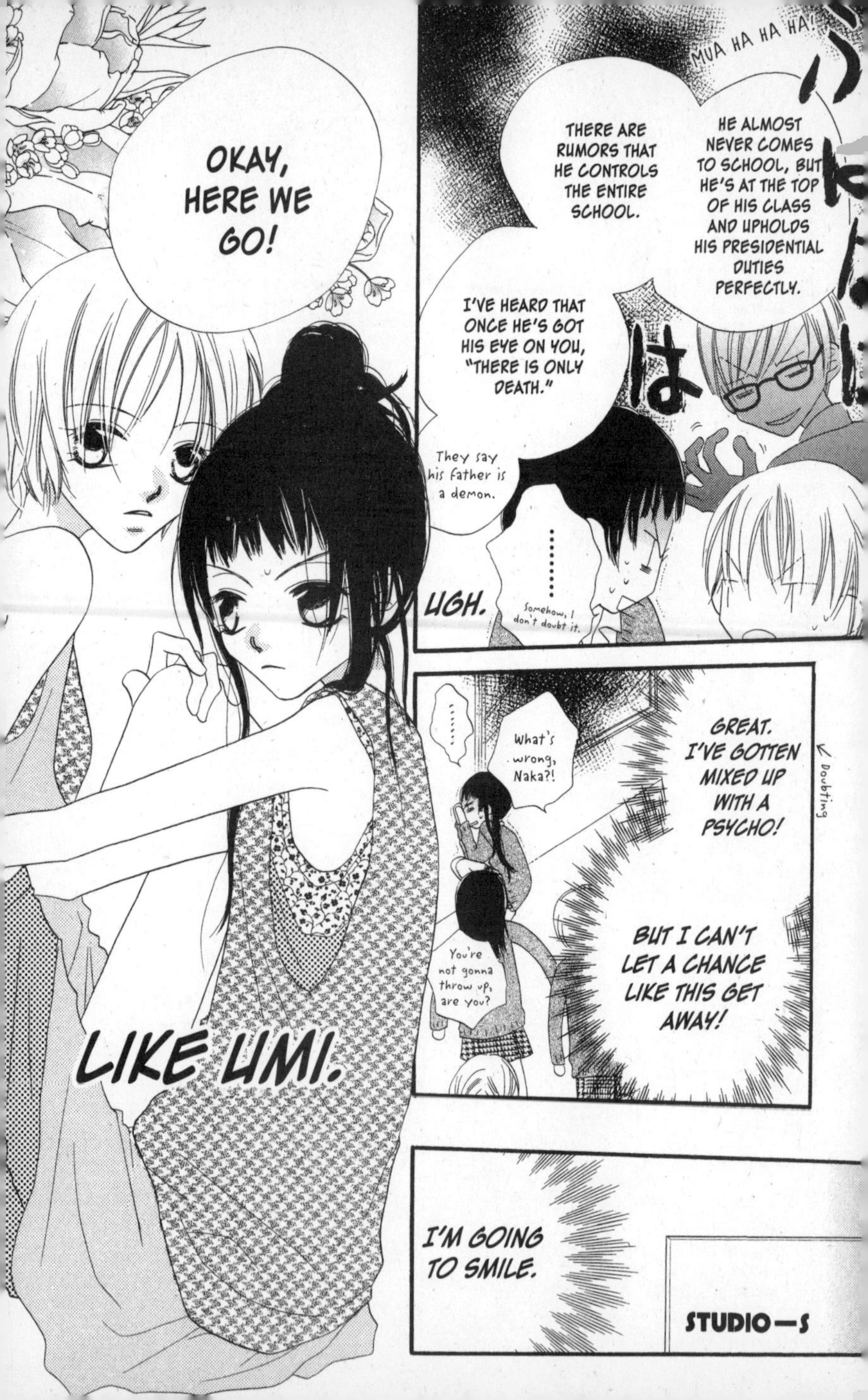
MUA HA HA HA!
は
HE ALMOST NEVER COMES TO SCHOOL, BUT HE'S AT THE TOP OF HIS CLASS AND UPHOLDS HIS PRESIDENTIAL DUTIES PERFECTLY.
THERE ARE RUMORS THAT HE CONTROLS THE ENTIRE SCHOOL.
I'VE HEARD THAT ONCE HE'S GOT HIS EYE ON YOU, "THERE IS ONLY DEATH."
They say his father is a demon.
......
Somehow, I don't doubt it.
UGH.
GREAT. I'VE GOTTEN MIXED UP WITH A PSYCHO!
Doubting
What's wrong, Naka?!
......
BUT I CAN'T LET A CHANCE LIKE THIS GET AWAY!
You're not gonna throw up, are you?
I'M GOING TO SMILE.
STUDIO—S
OKAY, HERE WE GO!
LIKE UMI.

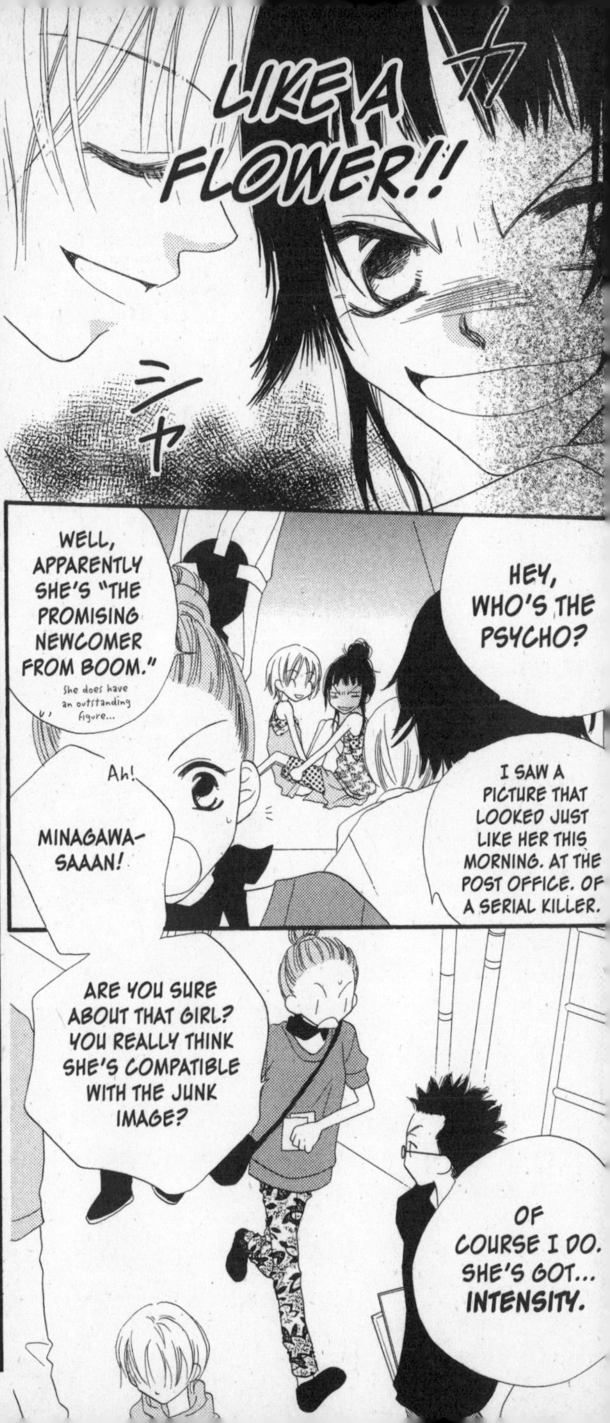
LIKE A FLOWER!!
ニヤ
HEY, WHO'S THE PSYCHO?
WELL, APPARENTLY SHE'S "THE PROMISING NEWCOMER FROM BOOM."
She does have an outstanding figure...
I SAW A PICTURE THAT LOOKED JUST LIKE HER THIS MORNING. AT THE POST OFFICE. OF A SERIAL KILLER.
Ah!
MINAGAWA-SAAAN!
ARE YOU SURE ABOUT THAT GIRL? YOU REALLY THINK SHE'S COMPATIBLE WITH THE JUNK IMAGE?
OF COURSE I DO. SHE'S GOT... INTENSITY.

1

Hello, and nice to meet you! My name is Ryoko Fukuyama.

This is my first comic, and I'm both happy and embarrassed to see Volume one published. My heart is beating like crazy and my hand is really shaking right now.

Let's see...I guess I should give you my vital stats.

Ryoko Fukuyama

- Born: January 5th Capricorn
- Blood type: A
- From: Wakayama Prefecture.
- Lives in: Kanagawa Prefecture.
- Personality: I jump to conclusions and get anxious all the time for no good reason. Also, I've got major stage fright. In other words, I'm shy.
- Height: 5'5"
- Shoe size: 8.5 to 9 women's
- Hair color: Chestnut
- Piercings: 5
- Favorite things: music, manga, clothes, cake, chocolate, curry, driving, Shibuya,* friends, the sky, my family, my computer, electronics, magazines, my camera, polka dots, the color red, convenience stores, bookstores, theatre, Japanese films, photo albums, clean sheets, comfy bed, sleep, motor bikes, the cities of Osaka and Kobe, and fonts. Oh! And I also really like TV dramas. And live shows!!

*High-fashion district in Tokyo.

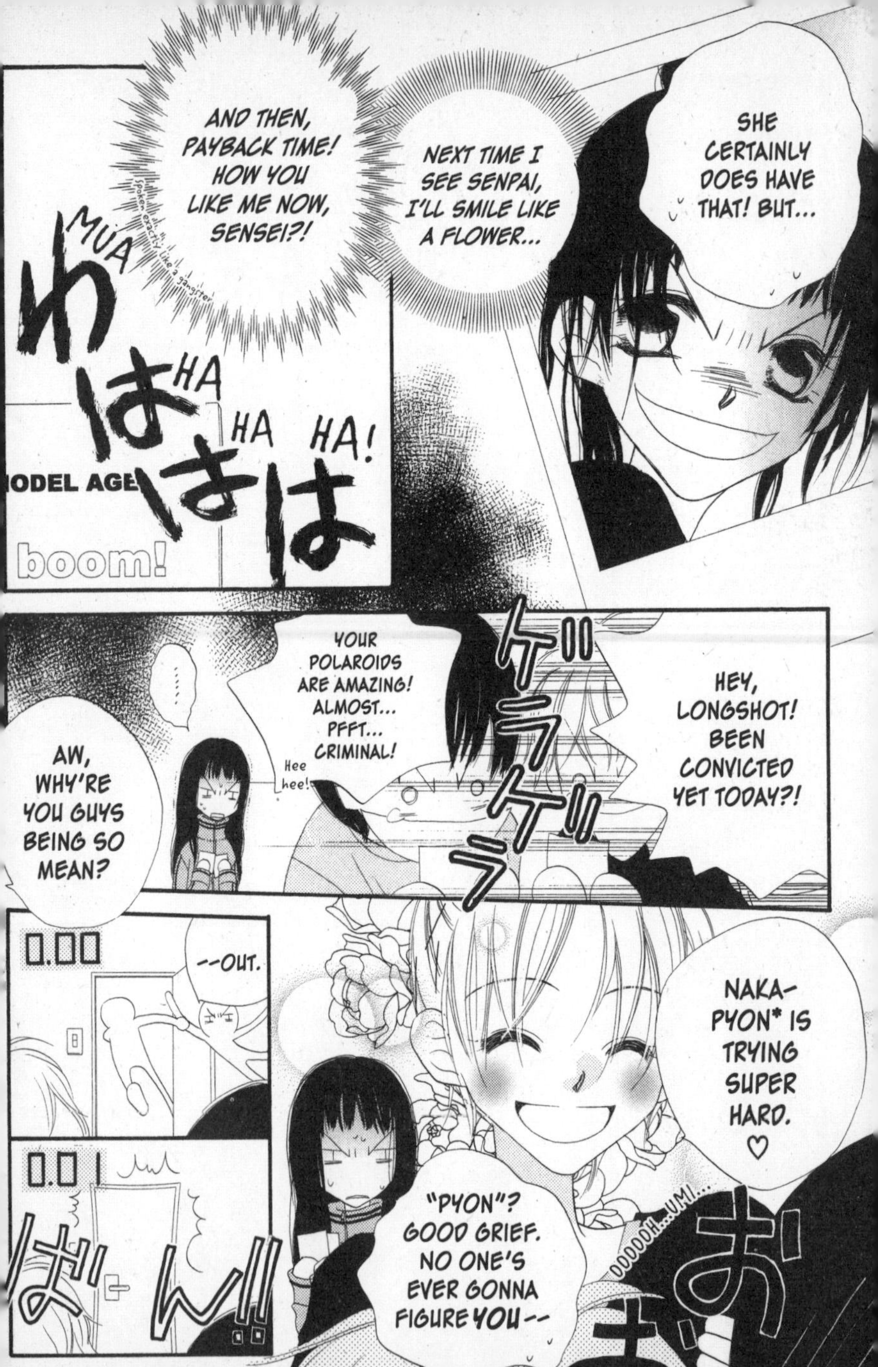
SHE CERTAINLY DOES HAVE THAT! BUT...
NEXT TIME I SEE SENPAI, I'LL SMILE LIKE A FLOWER...
AND THEN, PAYBACK TIME! HOW YOU LIKE ME NOW, SENSEI?!
spoken exactly like a gangster
MUA HA HA HA!
わははは
ODEL AGE
boom!
HEY, LONGSHOT! BEEN CONVICTED YET TODAY?!
ケラケラ
YOUR POLAROIDS ARE AMAZING! ALMOST... PFFT... CRIMINAL!
Hee hee!
......
AW, WHY'RE YOU GUYS BEING SO MEAN?
NAKA-PYON* IS TRYING SUPER HARD. ♡
OOOOOH... UMI...
おおお
"PYON"? GOOD GRIEF. NO ONE'S EVER GONNA FIGURE YOU--
0.00
--OUT.
0.01
ばん!!

*"Pyon" is a slang honorific that's even cutesier than "chan." Umi uses it when he wants to be extra girly.

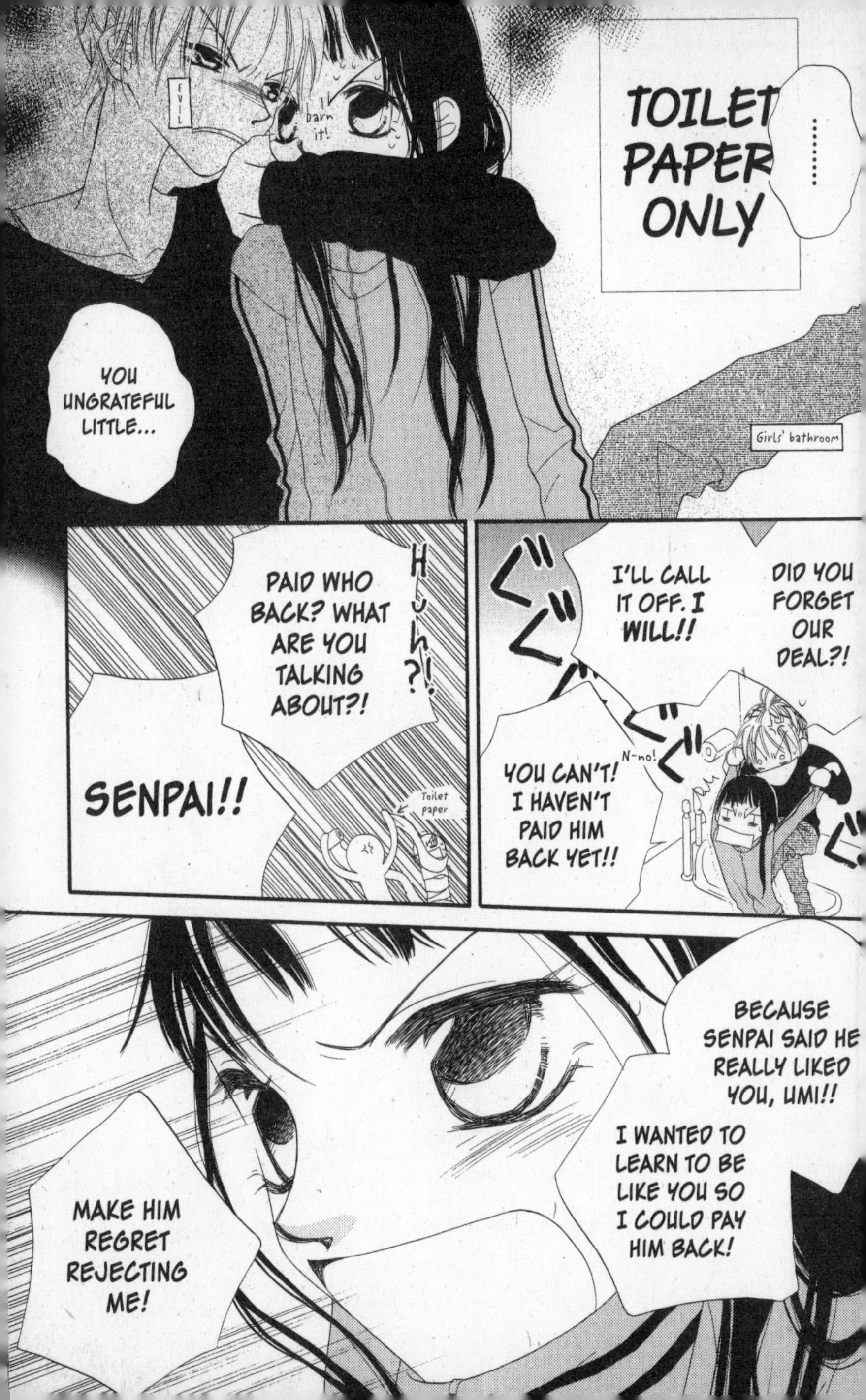

TOILET PAPER ONLY
......
Darn it!
EVIL
YOU UNGRATEFUL LITTLE...
Girls' bathroom
DID YOU FORGET OUR DEAL?!
I'LL CALL IT OFF. I WILL!!
N-no!
YOU CAN'T! I HAVEN'T PAID HIM BACK YET!!
Huh?!!
PAID WHO BACK? WHAT ARE YOU TALKING ABOUT?!
SENPAI!!
Toilet paper
BECAUSE SENPAI SAID HE REALLY LIKED YOU, UMI!!
I WANTED TO LEARN TO BE LIKE YOU SO I COULD PAY HIM BACK!
MAKE HIM REGRET REJECTING ME!

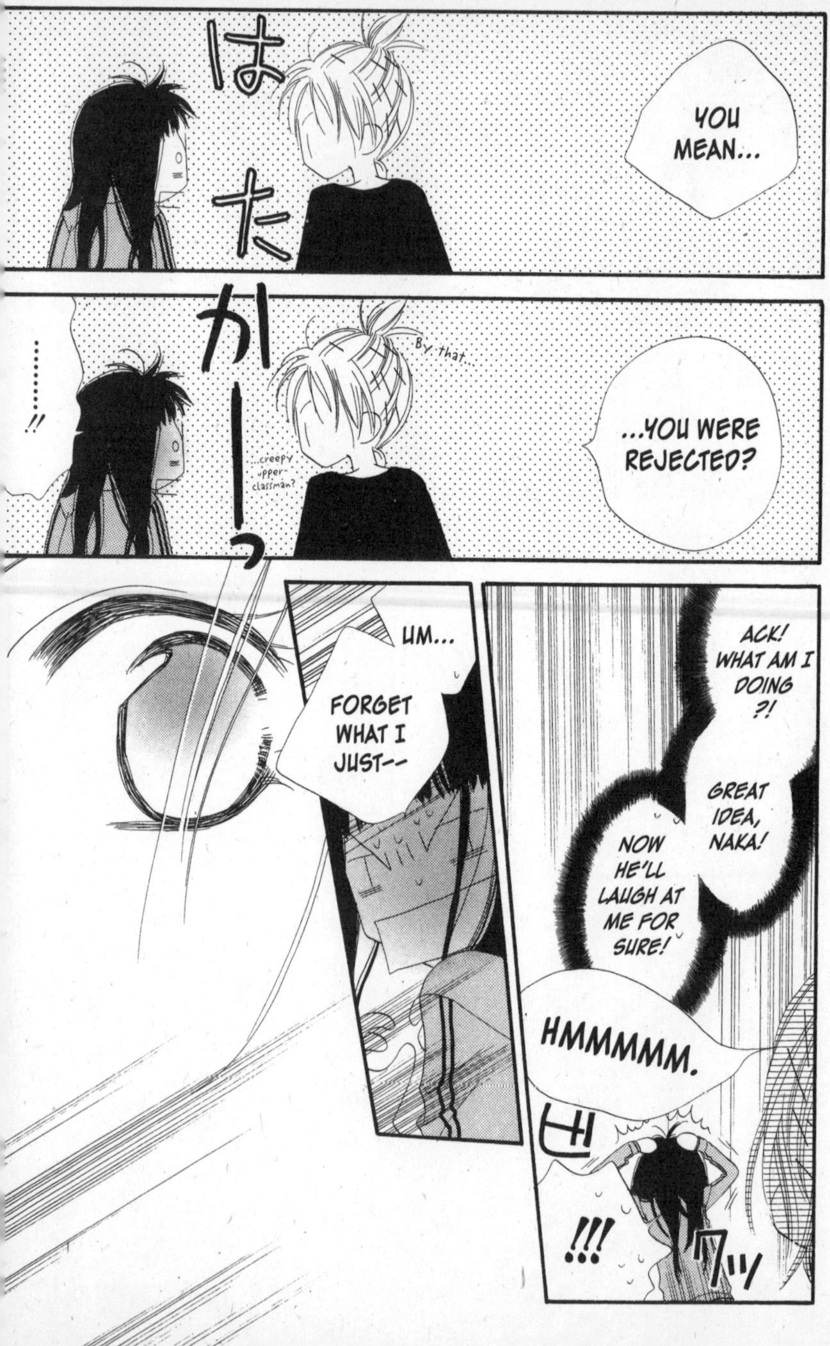

YOU MEAN...
はた
...YOU WERE REJECTED?
By that...
...creepy upperclassman?
......!!
かーっ
ACK! WHAT AM I DOING?!
GREAT IDEA, NAKA!
NOW HE'LL LAUGH AT ME FOR SURE!
HMMMMM.
!!!
ワッ
UM...
FORGET WHAT I JUST--

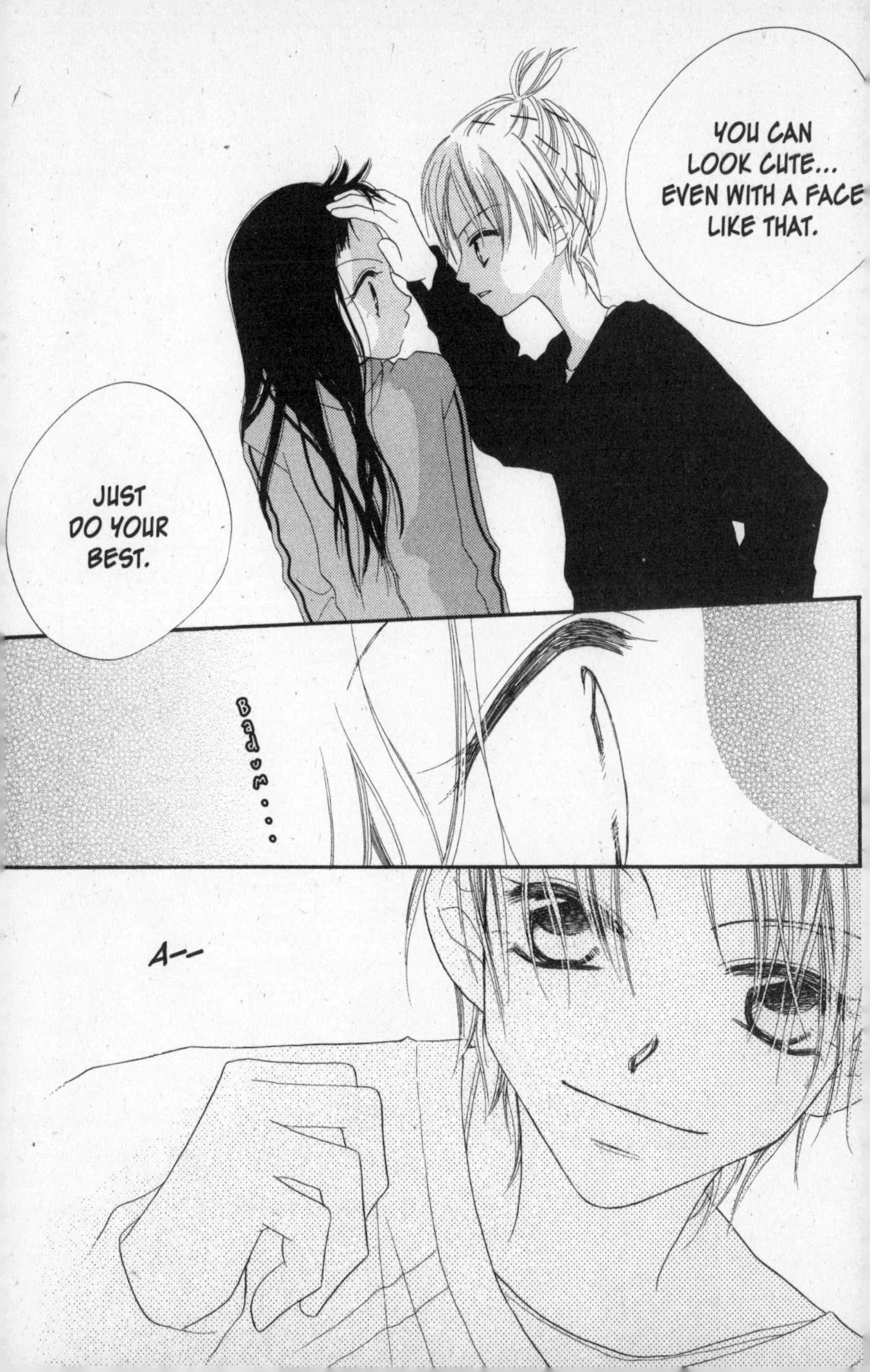
YOU CAN LOOK CUTE... EVEN WITH A FACE LIKE THAT.
JUST DO YOUR BEST.
Badum...
A--

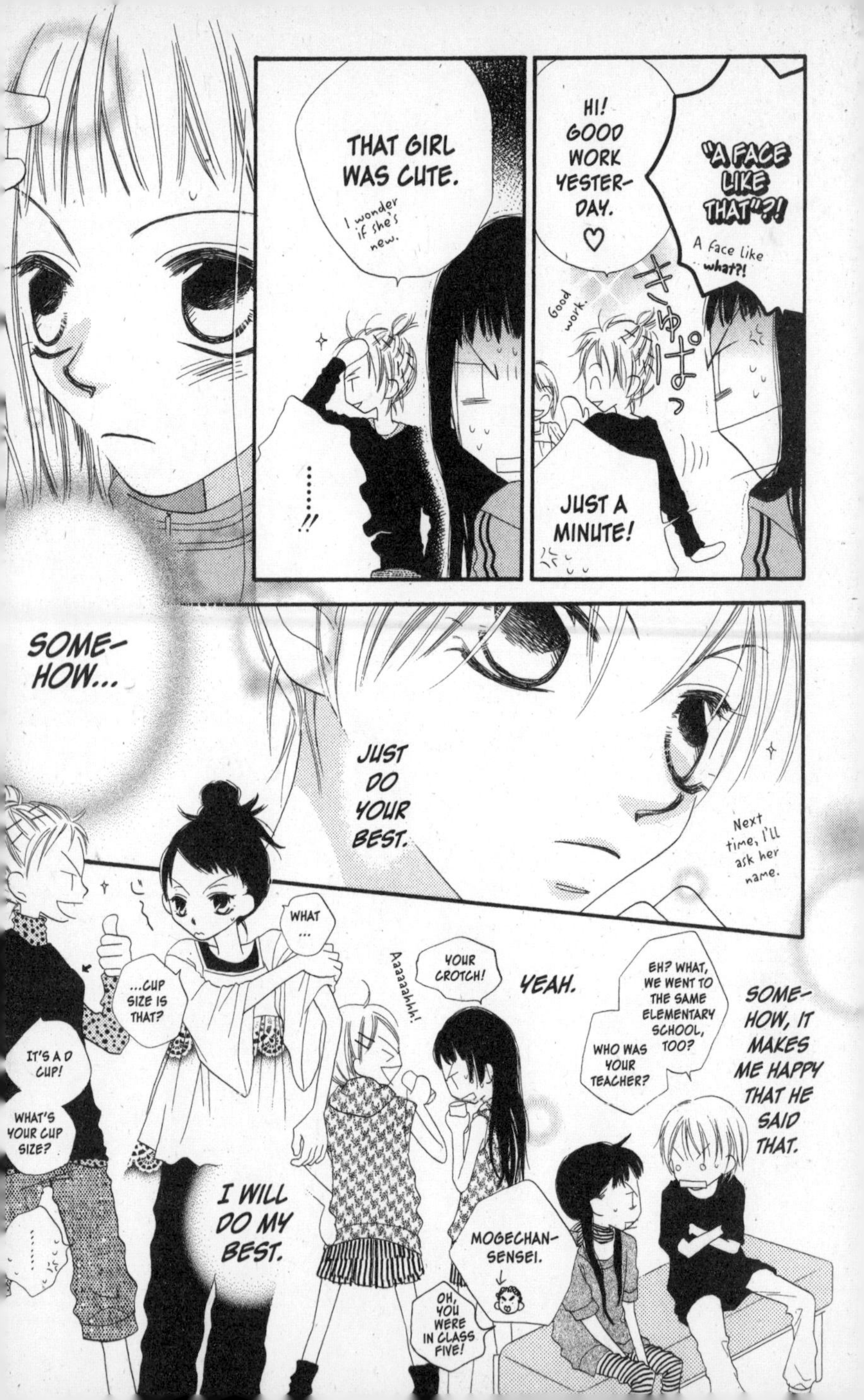
"A FACE LIKE THAT"?!
A face like what?!
HI! GOOD WORK YESTER-DAY. ♡
きゅぱっ
Good work.
JUST A MINUTE!
THAT GIRL WAS CUTE.
I wonder if she's new.
......!!
Next time, I'll ask her name.
JUST DO YOUR BEST.
SOME-HOW...
SOME-HOW, IT MAKES ME HAPPY THAT HE SAID THAT.
EH? WHAT, WE WENT TO THE SAME ELEMENTARY SCHOOL, TOO?
WHO WAS YOUR TEACHER?
MOGECHAN-SENSEI.
OH, YOU WERE IN CLASS FIVE!
YEAH.
YOUR CROTCH!
Aaaaaahhh!
I WILL DO MY BEST.
WHAT ...
...CUP SIZE IS THAT?
IT'S A D CUP!
WHAT'S YOUR CUP SIZE?
......

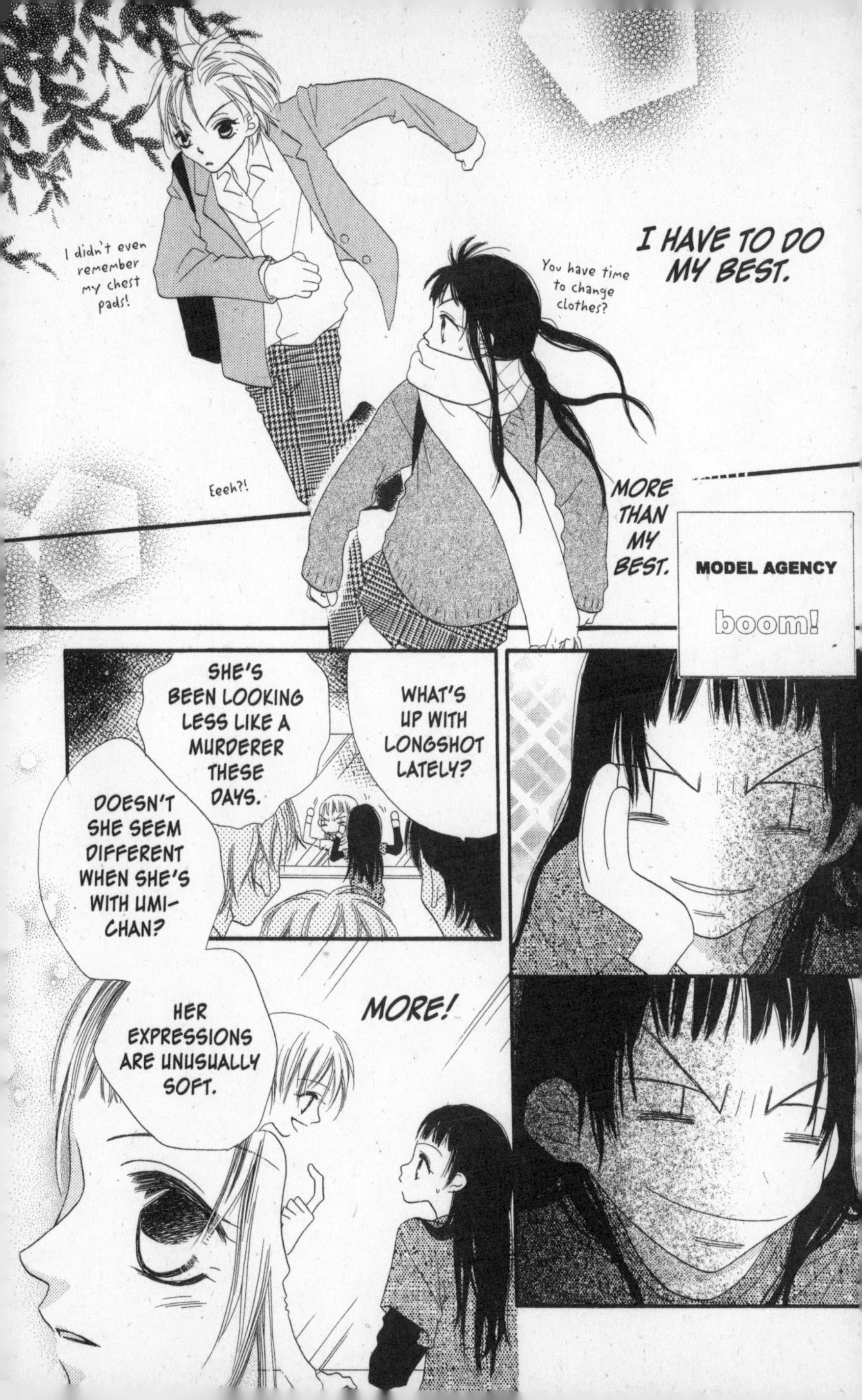
I HAVE TO DO MY BEST.
You have time to change clothes?
I didn't even remember my chest pads!
Eeeh?!
MORE THAN MY BEST.
MODEL AGENCY
boom!
WHAT'S UP WITH LONGSHOT LATELY?
SHE'S BEEN LOOKING LESS LIKE A MURDERER THESE DAYS.
DOESN'T SHE SEEM DIFFERENT WHEN SHE'S WITH UMI-CHAN?
MORE!
HER EXPRESSIONS ARE UNUSUALLY SOFT.

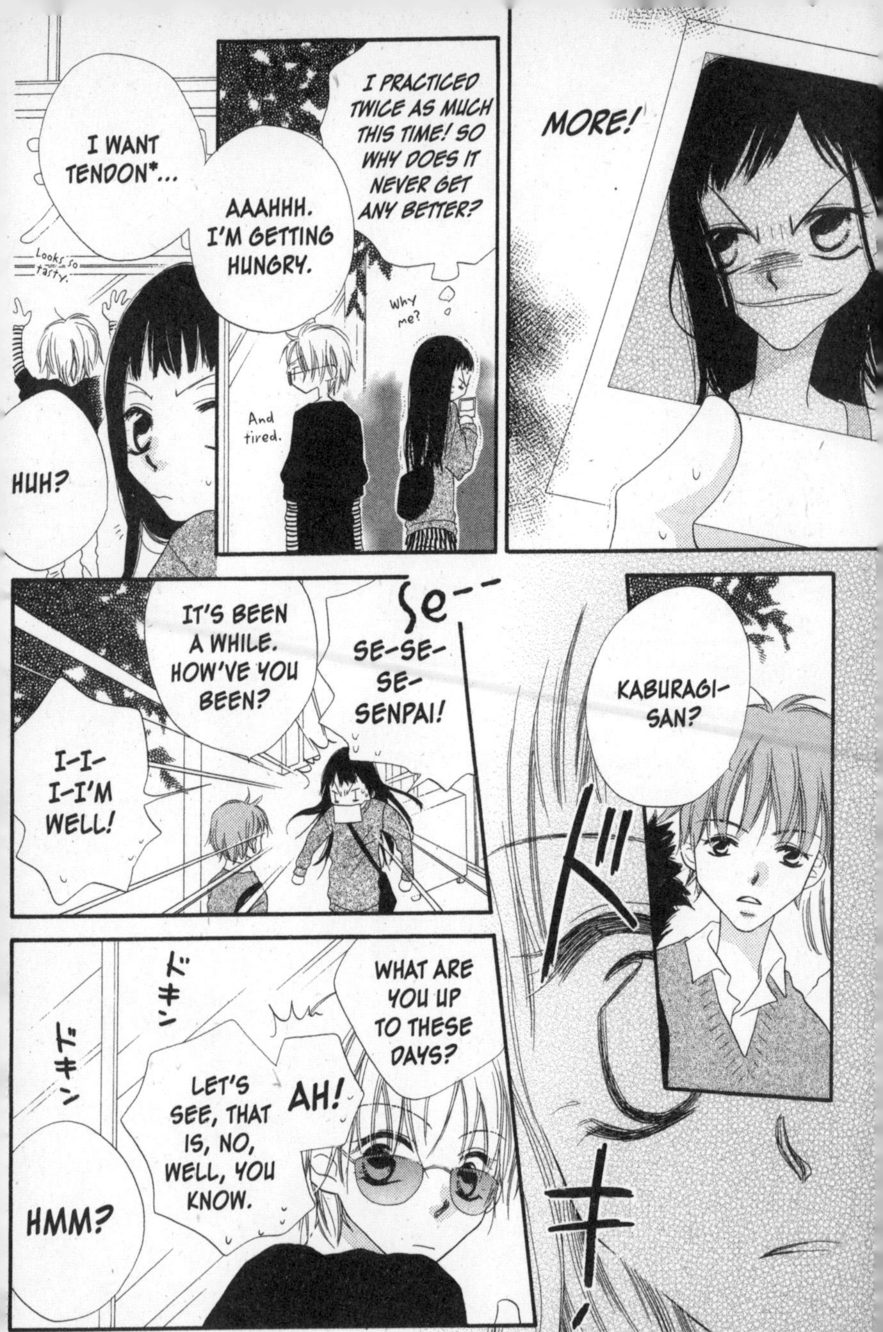
MORE!
I PRACTICED TWICE AS MUCH THIS TIME! SO WHY DOES IT NEVER GET ANY BETTER?
Why me?
And tired.
AAAHHH. I'M GETTING HUNGRY.
I WANT TENDON*...
Looks so tasty.
HUH?
KABURAGI-SAN?
ドキ
Se---
SE-SE-SE-SENPAI!
IT'S BEEN A WHILE. HOW'VE YOU BEEN?
I-I-I-I'M WELL!
WHAT ARE YOU UP TO THESE DAYS?
ドキン
ドキン
AH!
LET'S SEE, THAT IS, NO, WELL, YOU KNOW.
HMM?

*A rice and tempura dish.

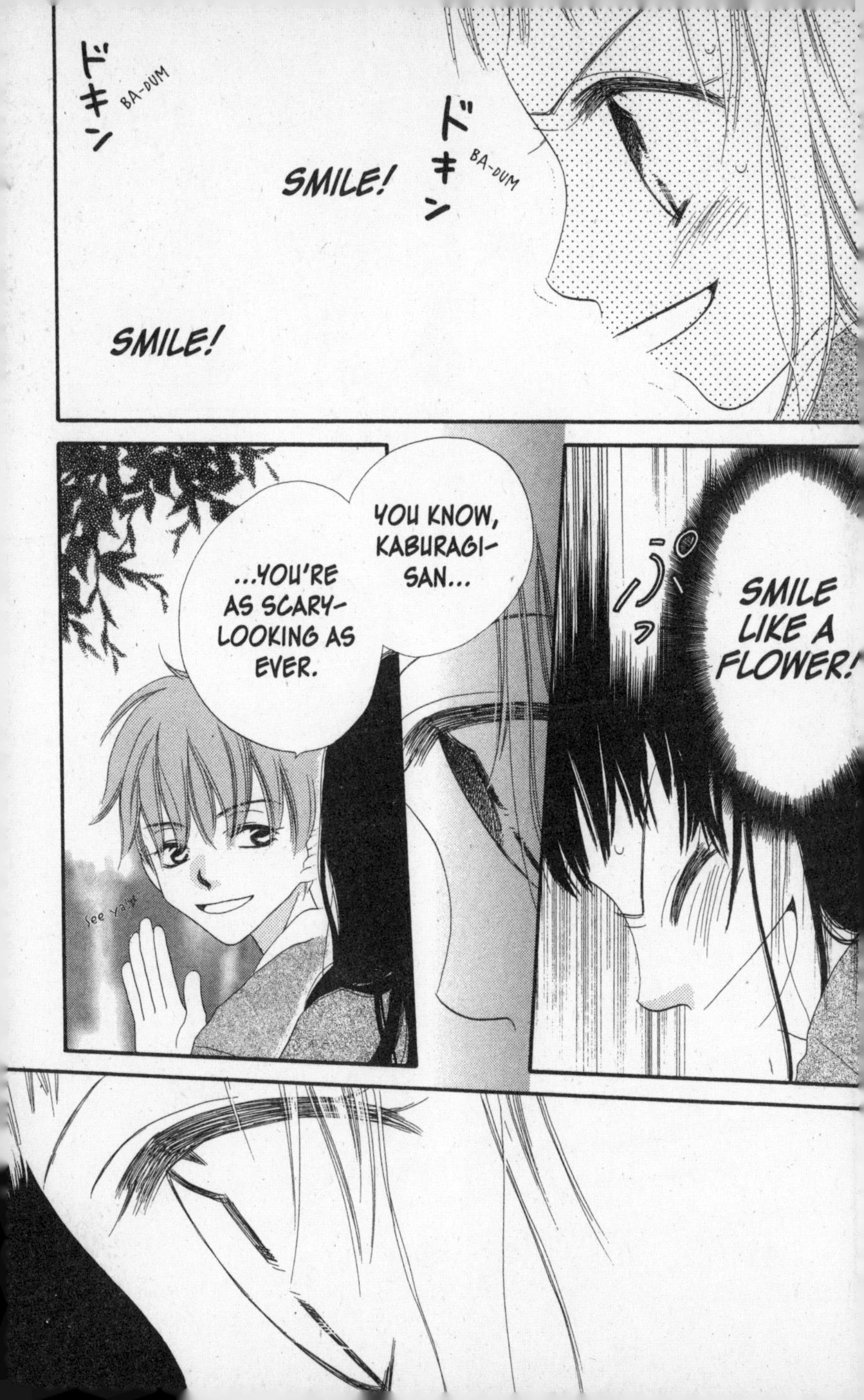

ドキン
BA-DUM
SMILE!
ドキン
BA-DUM
SMILE!
ぱっ
SMILE LIKE A FLOWER!
YOU KNOW, KABURAGI-SAN...
...YOU'RE AS SCARY-LOOKING AS EVER.
See ya!

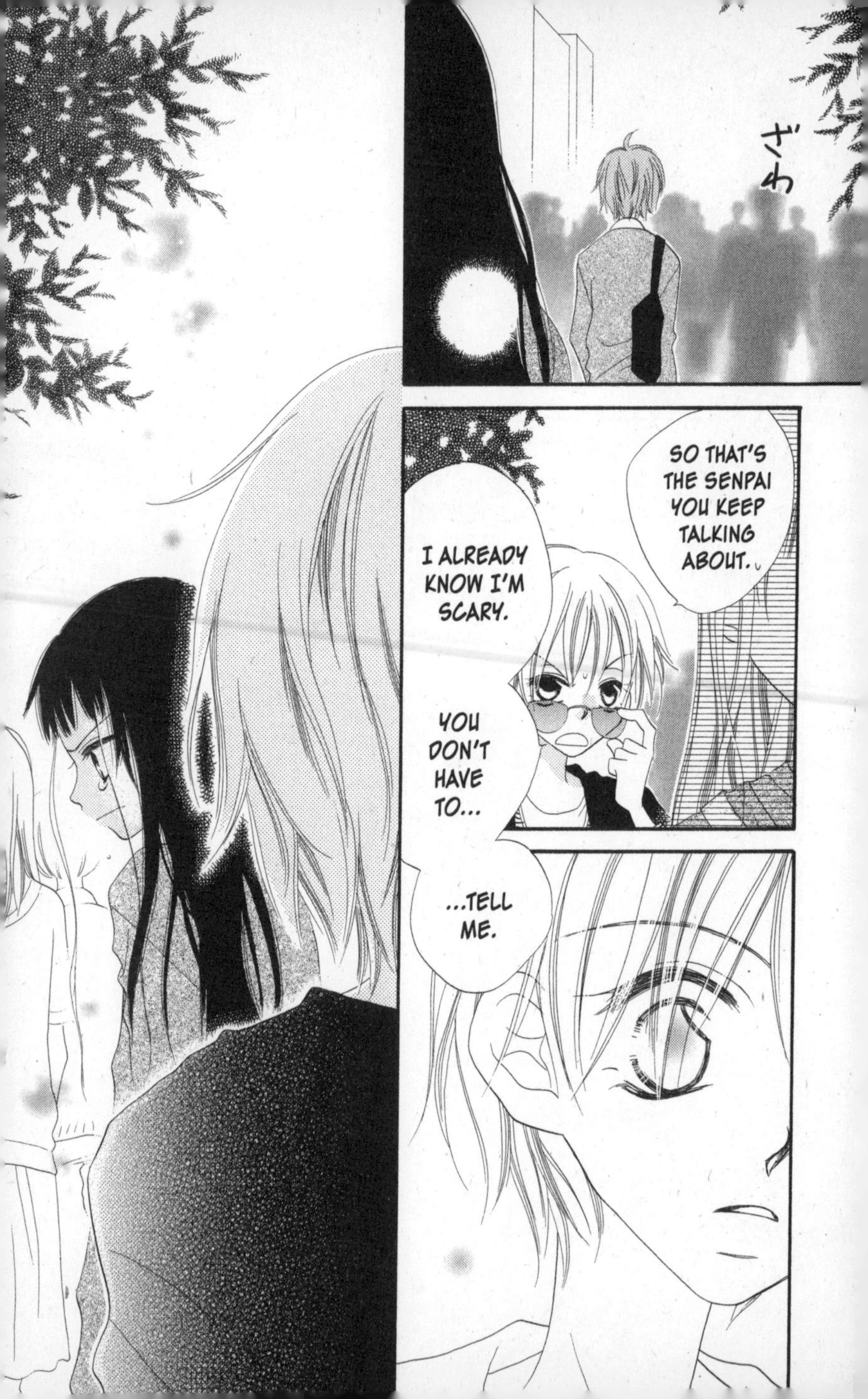
ざわ
SO THAT'S THE SENPAI YOU KEEP TALKING ABOUT.
I ALREADY KNOW I'M SCARY.
YOU DON'T HAVE TO...
...TELL ME.

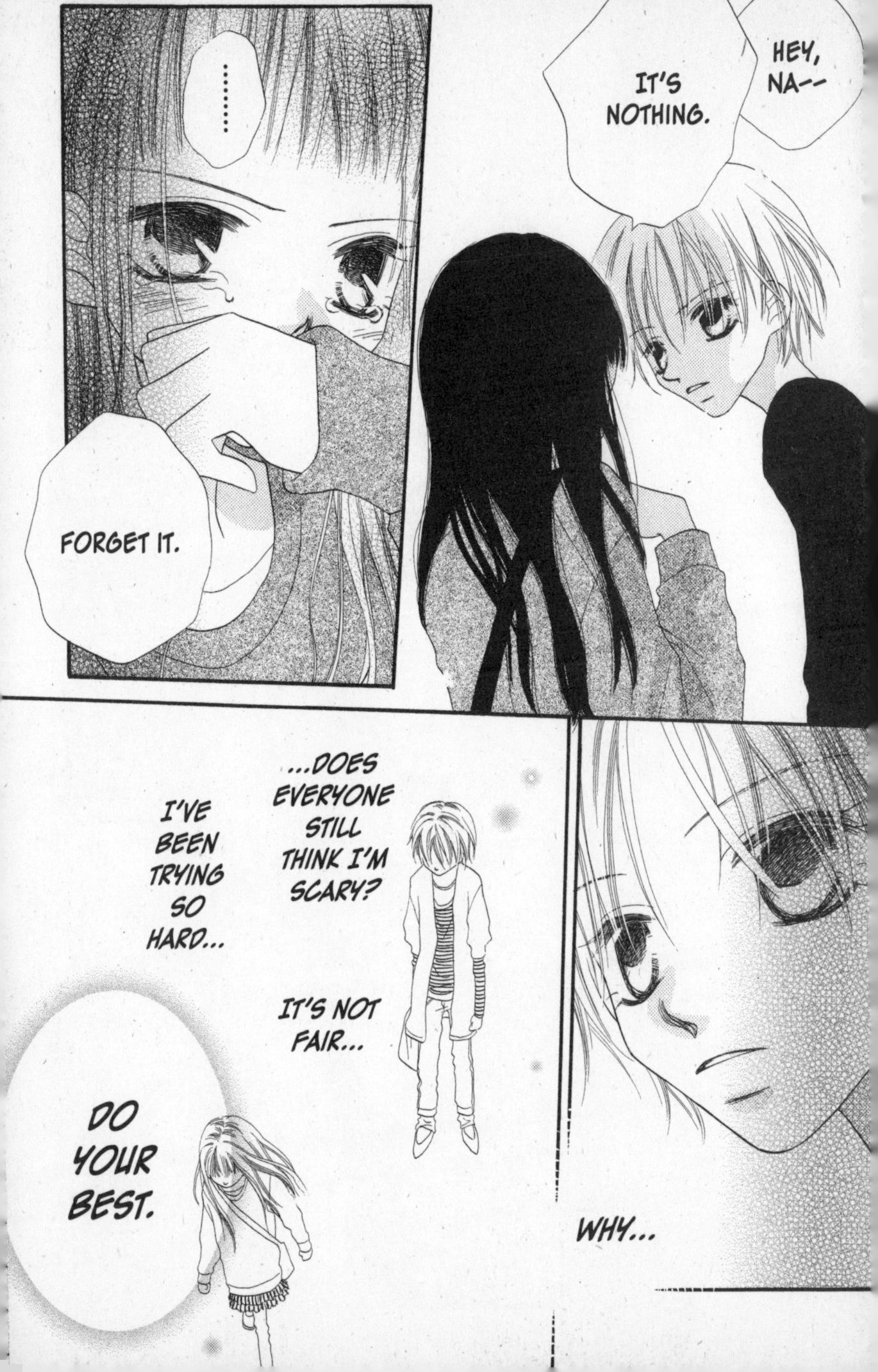
HEY, NA--
IT'S NOTHING.
......
FORGET IT.
WHY...
...DOES EVERYONE STILL THINK I'M SCARY?
I'VE BEEN TRYING SO HARD...
IT'S NOT FAIR...
DO YOUR BEST.

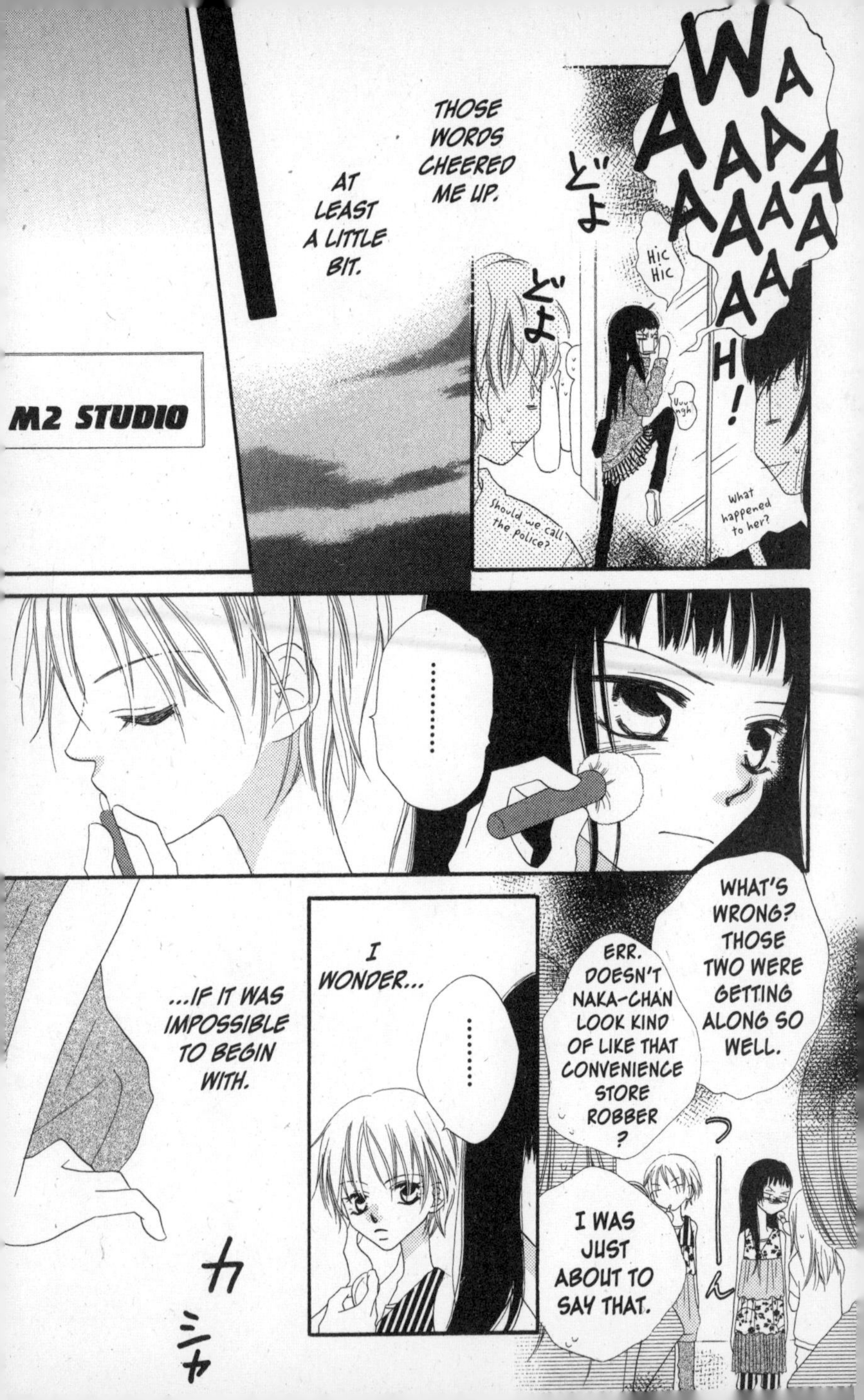
AWAAAAAAAAAAAAAH!
どよ
どよ
Hic Hic
Uuu ngh
What happened to her?
Should we call the police?
THOSE WORDS CHEERED ME UP.
AT LEAST A LITTLE BIT.
M2 STUDIO
......
WHAT'S WRONG? THOSE TWO WERE GETTING ALONG SO WELL.
ERR. DOESN'T NAKA-CHAN LOOK KIND OF LIKE THAT CONVENIENCE STORE ROBBER?
I WAS JUST ABOUT TO SAY THAT.
つーん
I WONDER...
......
...IF IT WAS IMPOSSIBLE TO BEGIN WITH.
カシャ

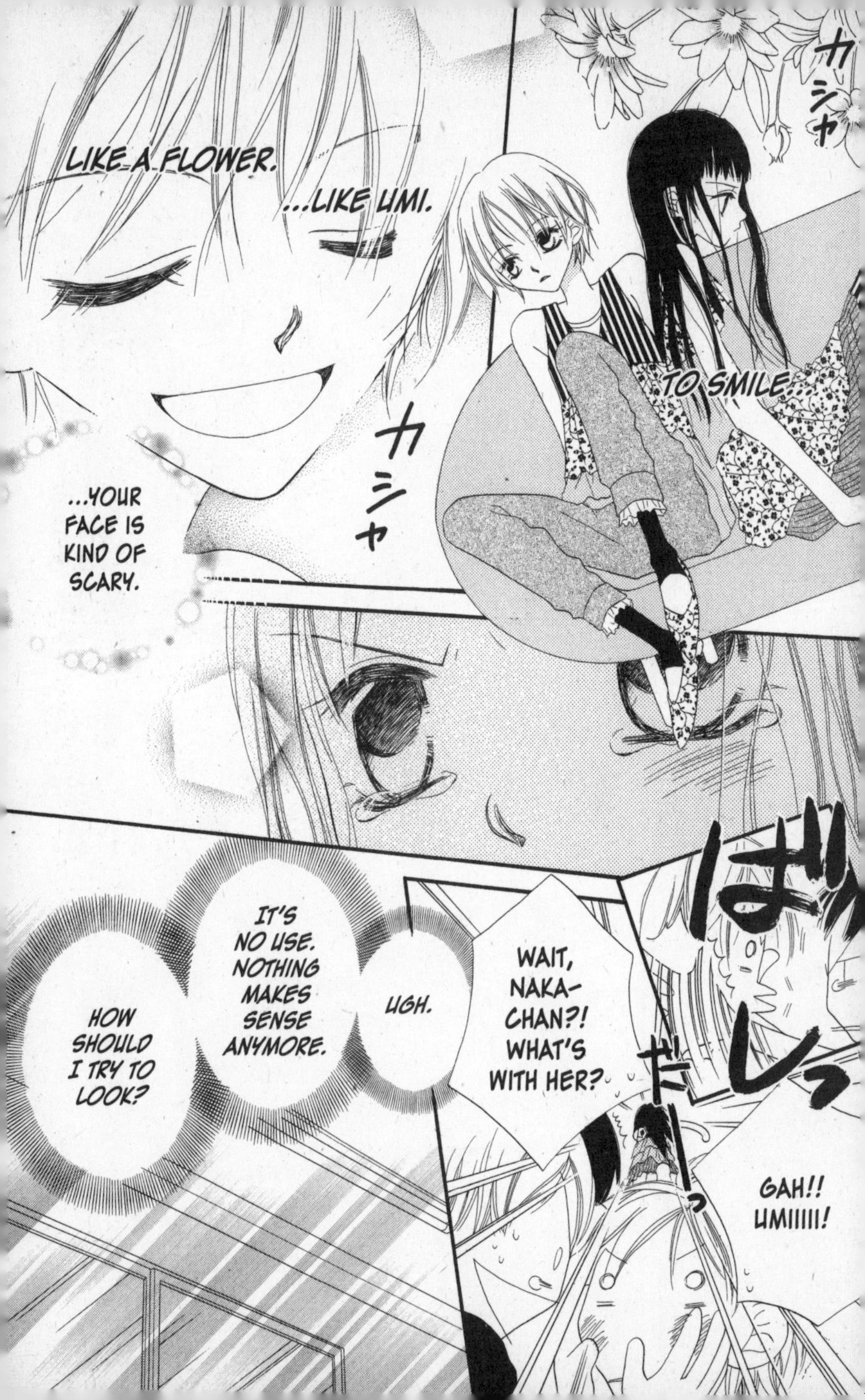

カシャ
TO SMILE...
LIKE A FLOWER.
...LIKE UMI.
カシャ
...YOUR FACE IS KIND OF SCARY.
WAIT, NAKA-CHAN?! WHAT'S WITH HER?
だーっ
GAH!! UMIIIIII!
UGH.
IT'S NO USE. NOTHING MAKES SENSE ANYMORE.
HOW SHOULD I TRY TO LOOK?

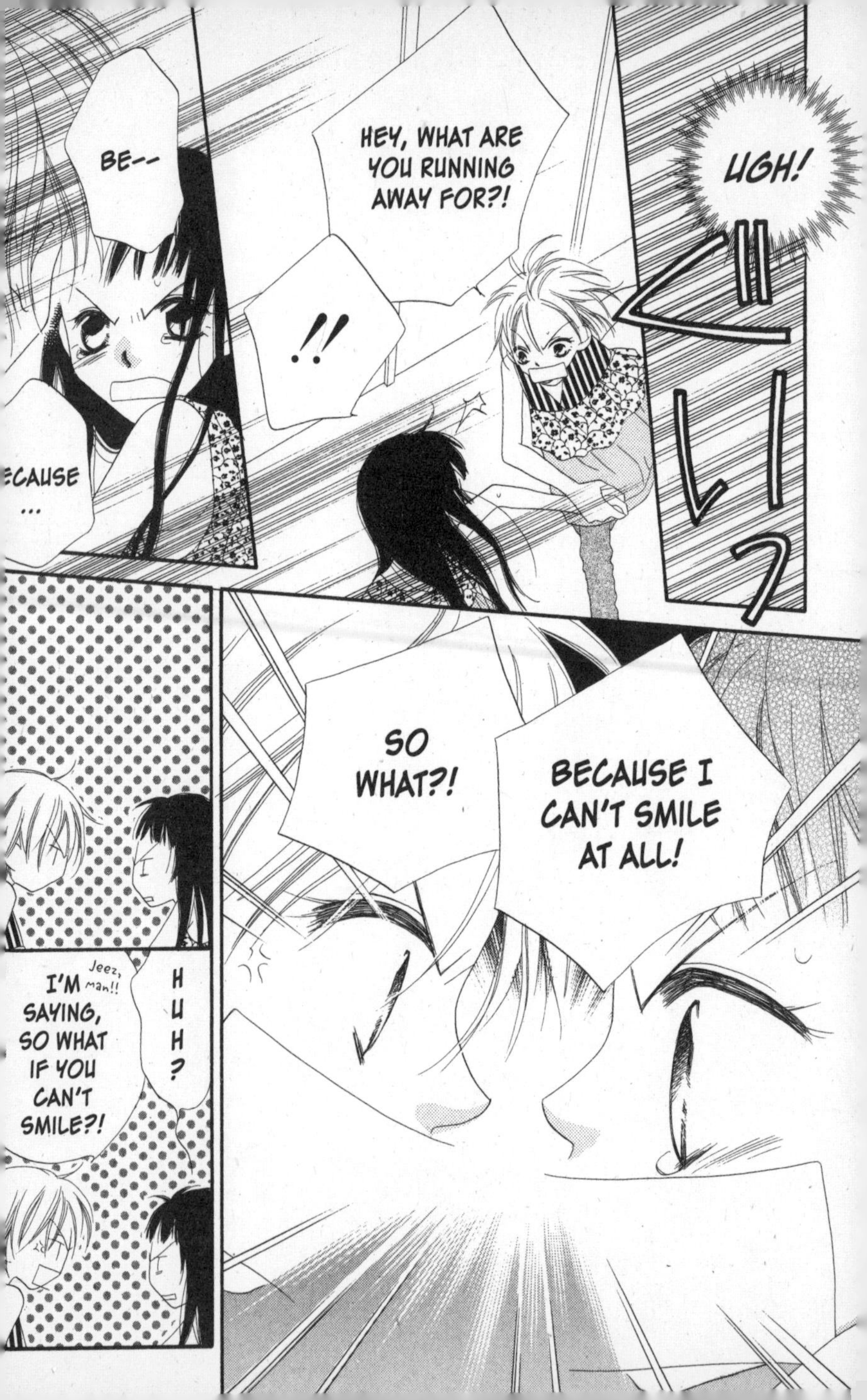
UGH!
HEY, WHAT ARE YOU RUNNING AWAY FOR?!
!!
BE--
ECAUSE …
BECAUSE I CAN'T SMILE AT ALL!
SO WHAT?!
HUH?
I'M SAYING, SO WHAT IF YOU CAN'T SMILE?!
Jeez, man!!

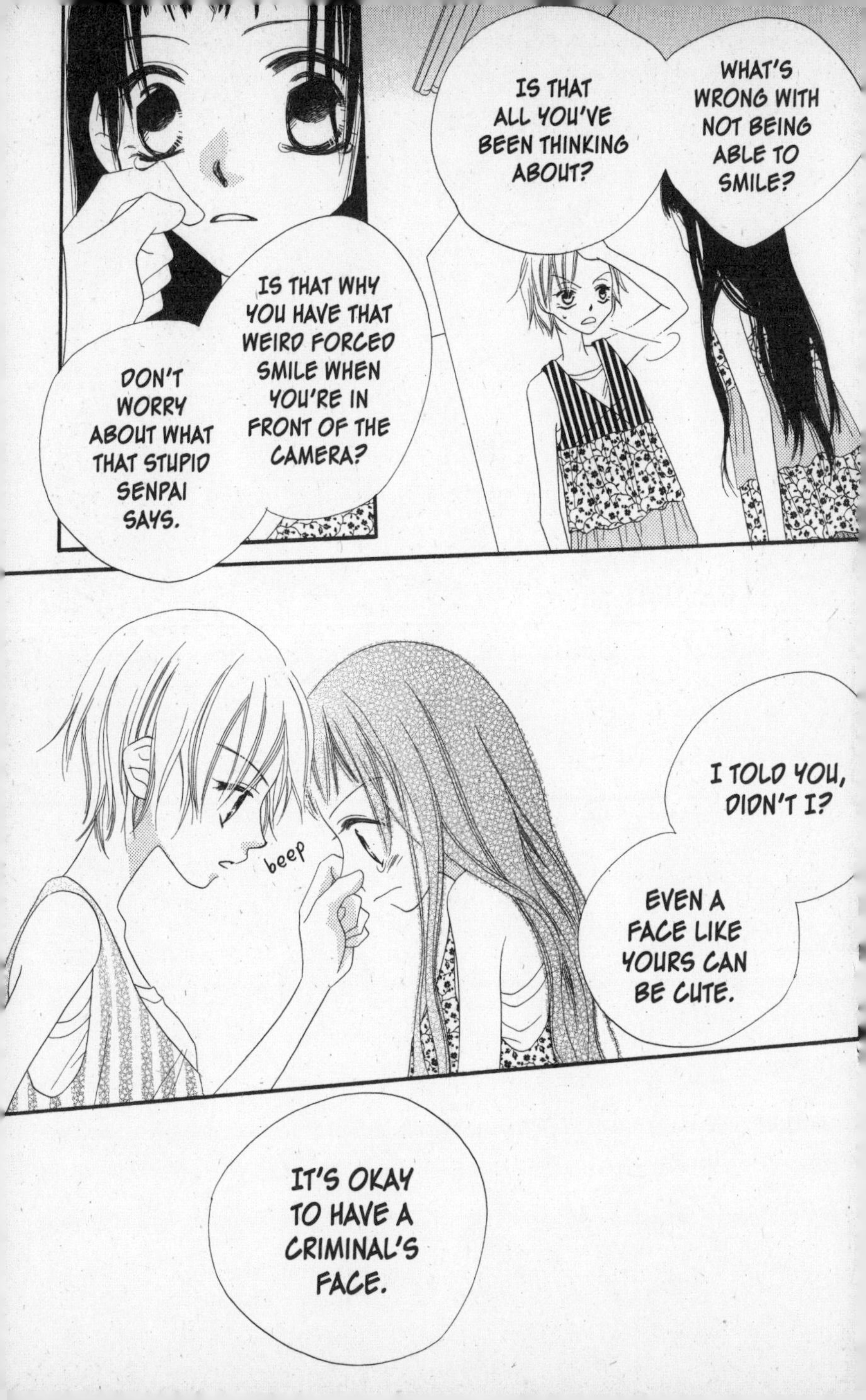
WHAT'S WRONG WITH NOT BEING ABLE TO SMILE?
IS THAT ALL YOU'VE BEEN THINKING ABOUT?
IS THAT WHY YOU HAVE THAT WEIRD FORCED SMILE WHEN YOU'RE IN FRONT OF THE CAMERA?
DON'T WORRY ABOUT WHAT THAT STUPID SENPAI SAYS.
I TOLD YOU, DIDN'T I?
EVEN A FACE LIKE YOURS CAN BE CUTE.
beep
IT'S OKAY TO HAVE A CRIMINAL'S FACE.

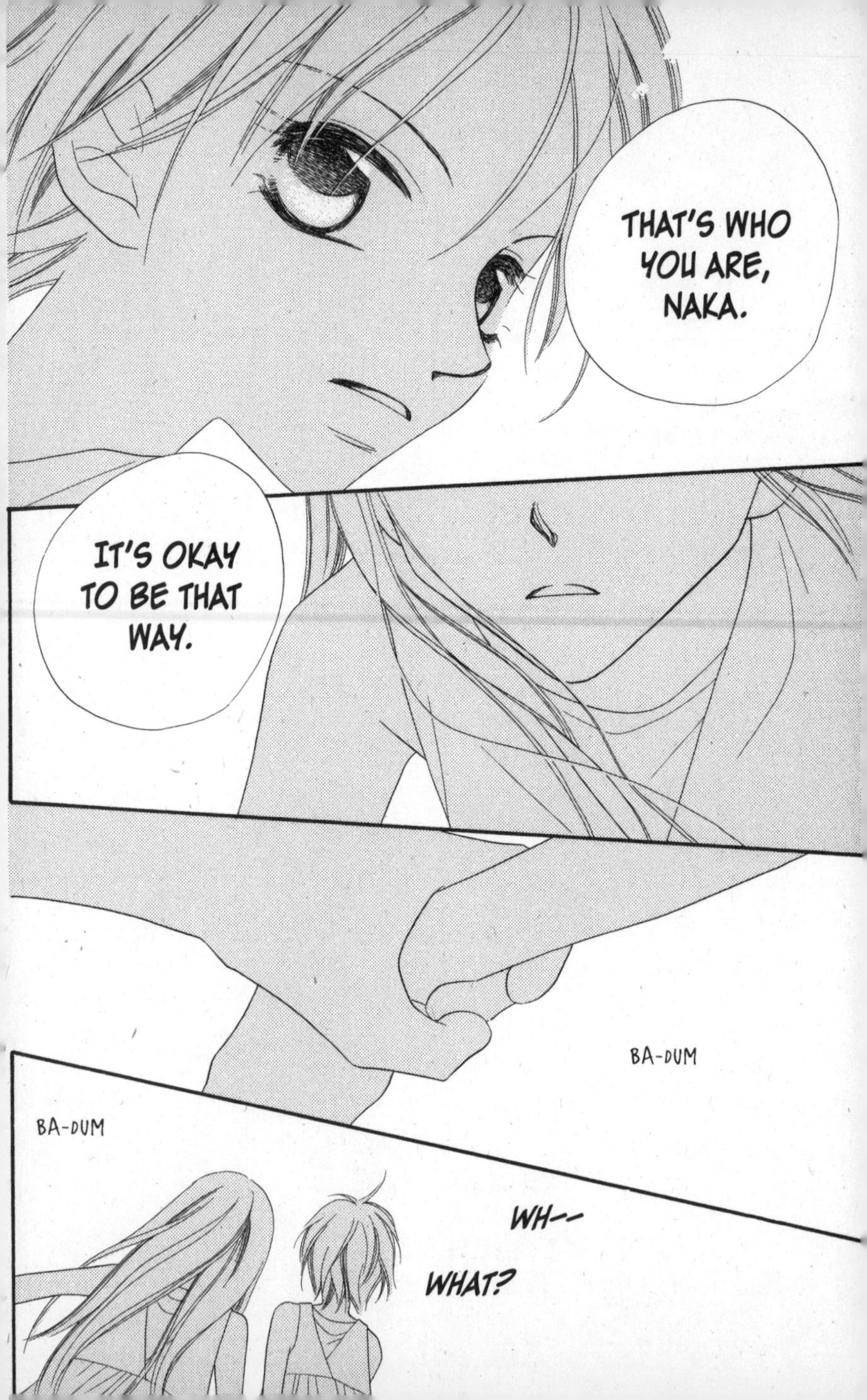
THAT'S WHO YOU ARE, NAKA.
IT'S OKAY TO BE THAT WAY.
BA-DUM
BA-DUM
WH--
WHAT?

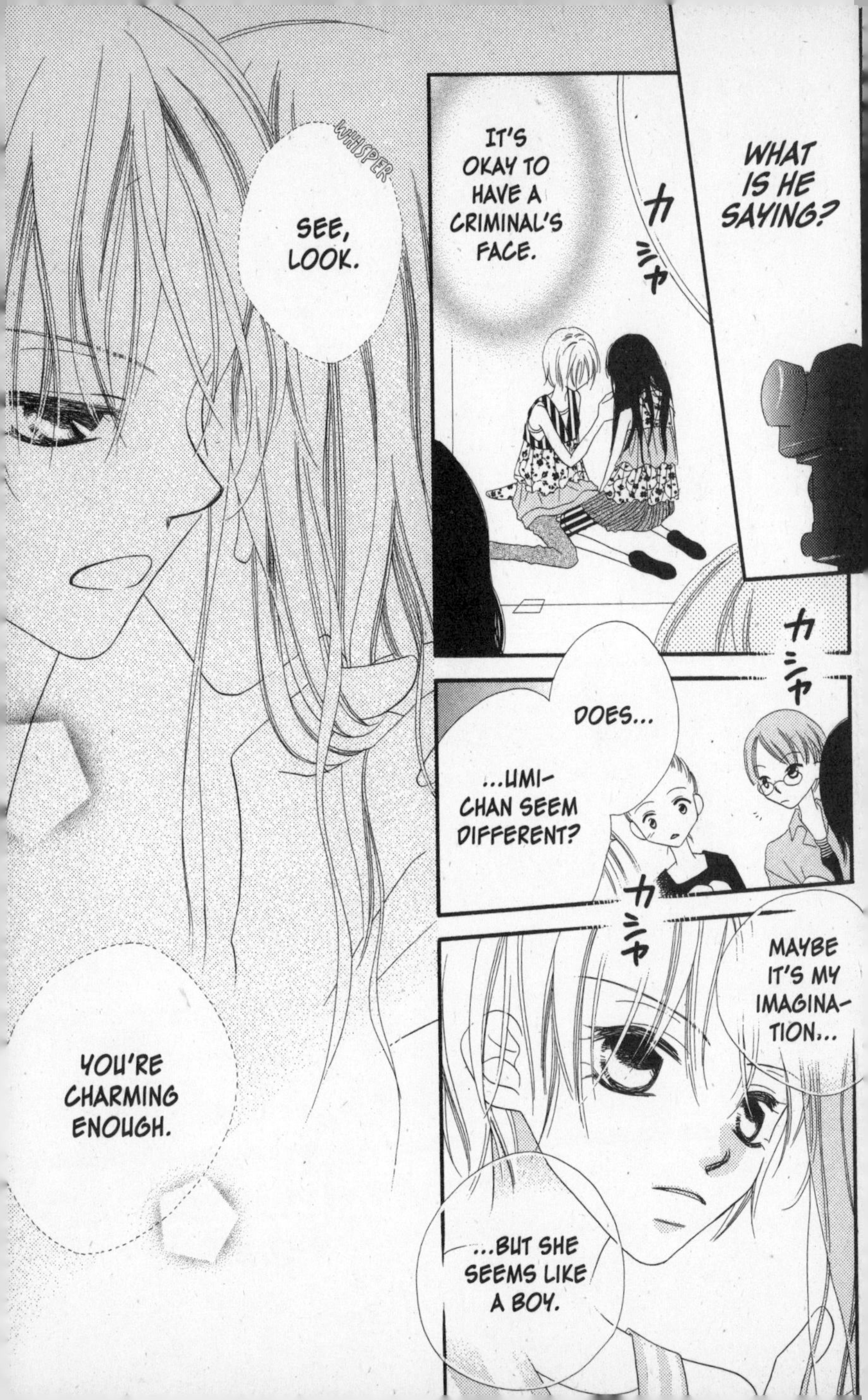
WHAT IS HE SAYING?
カシャ
IT'S OKAY TO HAVE A CRIMINAL'S FACE.
カシャ
DOES...
...UMI-CHAN SEEM DIFFERENT?
カシャ
MAYBE IT'S MY IMAGINATION...
...BUT SHE SEEMS LIKE A BOY.
WHISPER
SEE, LOOK.
YOU'RE CHARMING ENOUGH.

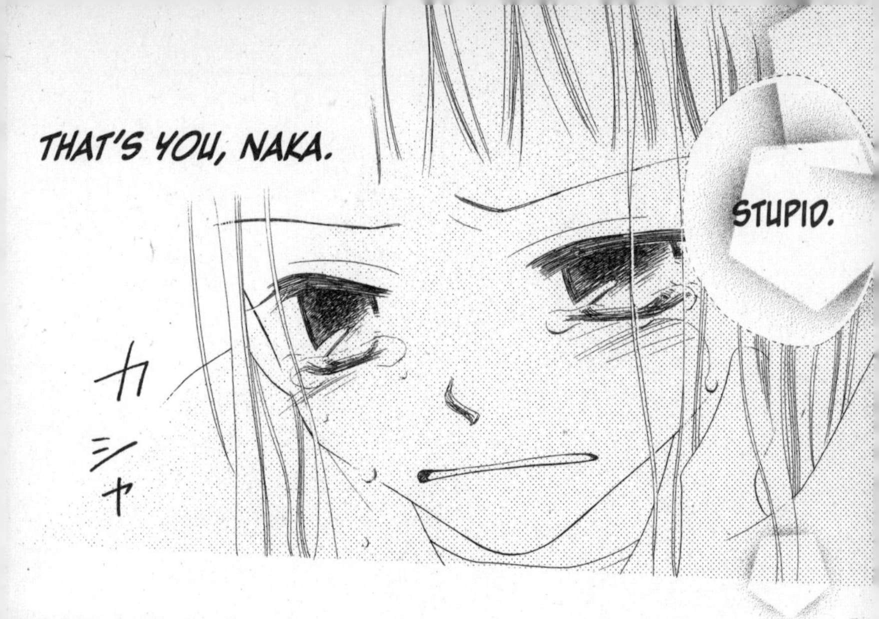
STUPID.
THAT'S YOU, NAKA.
カシャ
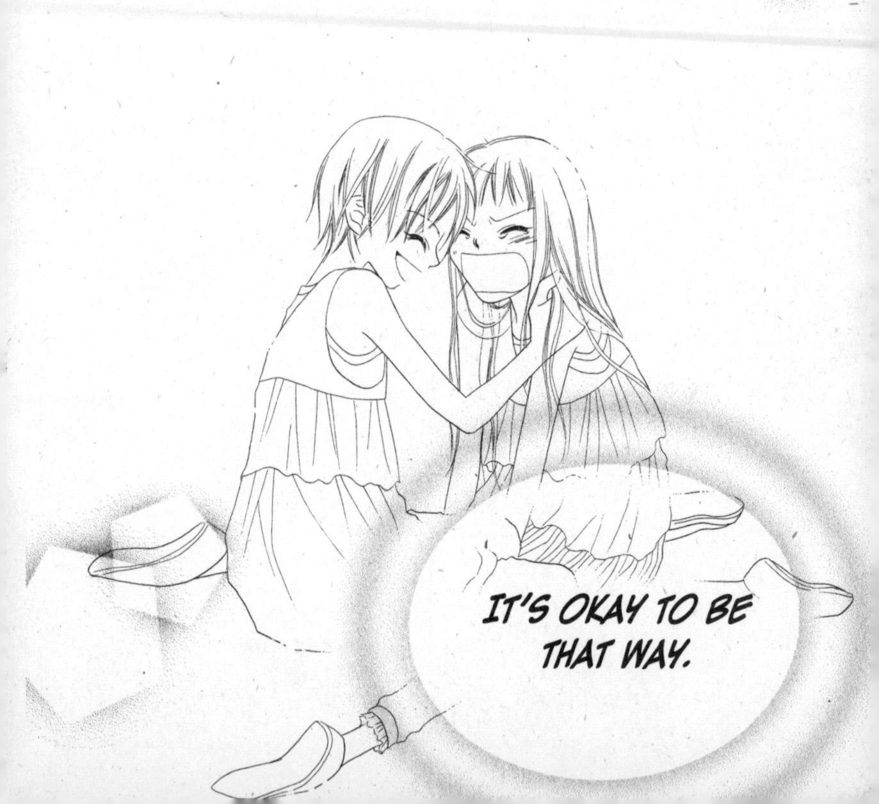
IT'S OKAY TO BE THAT WAY.

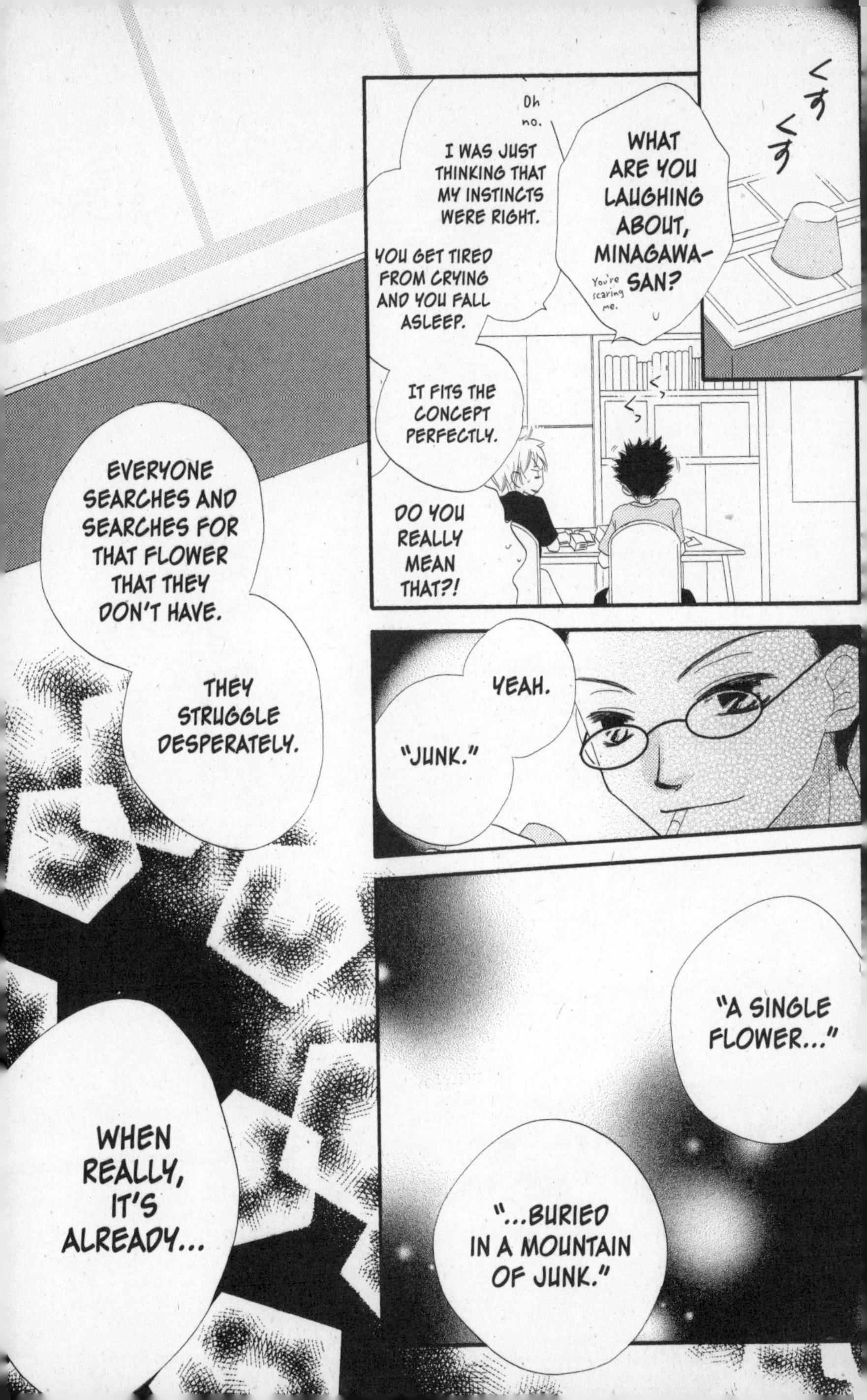
くす くす
WHAT ARE YOU LAUGHING ABOUT, MINAGAWA-SAN?
You're scaring me.
Oh no.
I WAS JUST THINKING THAT MY INSTINCTS WERE RIGHT.
YOU GET TIRED FROM CRYING AND YOU FALL ASLEEP.
IT FITS THE CONCEPT PERFECTLY.
くっ くっ
DO YOU REALLY MEAN THAT?!
YEAH.
"JUNK."
"A SINGLE FLOWER..."
"...BURIED IN A MOUNTAIN OF JUNK."
EVERYONE SEARCHES AND SEARCHES FOR THAT FLOWER THAT THEY DON'T HAVE.
THEY STRUGGLE DESPERATELY.
WHEN REALLY, IT'S ALREADY...

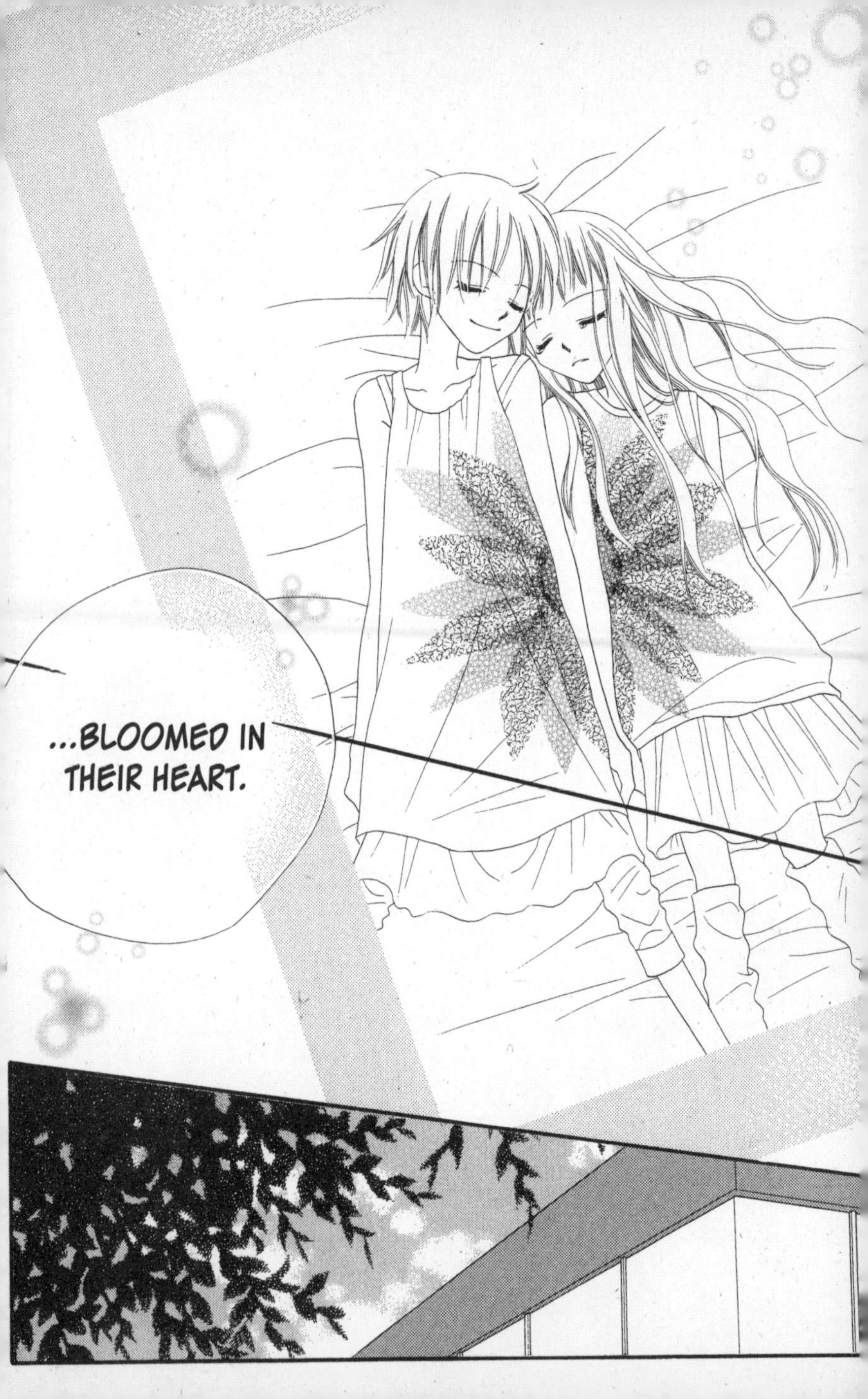
...BLOOMED IN THEIR HEART.

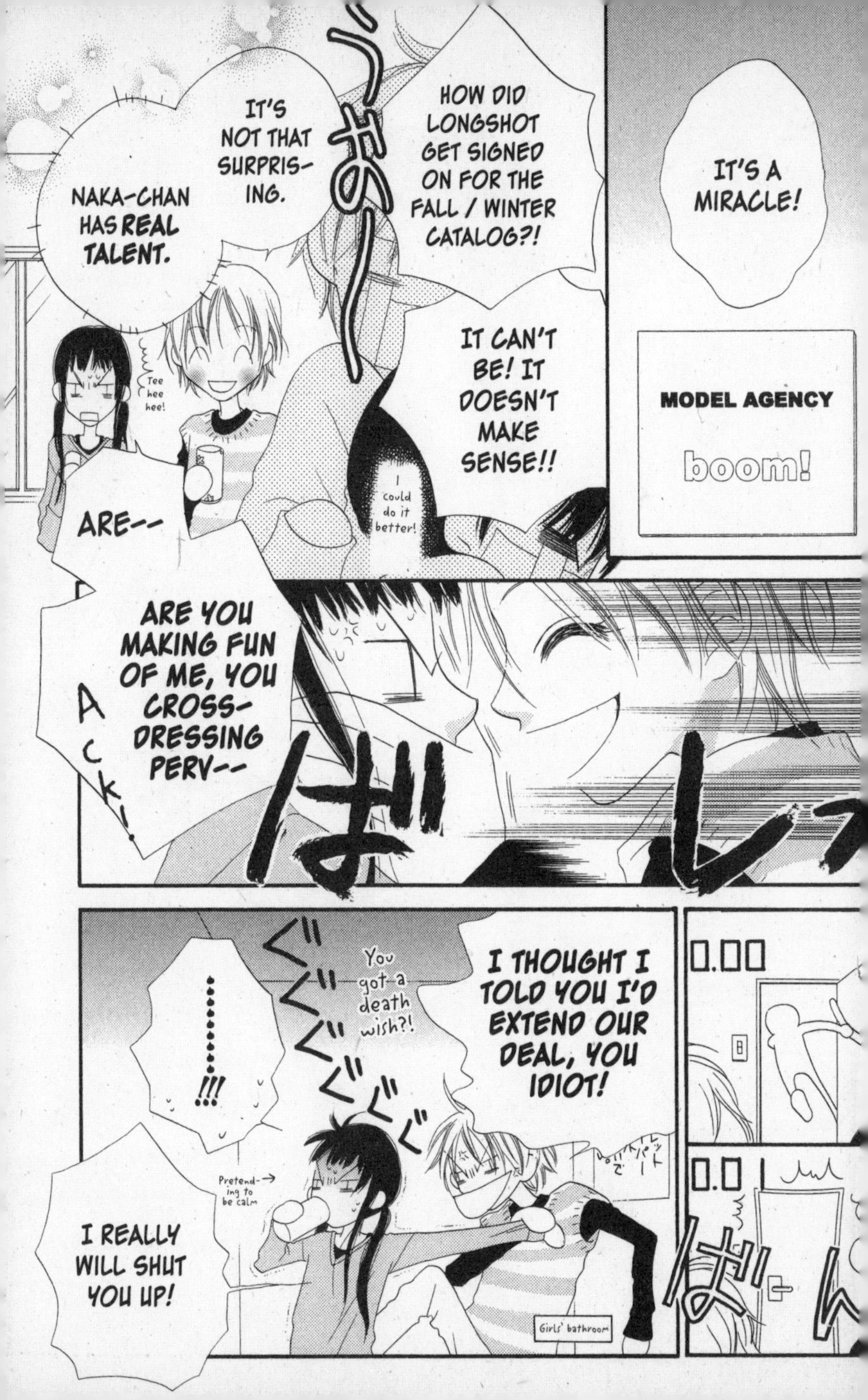
IT'S A MIRACLE!
MODEL AGENCY
boom!
HOW DID LONGSHOT GET SIGNED ON FOR THE FALL / WINTER CATALOG?!
IT CAN'T BE! IT DOESN'T MAKE SENSE!!
I could do it better!
IT'S NOT THAT SURPRISING.
NAKA-CHAN HAS REAL TALENT.
Tee hee hee!
ARE--
ARE YOU MAKING FUN OF ME, YOU CROSS-DRESSING PERV--
Ack!
I THOUGHT I TOLD YOU I'D EXTEND OUR DEAL, YOU IDIOT!
You got a death wish?!
.........!!!
Pretending to be calm
I REALLY WILL SHUT YOU UP!
Girls' bathroom

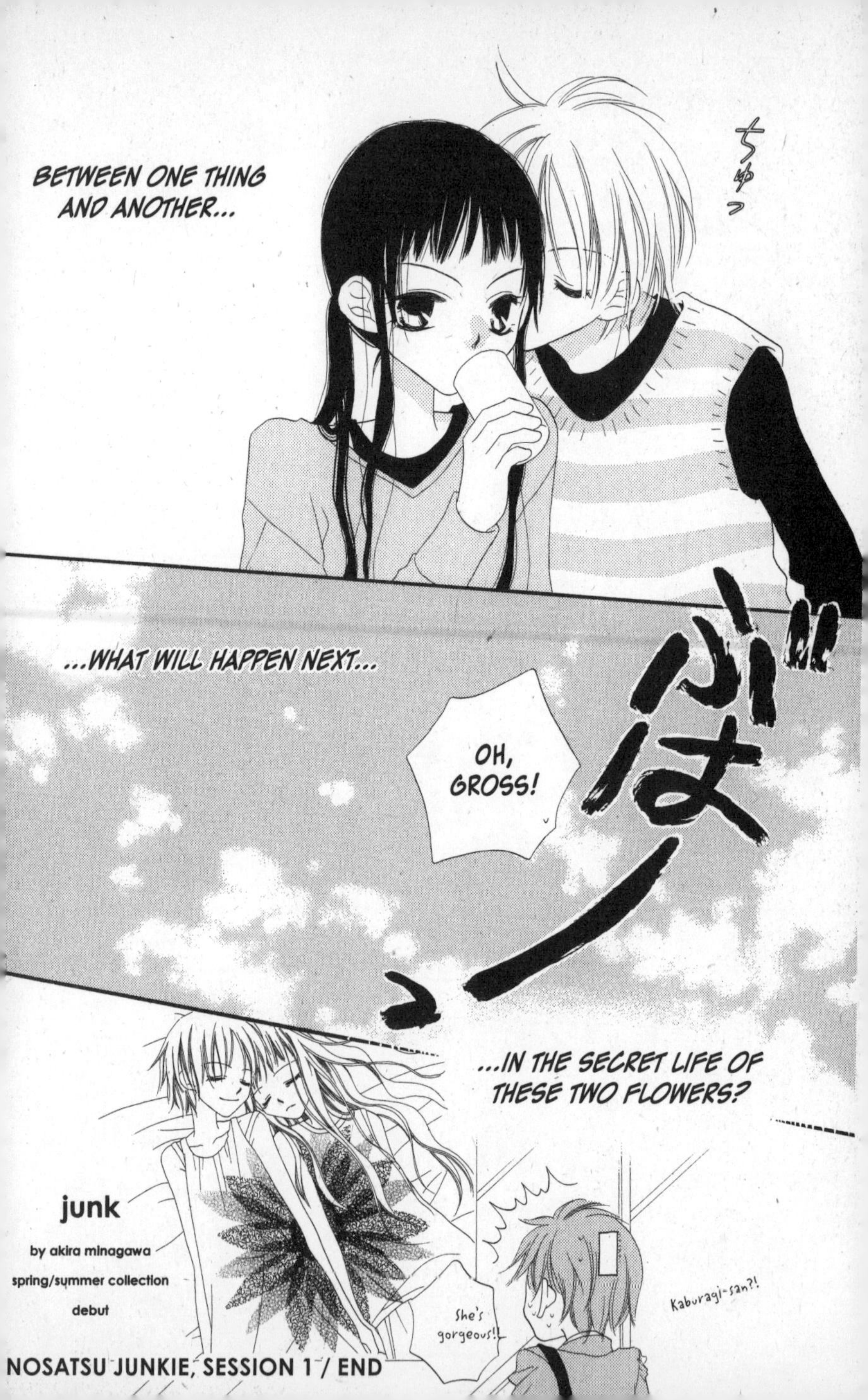

BETWEEN ONE THING AND ANOTHER...
ちゅっ
...WHAT WILL HAPPEN NEXT...
ぶはーっ
OH, GROSS!
...IN THE SECRET LIFE OF THESE TWO FLOWERS?
Kaburagi-san?!
She's gorgeous!!
junk
by akira minagawa
spring/summer collection
debut

NOSATSU JUNKIE, SESSION 1 / END

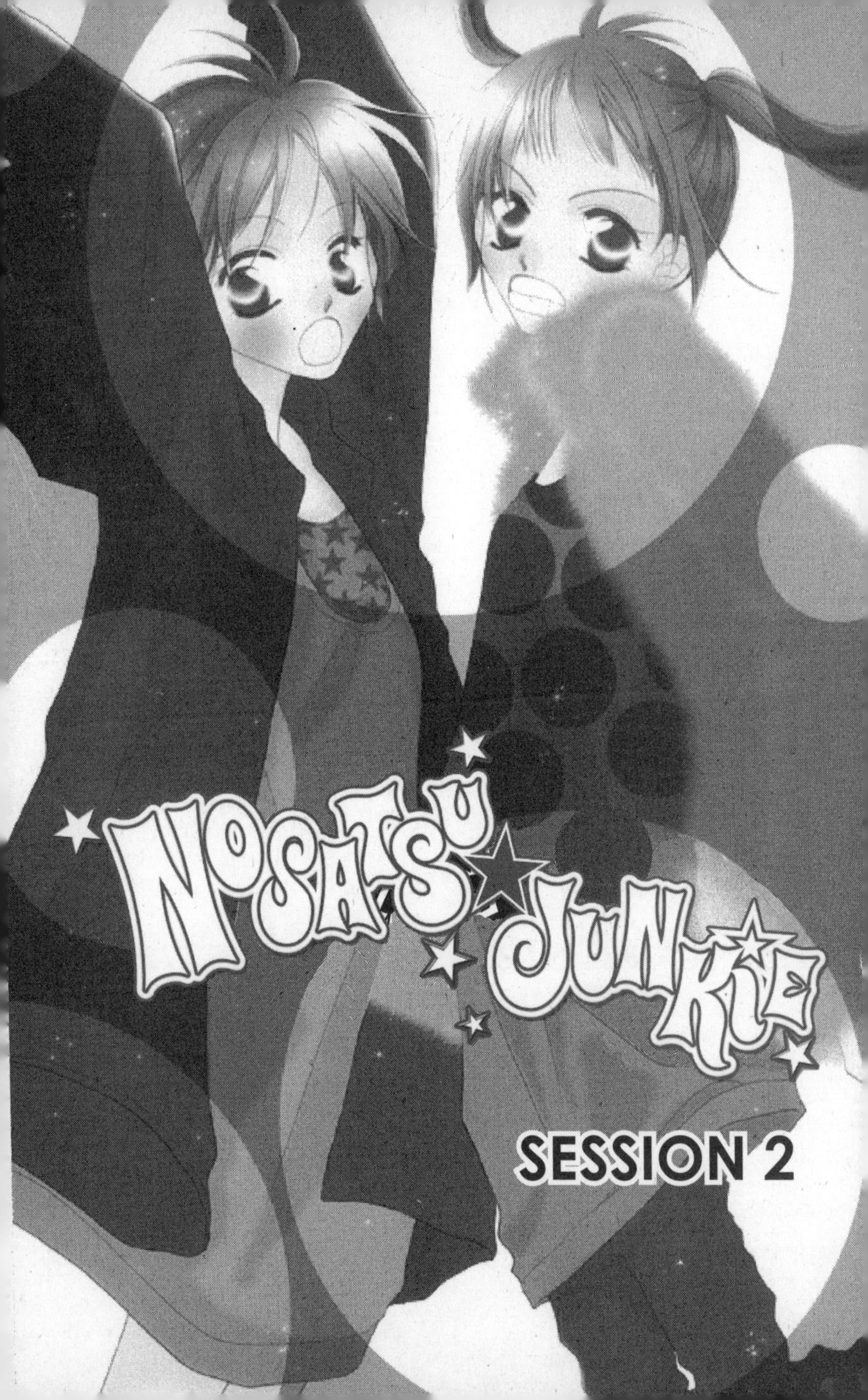
NOSATSU JUNKIE
SESSION 2

★ SESSION 2-5 PREVIEW! ★

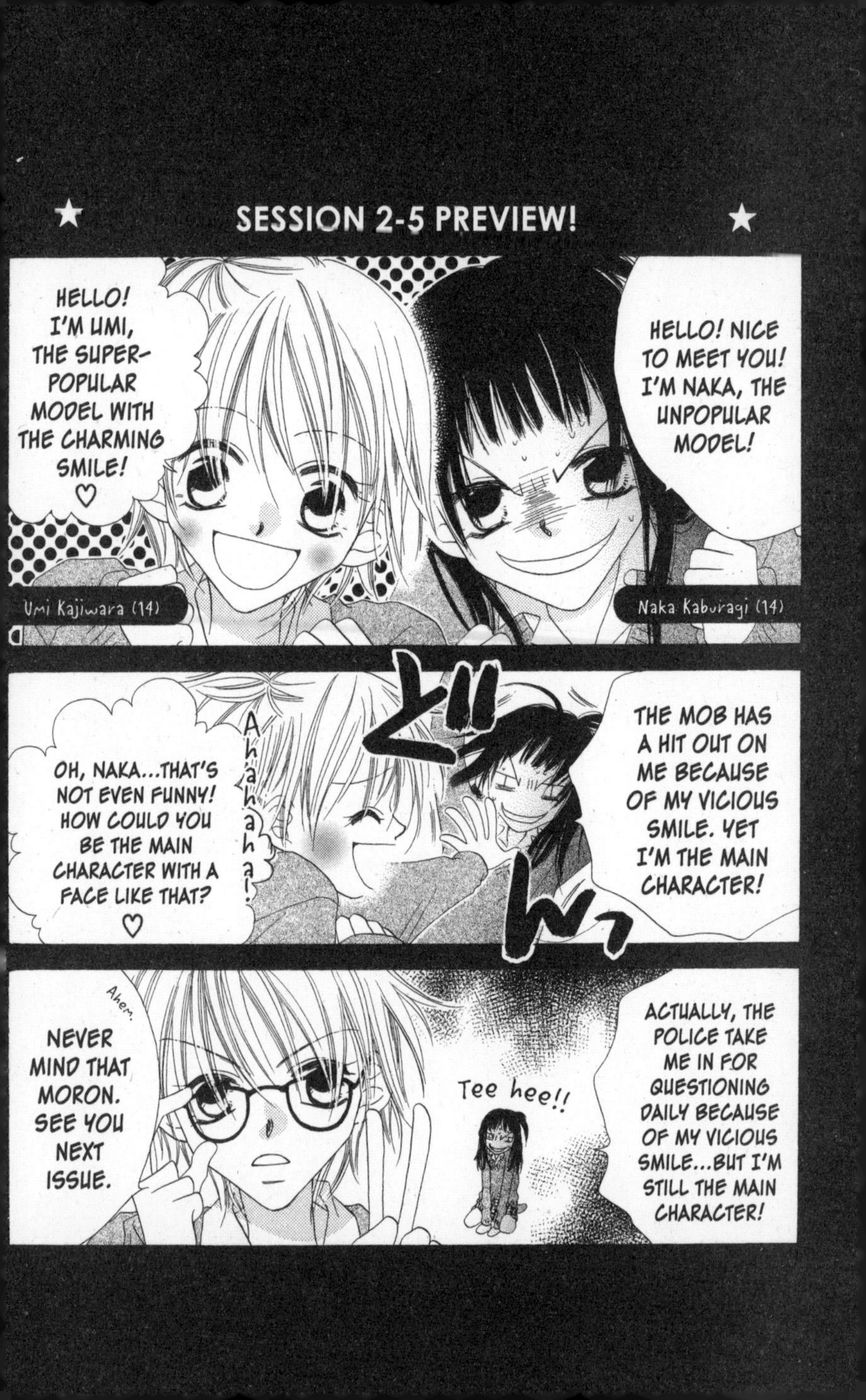
HELLO! NICE TO MEET YOU! I'M NAKA, THE UNPOPULAR MODEL!
Naka Kaburagi (14)
HELLO! I'M UMI, THE SUPER-POPULAR MODEL WITH THE CHARMING SMILE! ♡
Umi Kajiwara (14)
THE MOB HAS A HIT OUT ON ME BECAUSE OF MY VICIOUS SMILE. YET I'M THE MAIN CHARACTER!
Ahahaha!
OH, NAKA...THAT'S NOT EVEN FUNNY! HOW COULD YOU BE THE MAIN CHARACTER WITH A FACE LIKE THAT? ♡
ACTUALLY, THE POLICE TAKE ME IN FOR QUESTIONING DAILY BECAUSE OF MY VICIOUS SMILE...BUT I'M STILL THE MAIN CHARACTER!
Tee hee!!
Ahem.
NEVER MIND THAT MORON. SEE YOU NEXT ISSUE.

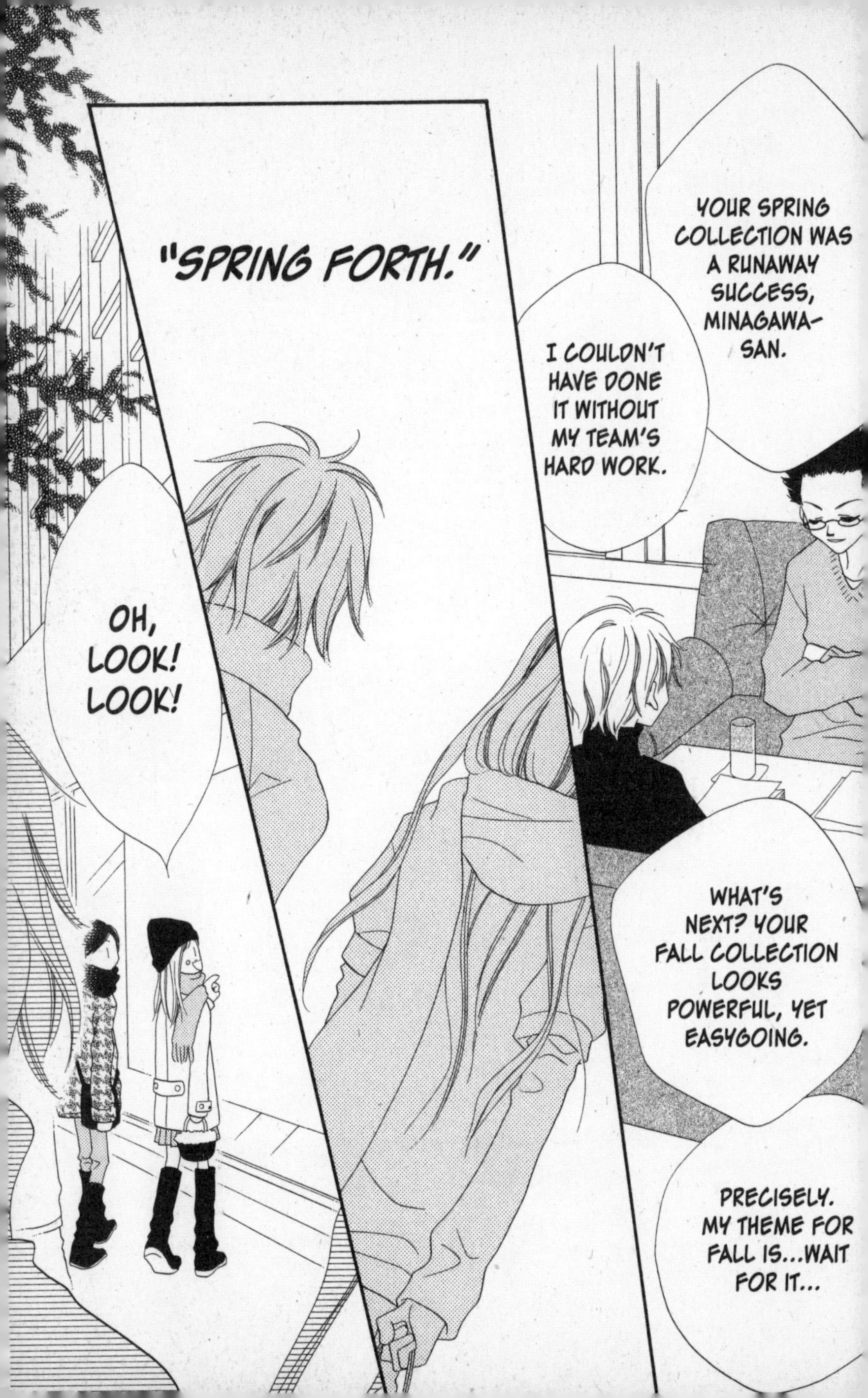
YOUR SPRING COLLECTION WAS A RUNAWAY SUCCESS, MINAGAWA-SAN.
I COULDN'T HAVE DONE IT WITHOUT MY TEAM'S HARD WORK.
WHAT'S NEXT? YOUR FALL COLLECTION LOOKS POWERFUL, YET EASYGOING.
PRECISELY. MY THEME FOR FALL IS...WAIT FOR IT...
"SPRING FORTH."
OH, LOOK! LOOK!

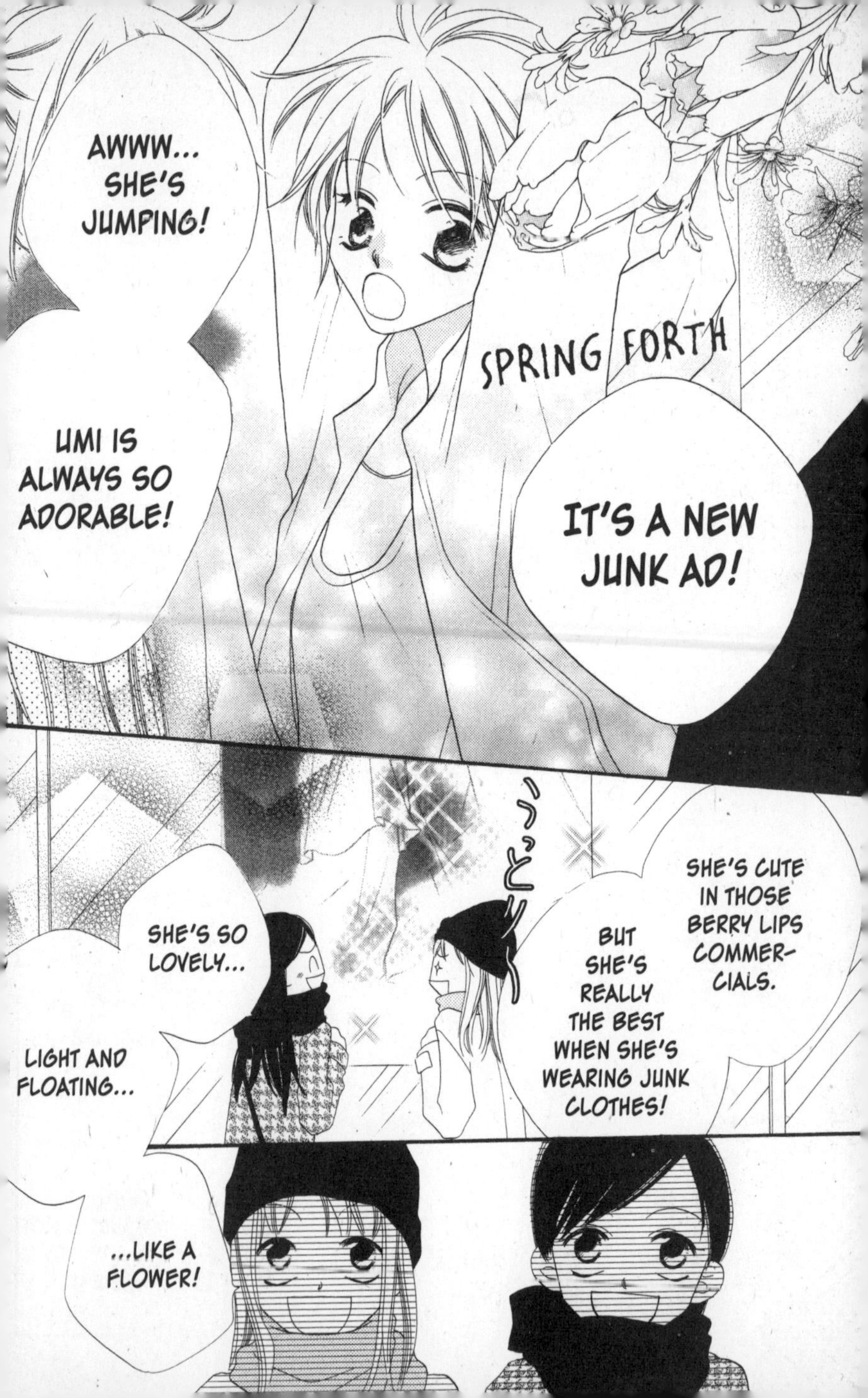
SPRING FORTH
IT'S A NEW JUNK AD!
AWWW... SHE'S JUMPING!
UMI IS ALWAYS SO ADORABLE!
SHE'S CUTE IN THOSE BERRY LIPS COMMER-CIALS.
BUT SHE'S REALLY THE BEST WHEN SHE'S WEARING JUNK CLOTHES!
SHE'S SO LOVELY...
LIGHT AND FLOATING...
...LIKE A FLOWER!

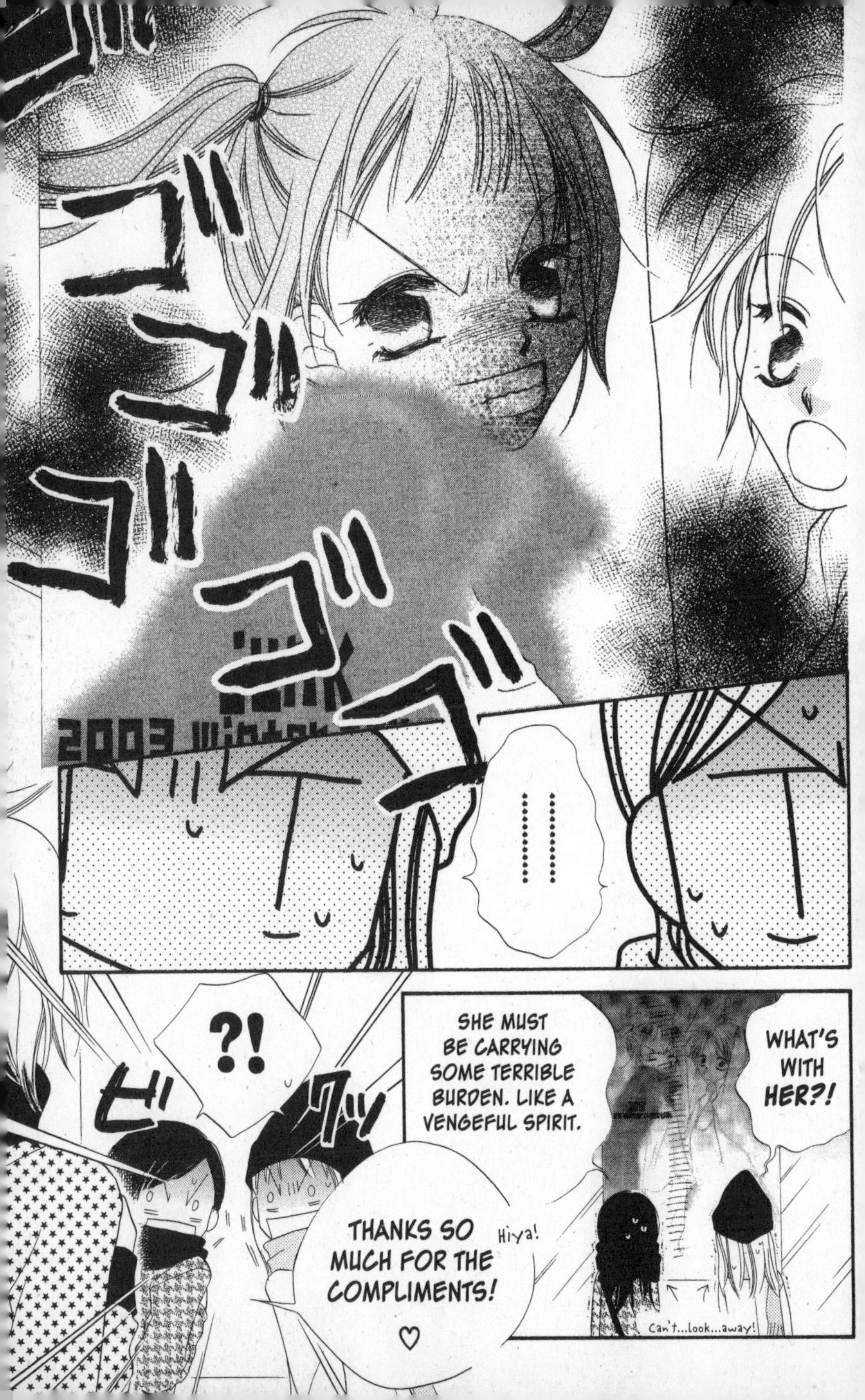
ゴゴゴゴゴ
......
WHAT'S WITH HER?!
SHE MUST BE CARRYING SOME TERRIBLE BURDEN. LIKE A VENGEFUL SPIRIT.
Can't...look...away!
?!
ビクッ
THANKS SO MUCH FOR THE COMPLIMENTS! ♡
Hiya!

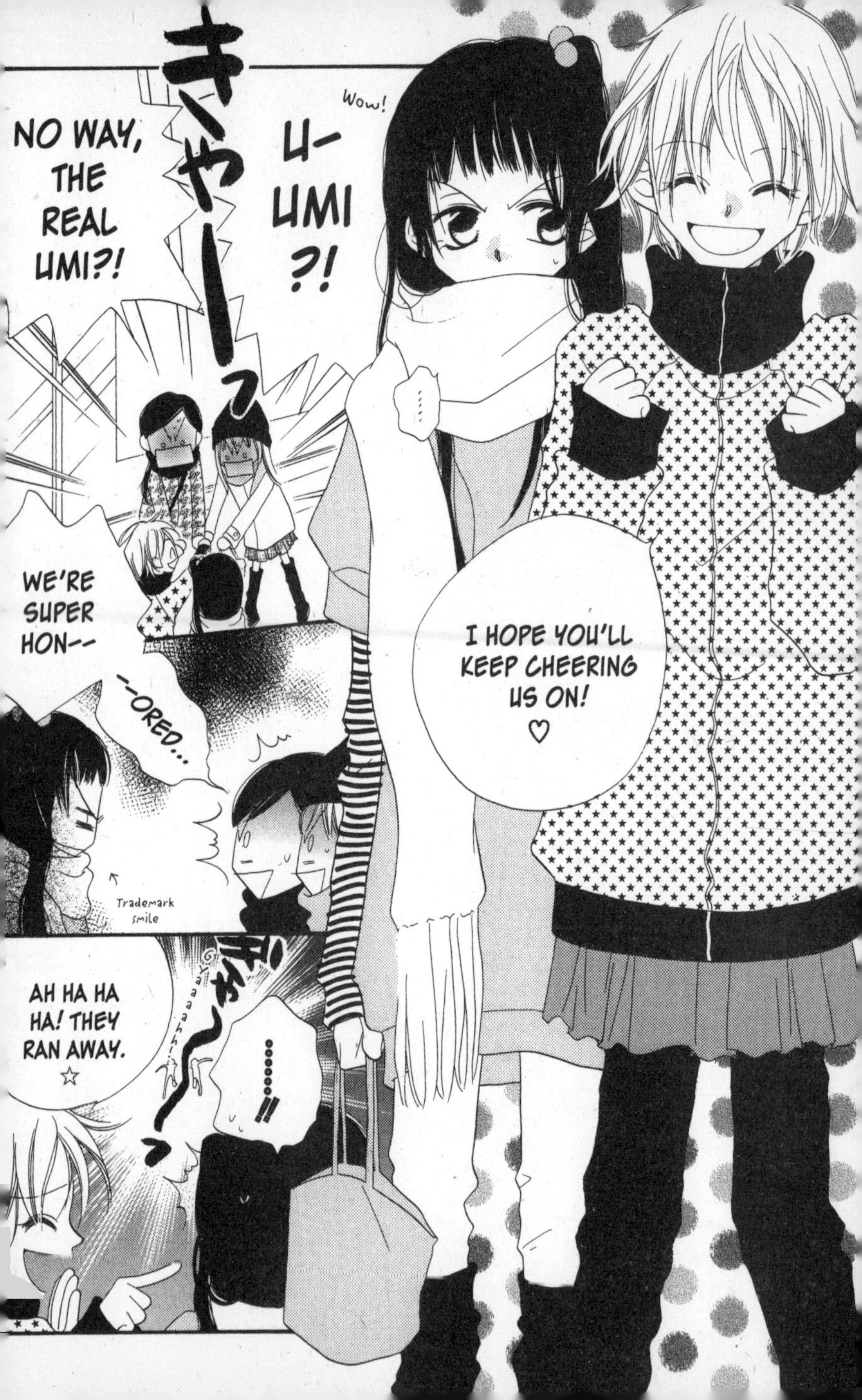
I HOPE YOU'LL KEEP CHEERING US ON! ♡
....
Wow!
U-UMI?!
きゃーっ
NO WAY, THE REAL UMI?!
WE'RE SUPER HON--
--ORED...
Trademark smile
ぎゃ～っ
Gyaaaaahh...
OOOOOO!!
AH HA HA HA! THEY RAN AWAY. ☆

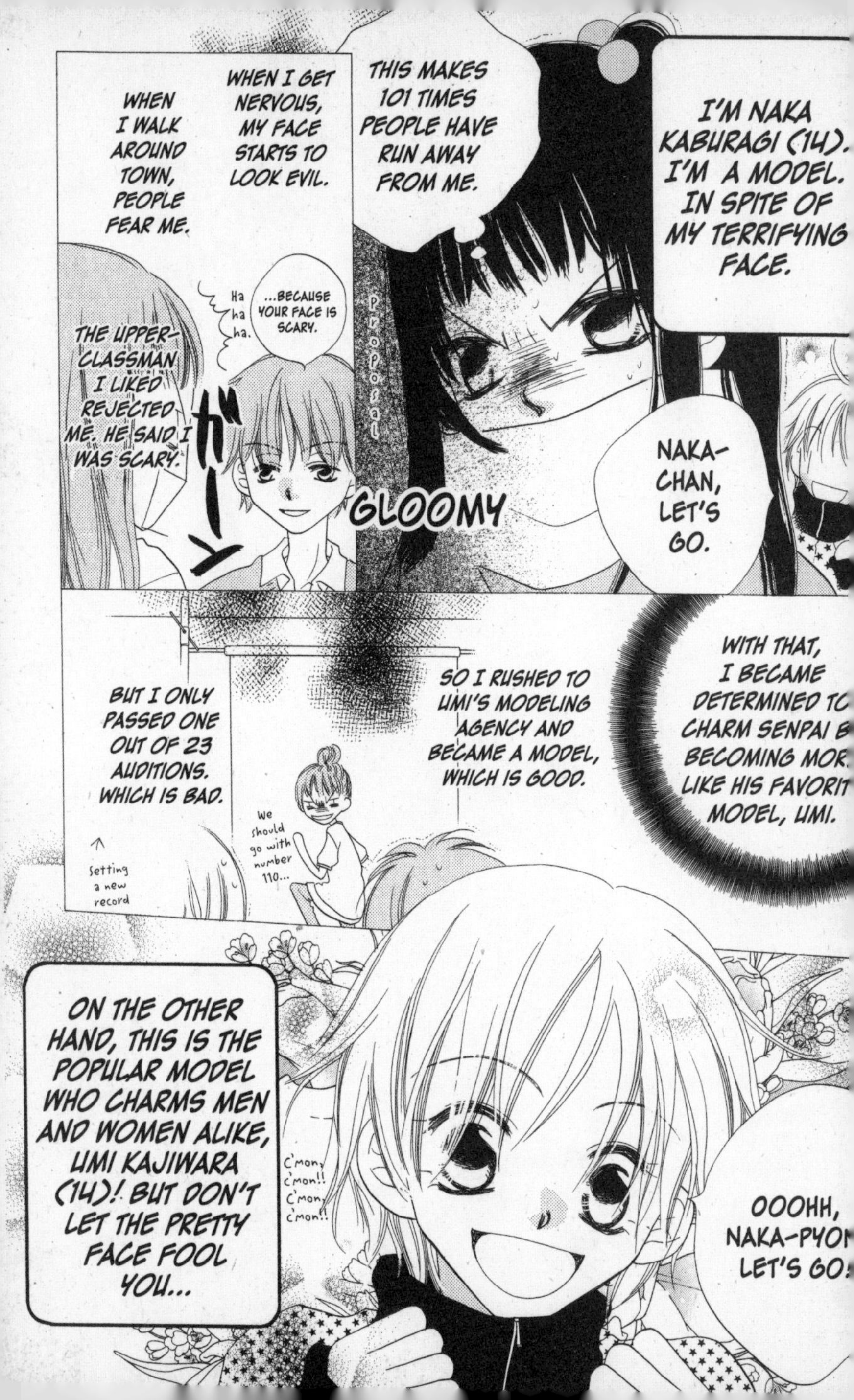
I'M NAKA KABURAGI (14). I'M A MODEL. IN SPITE OF MY TERRIFYING FACE.
THIS MAKES 101 TIMES PEOPLE HAVE RUN AWAY FROM ME.
NAKA-CHAN, LET'S GO.
GLOOMY
WHEN I GET NERVOUS, MY FACE STARTS TO LOOK EVIL.
WHEN I WALK AROUND TOWN, PEOPLE FEAR ME.
Proposal
...BECAUSE YOUR FACE IS SCARY.
Ha ha ha.
ガーン
THE UPPER-CLASSMAN I LIKED REJECTED ME. HE SAID I WAS SCARY.
WITH THAT, I BECAME DETERMINED TO CHARM SENPAI B BECOMING MOR LIKE HIS FAVORIT MODEL, UMI.
SO I RUSHED TO UMI'S MODELING AGENCY AND BECAME A MODEL, WHICH IS GOOD.
BUT I ONLY PASSED ONE OUT OF 23 AUDITIONS. WHICH IS BAD.
We should go with number 110...
Setting a new record
OOOHH, NAKA-PYO LET'S GO
C'mon, c'mon!! C'mon, c'mon!!
ON THE OTHER HAND, THIS IS THE POPULAR MODEL WHO CHARMS MEN AND WOMEN ALIKE, UMI KAJIWARA (14)! BUT DON'T LET THE PRETTY FACE FOOL YOU...

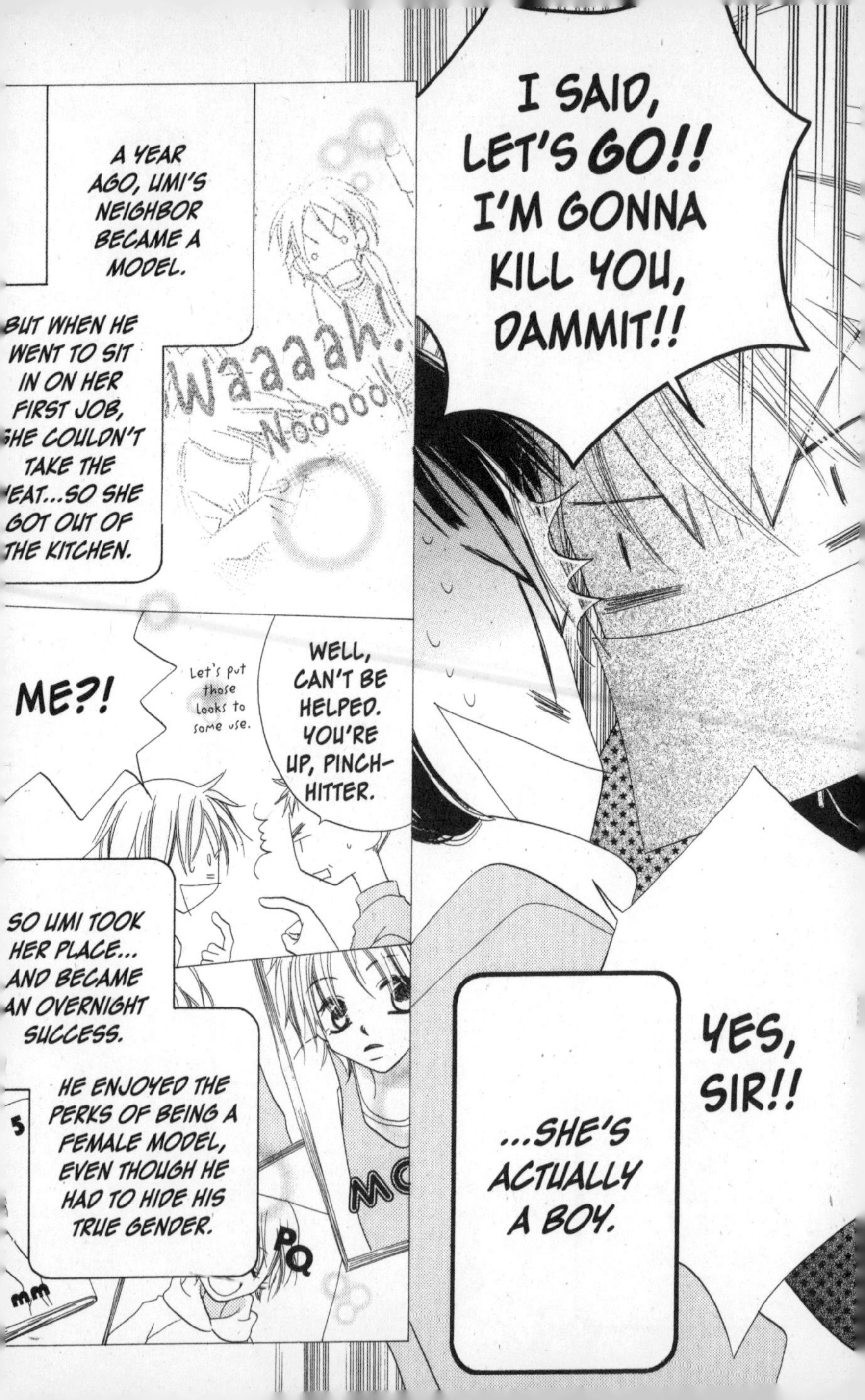
I SAID, LET'S GO!! I'M GONNA KILL YOU, DAMMIT!!
YES, SIR!!
...SHE'S ACTUALLY A BOY.
A YEAR AGO, UMI'S NEIGHBOR BECAME A MODEL.
Waaaah! Noooo!!
BUT WHEN HE WENT TO SIT IN ON HER FIRST JOB, SHE COULDN'T TAKE THE HEAT...SO SHE GOT OUT OF THE KITCHEN.
WELL, CAN'T BE HELPED. YOU'RE UP, PINCH-HITTER.
Let's put those looks to some use.
ME?!
SO UMI TOOK HER PLACE... AND BECAME AN OVERNIGHT SUCCESS.
HE ENJOYED THE PERKS OF BEING A FEMALE MODEL, EVEN THOUGH HE HAD TO HIDE HIS TRUE GENDER.

2

When I found out they would release this series in the graphic novel format, I had all these wild ideas about what to write in the fourth-space column. But now that the time to write is here, I don't know what I should say. Hmm.

"Nosatsu" is a story I wrote thinking, "Well, let's just enjoy drawing!!" Even now, I'm drawing, enjoying it immensely and grinning like an idiot. When trying to think up a particularly good name*, I'll stand up and walk around aimlessly. I look like a pretty dangerous person when you see me from the sidelines. Grrrr!

Generally, I sit at my desk when I think about the story. But things really come to me when I'm taking a shower! I guess that's when I'm the most relaxed. Thinking of a story while completely naked can be pretty dangerous when viewed from the sidelines, too.

I used to look pretty lousy when I was drawing, but I started to get depressed whenever I saw myself in the mirror, so I'm trying to wear slightly better clothes. When I did, the change was amazing! I get the feeling I look healthier now. Ha ha ha. It's probably all in my head, though. Yeah.

*The roughest draft of a manga, where the script is laid out in balloons but no art is filled in yet.

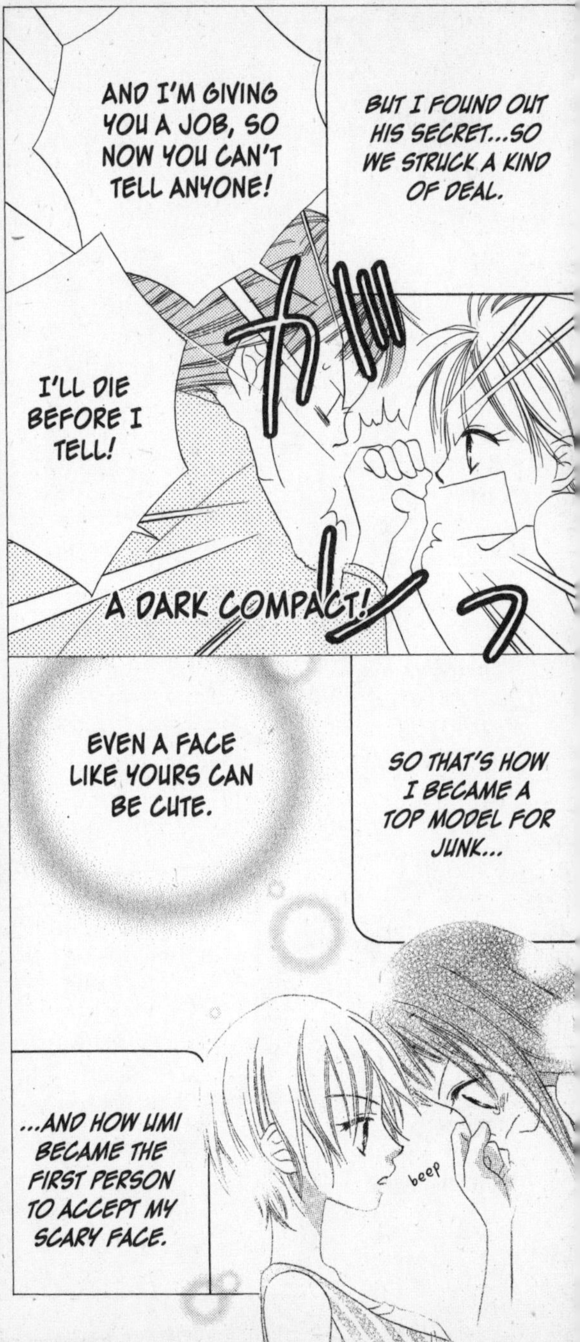
BUT I FOUND OUT HIS SECRET...SO WE STRUCK A KIND OF DEAL.
AND I'M GIVING YOU A JOB, SO NOW YOU CAN'T TELL ANYONE!
I'LL DIE BEFORE I TELL!
A DARK COMPACT!
SO THAT'S HOW I BECAME A TOP MODEL FOR JUNK...
EVEN A FACE LIKE YOURS CAN BE CUTE.
...AND HOW UMI BECAME THE FIRST PERSON TO ACCEPT MY SCARY FACE.
beep

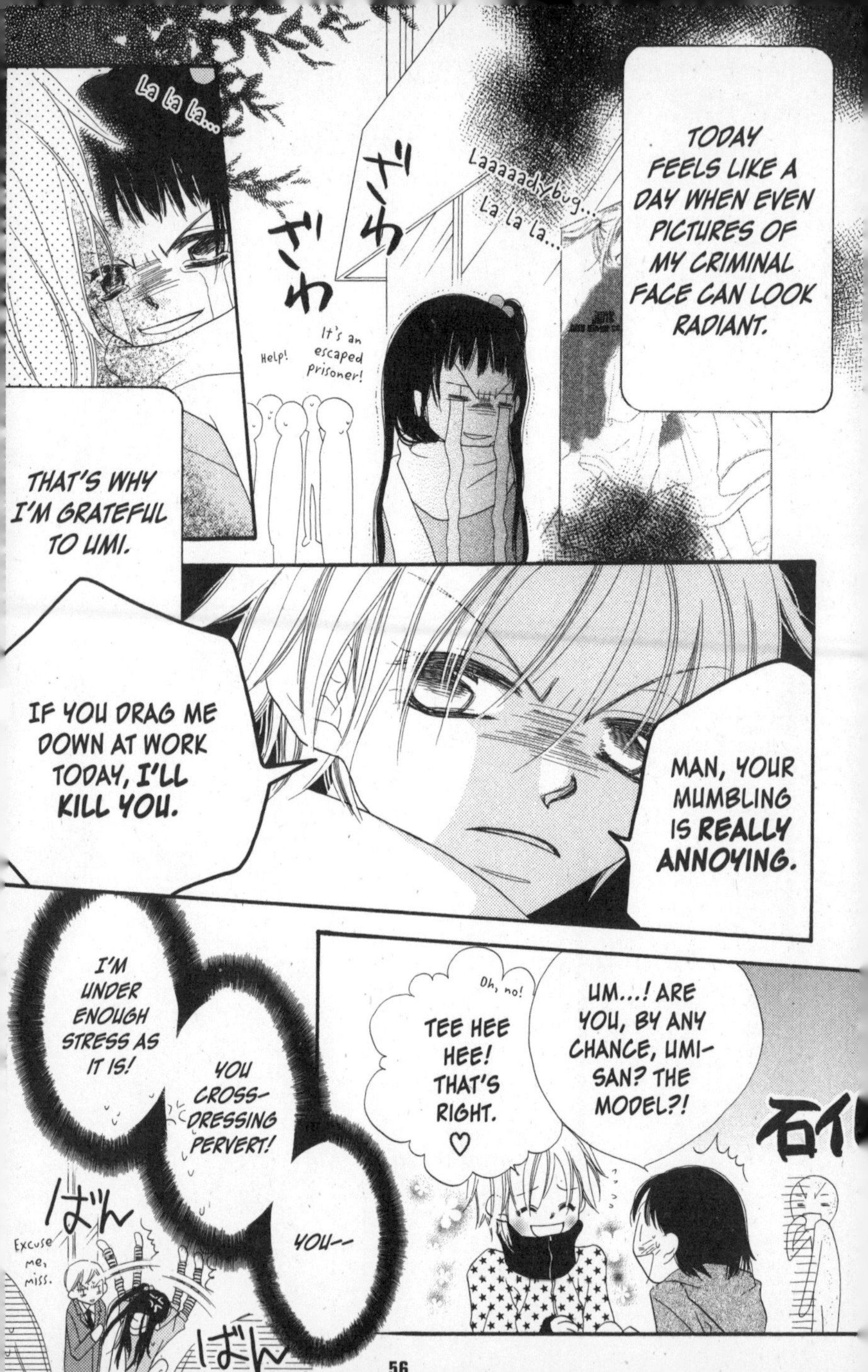
TODAY FEELS LIKE A DAY WHEN EVEN PICTURES OF MY CRIMINAL FACE CAN LOOK RADIANT.
Laaaaadybug... La la la...
ざわざわ
It's an escaped prisoner!
Help!
La la la...
THAT'S WHY I'M GRATEFUL TO UMI.
MAN, YOUR MUMBLING IS **REALLY ANNOYING.**
IF YOU DRAG ME DOWN AT WORK TODAY, **I'LL KILL YOU.**
石イ
UM...! ARE YOU, BY ANY CHANCE, UMI-SAN? THE MODEL?!
Oh, no!
TEE HEE HEE! THAT'S RIGHT. ♡
I'M UNDER ENOUGH STRESS AS IT IS!
YOU CROSS-DRESSING PERVERT!
YOU--
ばん
Excuse me, miss.
ばん

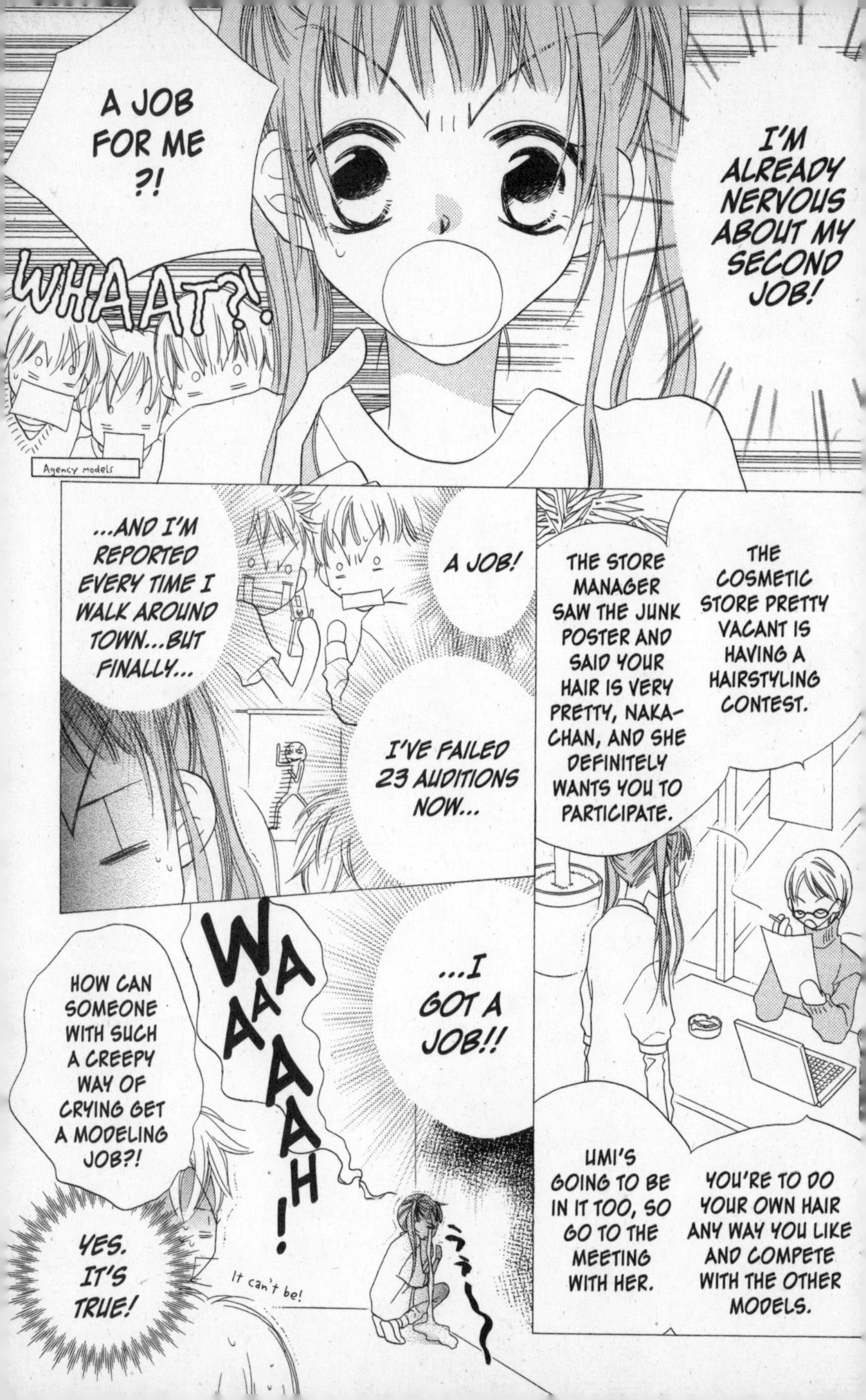

I'M ALREADY NERVOUS ABOUT MY SECOND JOB!
A JOB FOR ME ?!
WHAAAT?!
Agency models
THE COSMETIC STORE PRETTY VACANT IS HAVING A HAIRSTYLING CONTEST.
THE STORE MANAGER SAW THE JUNK POSTER AND SAID YOUR HAIR IS VERY PRETTY, NAKA-CHAN, AND SHE DEFINITELY WANTS YOU TO PARTICIPATE.
A JOB!
...AND I'M REPORTED EVERY TIME I WALK AROUND TOWN...BUT FINALLY...
I'VE FAILED 23 AUDITIONS NOW...
YOU'RE TO DO YOUR OWN HAIR ANY WAY YOU LIKE AND COMPETE WITH THE OTHER MODELS.
UMI'S GOING TO BE IN IT TOO, SO GO TO THE MEETING WITH HER.
...I GOT A JOB!!
WAAAAAH!
HOW CAN SOMEONE WITH SUCH A CREEPY WAY OF CRYING GET A MODELING JOB?!
YES. IT'S TRUE!
It can't be!

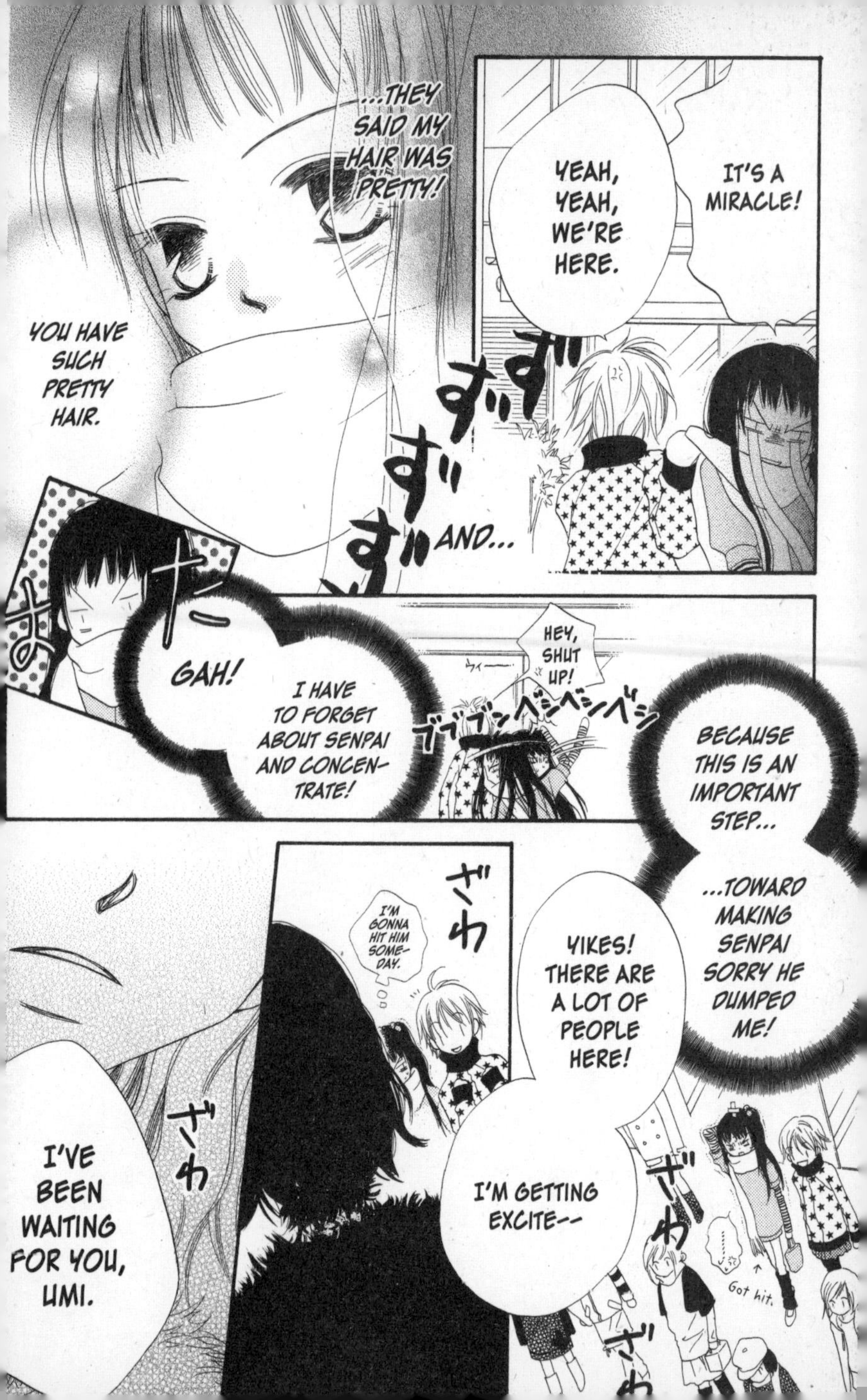
IT'S A MIRACLE!
YEAH, YEAH, WE'RE HERE.
...THEY SAID MY HAIR WAS PRETTY!
YOU HAVE SUCH PRETTY HAIR.
AND...
BECAUSE THIS IS AN IMPORTANT STEP...
HEY, SHUT UP!
I HAVE TO FORGET ABOUT SENPAI AND CONCENTRATE!
GAH!
...TOWARD MAKING SENPAI SORRY HE DUMPED ME!
YIKES! THERE ARE A LOT OF PEOPLE HERE!
I'M GETTING EXCITE--
Got hit.
I'M GONNA HIT HIM SOMEDAY.
I'VE BEEN WAITING FOR YOU, UMI.

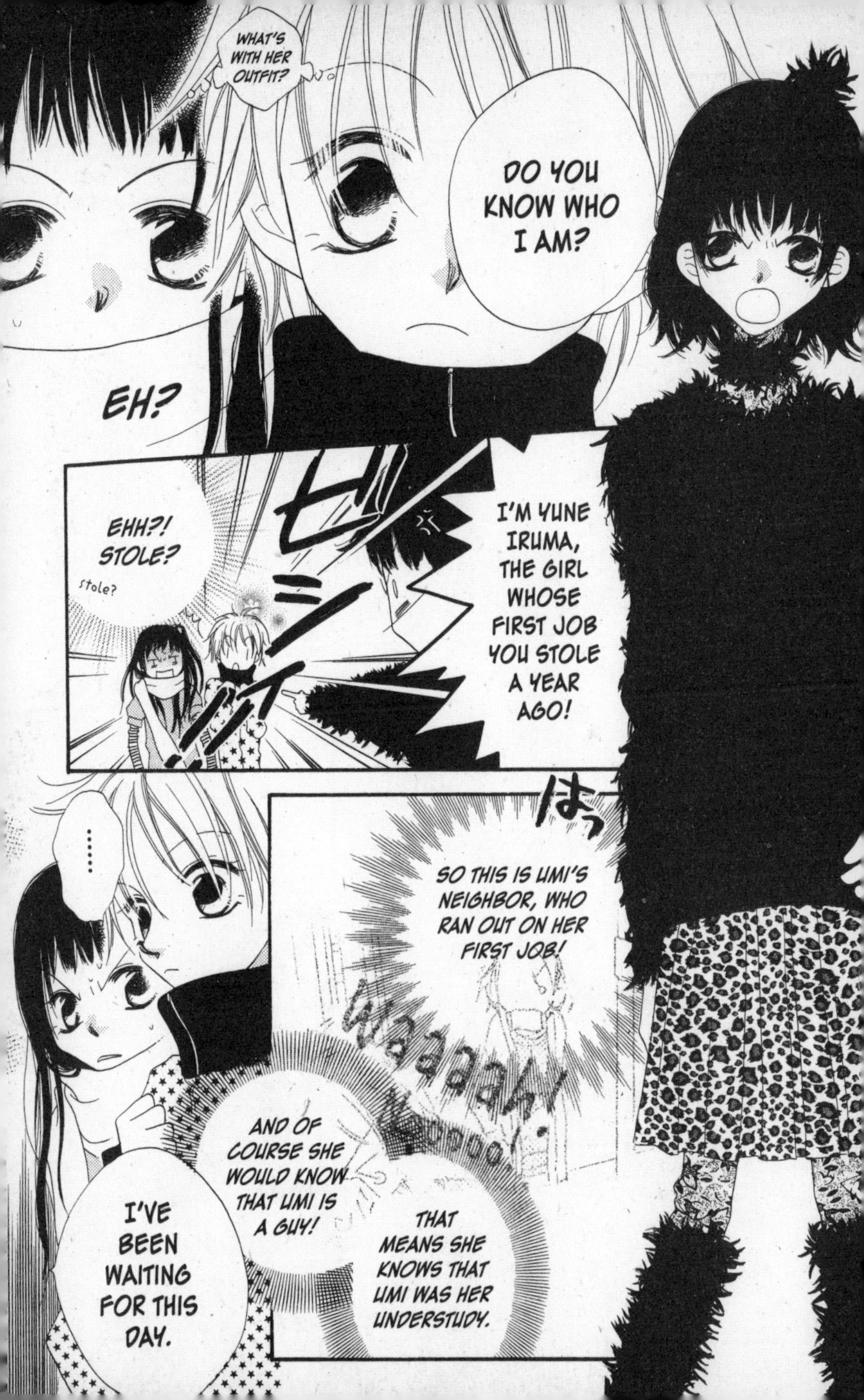
DO YOU KNOW WHO I AM?
WHAT'S WITH HER OUTFIT?
EH?
I'M YUNE IRUMA, THE GIRL WHOSE FIRST JOB YOU STOLE A YEAR AGO!
EHH?! STOLE?
stole?
はっ
SO THIS IS UMI'S NEIGHBOR, WHO RAN OUT ON HER FIRST JOB!
Waaaah!
THAT MEANS SHE KNOWS THAT UMI WAS HER UNDERSTUDY.
AND OF COURSE SHE WOULD KNOW THAT UMI IS A GUY!
……
I'VE BEEN WAITING FOR THIS DAY.

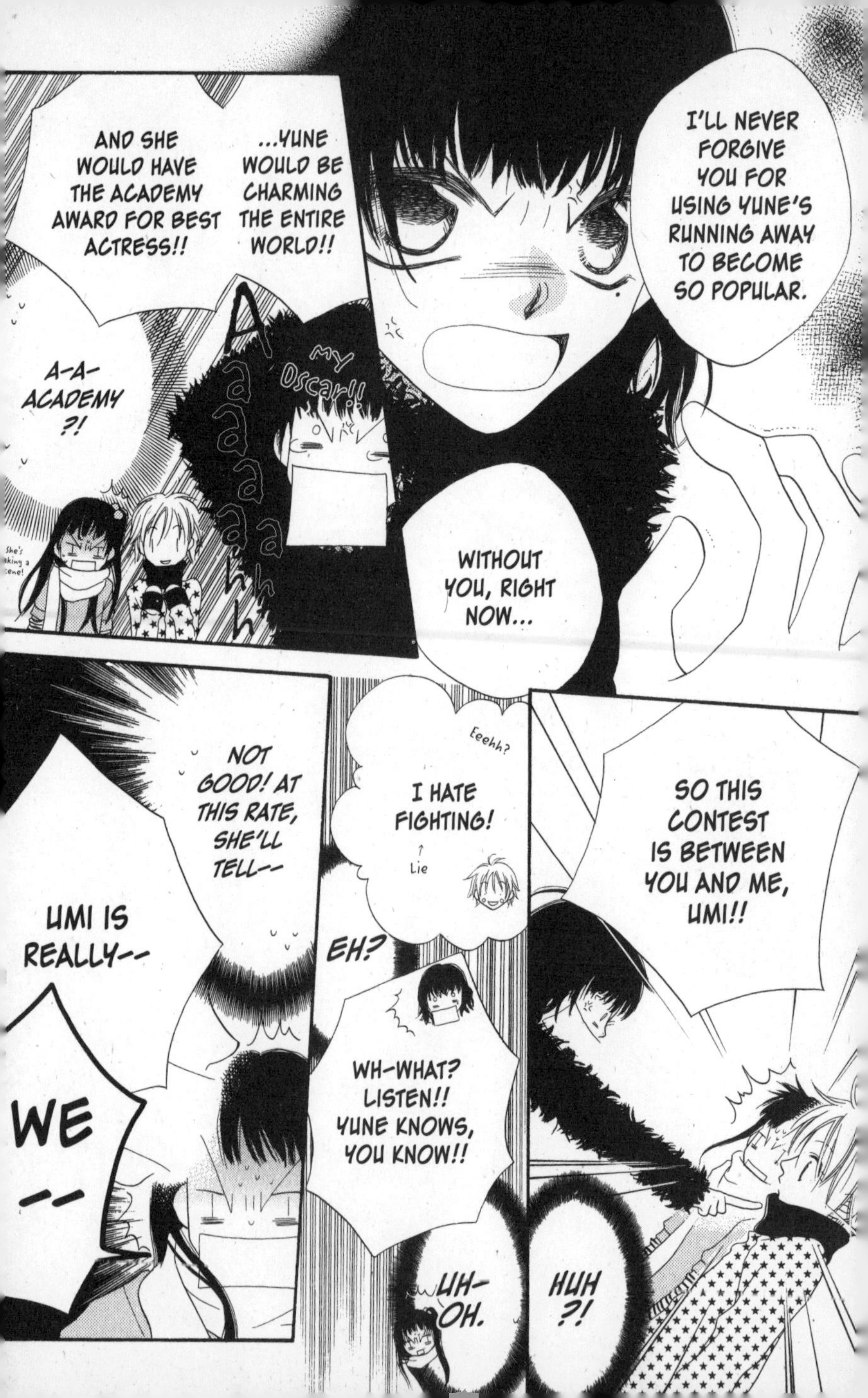
I'LL NEVER FORGIVE YOU FOR USING YUNE'S RUNNING AWAY TO BECOME SO POPULAR.
WITHOUT YOU, RIGHT NOW...
...YUNE WOULD BE CHARMING THE ENTIRE WORLD!!
AND SHE WOULD HAVE THE ACADEMY AWARD FOR BEST ACTRESS!!
Aaaaaaahh
my Oscar!!
A-A-ACADEMY?!
SO THIS CONTEST IS BETWEEN YOU AND ME, UMI!!
HUH?!
Eeehh?
I HATE FIGHTING!
Lie
EH?
WH-WHAT? LISTEN!! YUNE KNOWS, YOU KNOW!!
UH-OH.
NOT GOOD! AT THIS RATE, SHE'LL TELL--
UMI IS REALLY--
WE --

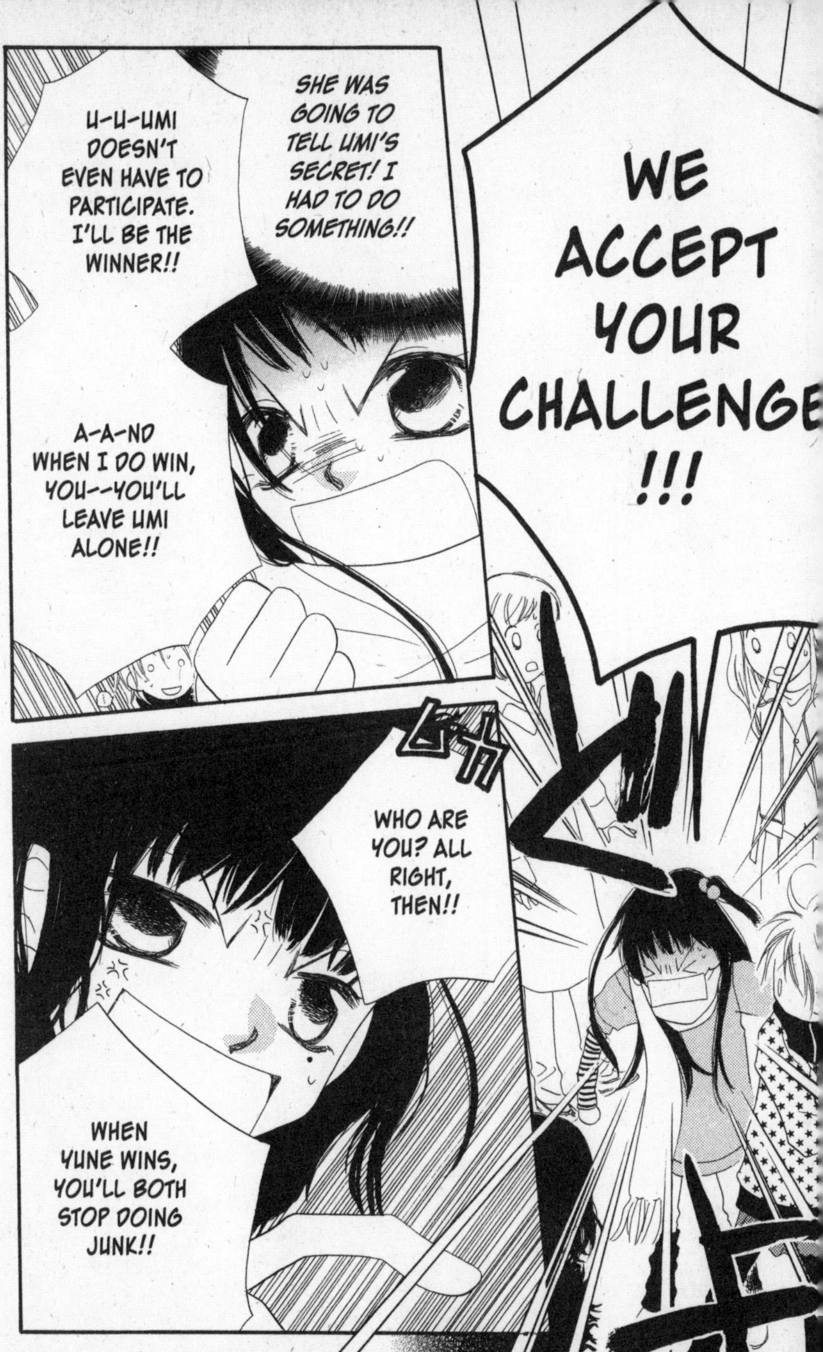
WE ACCEPT YOUR CHALLENGE!!!
SHE WAS GOING TO TELL UMI'S SECRET! I HAD TO DO SOMETHING!!
U-U-UMI DOESN'T EVEN HAVE TO PARTICIPATE. I'LL BE THE WINNER!!
A-A-ND WHEN I DO WIN, YOU--YOU'LL LEAVE UMI ALONE!!
WHO ARE YOU? ALL RIGHT, THEN!!
WHEN YUNE WINS, YOU'LL BOTH STOP DOING JUNK!!

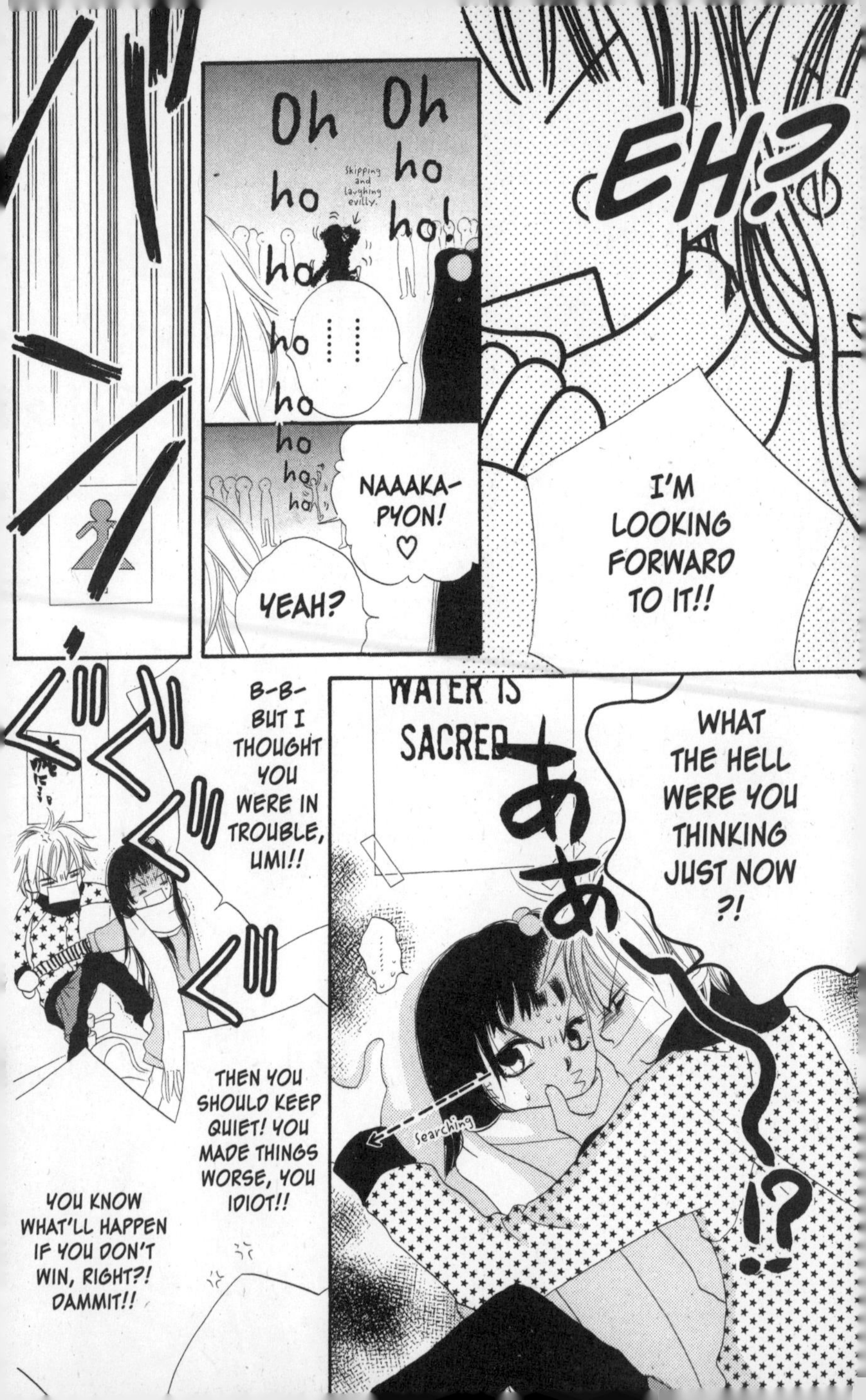
EH?
I'M LOOKING FORWARD TO IT!!
Oh ho ho!
Oh ho ho ho ho ho ho ho
Skipping and laughing evilly.
......
NAAAKA-PYON! ♡
YEAH?
WATER IS SACRED
あぁ～～!?
WHAT THE HELL WERE YOU THINKING JUST NOW ?!
Searching
B-B-BUT I THOUGHT YOU WERE IN TROUBLE, UMI!!
THEN YOU SHOULD KEEP QUIET! YOU MADE THINGS WORSE, YOU IDIOT!!
YOU KNOW WHAT'LL HAPPEN IF YOU DON'T WIN, RIGHT?! DAMMIT!!

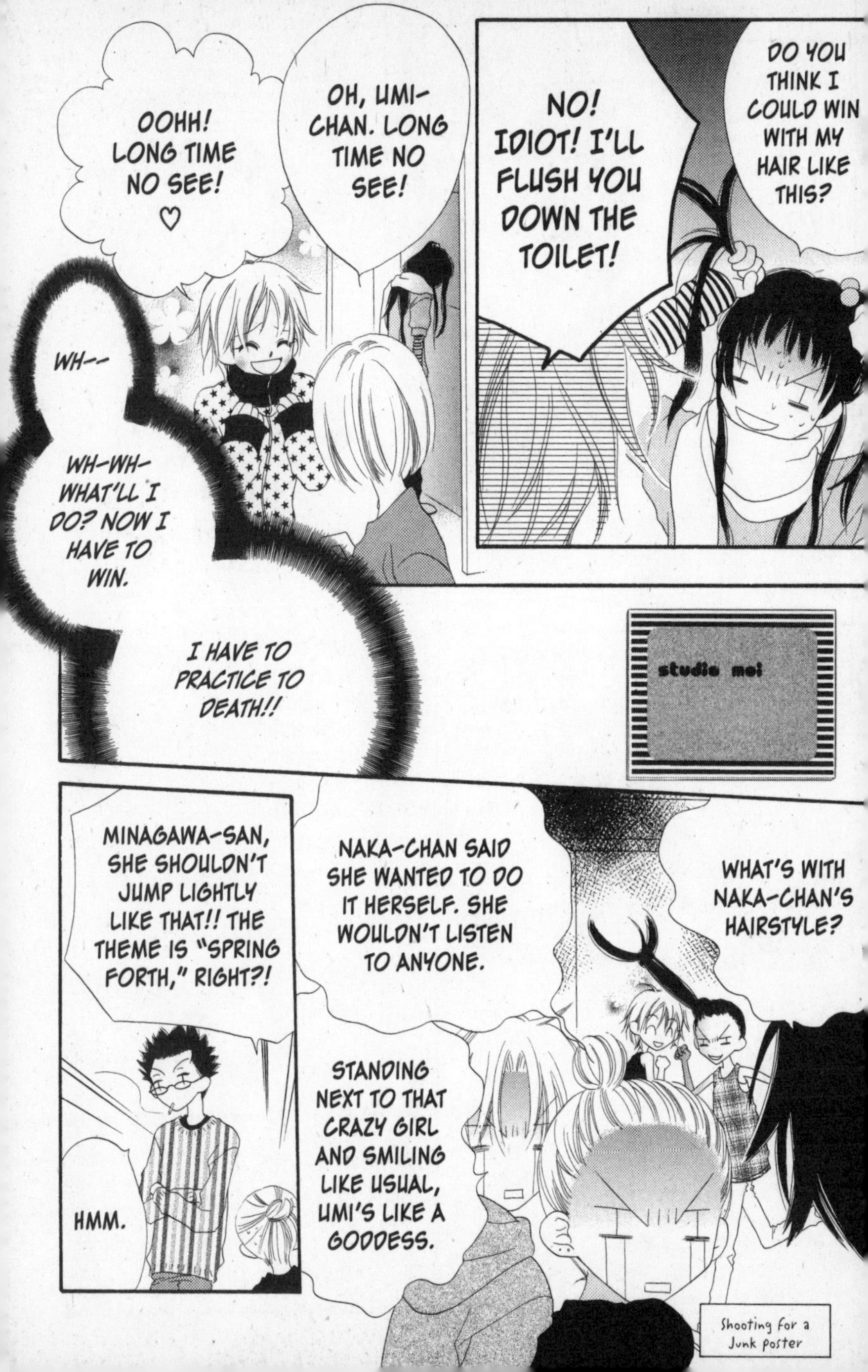
DO YOU THINK I COULD WIN WITH MY HAIR LIKE THIS?
NO! IDIOT! I'LL FLUSH YOU DOWN THE TOILET!
OH, UMI-CHAN. LONG TIME NO SEE!
OOHH! LONG TIME NO SEE! ♡
WH--
WH-WH-WHAT'LL I DO? NOW I HAVE TO WIN.
studio moi
I HAVE TO PRACTICE TO DEATH!!
WHAT'S WITH NAKA-CHAN'S HAIRSTYLE?
NAKA-CHAN SAID SHE WANTED TO DO IT HERSELF. SHE WOULDN'T LISTEN TO ANYONE.
STANDING NEXT TO THAT CRAZY GIRL AND SMILING LIKE USUAL, UMI'S LIKE A GODDESS.
Shooting for a Junk poster
MINAGAWA-SAN, SHE SHOULDN'T JUMP LIGHTLY LIKE THAT!! THE THEME IS "SPRING FORTH," RIGHT?!
HMM.

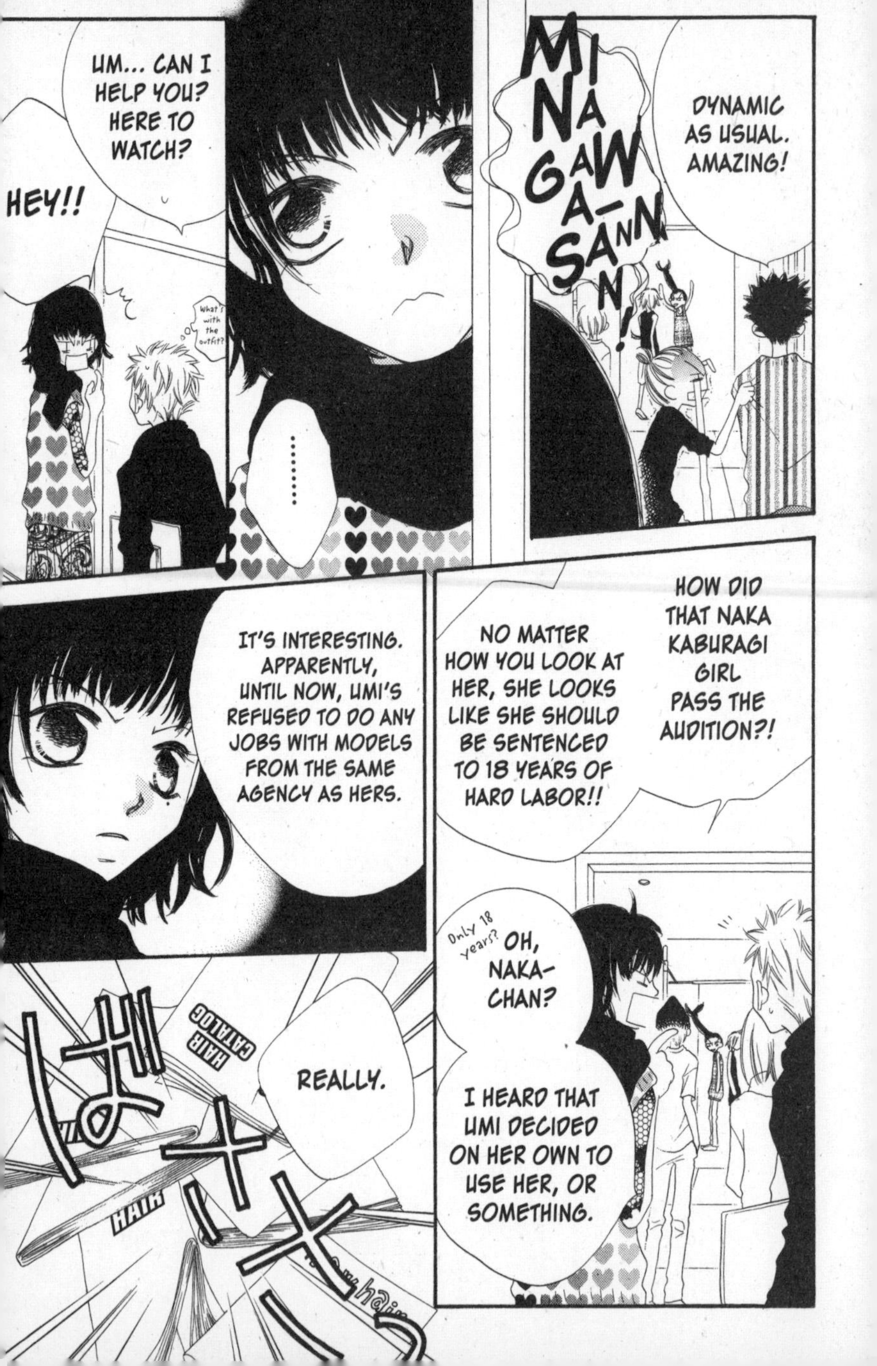
DYNAMIC AS USUAL. AMAZING!
MINAGAWA-SANNN!
....
UM... CAN I HELP YOU? HERE TO WATCH?
What's with the outfit?
HEY!!
HOW DID THAT NAKA KABURAGI GIRL PASS THE AUDITION?!
NO MATTER HOW YOU LOOK AT HER, SHE LOOKS LIKE SHE SHOULD BE SENTENCED TO 18 YEARS OF HARD LABOR!!
OH, NAKA-CHAN?
Only 18 years?
I HEARD THAT UMI DECIDED ON HER OWN TO USE HER, OR SOMETHING.
IT'S INTERESTING. APPARENTLY, UNTIL NOW, UMI'S REFUSED TO DO ANY JOBS WITH MODELS FROM THE SAME AGENCY AS HERS.
REALLY.
HAIR CATALOG
HAIR

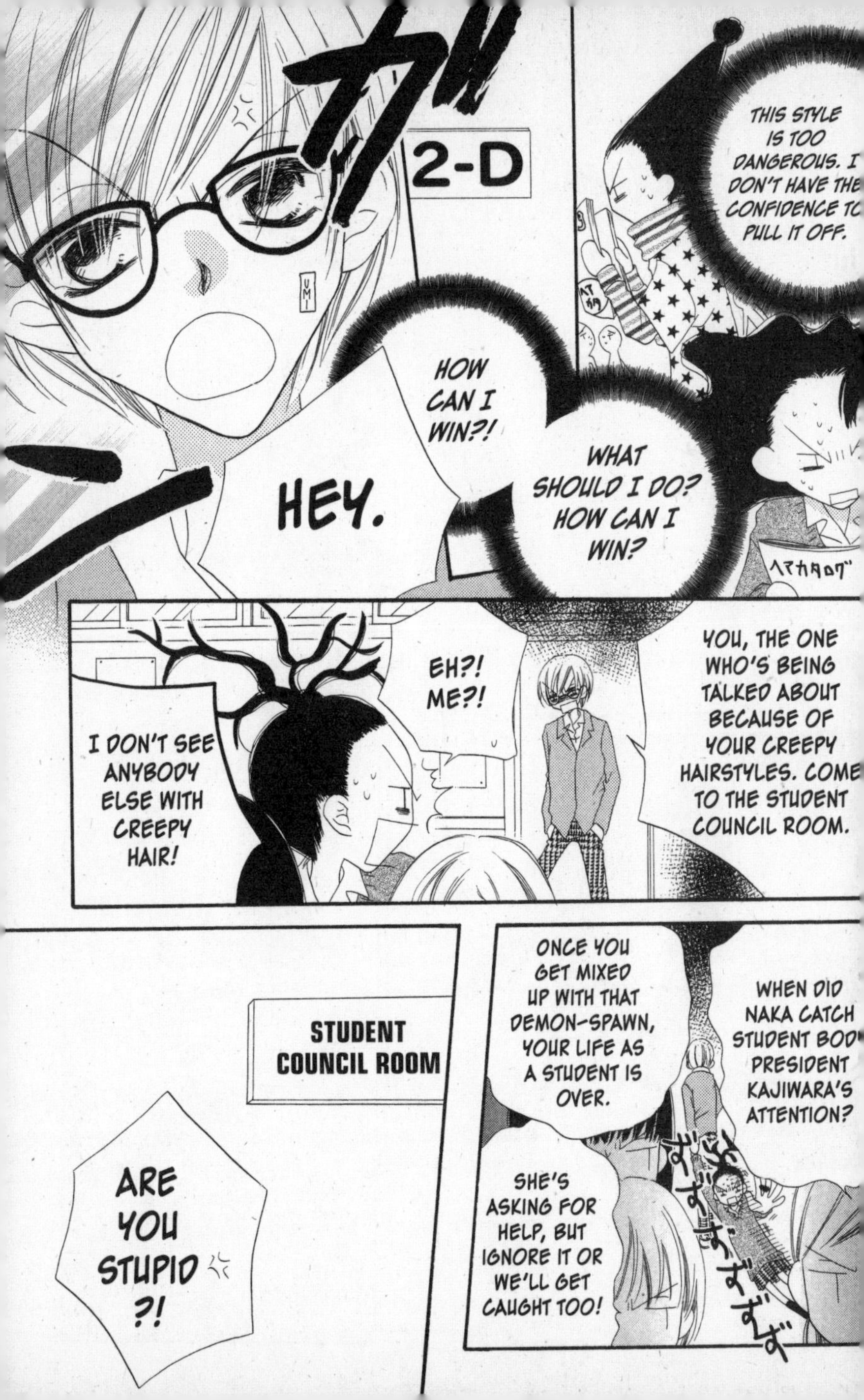

THIS STYLE IS TOO DANGEROUS. I DON'T HAVE THE CONFIDENCE TO PULL IT OFF.
ヘアカタログ
WHAT SHOULD I DO? HOW CAN I WIN?
HOW CAN I WIN?!
2-D
HEY.
YOU, THE ONE WHO'S BEING TALKED ABOUT BECAUSE OF YOUR CREEPY HAIRSTYLES. COME TO THE STUDENT COUNCIL ROOM.
EH?! ME?!
I DON'T SEE ANYBODY ELSE WITH CREEPY HAIR!
WHEN DID NAKA CATCH STUDENT BOD PRESIDENT KAJIWARA'S ATTENTION?
ONCE YOU GET MIXED UP WITH THAT DEMON-SPAWN, YOUR LIFE AS A STUDENT IS OVER.
SHE'S ASKING FOR HELP, BUT IGNORE IT OR WE'LL GET CAUGHT TOO!
STUDENT COUNCIL ROOM
ARE YOU STUPID?!

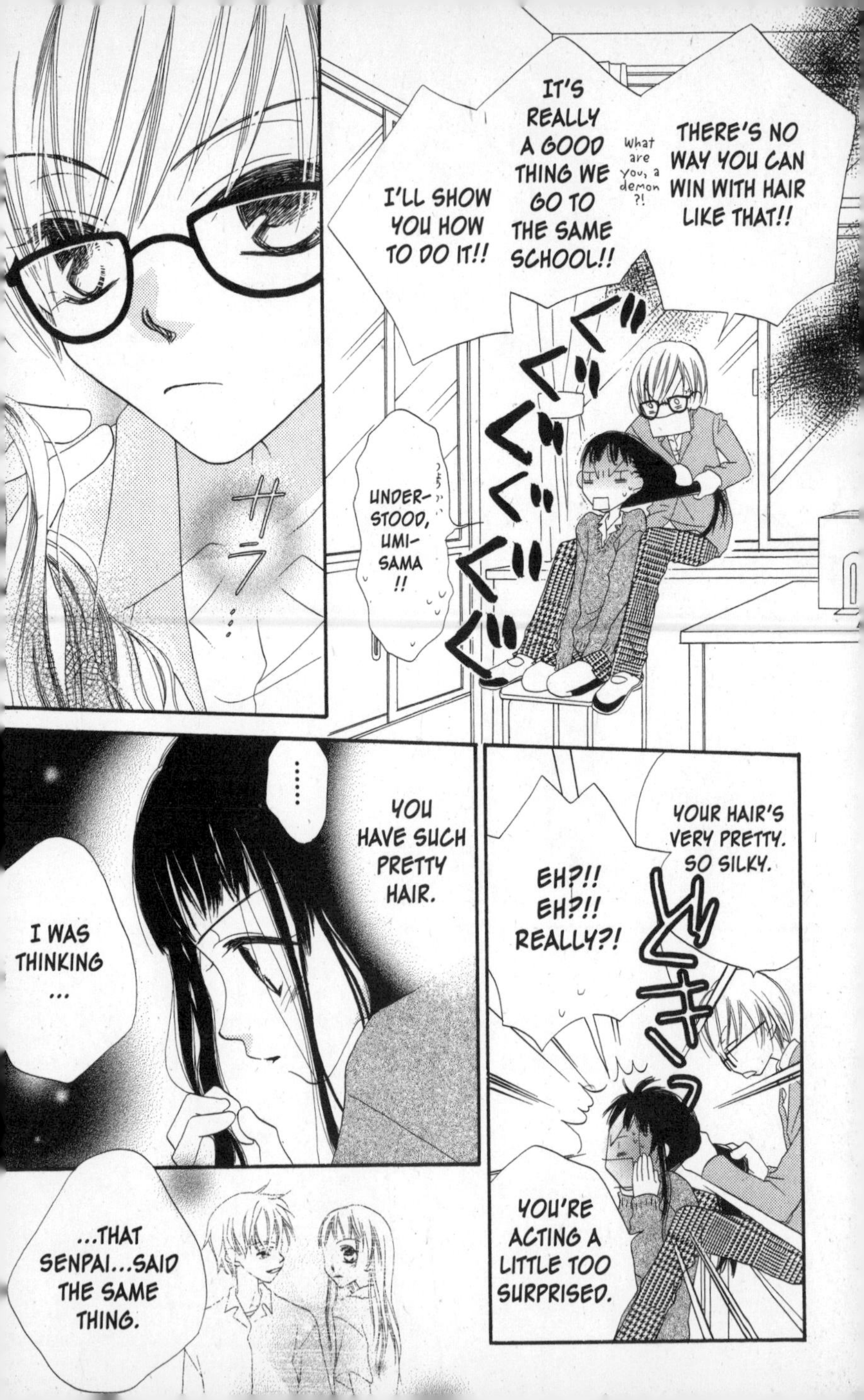
THERE'S NO WAY YOU CAN WIN WITH HAIR LIKE THAT!!
What are you, a demon?!
IT'S REALLY A GOOD THING WE GO TO THE SAME SCHOOL!!
I'LL SHOW YOU HOW TO DO IT!!
UNDERSTOOD, UMI-SAMA!!
サラ…
YOUR HAIR'S VERY PRETTY. SO SILKY.
ドキッ
EH?!! EH?!! REALLY?!
YOU'RE ACTING A LITTLE TOO SURPRISED.
……
YOU HAVE SUCH PRETTY HAIR.
I WAS THINKING ...
...THAT SENPAI...SAID THE SAME THING.

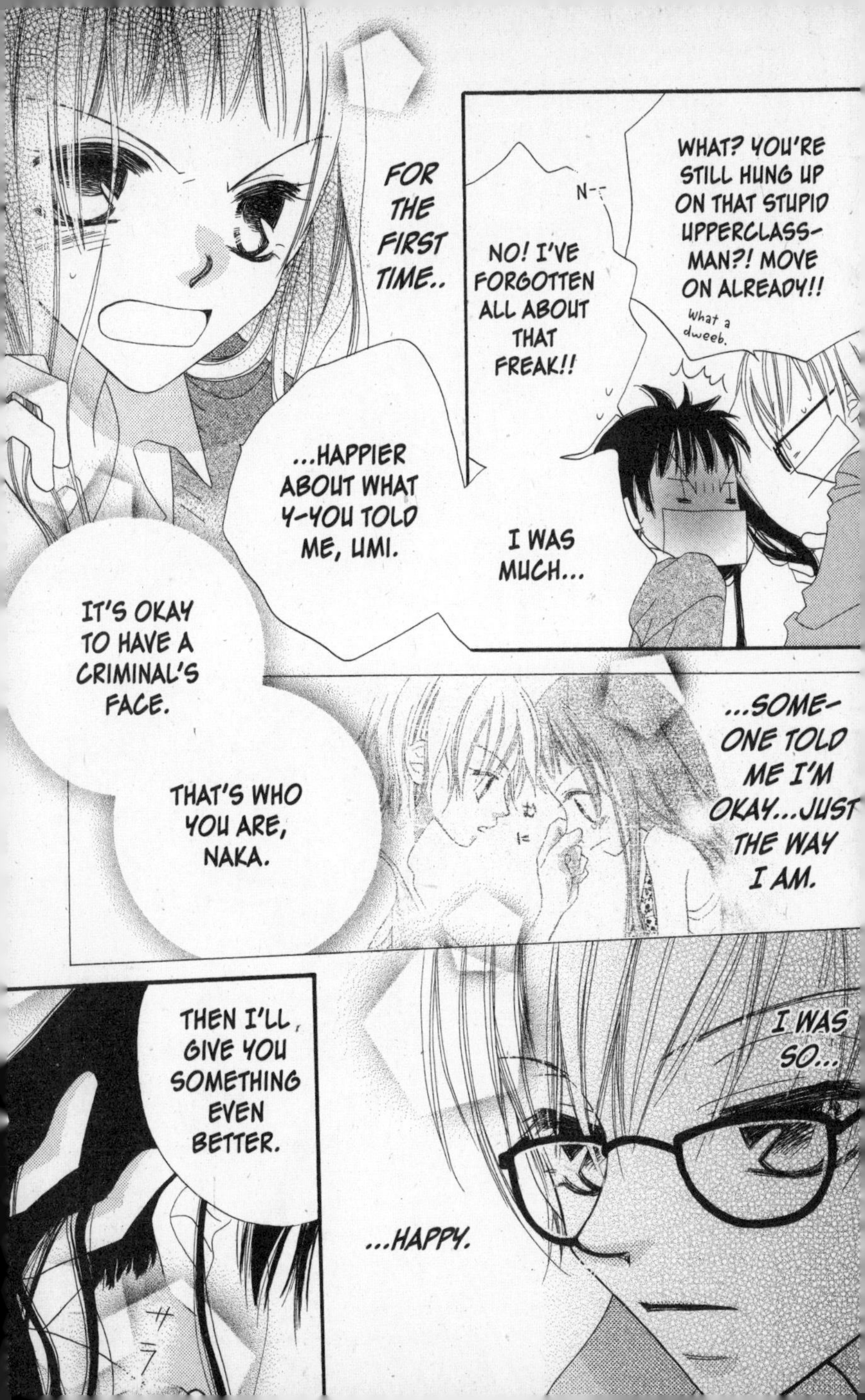
WHAT? YOU'RE STILL HUNG UP ON THAT STUPID UPPERCLASS-MAN?! MOVE ON ALREADY!!
What a dweeb.
N--
NO! I'VE FORGOTTEN ALL ABOUT THAT FREAK!!
I WAS MUCH...
...HAPPIER ABOUT WHAT Y-YOU TOLD ME, UMI.
FOR THE FIRST TIME..
...SOME-ONE TOLD ME I'M OKAY...JUST THE WAY I AM.
IT'S OKAY TO HAVE A CRIMINAL'S FACE.
THAT'S WHO YOU ARE, NAKA.
I WAS SO...
...HAPPY.
THEN I'LL GIVE YOU SOMETHING EVEN BETTER.

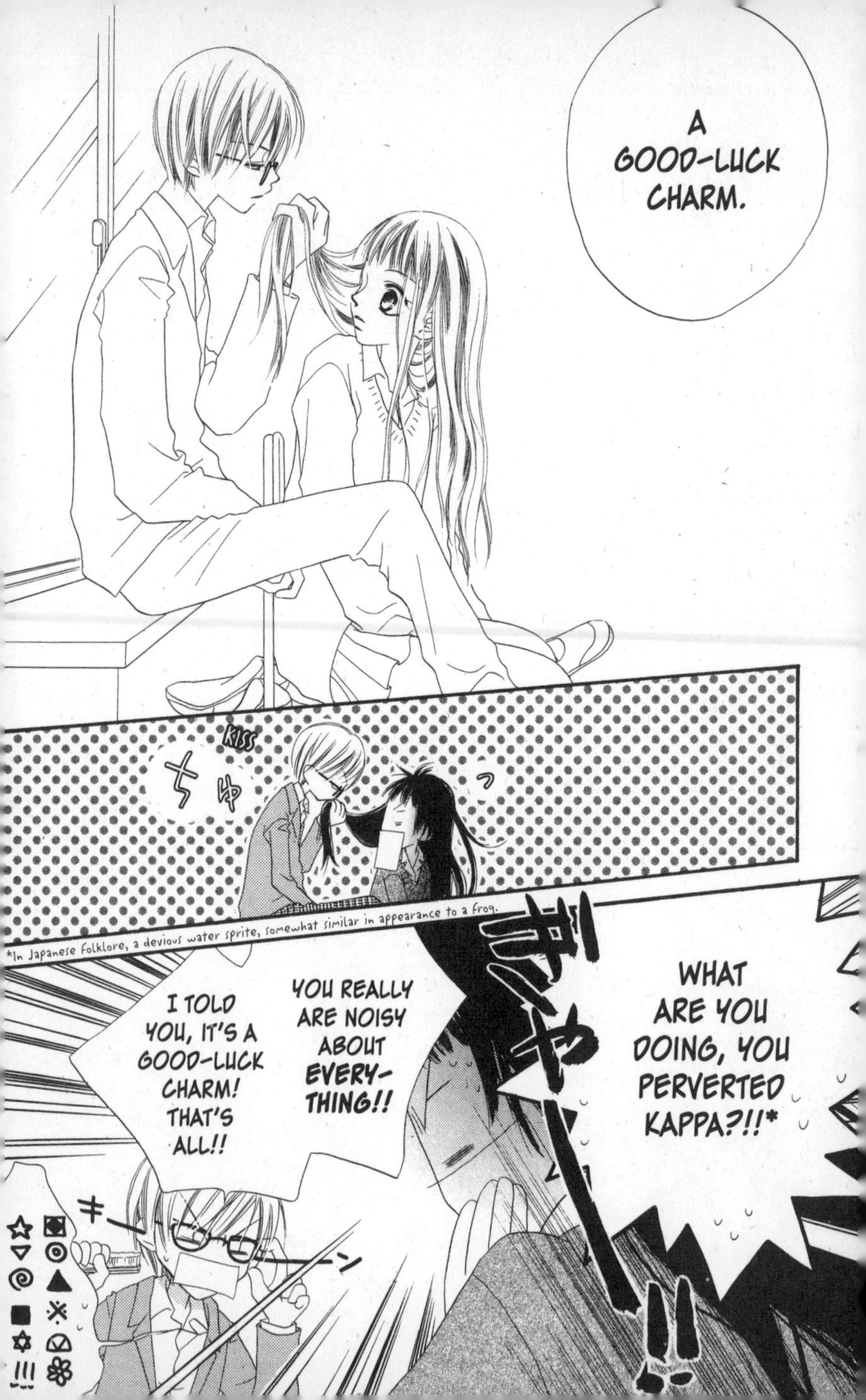
A GOOD-LUCK CHARM.
KISS
ちゅっ
WHAT ARE YOU DOING, YOU PERVERTED KAPPA?!!*
YOU REALLY ARE NOISY ABOUT EVERYTHING!!
I TOLD YOU, IT'S A GOOD-LUCK CHARM! THAT'S ALL!!

*In Japanese folklore, a devious water sprite, somewhat similar in appearance to a frog.

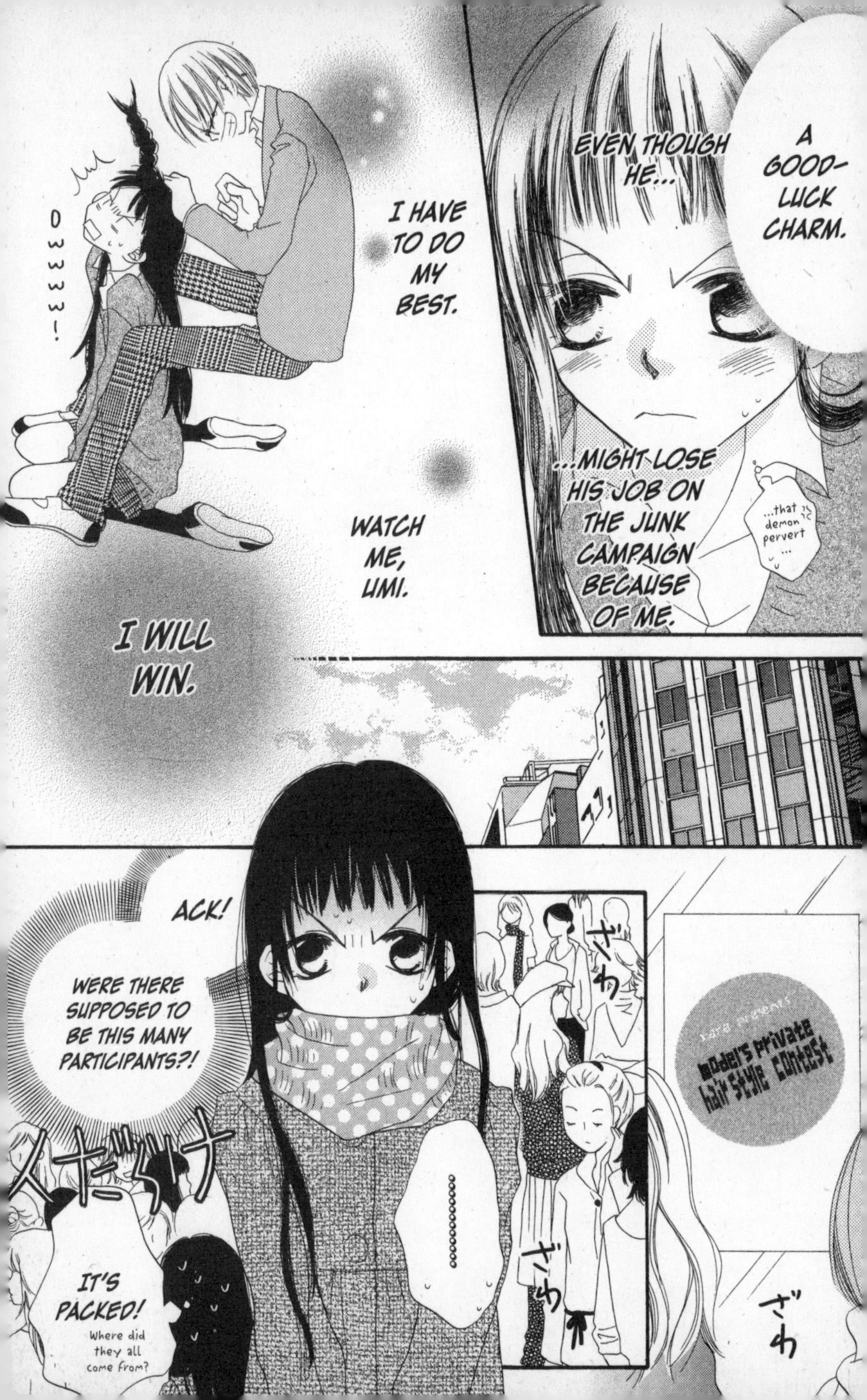
A GOOD-LUCK CHARM.
EVEN THOUGH HE...
...MIGHT LOSE HIS JOB ON THE JUNK CAMPAIGN BECAUSE OF ME.
...that demon pervert...
I HAVE TO DO MY BEST.
WATCH ME, UMI.
OWWWWW!
I WILL WIN.
model's private hair style contest
ACK!
WERE THERE SUPPOSED TO BE THIS MANY PARTICIPANTS?!
....
IT'S PACKED!
Where did they all come from?

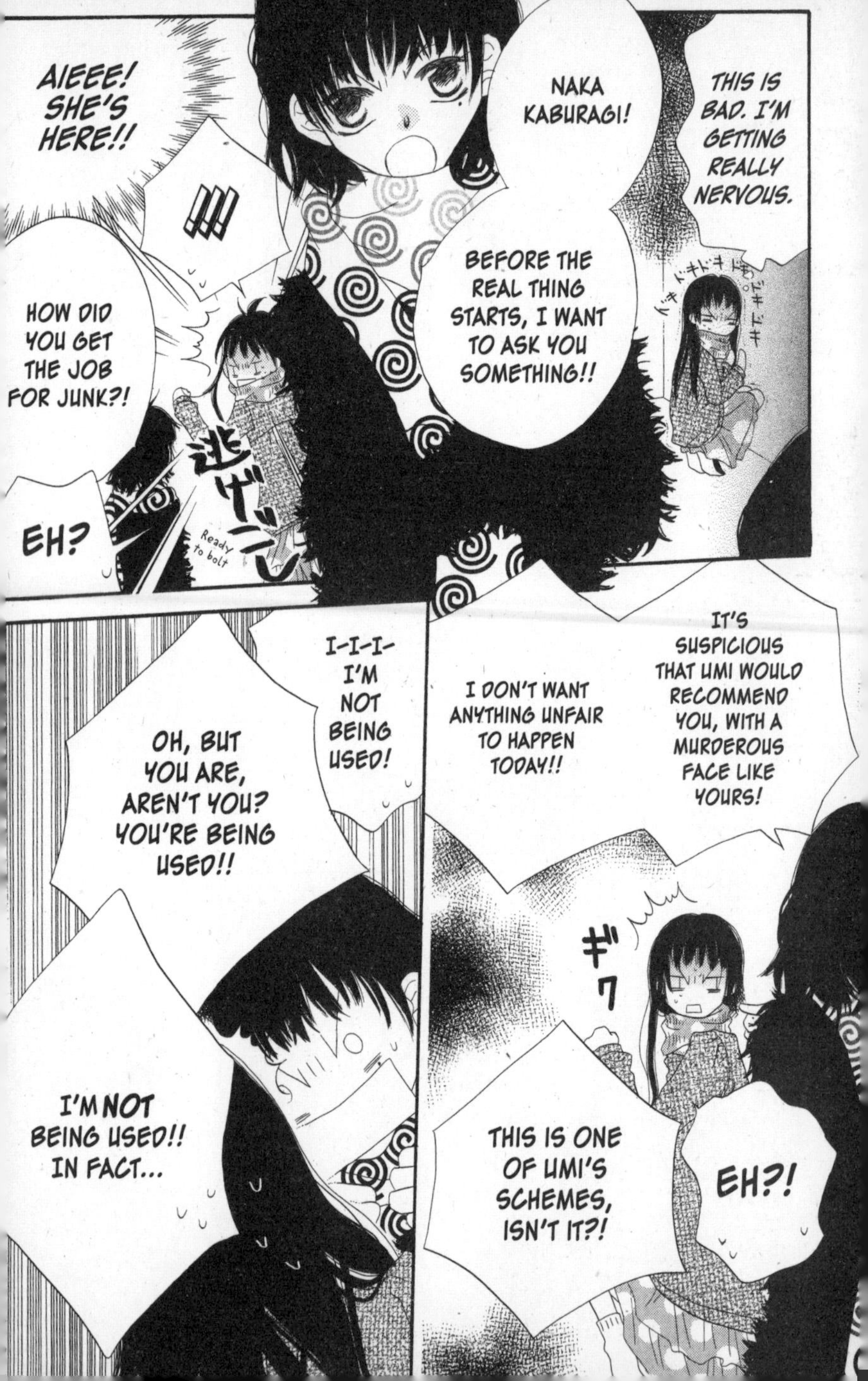
THIS IS BAD. I'M GETTING REALLY NERVOUS.
ドキドキ
NAKA KABURAGI!
BEFORE THE REAL THING STARTS, I WANT TO ASK YOU SOMETHING!!
AIEEE! SHE'S HERE!!
!!!
HOW DID YOU GET THE JOB FOR JUNK?!
EH?
逃げ
Ready to bolt
IT'S SUSPICIOUS THAT UMI WOULD RECOMMEND YOU, WITH A MURDEROUS FACE LIKE YOURS!
I DON'T WANT ANYTHING UNFAIR TO HAPPEN TODAY!!
ギク
THIS IS ONE OF UMI'S SCHEMES, ISN'T IT?!
EH?!
I-I-I- I'M NOT BEING USED!
OH, BUT YOU ARE, AREN'T YOU? YOU'RE BEING USED!!
I'M NOT BEING USED!! IN FACT...

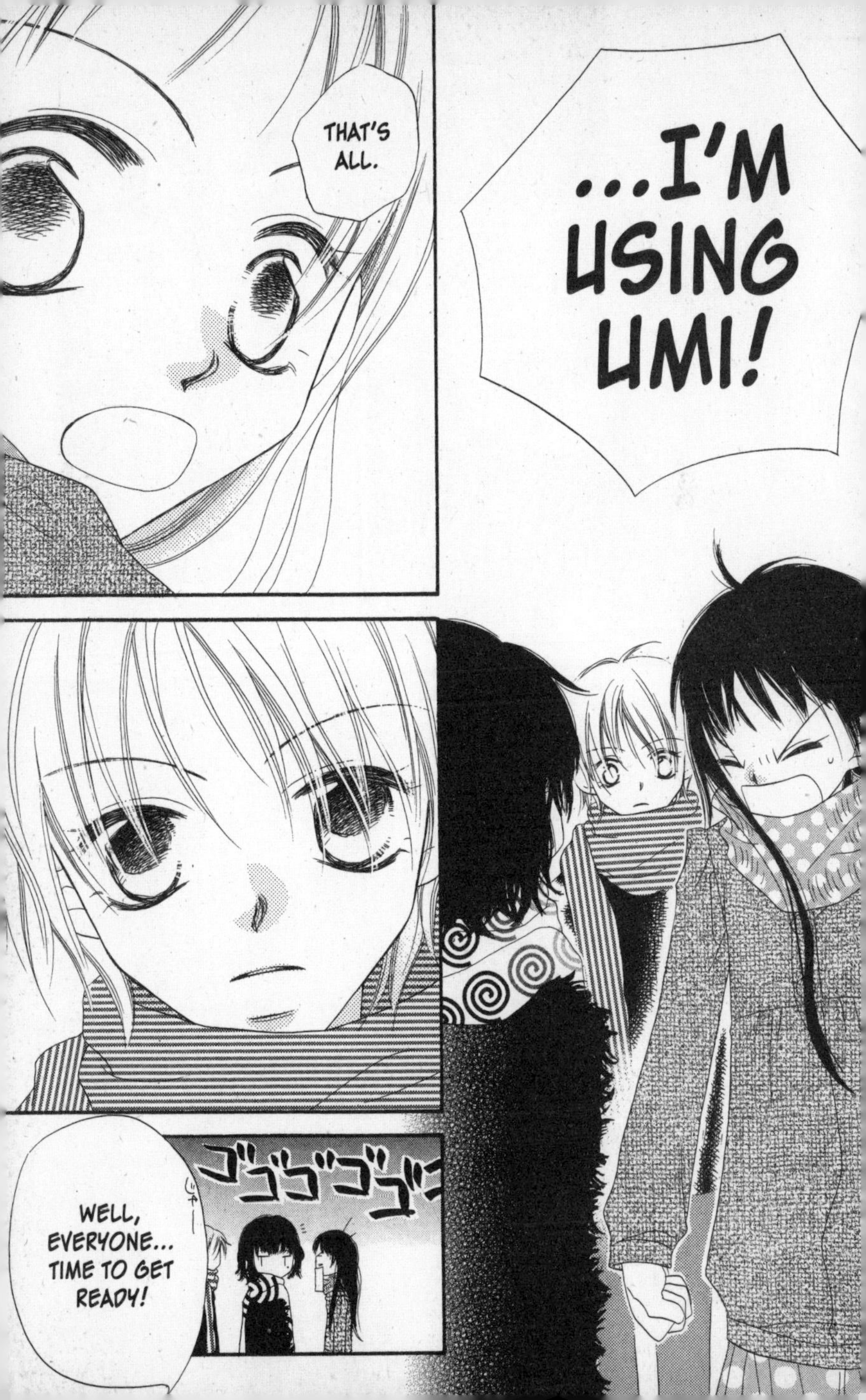
...I'M USING UMI!
THAT'S ALL.
WELL, EVERYONE... TIME TO GET READY!
ゴゴゴゴゴ

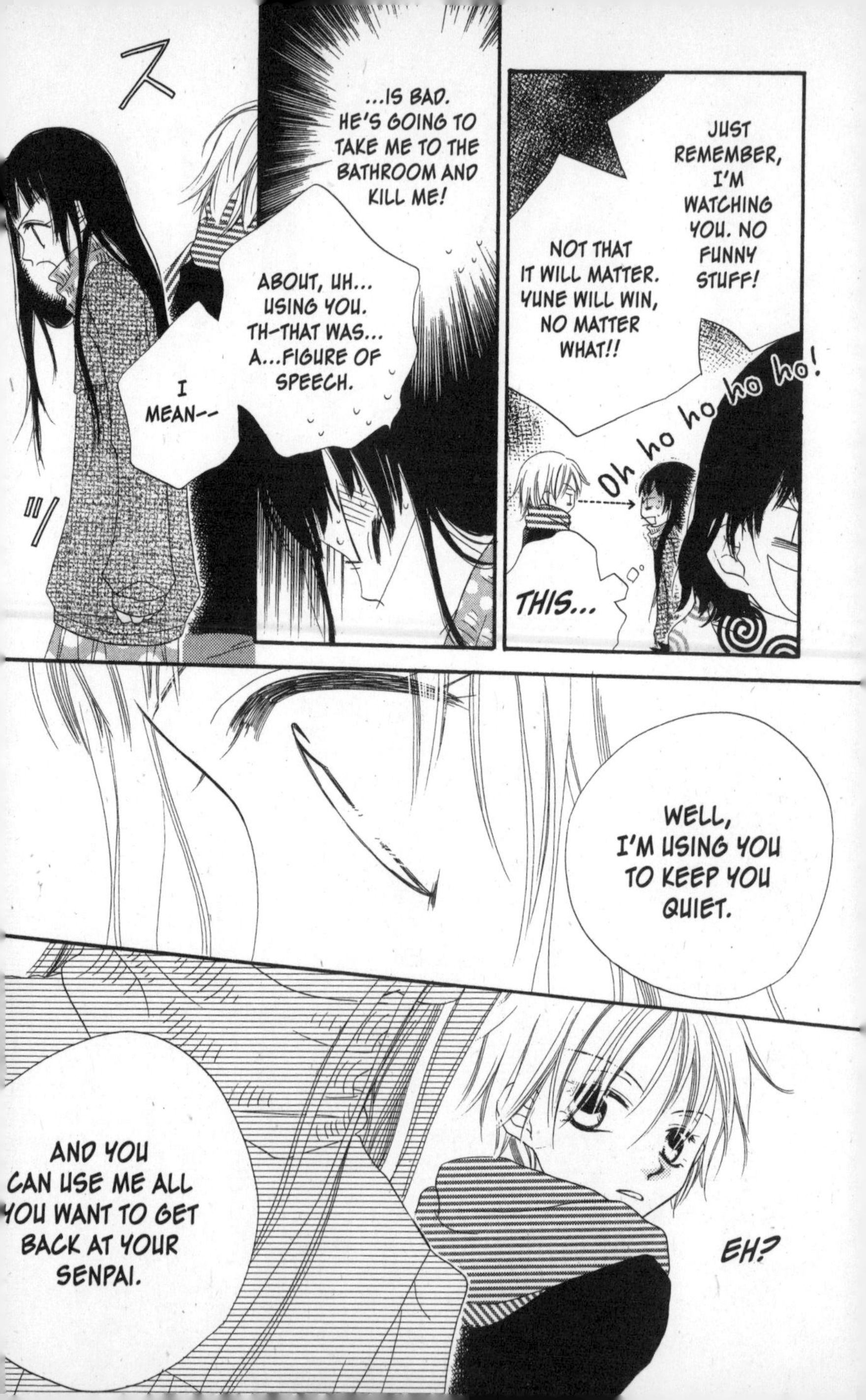
JUST REMEMBER, I'M WATCHING YOU. NO FUNNY STUFF!
NOT THAT IT WILL MATTER. YUNE WILL WIN, NO MATTER WHAT!!
Oh ho ho ho ho ho!
THIS...
...IS BAD. HE'S GOING TO TAKE ME TO THE BATHROOM AND KILL ME!
ABOUT, UH... USING YOU. TH-THAT WAS... A...FIGURE OF SPEECH.
I MEAN--
ス
WELL, I'M USING YOU TO KEEP YOU QUIET.
EH?
AND YOU CAN USE ME ALL YOU WANT TO GET BACK AT YOUR SENPAI.

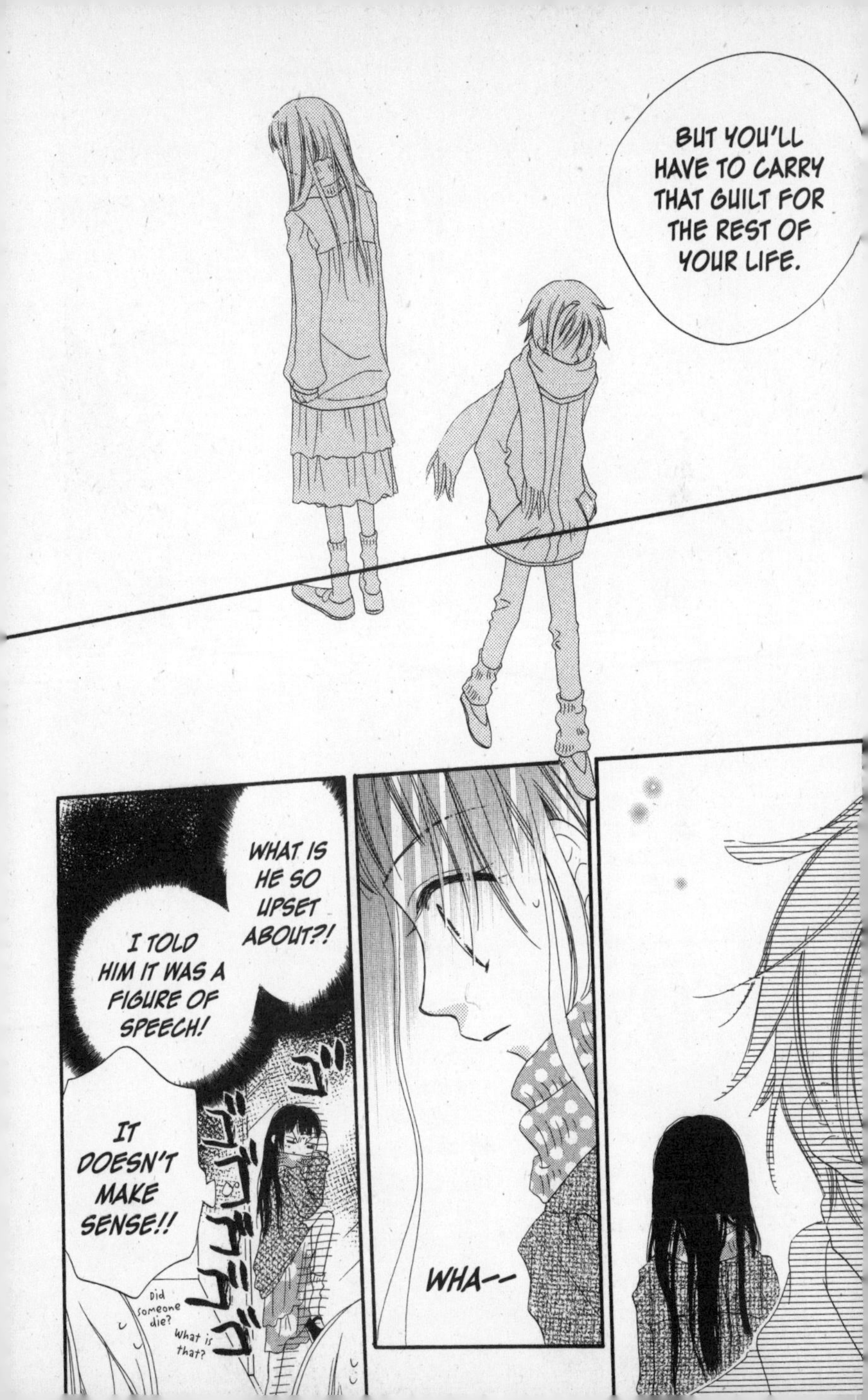
BUT YOU'LL HAVE TO CARRY THAT GUILT FOR THE REST OF YOUR LIFE.
WHA--
WHAT IS HE SO UPSET ABOUT?!
I TOLD HIM IT WAS A FIGURE OF SPEECH!
IT DOESN'T MAKE SENSE!!
Did someone die?
What is that?

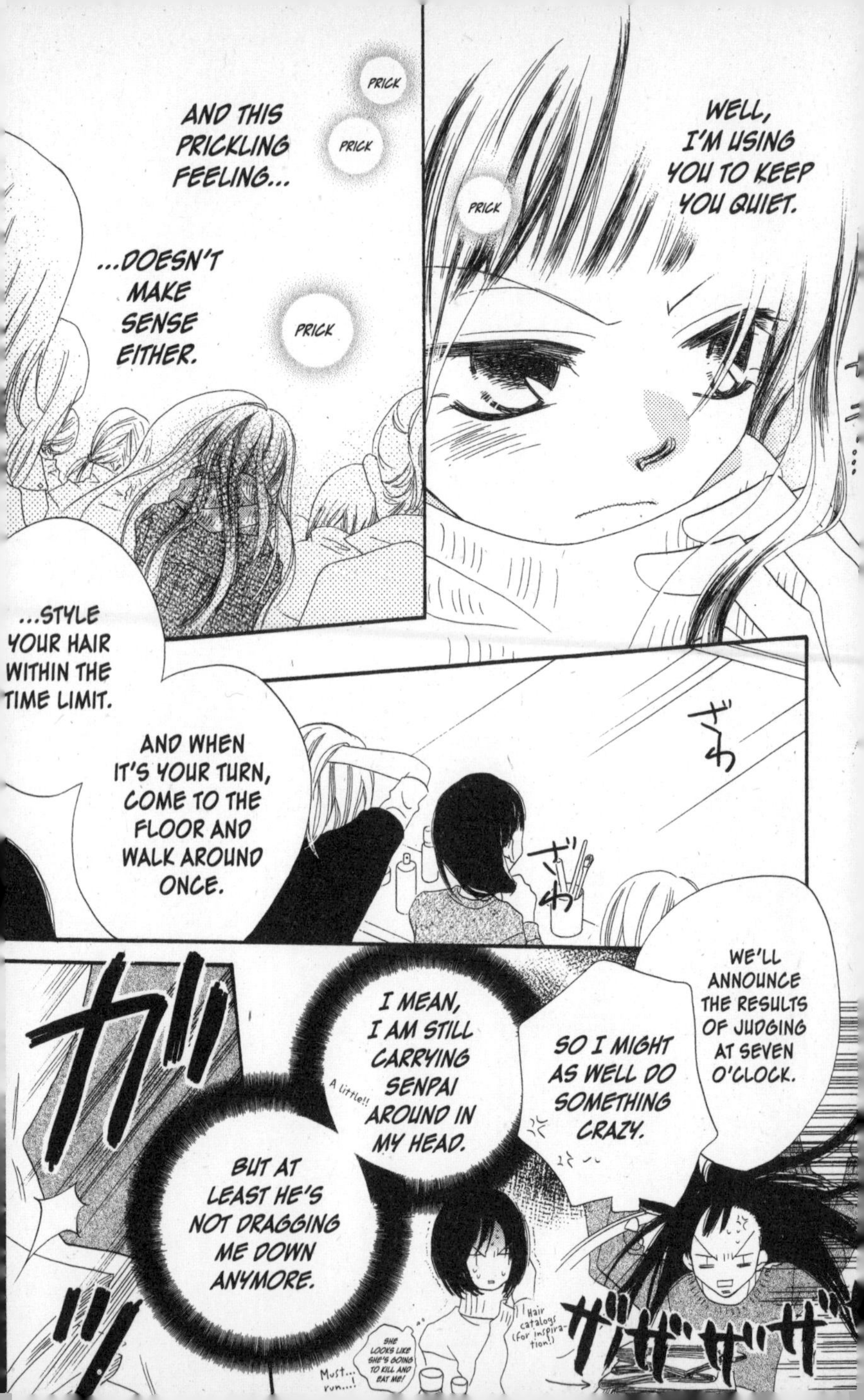
WELL, I'M USING YOU TO KEEP YOU QUIET.
PRICK
PRICK
AND THIS PRICKLING FEELING...
PRICK
...DOESN'T MAKE SENSE EITHER.
PRICK
ざわ
ざわ
...STYLE YOUR HAIR WITHIN THE TIME LIMIT.
AND WHEN IT'S YOUR TURN, COME TO THE FLOOR AND WALK AROUND ONCE.
WE'LL ANNOUNCE THE RESULTS OF JUDGING AT SEVEN O'CLOCK.
SO I MIGHT AS WELL DO SOMETHING CRAZY.
I MEAN, I AM STILL CARRYING SENPAI AROUND IN MY HEAD.
A little!!
BUT AT LEAST HE'S NOT DRAGGING ME DOWN ANYMORE.
ザザザザ
Hair catalogs (for inspira-tion!)
SHE LOOKS LIKE SHE'S GOING TO KILL AND EAT ME!
Must... run...!
ガッ

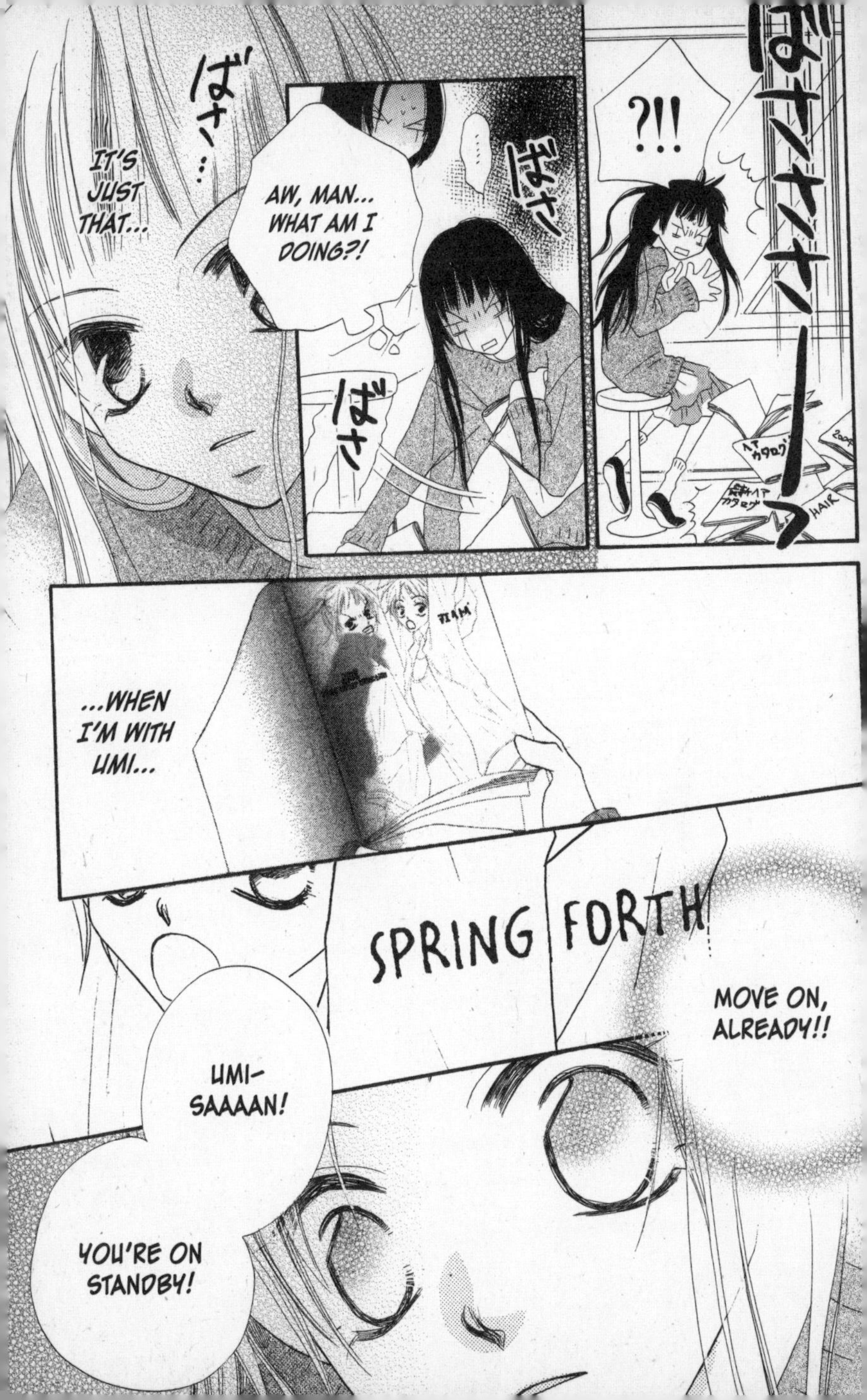
ばさささーっ
?!!
ヘア カタログ
HAIR
...
AW, MAN... WHAT AM I DOING?!
ばさ
ばさ
ばさ...
IT'S JUST THAT...
...WHEN I'M WITH UMI...
MOVE ON, ALREADY!!
SPRING FORTH
UMI-SAAAAN!
YOU'RE ON STANDBY!

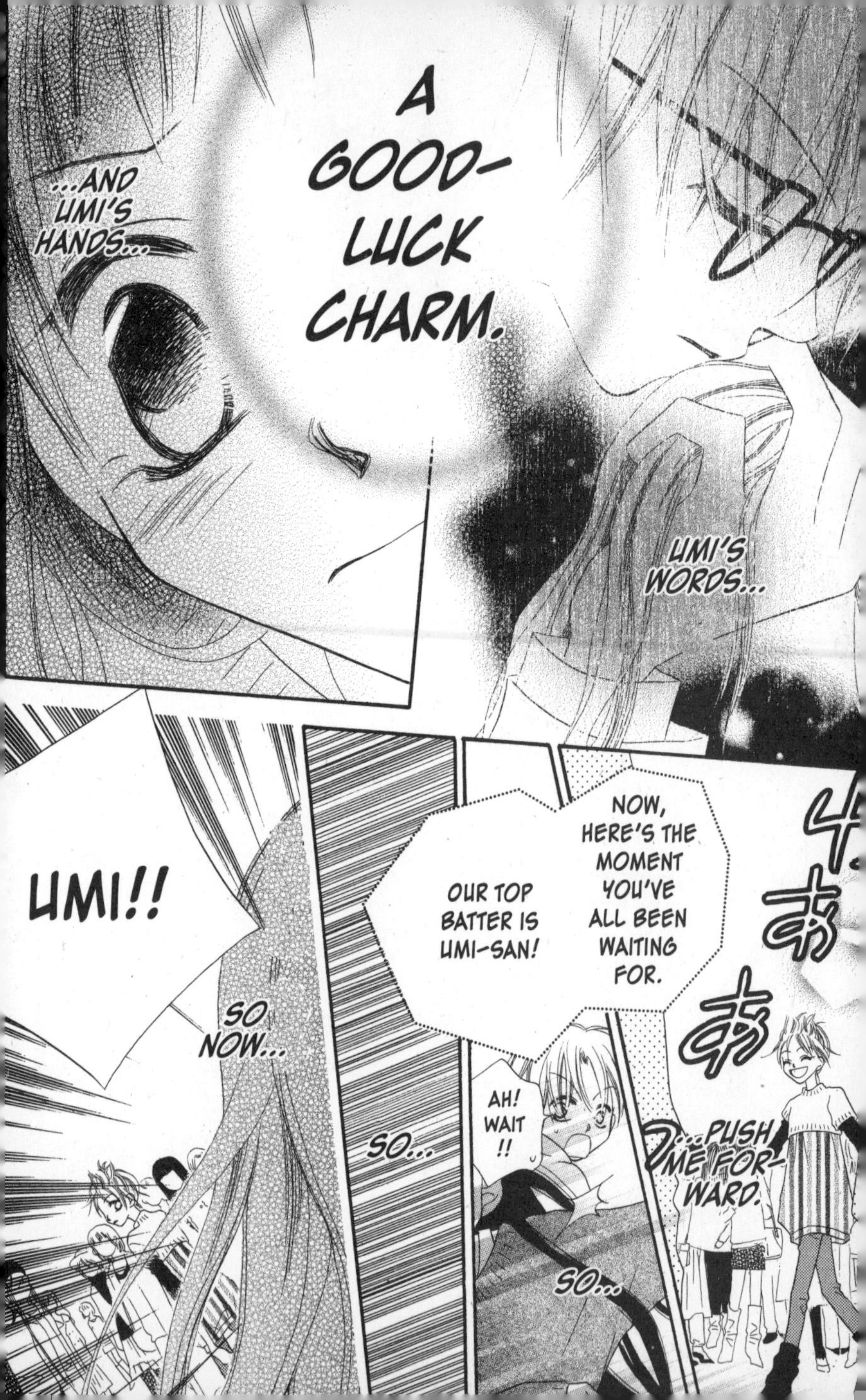
UMI'S WORDS...
A GOOD-LUCK CHARM.
...AND UMI'S HANDS...
NOW, HERE'S THE MOMENT YOU'VE ALL BEEN WAITING FOR.
OUR TOP BATTER IS UMI-SAN!
...PUSH ME FOR-WARD.
AH! WAIT !!
SO...
SO...
SO NOW...
UMI!!

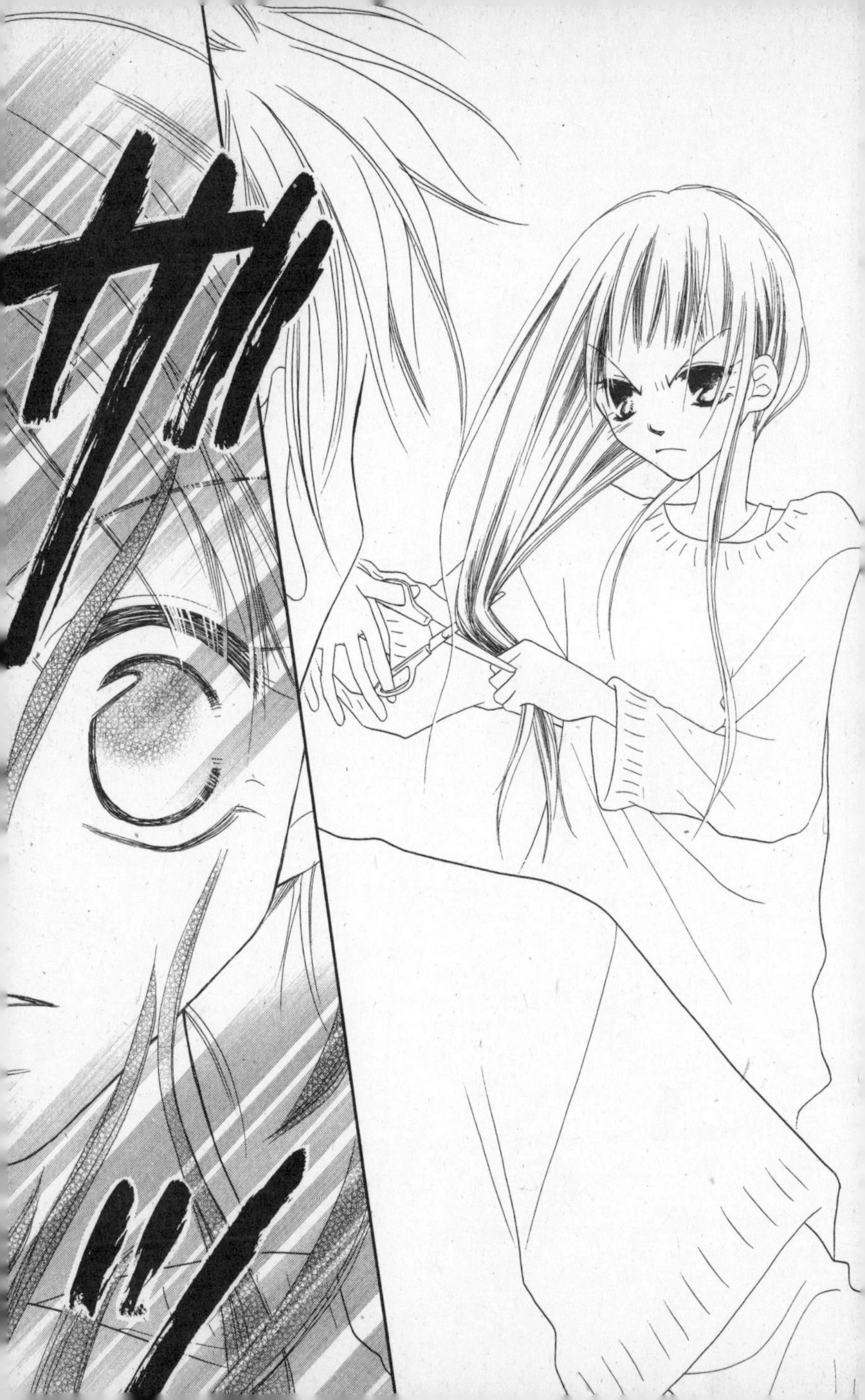
ザッ

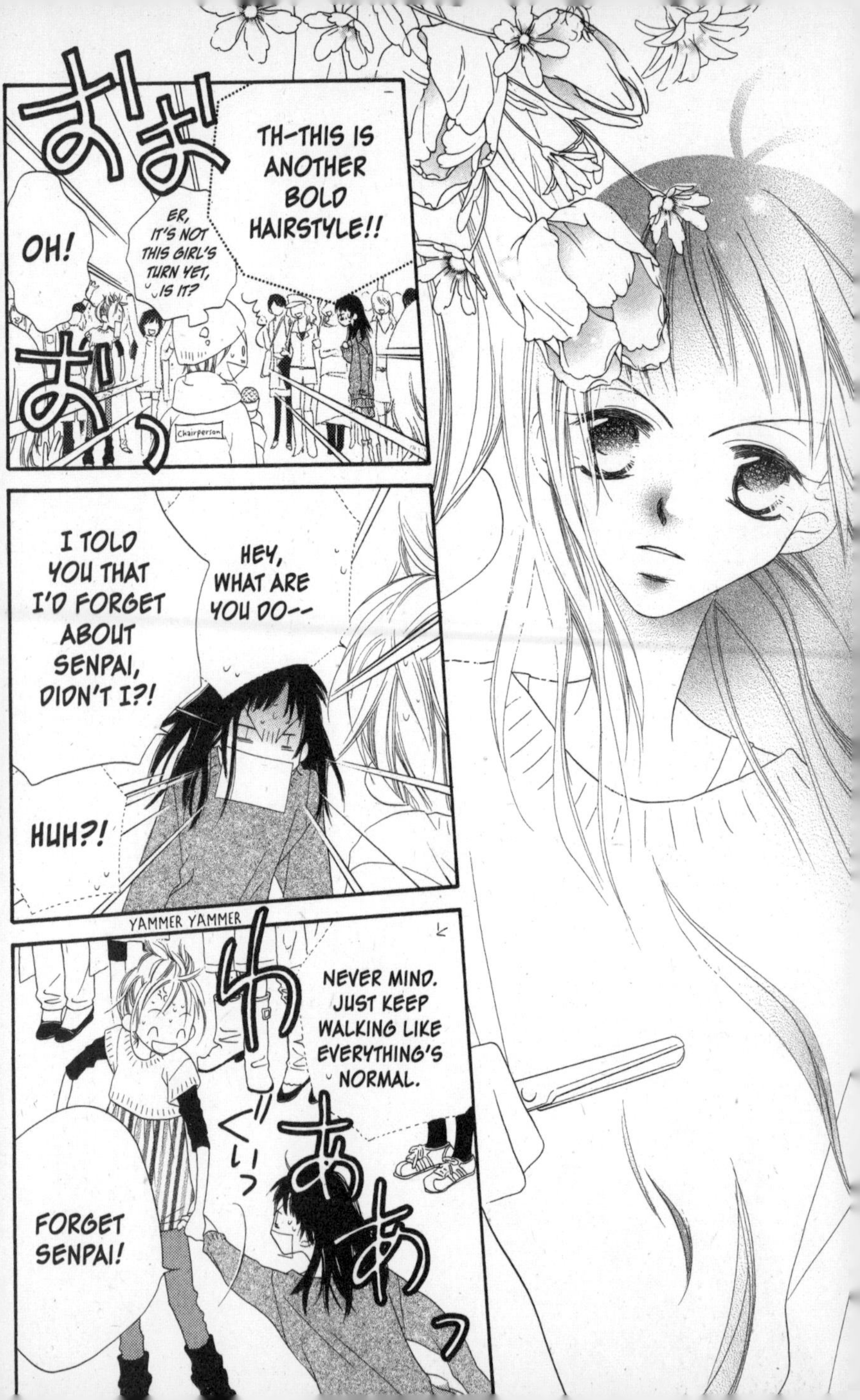

おぉ
TH-THIS IS ANOTHER BOLD HAIRSTYLE!!
ER, IT'S NOT THIS GIRL'S TURN YET, IS IT?
OH!
ぉっ
Chairperson
HEY, WHAT ARE YOU DO--
I TOLD YOU THAT I'D FORGET ABOUT SENPAI, DIDN'T I?!
HUH?!
YAMMER YAMMER
NEVER MIND. JUST KEEP WALKING LIKE EVERYTHING'S NORMAL.
ゆ
ああっ
ぐいっ
FORGET SENPAI!

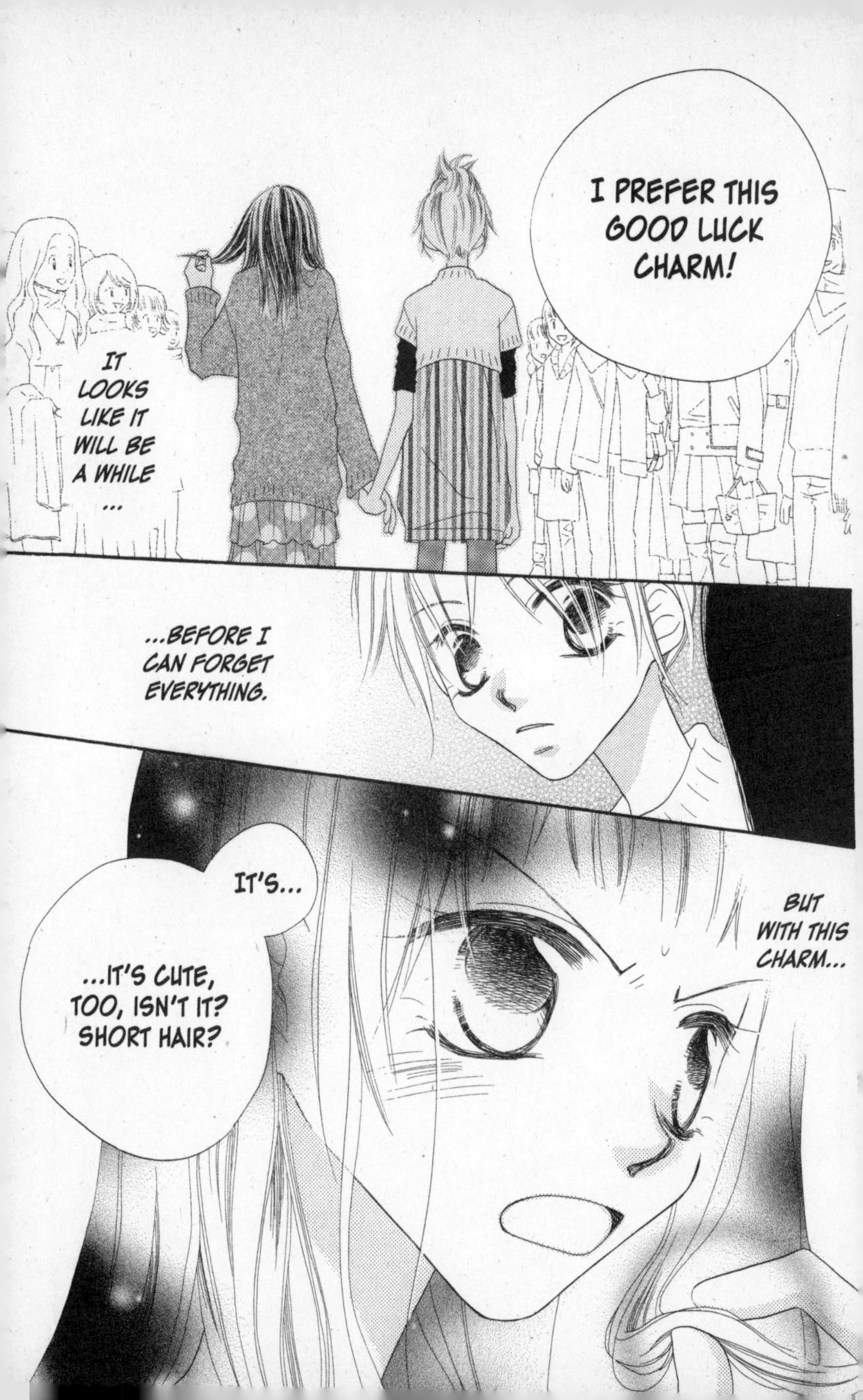
I PREFER THIS GOOD LUCK CHARM!
IT LOOKS LIKE IT WILL BE A WHILE ...
...BEFORE I CAN FORGET EVERYTHING.
BUT WITH THIS CHARM...
IT'S...
...IT'S CUTE, TOO, ISN'T IT? SHORT HAIR?

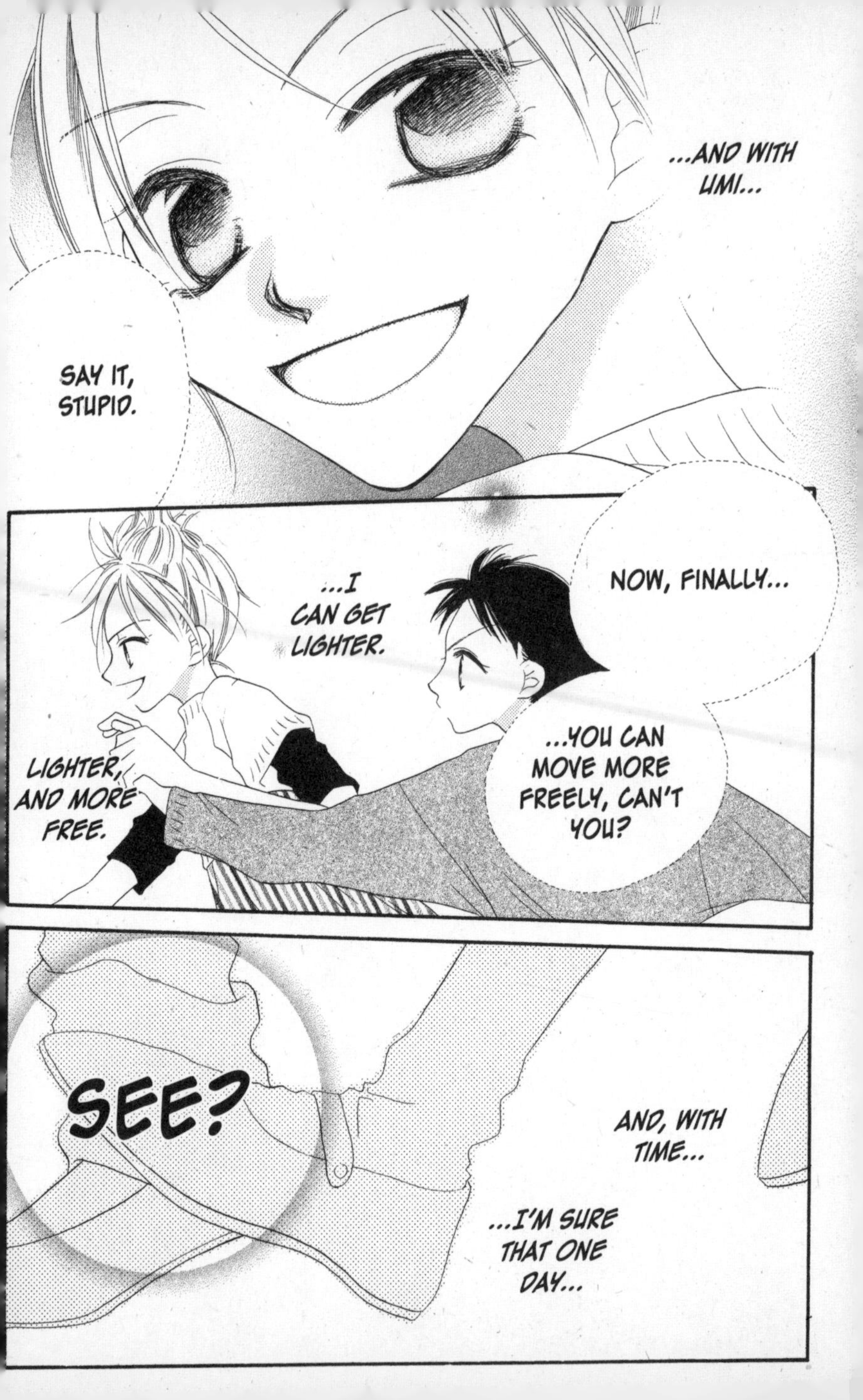

...AND WITH UMI...
SAY IT, STUPID.
NOW, FINALLY...
...YOU CAN MOVE MORE FREELY, CAN'T YOU?
...I CAN GET LIGHTER.
LIGHTER, AND MORE FREE.
AND, WITH TIME...
...I'M SURE THAT ONE DAY...
SEE?

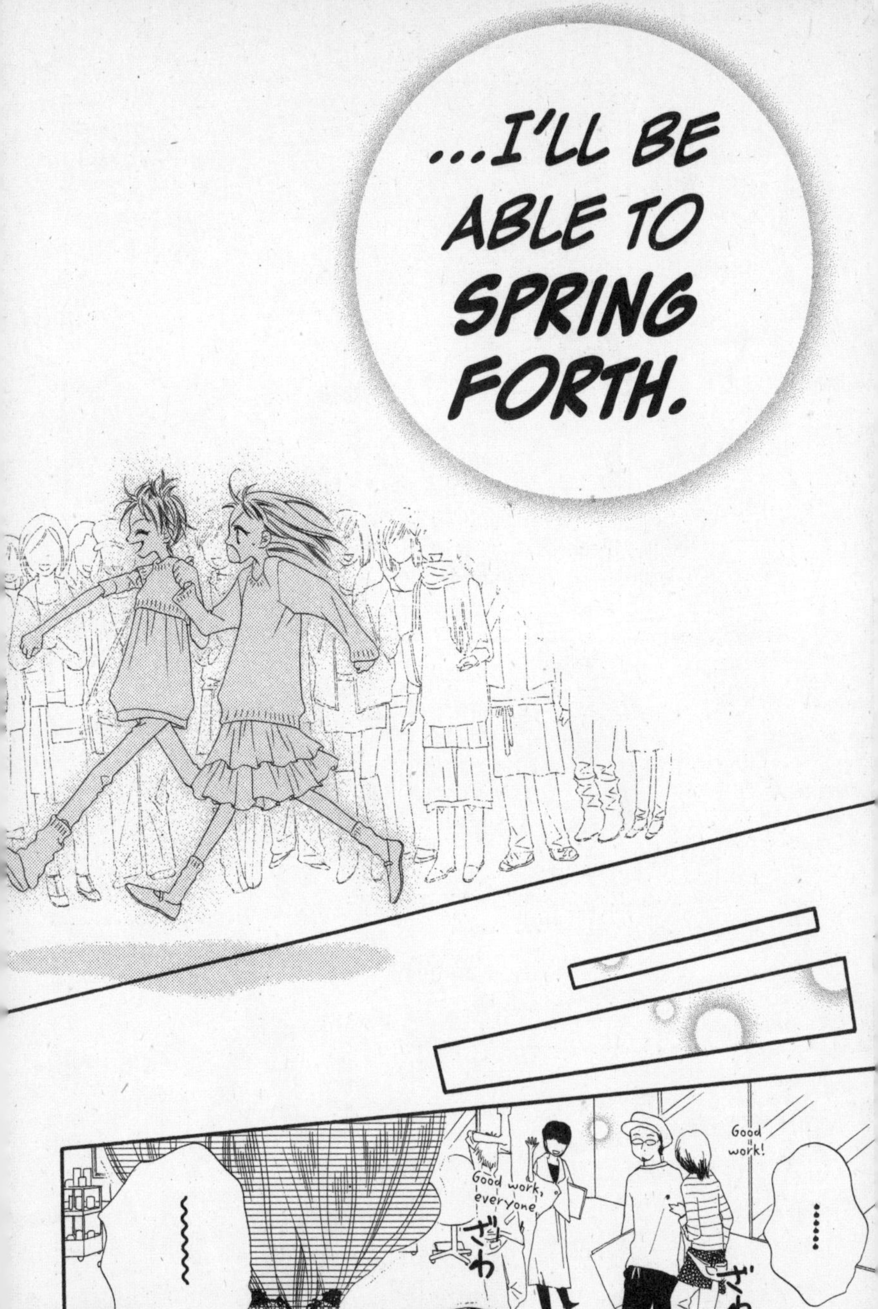
...I'LL BE ABLE TO SPRING FORTH.
......
Good work!
ざわ
Good work, everyone
ざわ

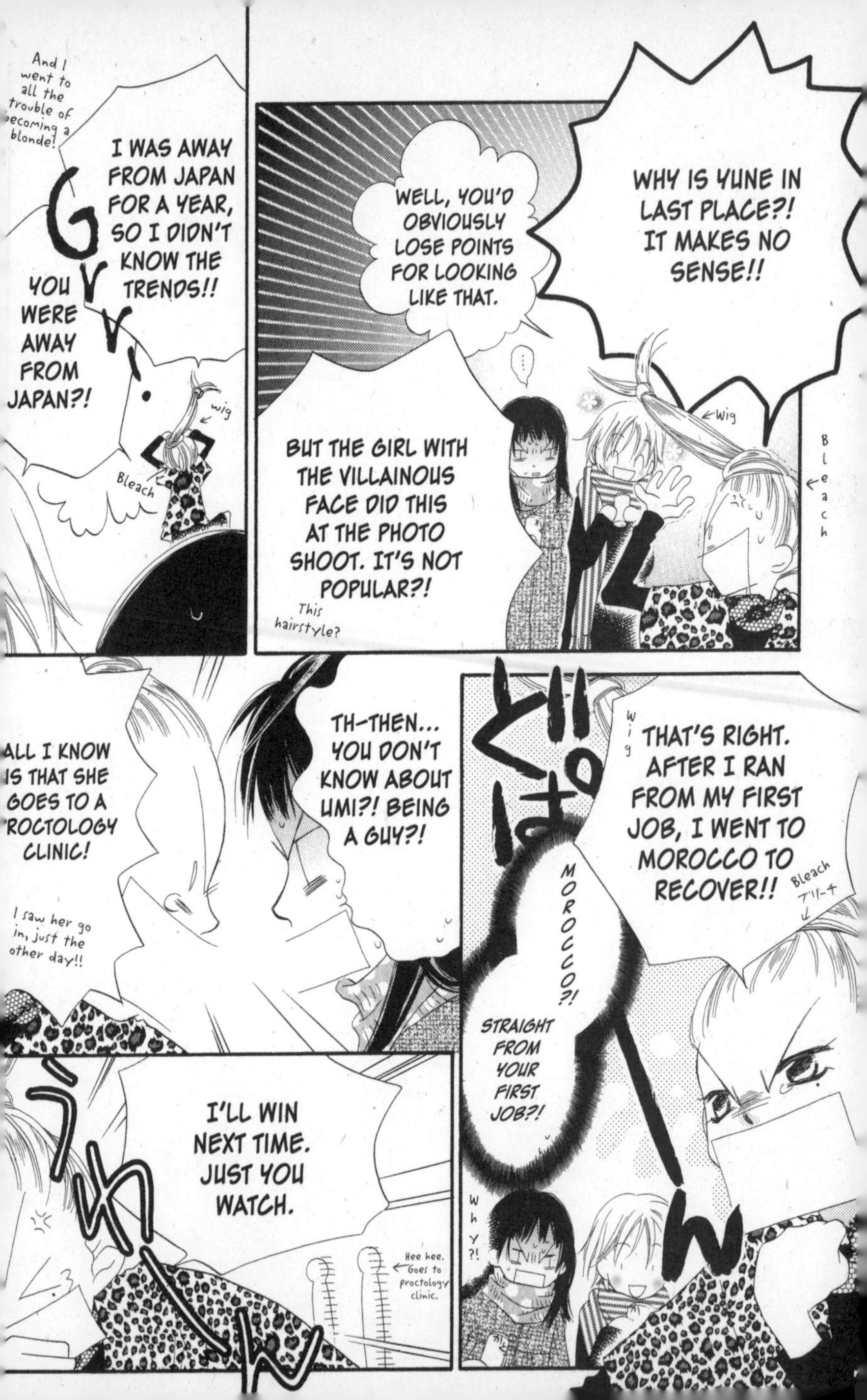
WHY IS YUNE IN LAST PLACE?! IT MAKES NO SENSE!!
WELL, YOU'D OBVIOUSLY LOSE POINTS FOR LOOKING LIKE THAT.
...
Wig
Bleach
BUT THE GIRL WITH THE VILLAINOUS FACE DID THIS AT THE PHOTO SHOOT. IT'S NOT POPULAR?!
This hairstyle?
I WAS AWAY FROM JAPAN FOR A YEAR, SO I DIDN'T KNOW THE TRENDS!!
And I went to all the trouble of becoming a blonde!
YOU WERE AWAY FROM JAPAN?!
wig
Bleach
THAT'S RIGHT. AFTER I RAN FROM MY FIRST JOB, I WENT TO MOROCCO TO RECOVER!!
Wig
Bleach
MOROCCO?!
STRAIGHT FROM YOUR FIRST JOB?!
Why?!
TH-THEN... YOU DON'T KNOW ABOUT UMI?! BEING A GUY?!
ALL I KNOW IS THAT SHE GOES TO A ROCTOLOGY CLINIC!
I saw her go in, just the other day!!
I'LL WIN NEXT TIME. JUST YOU WATCH.
Hee hee. Goes to proctology clinic.

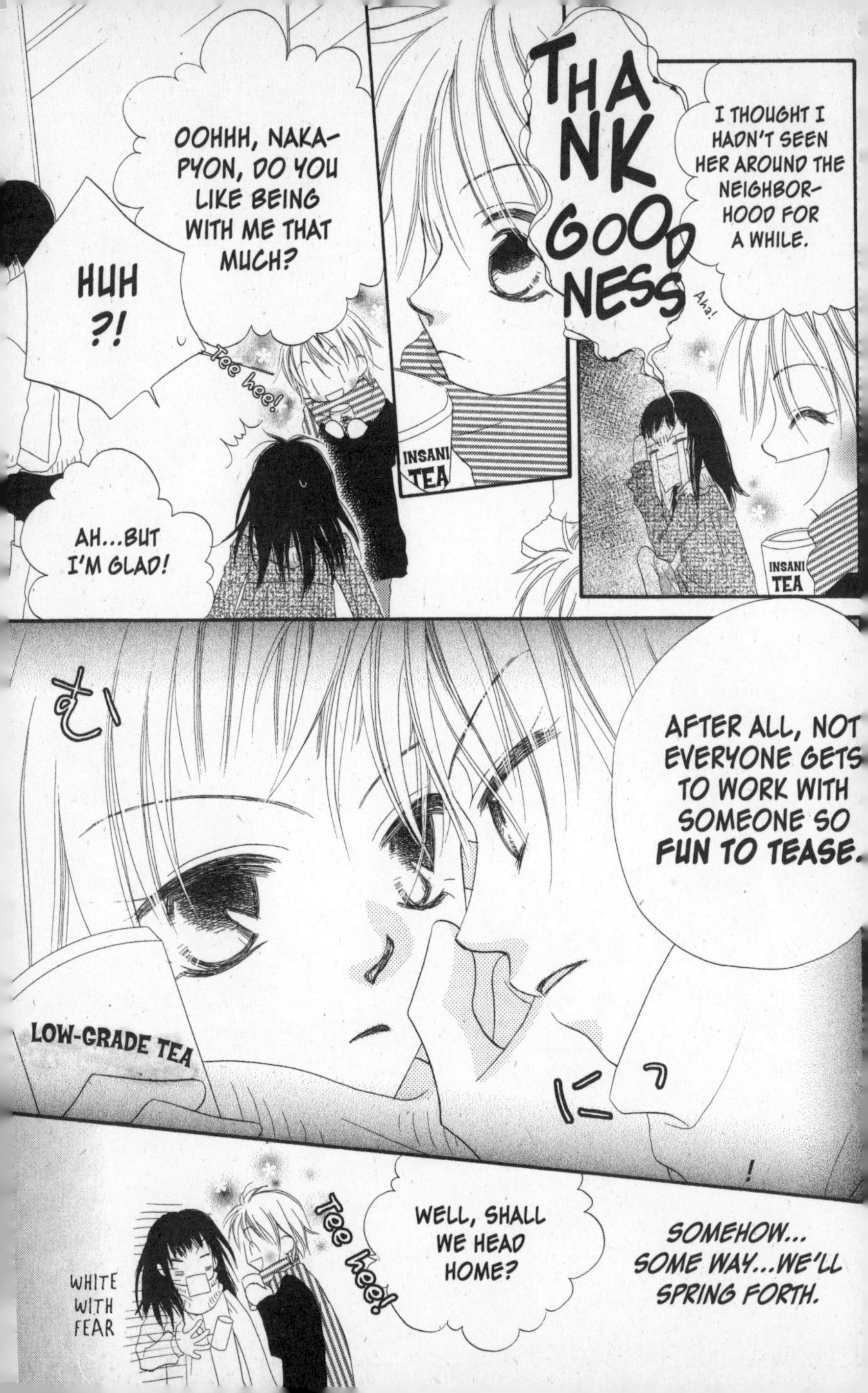
I THOUGHT I HADN'T SEEN HER AROUND THE NEIGHBOR-HOOD FOR A WHILE.
Aha!
THANK GOOODNESS
INSANI TEA
INSANI TEA
OOHHH, NAKA-PYON, DO YOU LIKE BEING WITH ME THAT MUCH?
HUH ?!
Tee hee!
AH...BUT I'M GLAD!
AFTER ALL, NOT EVERYONE GETS TO WORK WITH SOMEONE SO FUN TO TEASE.
むー
にーっ
LOW-GRADE TEA
!
SOMEHOW... SOME WAY...WE'LL SPRING FORTH.
WELL, SHALL WE HEAD HOME?
Tee hee!
WHITE WITH FEAR

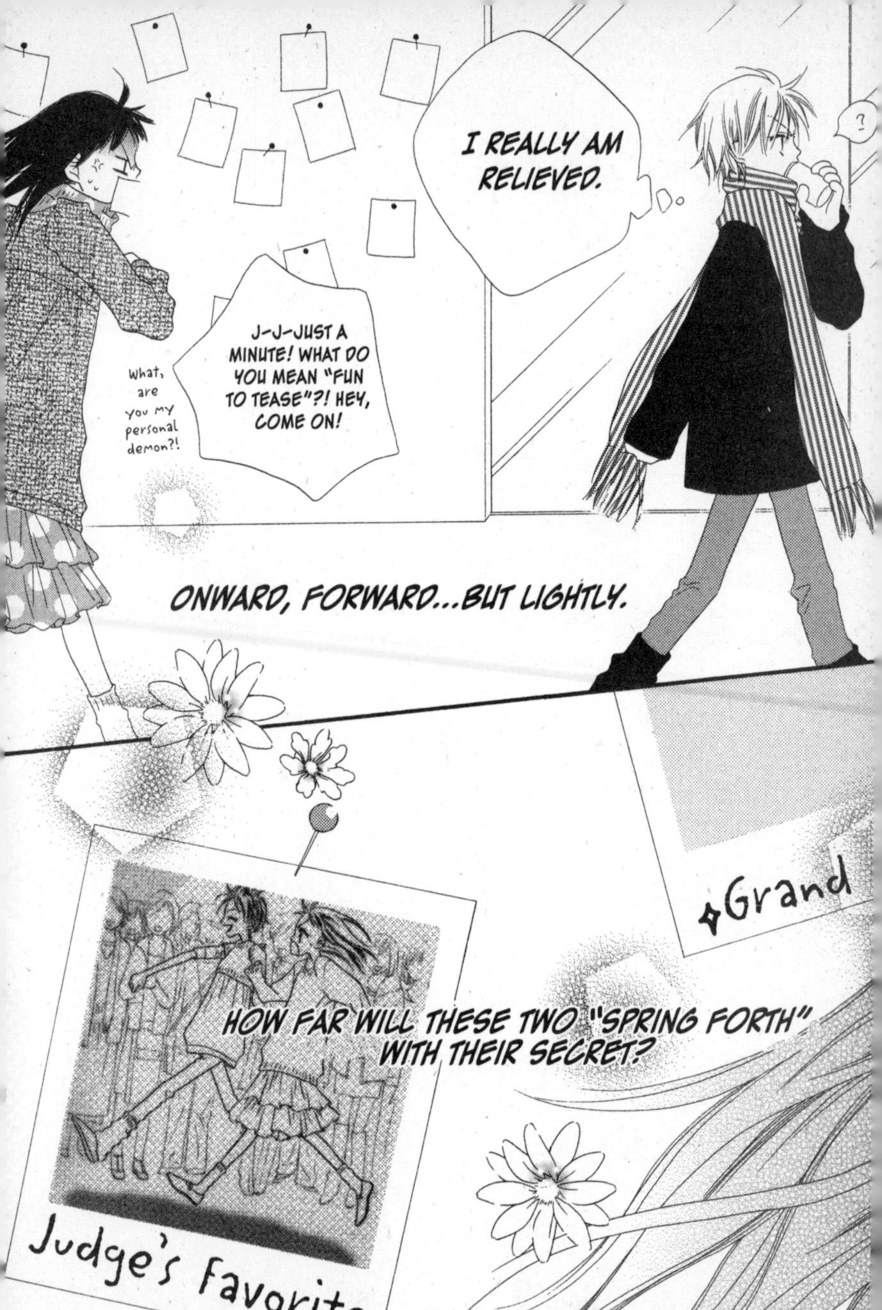
?
I REALLY AM RELIEVED.
J-J-JUST A MINUTE! WHAT DO YOU MEAN "FUN TO TEASE"?! HEY, COME ON!
What, are you my personal demon?!
ONWARD, FORWARD...BUT LIGHTLY.
Grand
HOW FAR WILL THESE TWO "SPRING FORTH" WITH THEIR SECRET?
Judge's Favorite

OSATSU JUNKIE, SESSION 2 / END

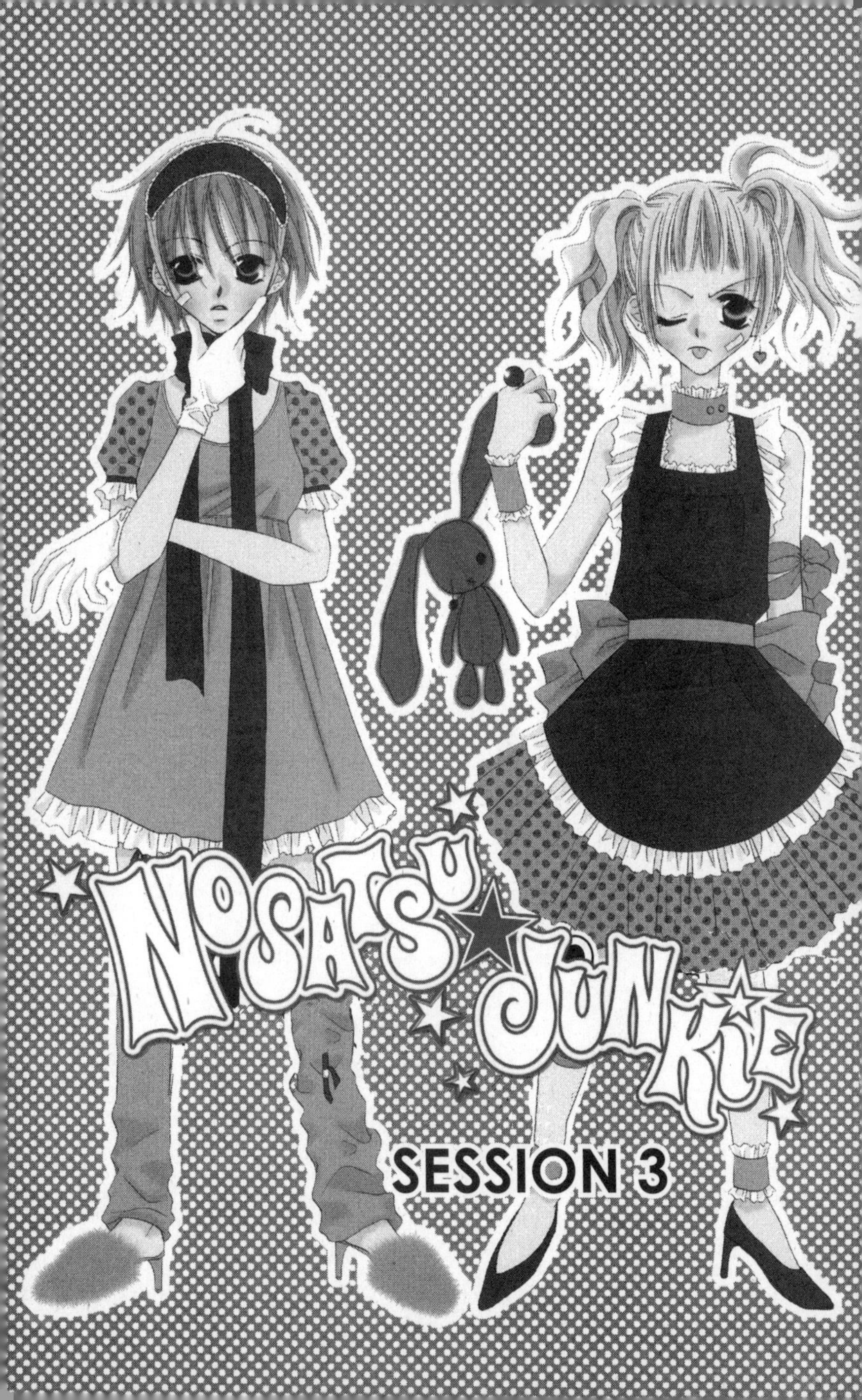
NOSATSU JUNKIE
SESSION 3

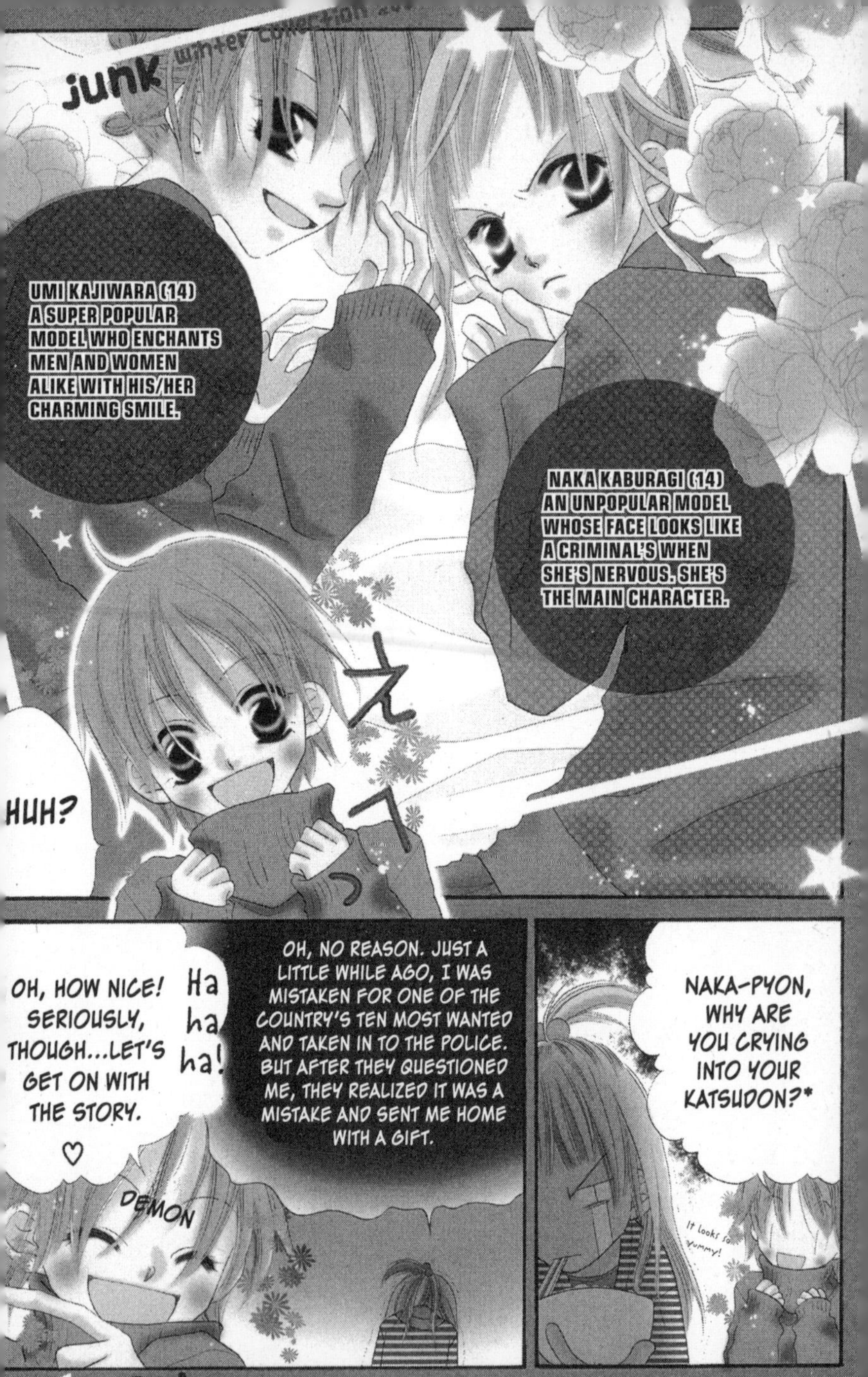
junk
UMI KAJIWARA (14) A SUPER POPULAR MODEL WHO ENCHANTS MEN AND WOMEN ALIKE WITH HIS/HER CHARMING SMILE.
NAKA KABURAGI (14) AN UNPOPULAR MODEL WHOSE FACE LOOKS LIKE A CRIMINAL'S WHEN SHE'S NERVOUS. SHE'S THE MAIN CHARACTER.
HUH?
NAKA-PYON, WHY ARE YOU CRYING INTO YOUR KATSUDON?*
It looks so yummy!
OH, NO REASON. JUST A LITTLE WHILE AGO, I WAS MISTAKEN FOR ONE OF THE COUNTRY'S TEN MOST WANTED AND TAKEN IN TO THE POLICE. BUT AFTER THEY QUESTIONED ME, THEY REALIZED IT WAS A MISTAKE AND SENT ME HOME WITH A GIFT.
Ha ha ha!
OH, HOW NICE! SERIOUSLY, THOUGH...LET'S GET ON WITH THE STORY. ♡
DEMON

*breaded, fried pork with rice.

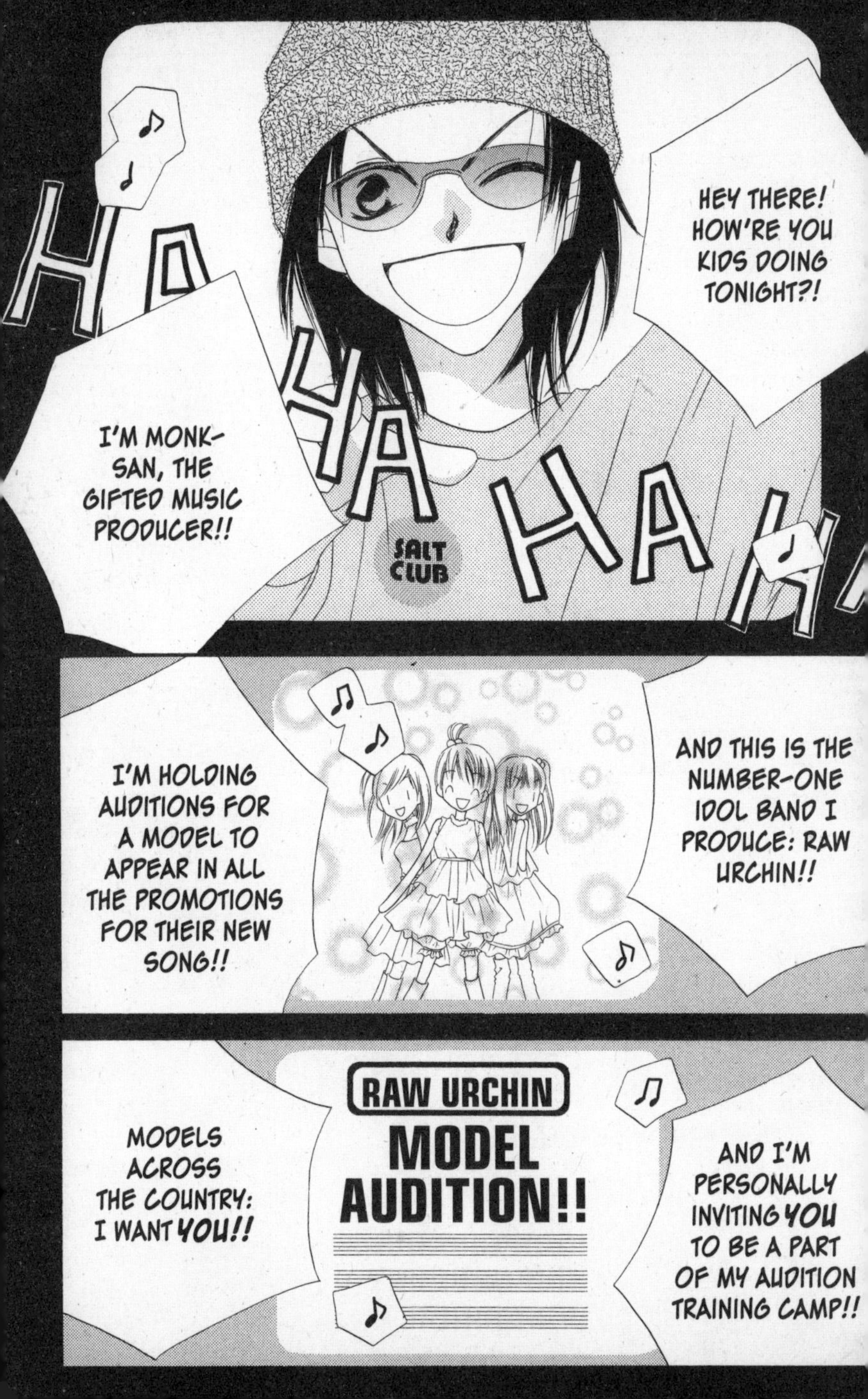
HEY THERE! HOW'RE YOU KIDS DOING TONIGHT?!
HA HA HA HA
I'M MONK-SAN, THE GIFTED MUSIC PRODUCER!!
SALT CLUB
AND THIS IS THE NUMBER-ONE IDOL BAND I PRODUCE: RAW URCHIN!!
I'M HOLDING AUDITIONS FOR A MODEL TO APPEAR IN ALL THE PROMOTIONS FOR THEIR NEW SONG!!
AND I'M PERSONALLY INVITING YOU TO BE A PART OF MY AUDITION TRAINING CAMP!!
RAW URCHIN
MODEL AUDITION!!
MODELS ACROSS THE COUNTRY: I WANT YOU!!

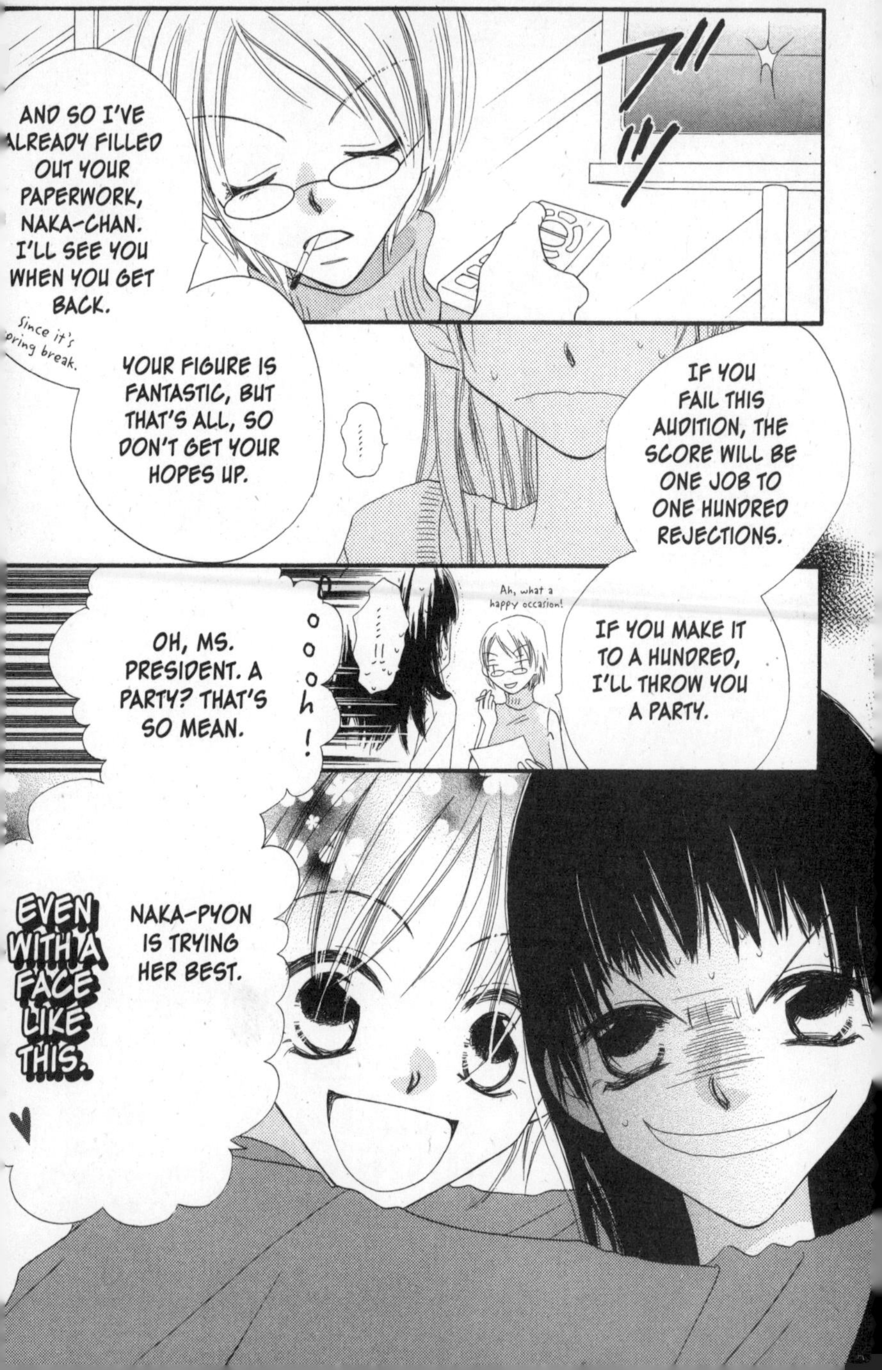
AND SO I'VE ALREADY FILLED OUT YOUR PAPERWORK, NAKA-CHAN. I'LL SEE YOU WHEN YOU GET BACK.
Since it's pring break.
IF YOU FAIL THIS AUDITION, THE SCORE WILL BE ONE JOB TO ONE HUNDRED REJECTIONS.
......
YOUR FIGURE IS FANTASTIC, BUT THAT'S ALL, SO DON'T GET YOUR HOPES UP.
IF YOU MAKE IT TO A HUNDRED, I'LL THROW YOU A PARTY.
Ah, what a happy occasion!
......!!
OOOh!
OH, MS. PRESIDENT. A PARTY? THAT'S SO MEAN.
NAKA-PYON IS TRYING HER BEST.
EVEN WITH A FACE LIKE THIS.

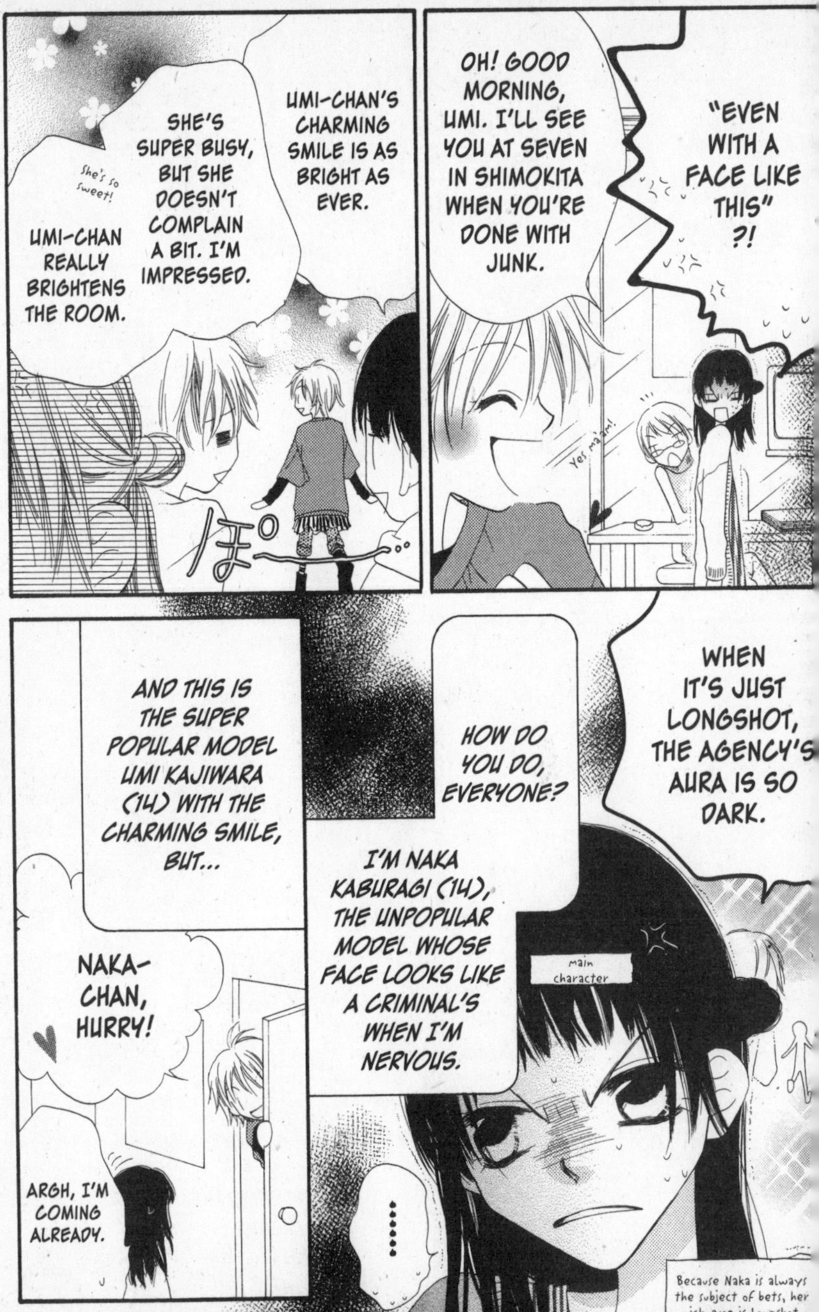
"EVEN WITH A FACE LIKE THIS"?!
OH! GOOD MORNING, UMI. I'LL SEE YOU AT SEVEN IN SHIMOKITA WHEN YOU'RE DONE WITH JUNK.
Yes ma'am!
UMI-CHAN'S CHARMING SMILE IS AS BRIGHT AS EVER.
SHE'S SUPER BUSY, BUT SHE DOESN'T COMPLAIN A BIT. I'M IMPRESSED.
She's so sweet!
UMI-CHAN REALLY BRIGHTENS THE ROOM.
ぽ~
WHEN IT'S JUST LONGSHOT, THE AGENCY'S AURA IS SO DARK.
HOW DO YOU DO, EVERYONE?
I'M NAKA KABURAGI (14), THE UNPOPULAR MODEL WHOSE FACE LOOKS LIKE A CRIMINAL'S WHEN I'M NERVOUS.
main character
......
Because Naka is always the subject of bets, her nickname is Longshot.
AND THIS IS THE SUPER POPULAR MODEL UMI KAJIWARA (14) WITH THE CHARMING SMILE, BUT...
NAKA-CHAN, HURRY!
ARGH, I'M COMING ALREADY.

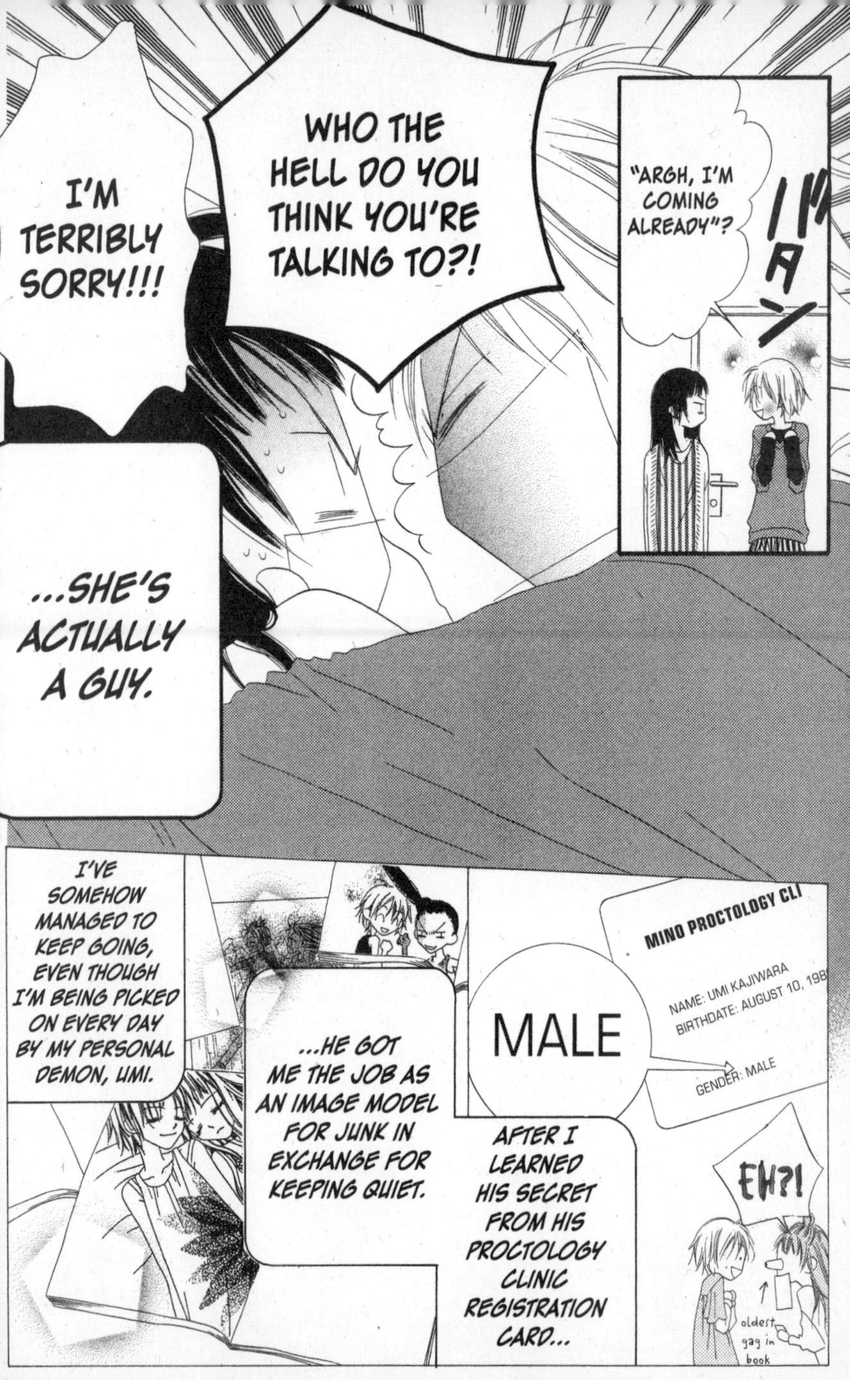
"ARGH, I'M COMING ALREADY"?
WHO THE HELL DO YOU THINK YOU'RE TALKING TO?!
I'M TERRIBLY SORRY!!!
...SHE'S ACTUALLY A GUY.
MINO PROCTOLOGY CLI
NAME: UMI KAJIWARA
BIRTHDATE: AUGUST 10, 198
GENDER: MALE
MALE
EH?!
oldest gag in book
AFTER I LEARNED HIS SECRET FROM HIS PROCTOLOGY CLINIC REGISTRATION CARD...
...HE GOT ME THE JOB AS AN IMAGE MODEL FOR JUNK IN EXCHANGE FOR KEEPING QUIET.
I'VE SOMEHOW MANAGED TO KEEP GOING, EVEN THOUGH I'M BEING PICKED ON EVERY DAY BY MY PERSONAL DEMON, UMI.

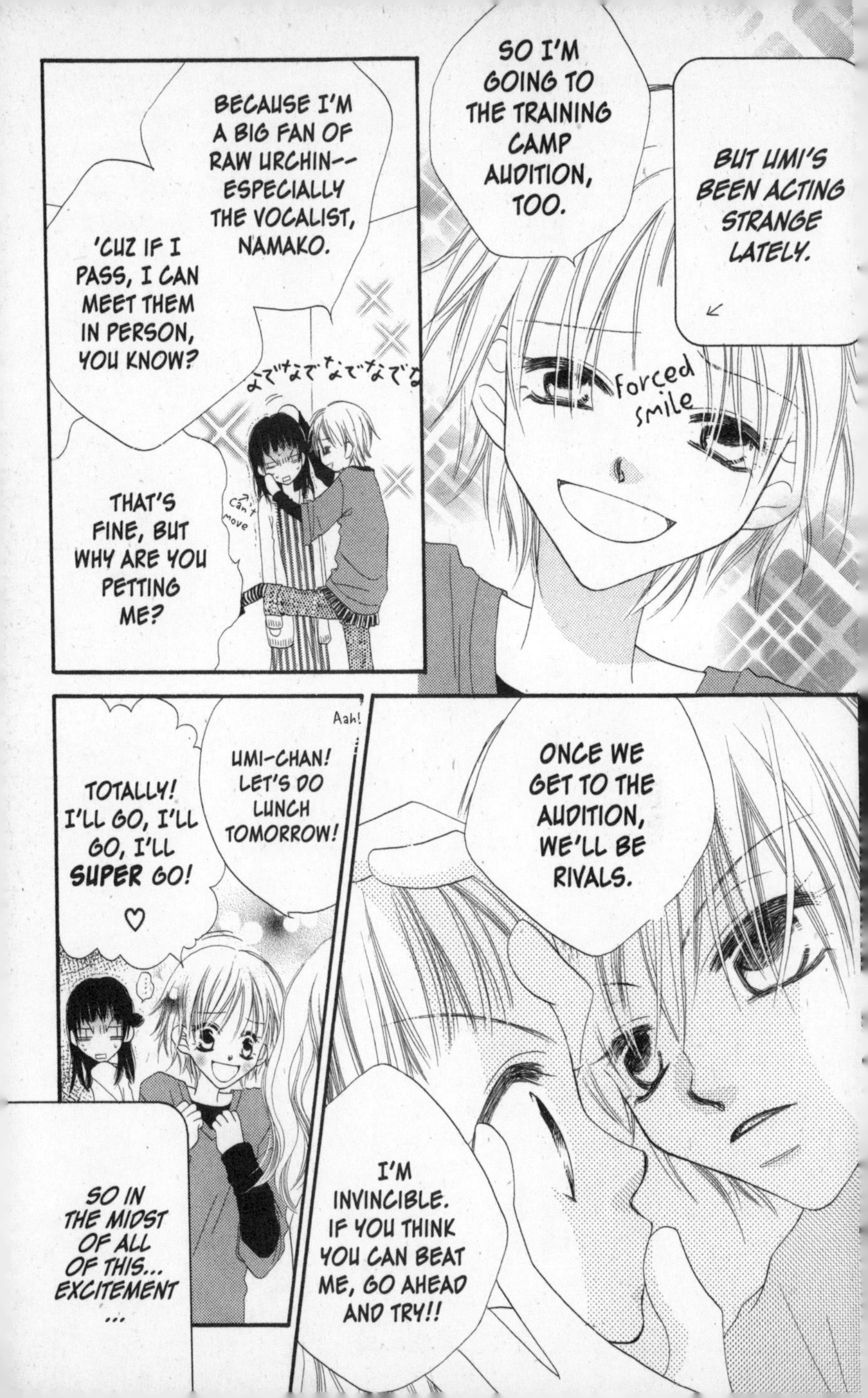
BUT UMI'S BEEN ACTING STRANGE LATELY.
SO I'M GOING TO THE TRAINING CAMP AUDITION, TOO.
Forced smile
BECAUSE I'M A BIG FAN OF RAW URCHIN--ESPECIALLY THE VOCALIST, NAMAKO.
'CUZ IF I PASS, I CAN MEET THEM IN PERSON, YOU KNOW?
なでなでなでなでな
Can't move
THAT'S FINE, BUT WHY ARE YOU PETTING ME?
ONCE WE GET TO THE AUDITION, WE'LL BE RIVALS.
I'M INVINCIBLE. IF YOU THINK YOU CAN BEAT ME, GO AHEAD AND TRY!!
Aah!
UMI-CHAN! LET'S DO LUNCH TOMORROW!
TOTALLY! I'LL GO, I'LL GO, I'LL SUPER GO! ♡
...
SO IN THE MIDST OF ALL OF THIS... EXCITEMENT ...

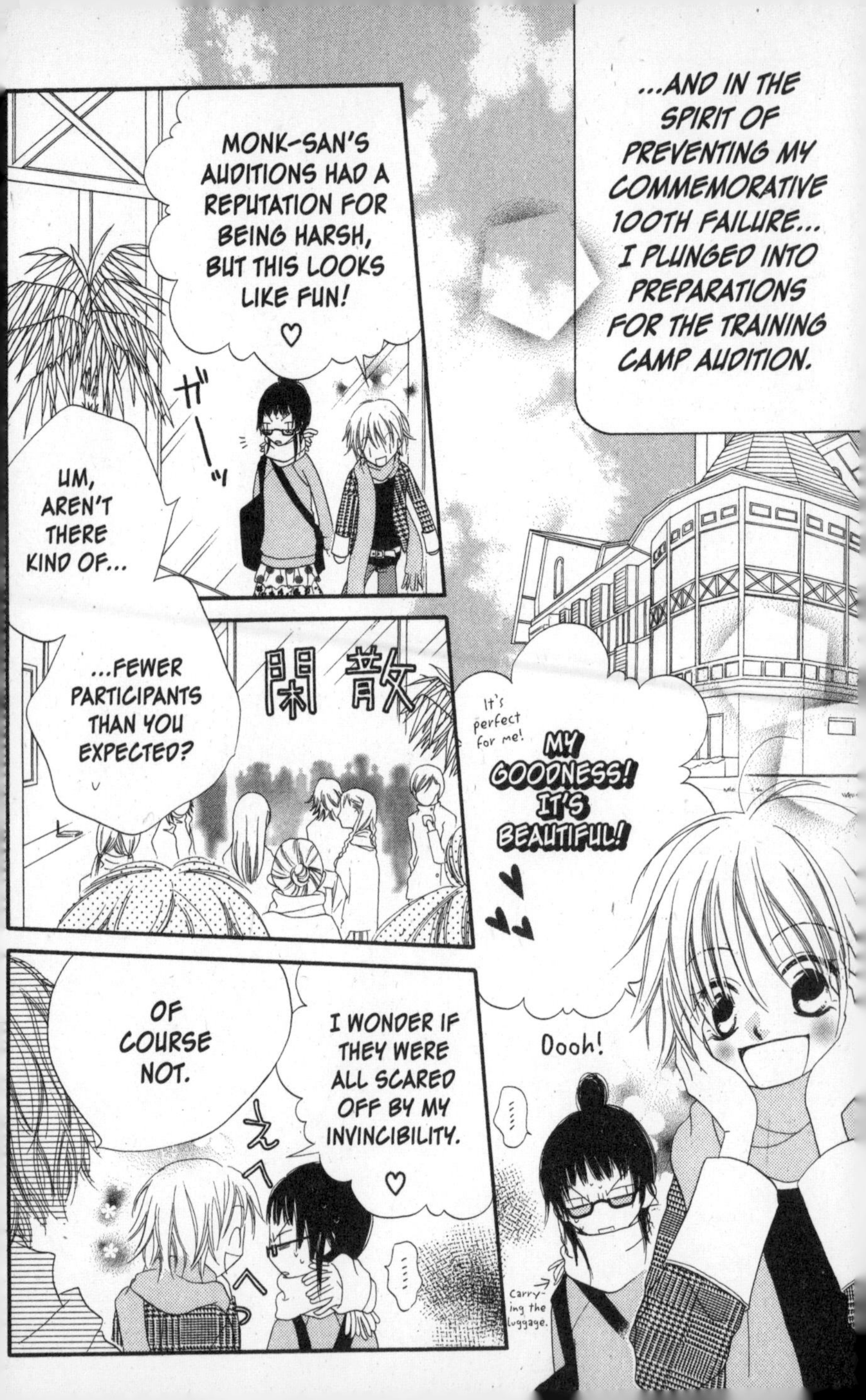
...AND IN THE SPIRIT OF PREVENTING MY COMMEMORATIVE 100TH FAILURE... I PLUNGED INTO PREPARATIONS FOR THE TRAINING CAMP AUDITION.
MY GOODNESS! IT'S BEAUTIFUL!
It's perfect for me!
Oooh!
......
Carrying the luggage.
MONK-SAN'S AUDITIONS HAD A REPUTATION FOR BEING HARSH, BUT THIS LOOKS LIKE FUN! ♡
ガーッ
UM, AREN'T THERE KIND OF...
...FEWER PARTICIPANTS THAN YOU EXPECTED?
閑散
I WONDER IF THEY WERE ALL SCARED OFF BY MY INVINCIBILITY. ♡
えへへ
OF COURSE NOT.
......

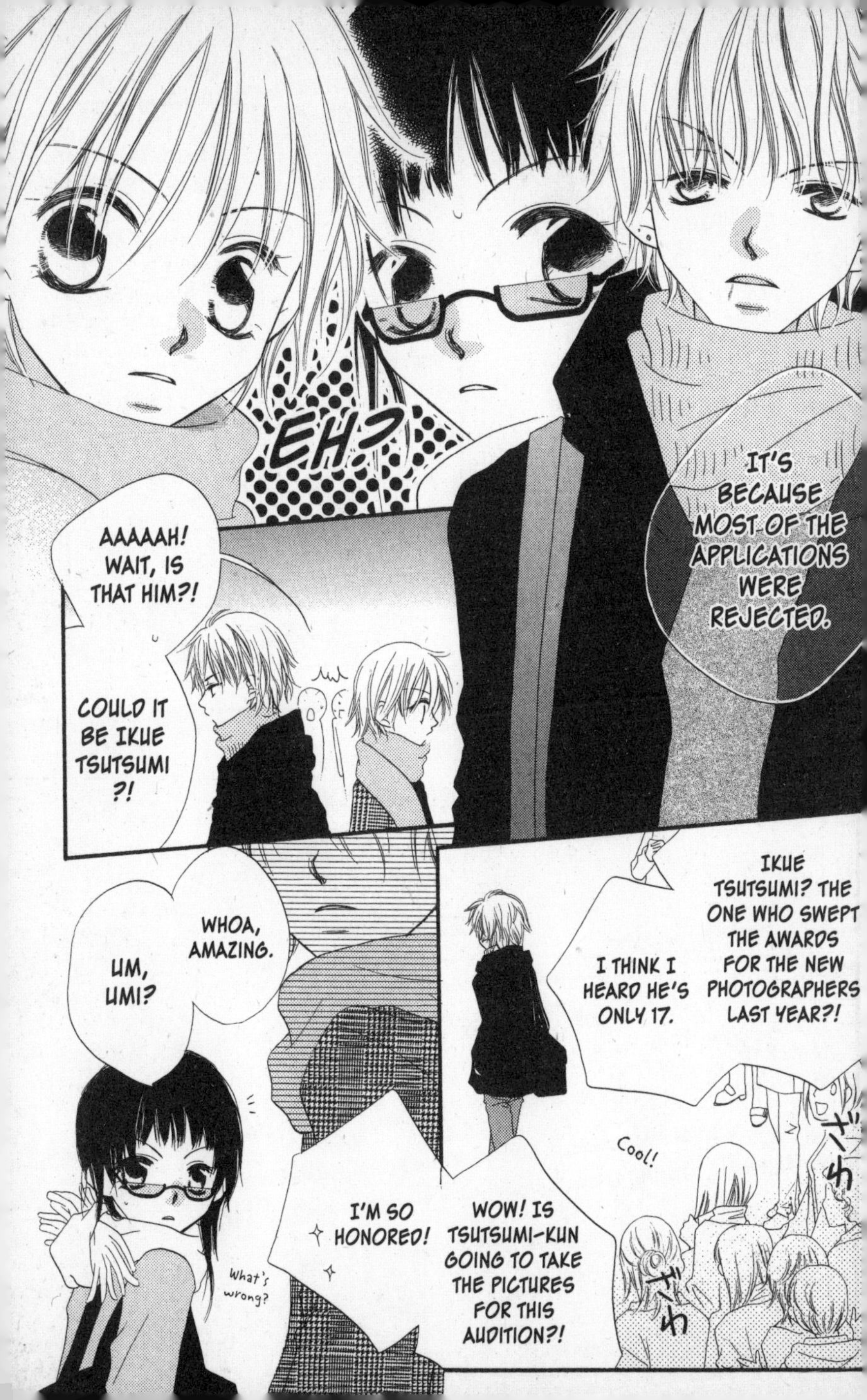
EH?
IT'S BECAUSE MOST OF THE APPLICATIONS WERE REJECTED.
AAAAAH! WAIT, IS THAT HIM?!
COULD IT BE IKUE TSUTSUMI ?!
IKUE TSUTSUMI? THE ONE WHO SWEPT THE AWARDS FOR THE NEW PHOTOGRAPHERS LAST YEAR?!
I THINK I HEARD HE'S ONLY 17.
Cool!
WOW! IS TSUTSUMI-KUN GOING TO TAKE THE PICTURES FOR THIS AUDITION?!
I'M SO HONORED!
WHOA, AMAZING.
UM, UMI?
What's wrong?

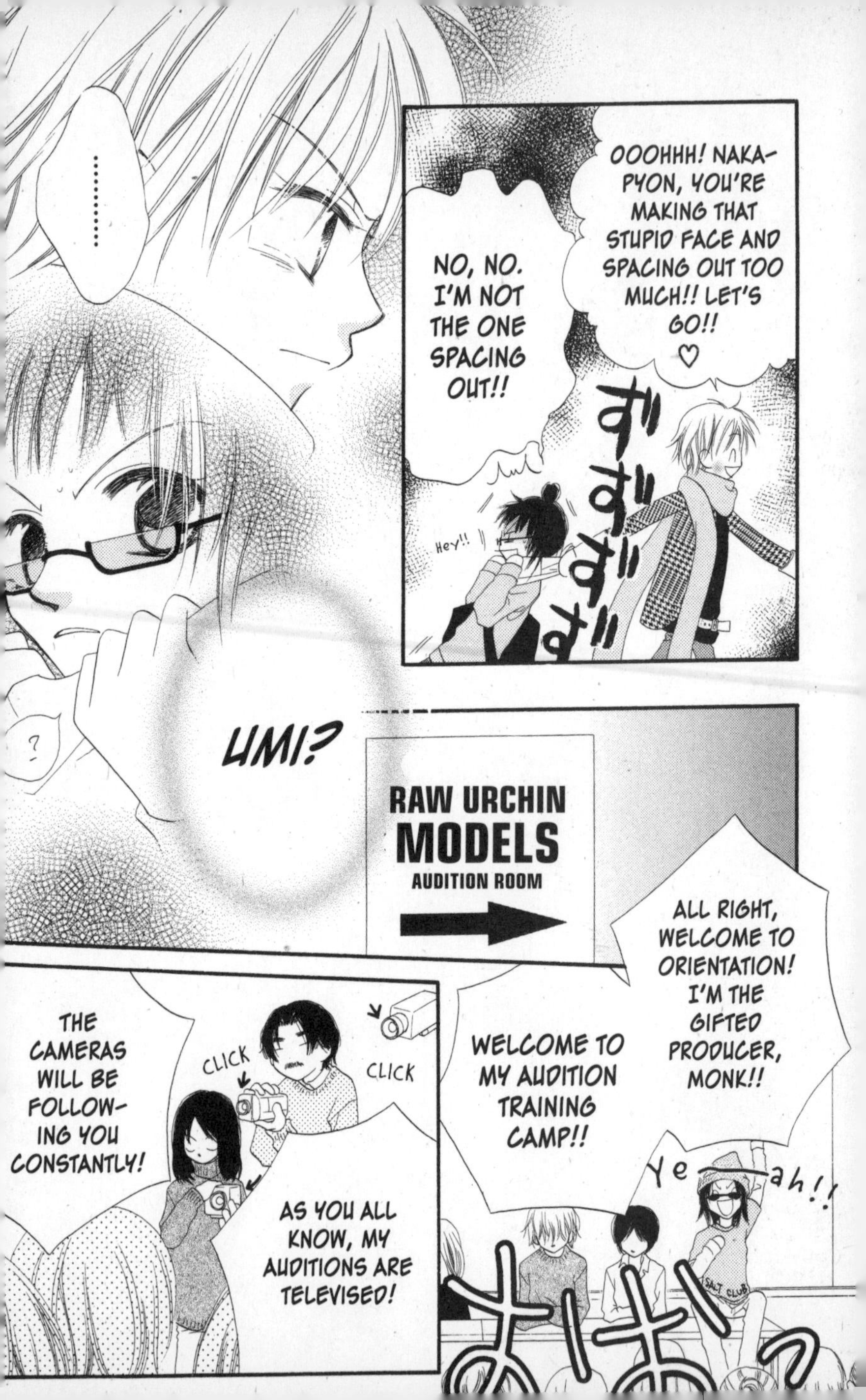
OOOHHH! NAKA-PYON, YOU'RE MAKING THAT STUPID FACE AND SPACING OUT TOO MUCH!! LET'S GO!! ♡
NO, NO. I'M NOT THE ONE SPACING OUT!!
ずずずず
Hey!!
RAW URCHIN
MODELS
AUDITION ROOM
......
UMI?
?
ALL RIGHT, WELCOME TO ORIENTATION! I'M THE GIFTED PRODUCER, MONK!!
WELCOME TO MY AUDITION TRAINING CAMP!!
Ye—ah!!
SALT CLUB
おおっ
CLICK
CLICK
AS YOU ALL KNOW, MY AUDITIONS ARE TELEVISED!
THE CAMERAS WILL BE FOLLOW-ING YOU CONSTANTLY!

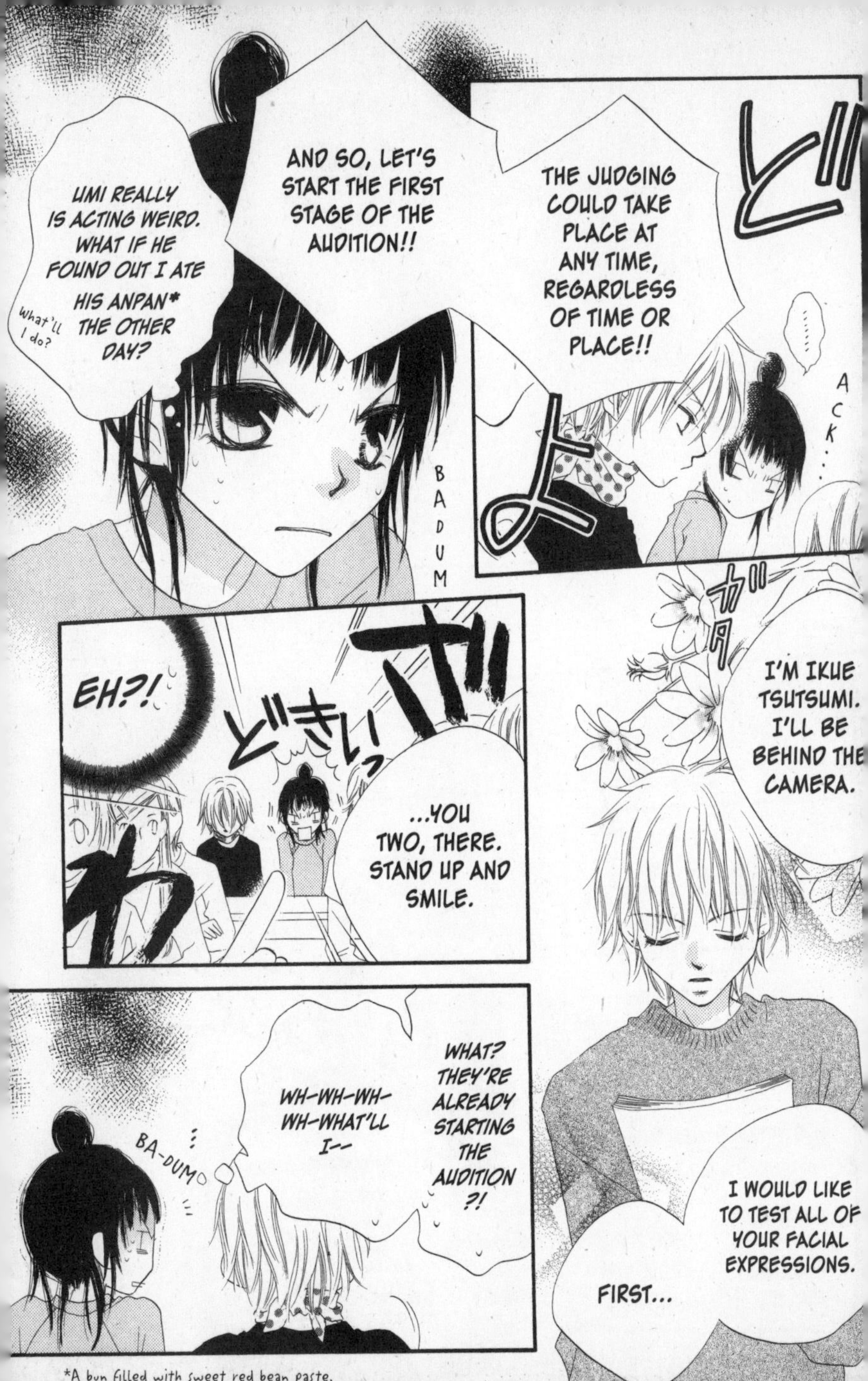
AND SO, LET'S START THE FIRST STAGE OF THE AUDITION!!
THE JUDGING COULD TAKE PLACE AT ANY TIME, REGARDLESS OF TIME OR PLACE!!
......
ACK...
UMI REALLY IS ACTING WEIRD. WHAT IF HE FOUND OUT I ATE HIS ANPAN* THE OTHER DAY?
What'll I do?
BADUM
I'M IKUE TSUTSUMI. I'LL BE BEHIND THE CAMERA.
I WOULD LIKE TO TEST ALL OF YOUR FACIAL EXPRESSIONS.
FIRST...
...YOU TWO, THERE. STAND UP AND SMILE.
EH?!
WHAT? THEY'RE ALREADY STARTING THE AUDITION ?!
WH-WH-WH-WH-WHAT'LL I--
BA-DUM

*A bun filled with sweet red bean paste.

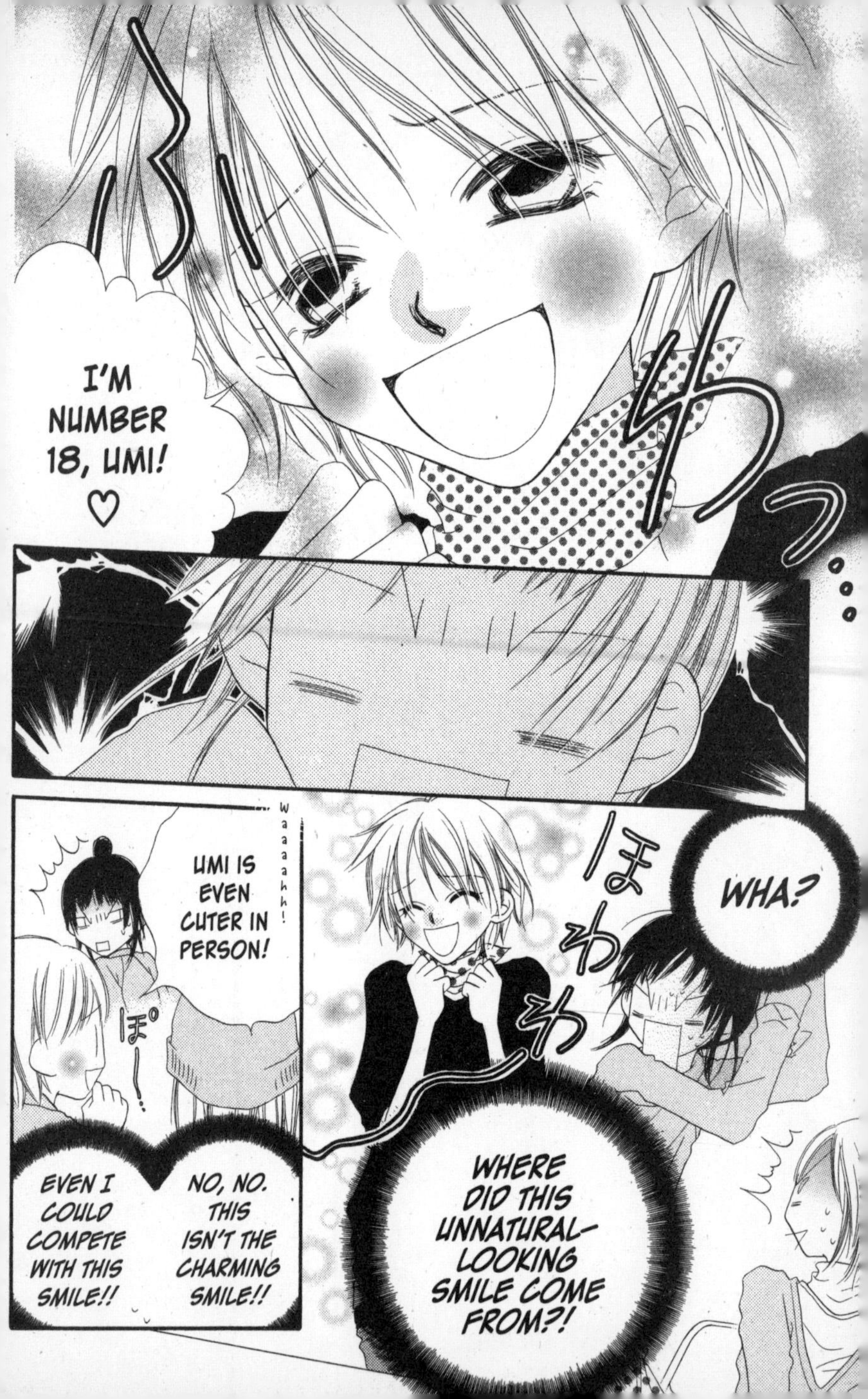
I'M NUMBER 18, UMI! ♡
WHA?
Waaaaahh!
UMI IS EVEN CUTER IN PERSON!
WHERE DID THIS UNNATURAL-LOOKING SMILE COME FROM?!
NO, NO. THIS ISN'T THE CHARMING SMILE!!
EVEN I COULD COMPETE WITH THIS SMILE!!

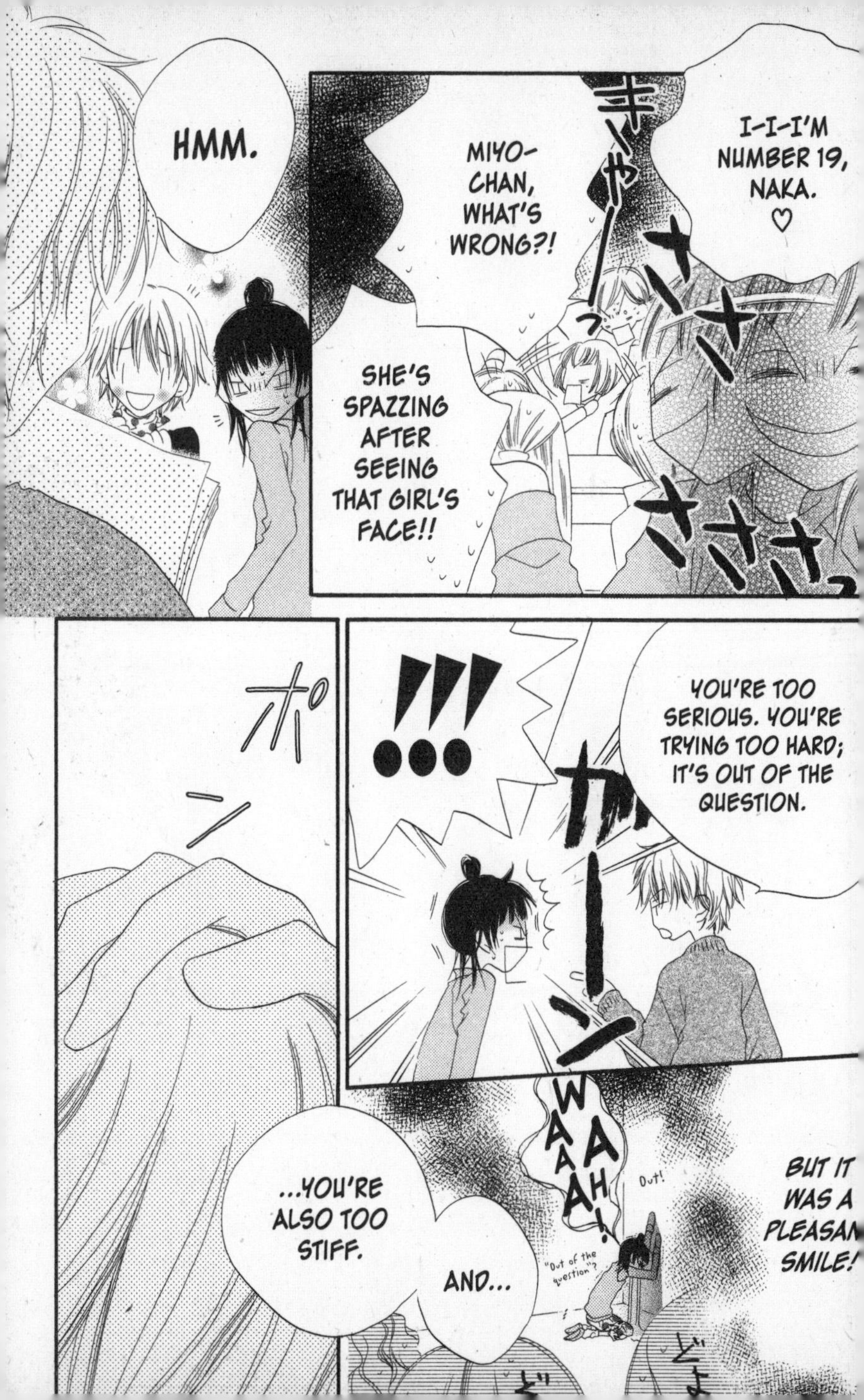
I-I-I'M NUMBER 19, NAKA. ♡
MIYO-CHAN, WHAT'S WRONG?!
SHE'S SPAZZING AFTER SEEING THAT GIRL'S FACE!!
HMM.
!!!...
YOU'RE TOO SERIOUS. YOU'RE TRYING TOO HARD; IT'S OUT OF THE QUESTION.
BUT IT WAS A PLEASAN SMILE!
WAAAAH!
Out!
"Out of the question"?
...YOU'RE ALSO TOO STIFF.
AND...

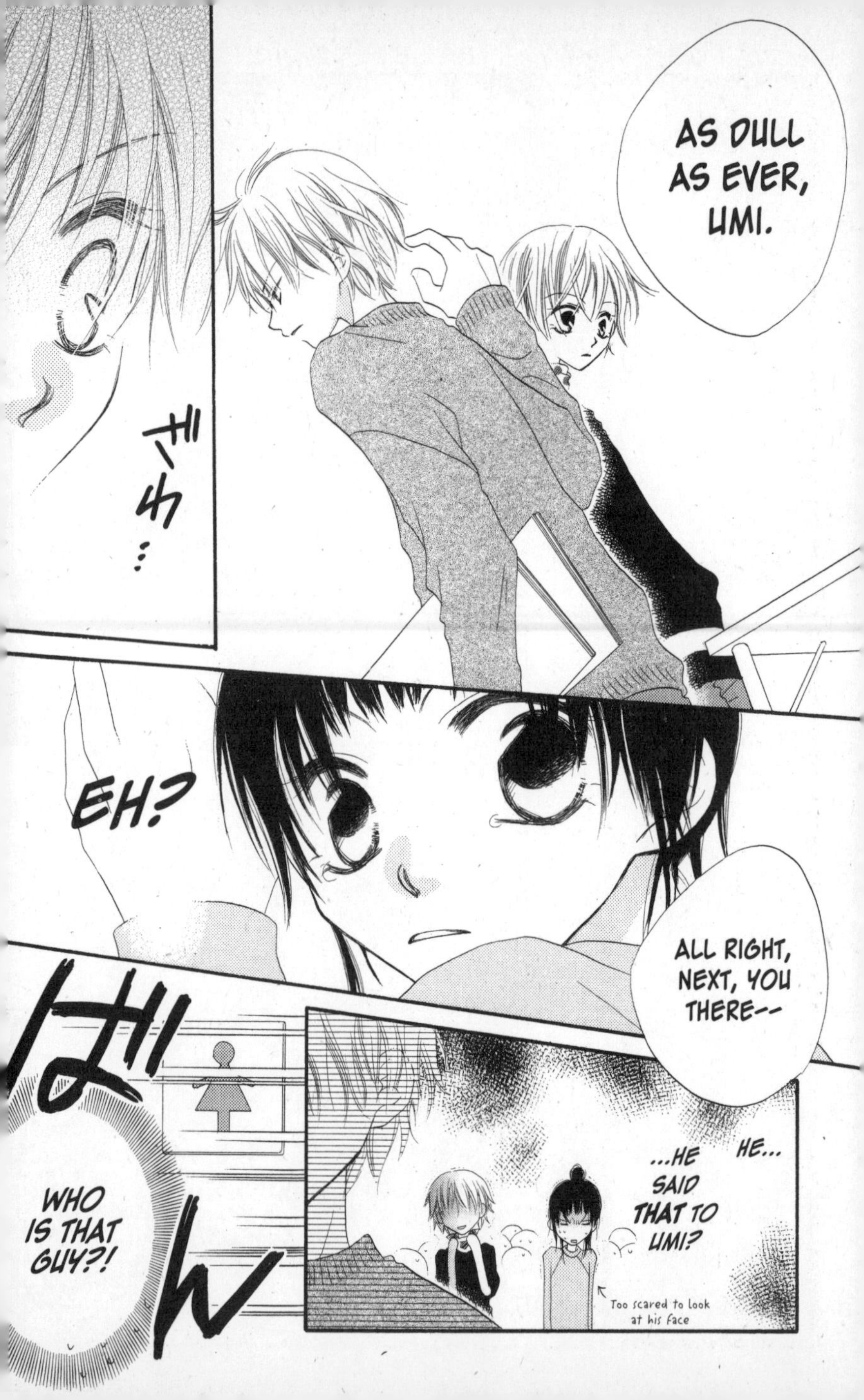
AS DULL AS EVER, UMI.
EH?
ALL RIGHT, NEXT, YOU THERE--
HE...
...HE SAID THAT TO UMI?
Too scared to look at his face
WHO IS THAT GUY?!

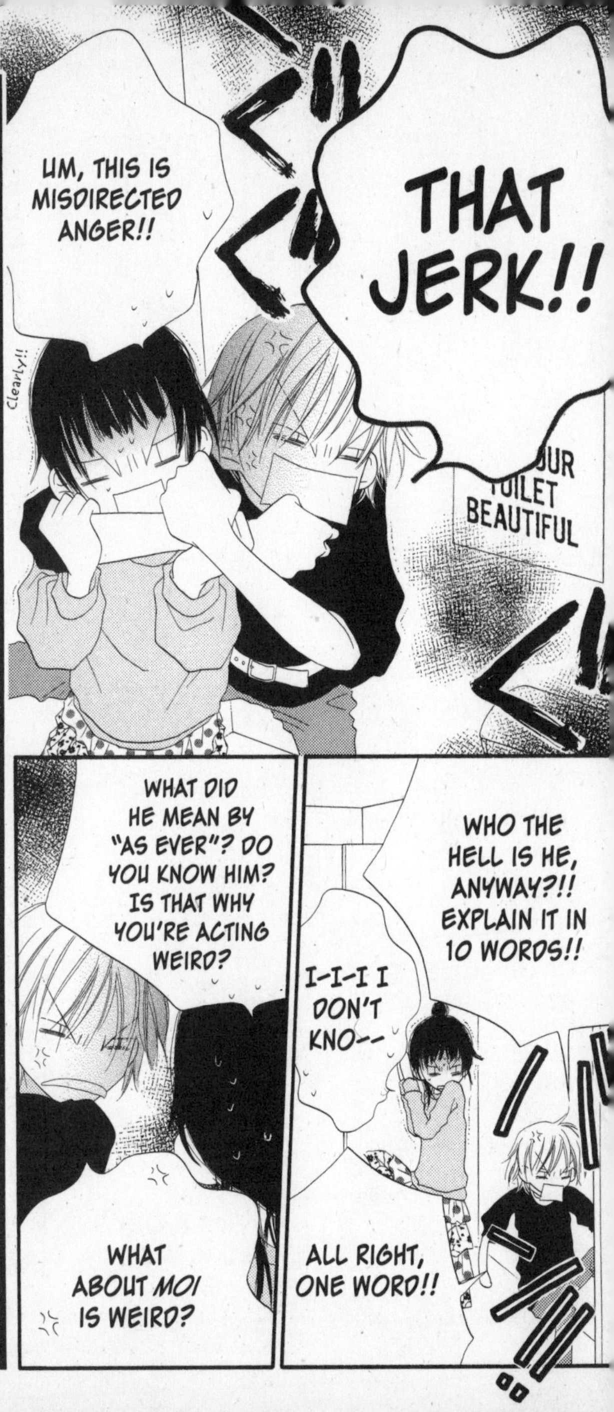
THAT JERK!!
UM, THIS IS MISDIRECTED ANGER!!
Clearly!!
OUR TOILET BEAUTIFUL
WHO THE HELL IS HE, ANYWAY?!! EXPLAIN IT IN 10 WORDS!!
I-I-I I DON'T KNO--
ALL RIGHT, ONE WORD!!
WHAT DID HE MEAN BY "AS EVER"? DO YOU KNOW HIM? IS THAT WHY YOU'RE ACTING WEIRD?
WHAT ABOUT *MOI* IS WEIRD?

3

Fukuyama

It's fun to draw clothes. Because I love to buy mugger-zines... I mean magazines. I get a lot of ideas while flipping through them. But since what I tend to like is set, I get the feeling that the clothes I draw all look pretty similar. It's hard because when I see a cute outfit in the store, then I draw a picture and it's not as cute. I have to concentrate.

Naka has that face, so I put her in a skirt as much as possible, and I put Umi in pants so that when he goes into guy-mode he doesn't look too much like a transvestite. The hard one is a certain photographer. No matter what I put him in, he looks like a gigolo. I wonder what's with him. Please send me ideas for clothes that look good on a guy with wavy hair. (Seriously!)

As characters, all three of them are extremely simple to move, so it's very easy. I wonder if it's a good balance, with sadism and masochism jumbled together. In a way, this is an S&M manga. By the way, is my handwriting too small? I'm sorry it's hard to read. I'll write bigger. Bigger. Oh yeah, recently I got a Sky Perfect channel called M-ON! I'm taping my favorite promos like crazy and am satisfied with my music life. It's cheap at less than a thousand yen a month!! I'm happy. Long live music!

Yay! Yay!

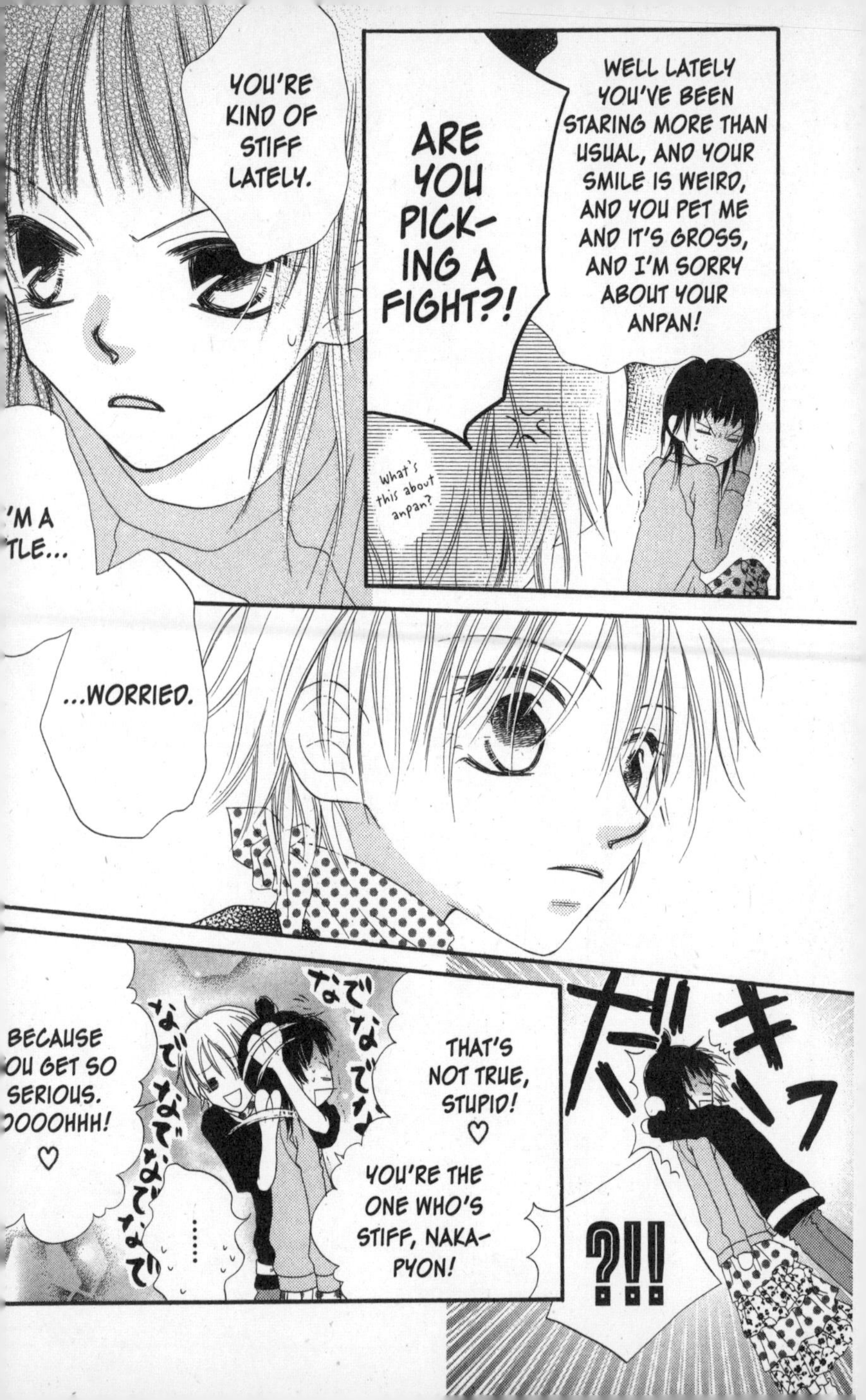
WELL LATELY YOU'VE BEEN STARING MORE THAN USUAL, AND YOUR SMILE IS WEIRD, AND YOU PET ME AND IT'S GROSS, AND I'M SORRY ABOUT YOUR ANPAN!
ARE YOU PICK-ING A FIGHT?!
What's this about anpan?
YOU'RE KIND OF STIFF LATELY.
'M A TLE...
...WORRIED.
ダキッ
?!!
THAT'S NOT TRUE, STUPID! ♡
YOU'RE THE ONE WHO'S STIFF, NAKA-PYON!
なでなでなで
なでなでなでなで
......
BECAUSE OU GET SO SERIOUS. OOOOHHH! ♡

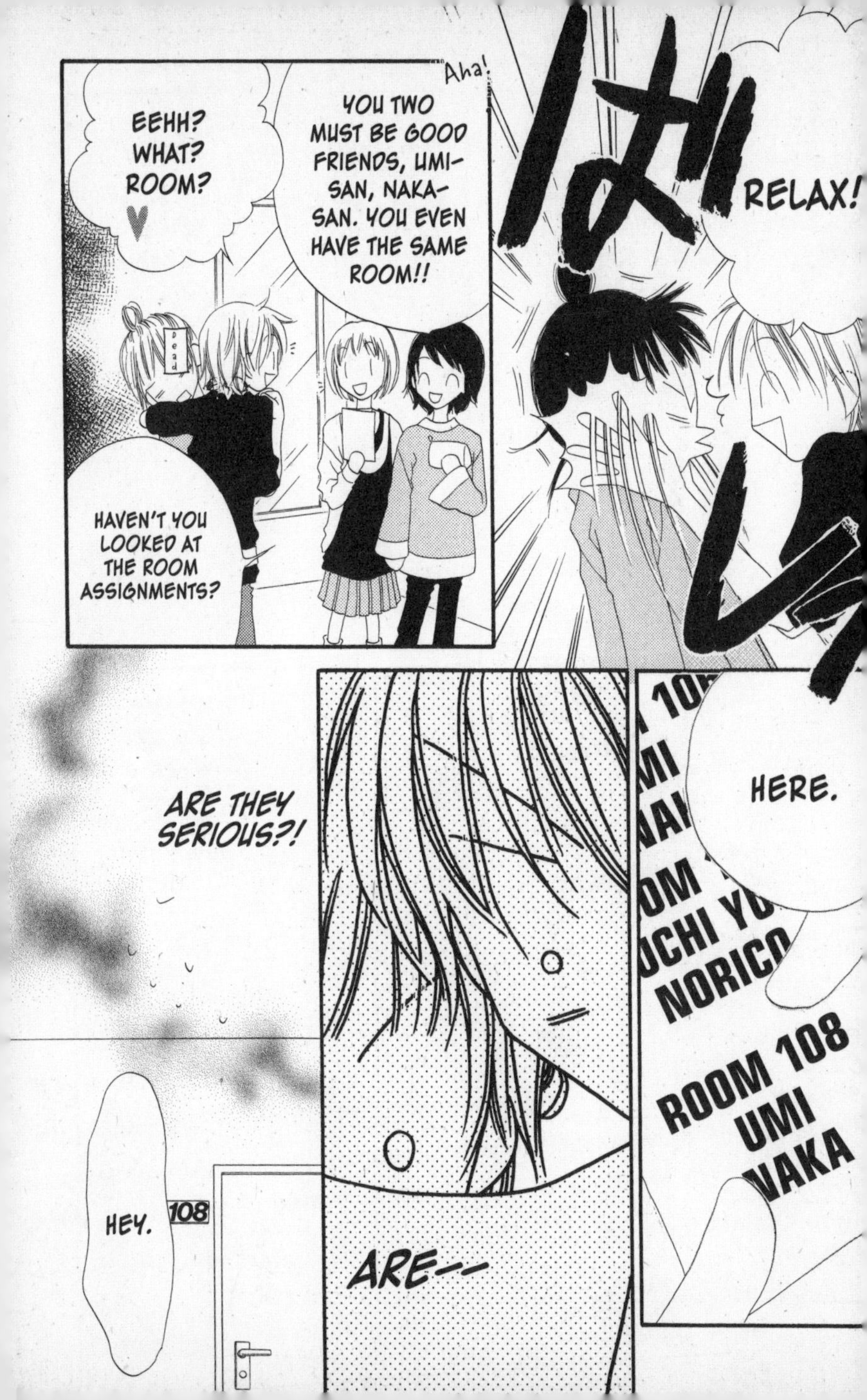
はい
RELAX!
Aha!
YOU TWO MUST BE GOOD FRIENDS, UMI-SAN, NAKA-SAN. YOU EVEN HAVE THE SAME ROOM!!
EEHH? WHAT? ROOM? ♥
Dead
HAVEN'T YOU LOOKED AT THE ROOM ASSIGNMENTS?
HERE.
NORICO
ROOM 108 UMI NAKA
ARE---
ARE THEY SERIOUS?!
HEY.
108

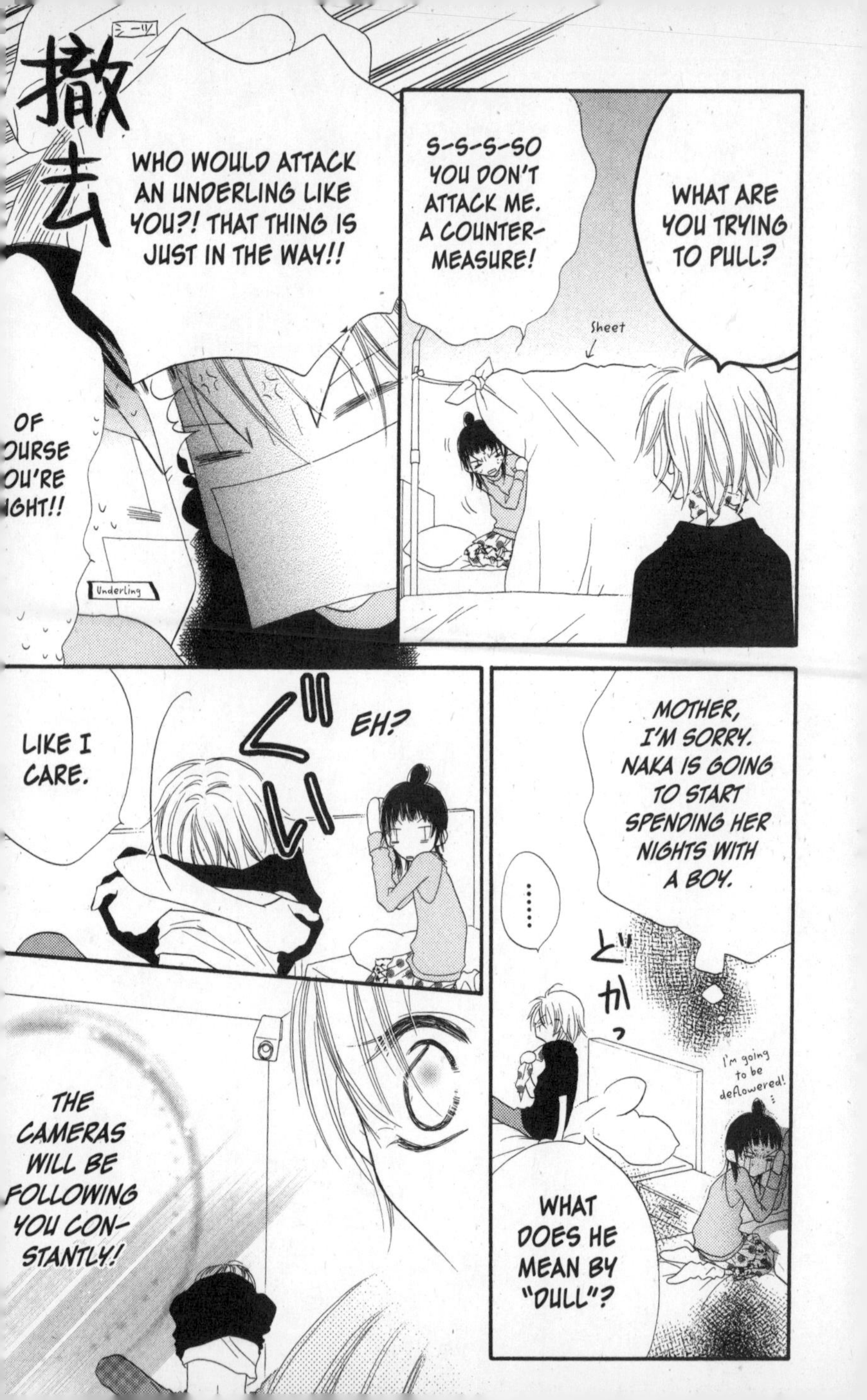
WHAT ARE YOU TRYING TO PULL?
S-S-S-SO YOU DON'T ATTACK ME. A COUNTER-MEASURE!
Sheet
撤去
WHO WOULD ATTACK AN UNDERLING LIKE YOU?! THAT THING IS JUST IN THE WAY!!
OF OURSE OU'RE IGHT!!
Underling
MOTHER, I'M SORRY. NAKA IS GOING TO START SPENDING HER NIGHTS WITH A BOY.
......
どかっ
I'm going to be deflowered!
WHAT DOES HE MEAN BY "DULL"?
LIKE I CARE.
ぐい
EH?
THE CAMERAS WILL BE FOLLOWING YOU CON-STANTLY!

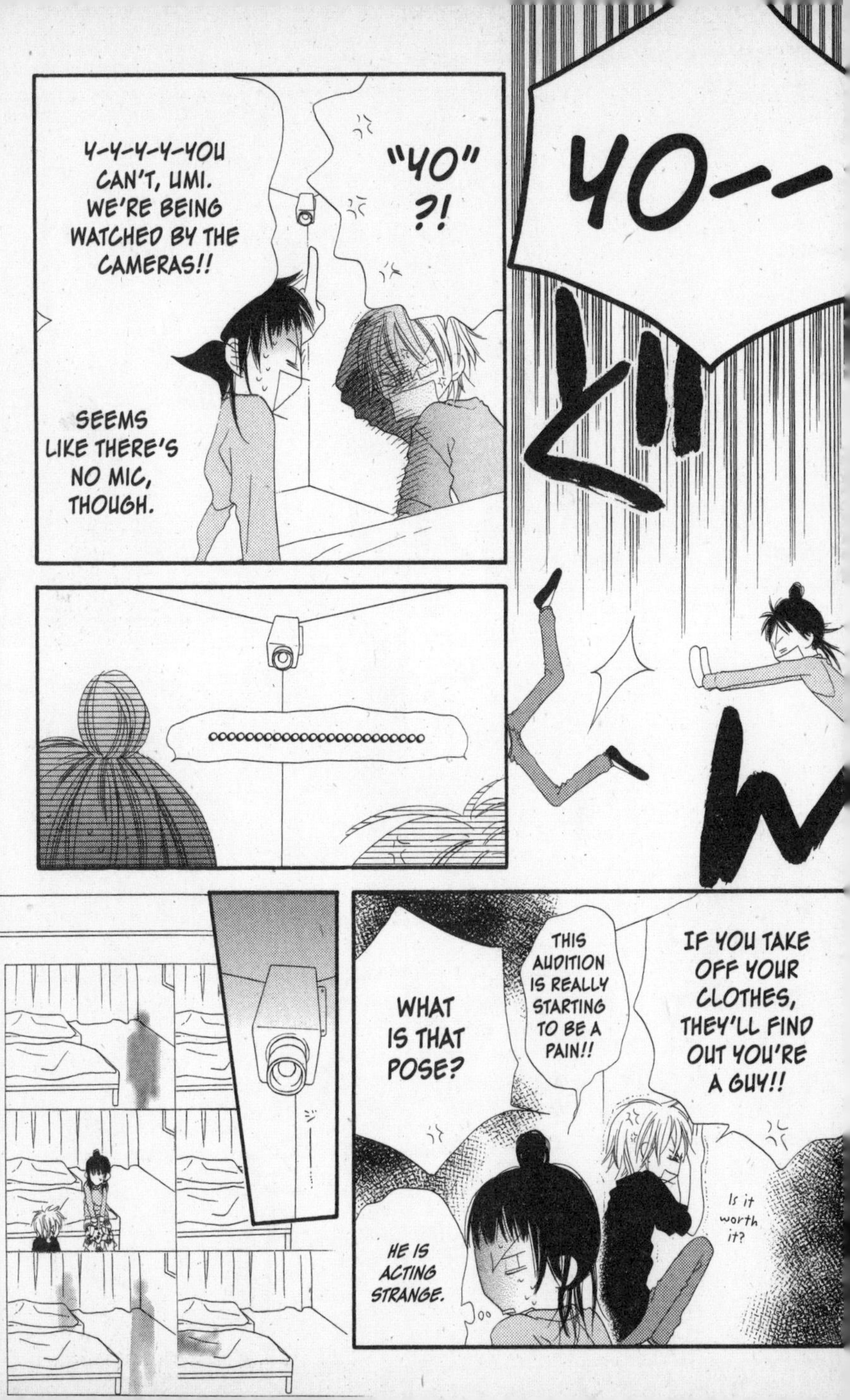
YO--
どん
"YO" ?!
Y-Y-Y-Y-YOU CAN'T, UMI. WE'RE BEING WATCHED BY THE CAMERAS!!
SEEMS LIKE THERE'S NO MIC, THOUGH.
oooooooooooooooooooooo
IF YOU TAKE OFF YOUR CLOTHES, THEY'LL FIND OUT YOU'RE A GUY!!
THIS AUDITION IS REALLY STARTING TO BE A PAIN!!
WHAT IS THAT POSE?
Is it worth it?
HE IS ACTING STRANGE.
ジー

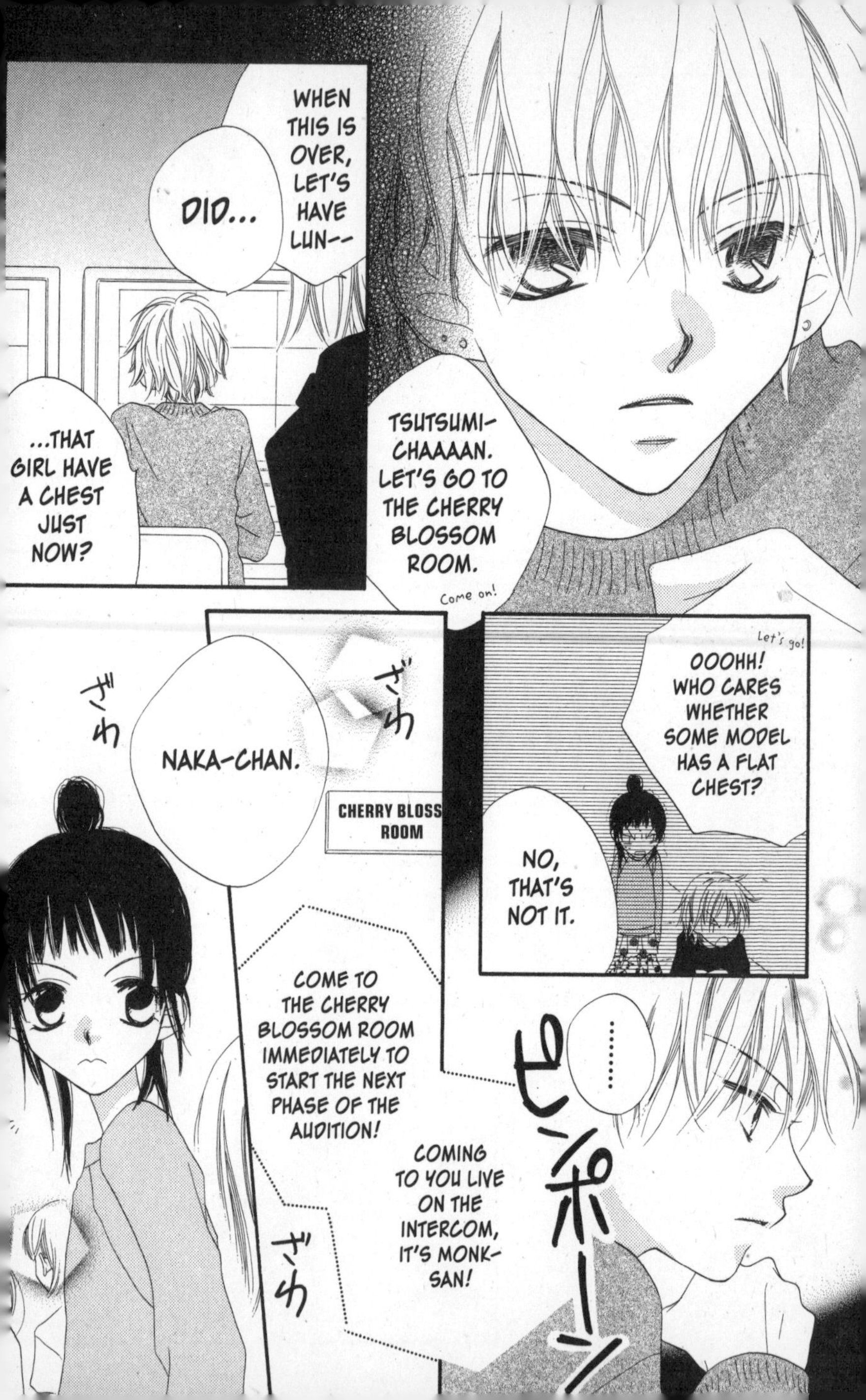
TSUTSUMI-CHAAAAN. LET'S GO TO THE CHERRY BLOSSOM ROOM.
Come on!
WHEN THIS IS OVER, LET'S HAVE LUN--
DID...
...THAT GIRL HAVE A CHEST JUST NOW?
Let's go!
OOOHH! WHO CARES WHETHER SOME MODEL HAS A FLAT CHEST?
NO, THAT'S NOT IT.
......
ピンポーン
COMING TO YOU LIVE ON THE INTERCOM, IT'S MONK-SAN!
COME TO THE CHERRY BLOSSOM ROOM IMMEDIATELY TO START THE NEXT PHASE OF THE AUDITION!
ざわ
ざわ
CHERRY BLOSS ROOM
NAKA-CHAN.
ざわ

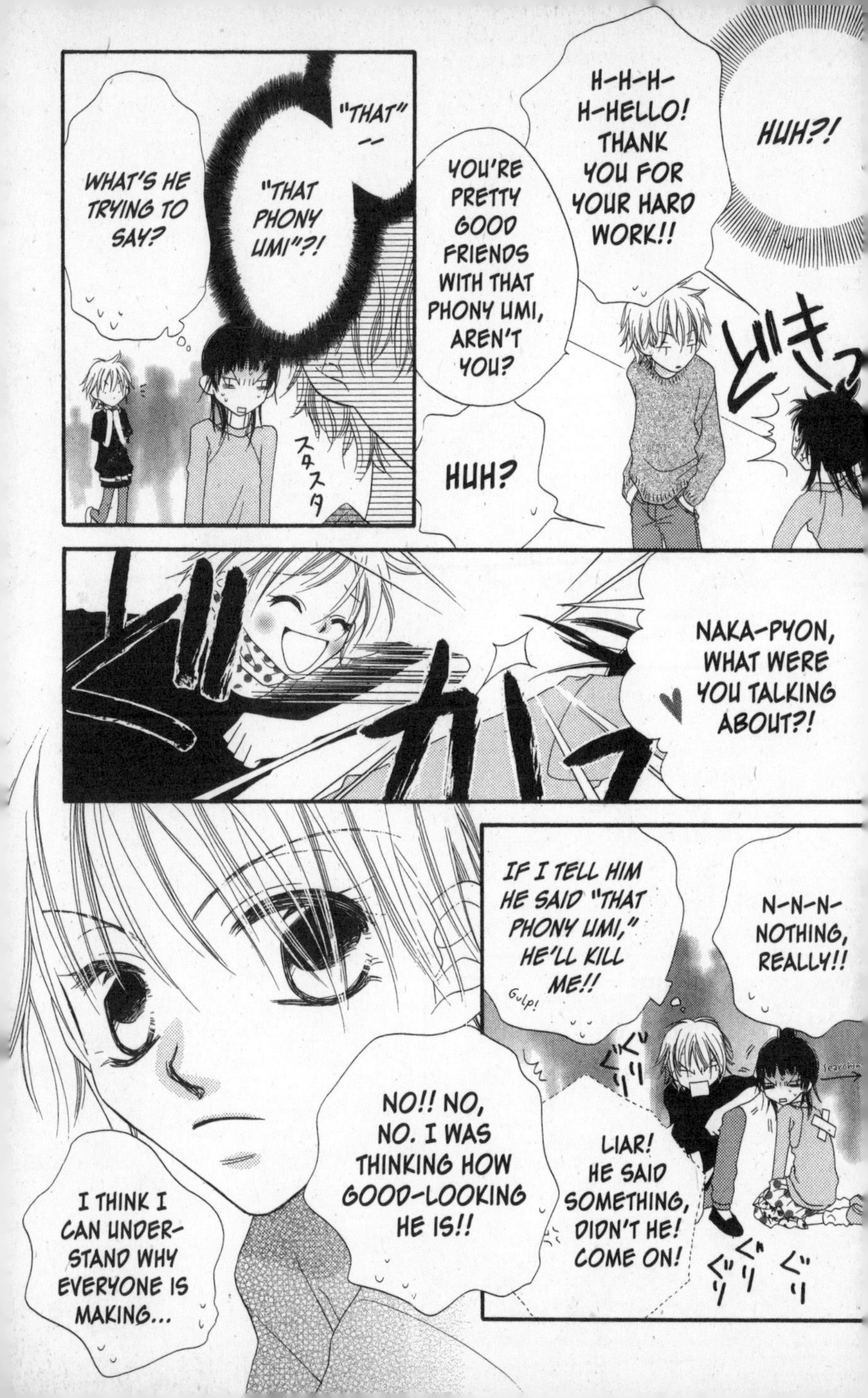
HUH?!
H-H-H-H-HELLO! THANK YOU FOR YOUR HARD WORK!!
どきっ
YOU'RE PRETTY GOOD FRIENDS WITH THAT PHONY UMI, AREN'T YOU?
HUH?
"THAT" --
"THAT PHONY UMI"?!
スタスタ
WHAT'S HE TRYING TO SAY?
NAKA-PYON, WHAT WERE YOU TALKING ABOUT?!
N-N-N-NOTHING, REALLY!!
IF I TELL HIM HE SAID "THAT PHONY UMI," HE'LL KILL ME!!
Gulp!
LIAR! HE SAID SOMETHING, DIDN'T HE! COME ON!
ぐりぐり
NO!! NO, NO. I WAS THINKING HOW GOOD-LOOKING HE IS!!
I THINK I CAN UNDERSTAND WHY EVERYONE IS MAKING...

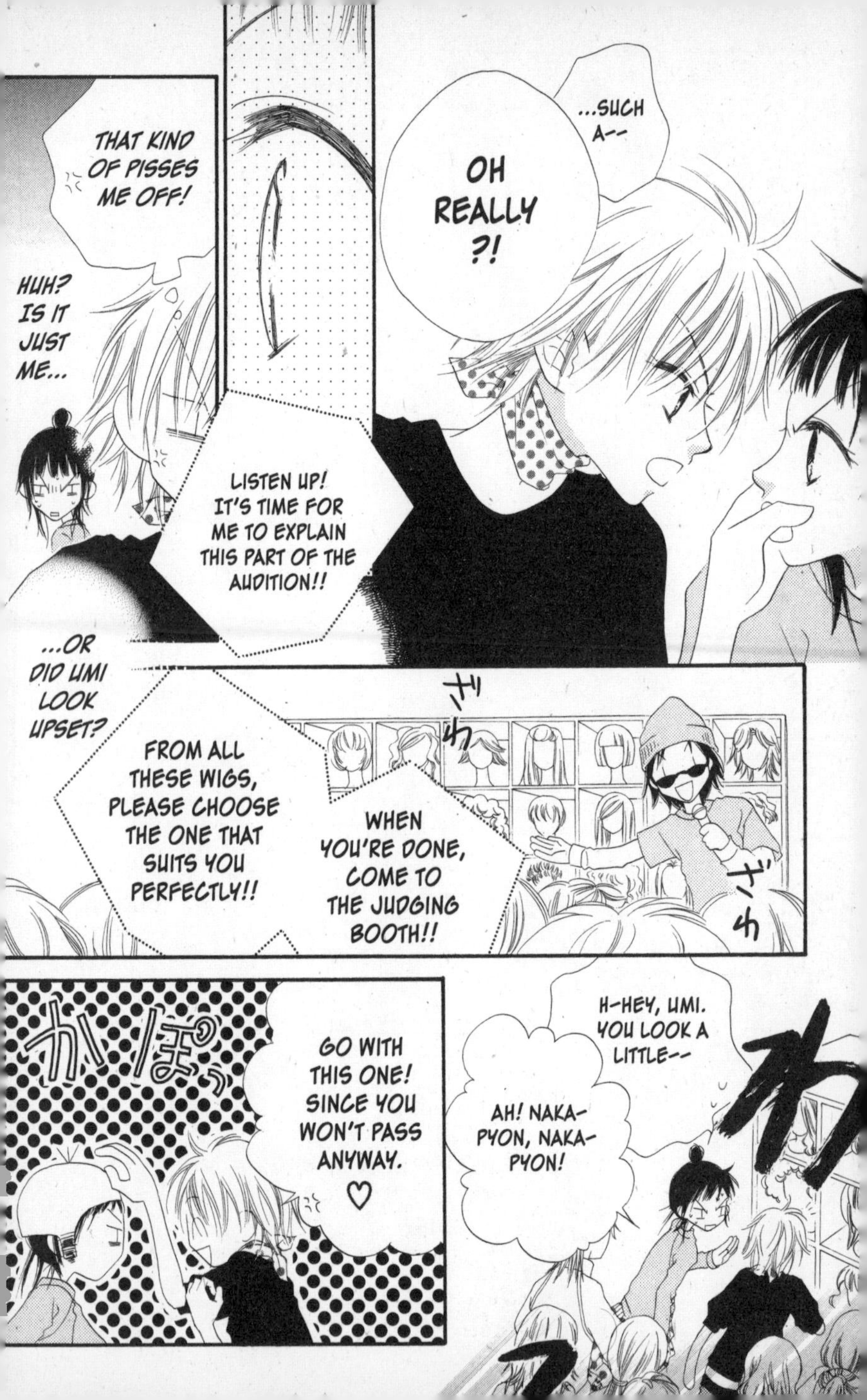
...SUCH A--
OH REALLY ?!
LISTEN UP! IT'S TIME FOR ME TO EXPLAIN THIS PART OF THE AUDITION!!
THAT KIND OF PISSES ME OFF!
HUH? IS IT JUST ME...
...OR DID UMI LOOK UPSET?
FROM ALL THESE WIGS, PLEASE CHOOSE THE ONE THAT SUITS YOU PERFECTLY!!
WHEN YOU'RE DONE, COME TO THE JUDGING BOOTH!!
H-HEY, UMI. YOU LOOK A LITTLE--
AH! NAKA-PYON, NAKA-PYON!
GO WITH THIS ONE! SINCE YOU WON'T PASS ANYWAY. ♡

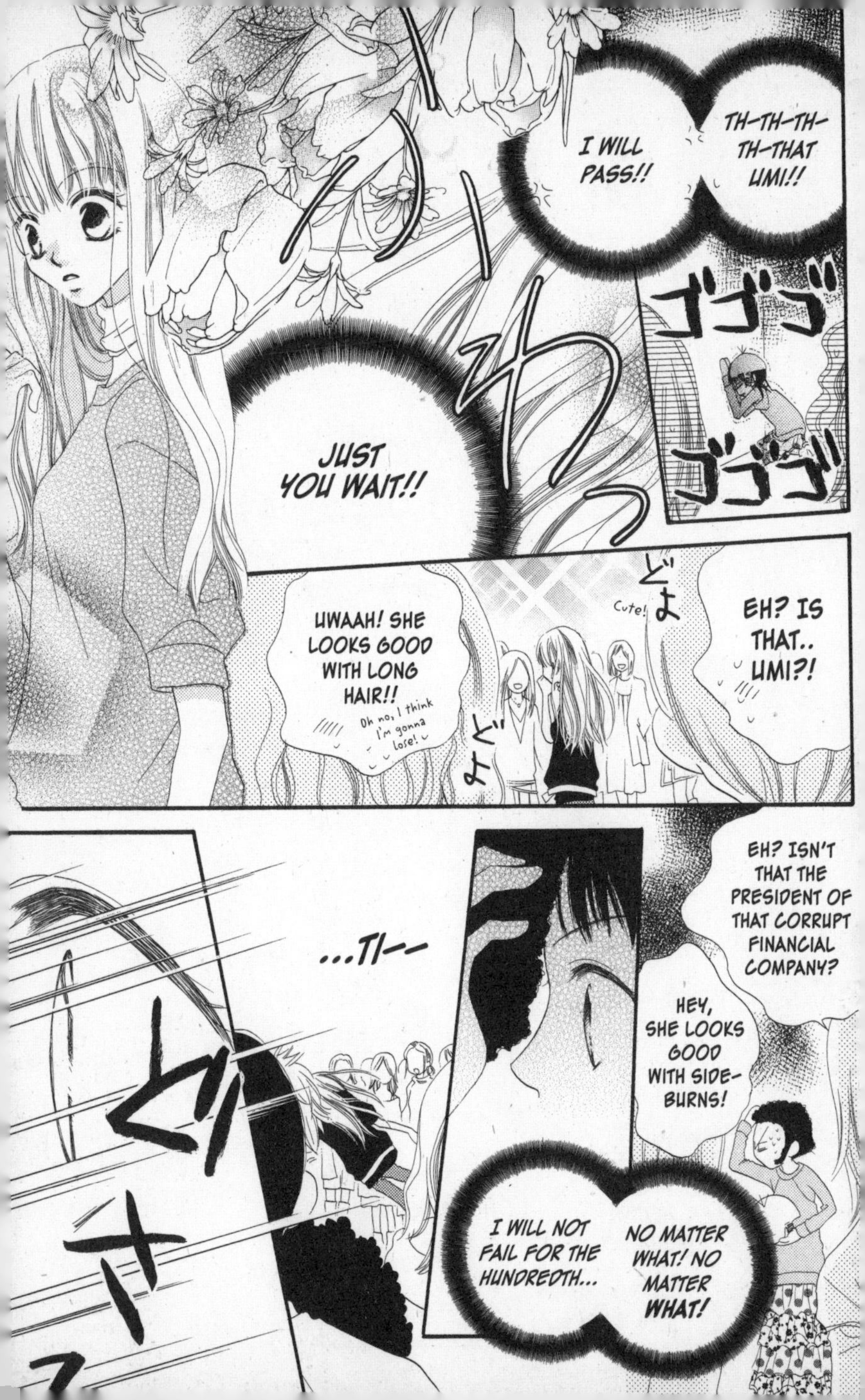
TH-TH-TH-
TH-THAT
UMI!!
I WILL
PASS!!
ゴゴゴ
ゴゴゴ
JUST
YOU WAIT!!
EH? IS
THAT..
UMI?!
どよ
Cute!
UWAAH! SHE
LOOKS GOOD
WITH LONG
HAIR!!
Oh no, I think
I'm gonna
lose!
どよ
EH? ISN'T
THAT THE
PRESIDENT OF
THAT CORRUPT
FINANCIAL
COMPANY?
HEY,
SHE LOOKS
GOOD
WITH SIDE-
BURNS!
...TI--
NO MATTER
WHAT! NO
MATTER
WHAT!
I WILL NOT
FAIL FOR THE
HUNDREDTH...

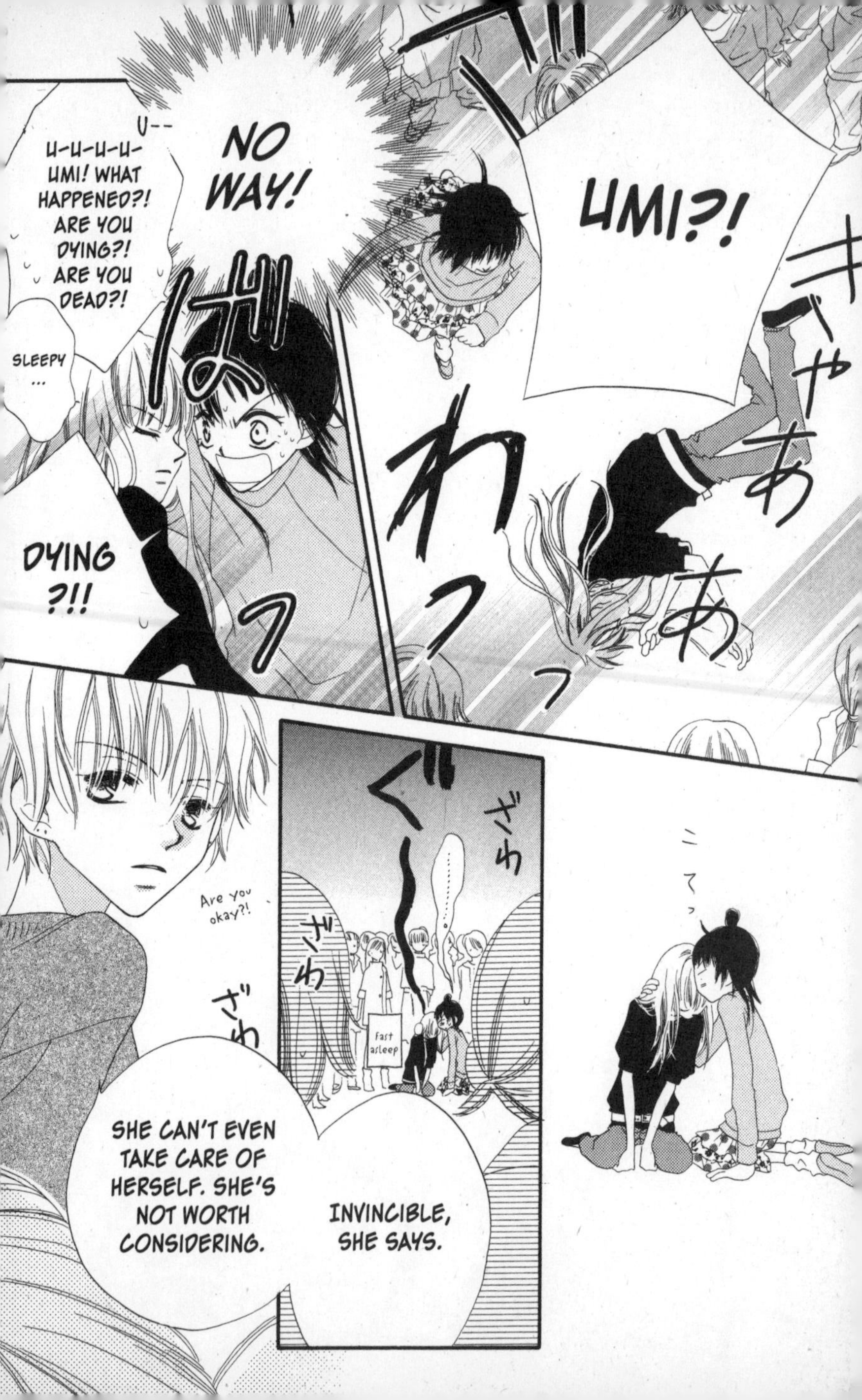
UMI?!
きゃあぁっ
わっ
NO WAY!
ばっ
U-- U-U-U-U-UMI! WHAT HAPPENED?! ARE YOU DYING?! ARE YOU DEAD?!
SLEEPY ...
DYING ?!!
こてっ
ざわ
ざわ
ぐ~~
......
Fast asleep
INVINCIBLE, SHE SAYS.
Are you okay?!
ざわ
SHE CAN'T EVEN TAKE CARE OF HERSELF. SHE'S NOT WORTH CONSIDERING.

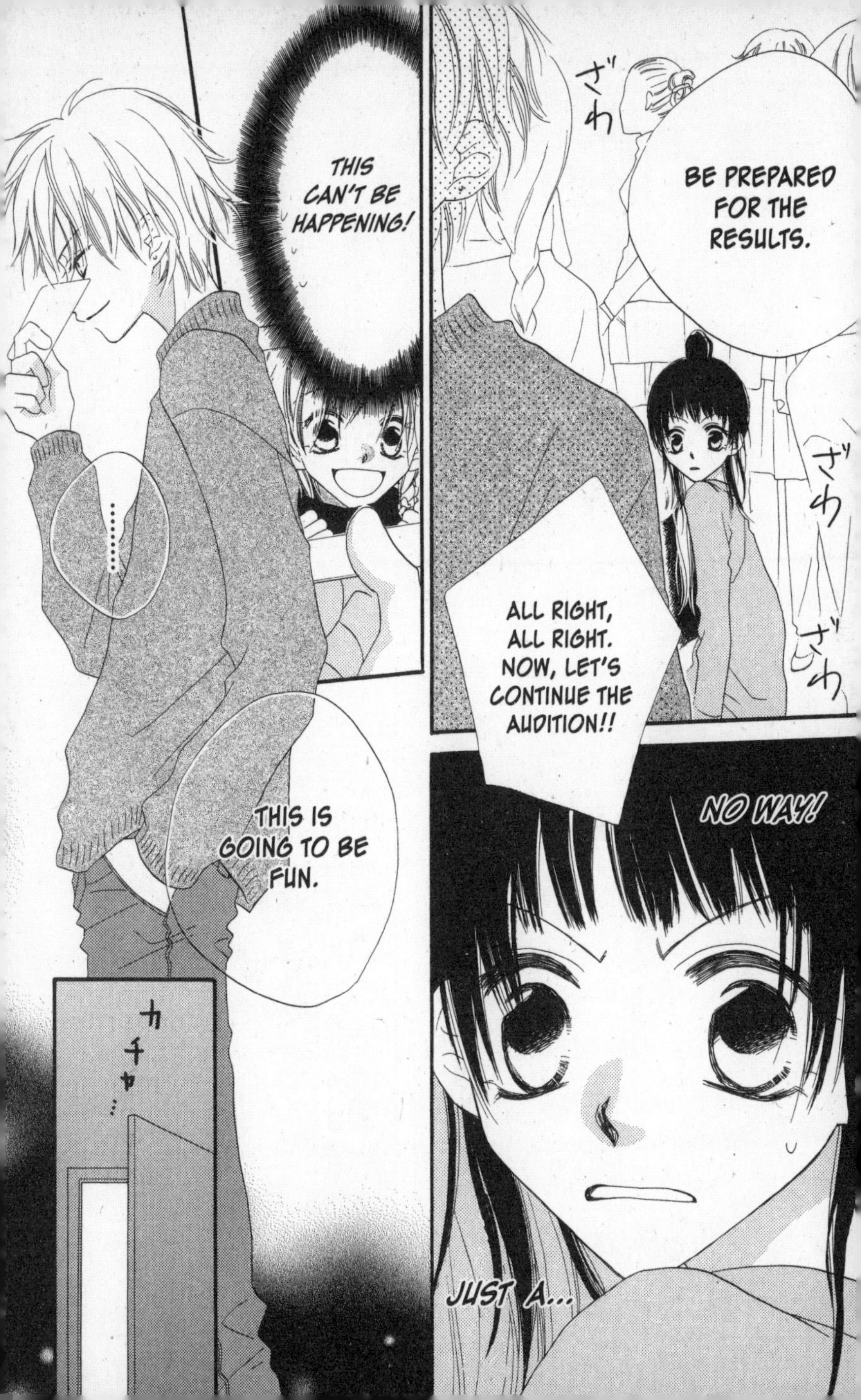
ざわ
BE PREPARED FOR THE RESULTS.
ざわ
ざわ
ALL RIGHT, ALL RIGHT. NOW, LET'S CONTINUE THE AUDITION!!
NO WAY!
JUST A...
THIS CAN'T BE HAPPENING!
THIS IS GOING TO BE FUN.
カチャ…

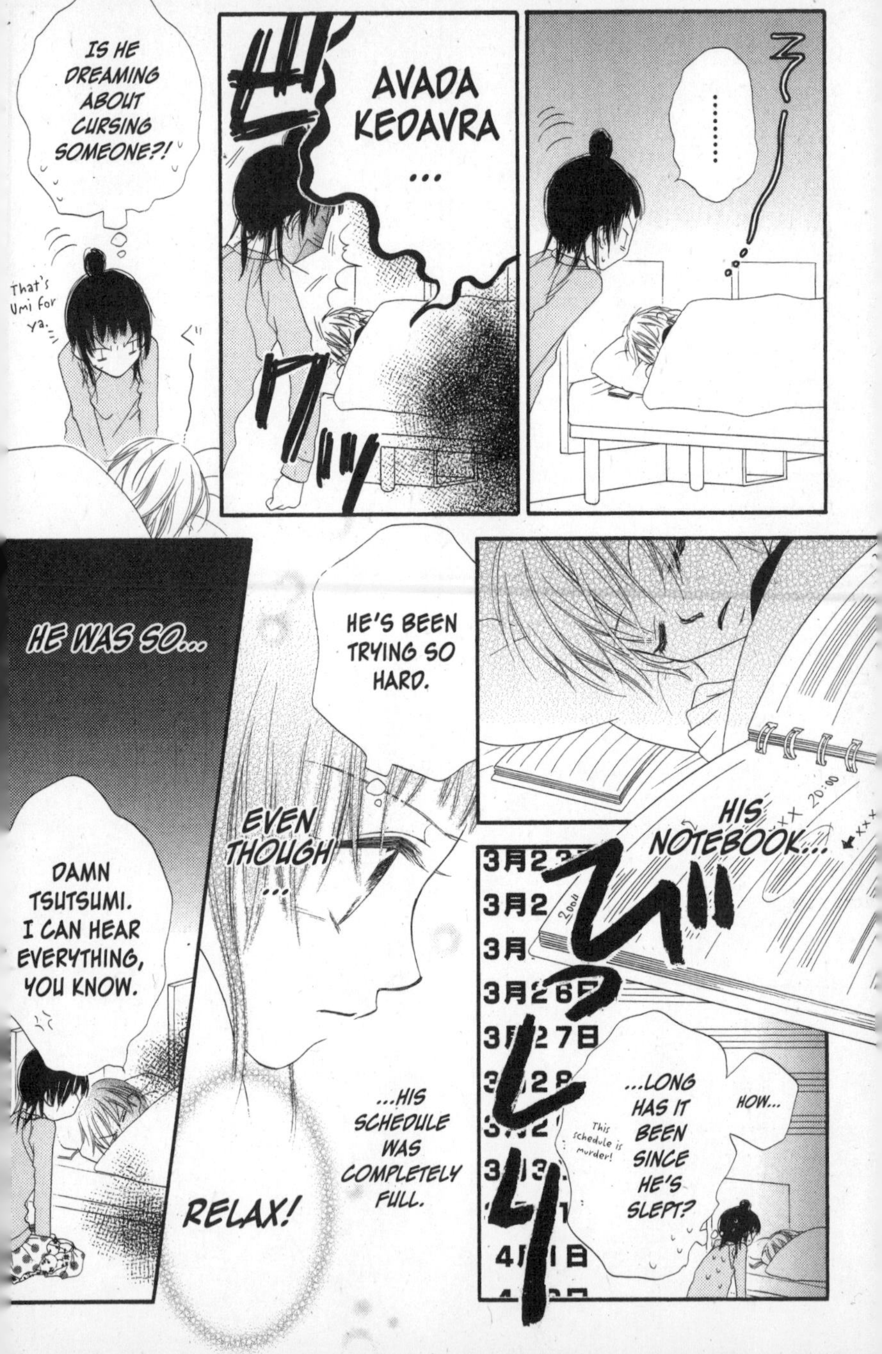
......
AVADA KEDAVRA ...
IS HE DREAMING ABOUT CURSING SOMEONE?!
That's Umi for ya.
HIS NOTEBOOK...
20:00
3月26日
3月27日
4月1日
HOW...
...LONG HAS IT BEEN SINCE HE'S SLEPT?
This schedule is murder!
HE'S BEEN TRYING SO HARD.
EVEN THOUGH...
...HIS SCHEDULE WAS COMPLETELY FULL.
RELAX!
HE WAS SO...
DAMN TSUTSUMI. I CAN HEAR EVERYTHING, YOU KNOW.

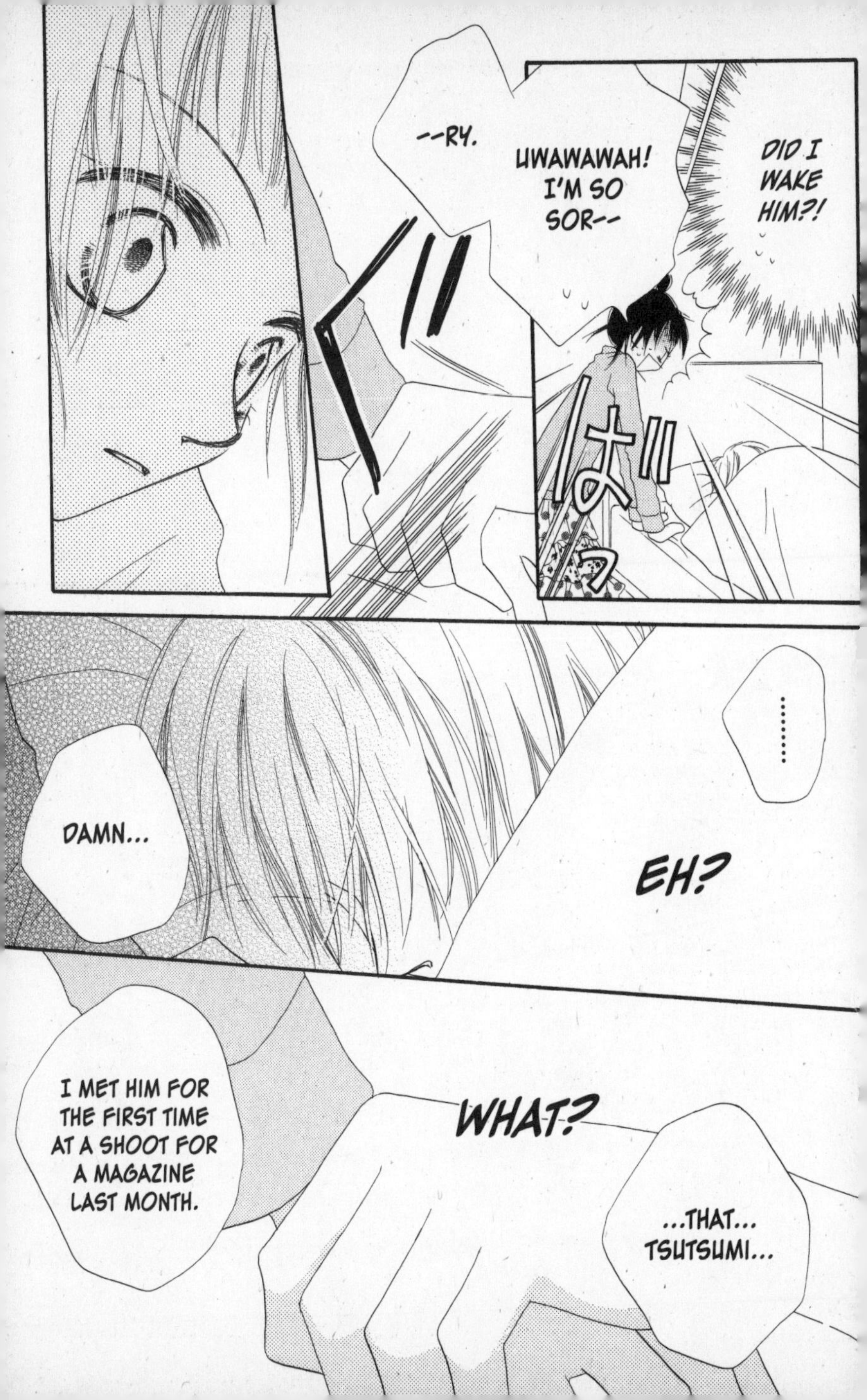
DID I WAKE HIM?!
UWAWAWAH! I'M SO SOR--
はっ
--RY.
......
EH?
DAMN...
...THAT... TSUTSUMI...
WHAT?
I MET HIM FOR THE FIRST TIME AT A SHOOT FOR A MAGAZINE LAST MONTH.

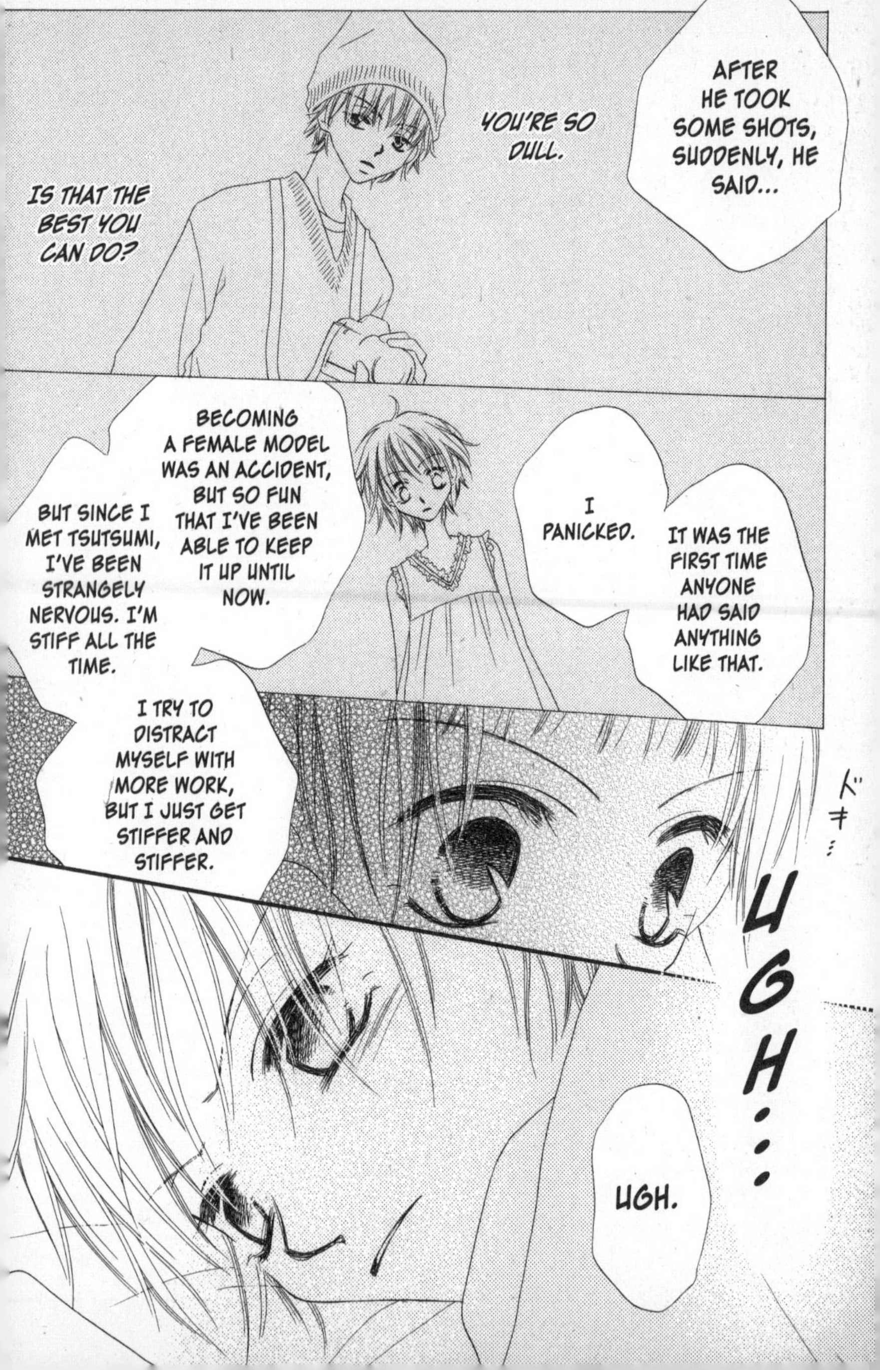
AFTER HE TOOK SOME SHOTS, SUDDENLY, HE SAID...
YOU'RE SO DULL.
IS THAT THE BEST YOU CAN DO?
IT WAS THE FIRST TIME ANYONE HAD SAID ANYTHING LIKE THAT.
I PANICKED.
BECOMING A FEMALE MODEL WAS AN ACCIDENT, BUT SO FUN THAT I'VE BEEN ABLE TO KEEP IT UP UNTIL NOW.
BUT SINCE I MET TSUTSUMI, I'VE BEEN STRANGELY NERVOUS. I'M STIFF ALL THE TIME.
I TRY TO DISTRACT MYSELF WITH MORE WORK, BUT I JUST GET STIFFER AND STIFFER.
ドキ…
UGH...
UGH.

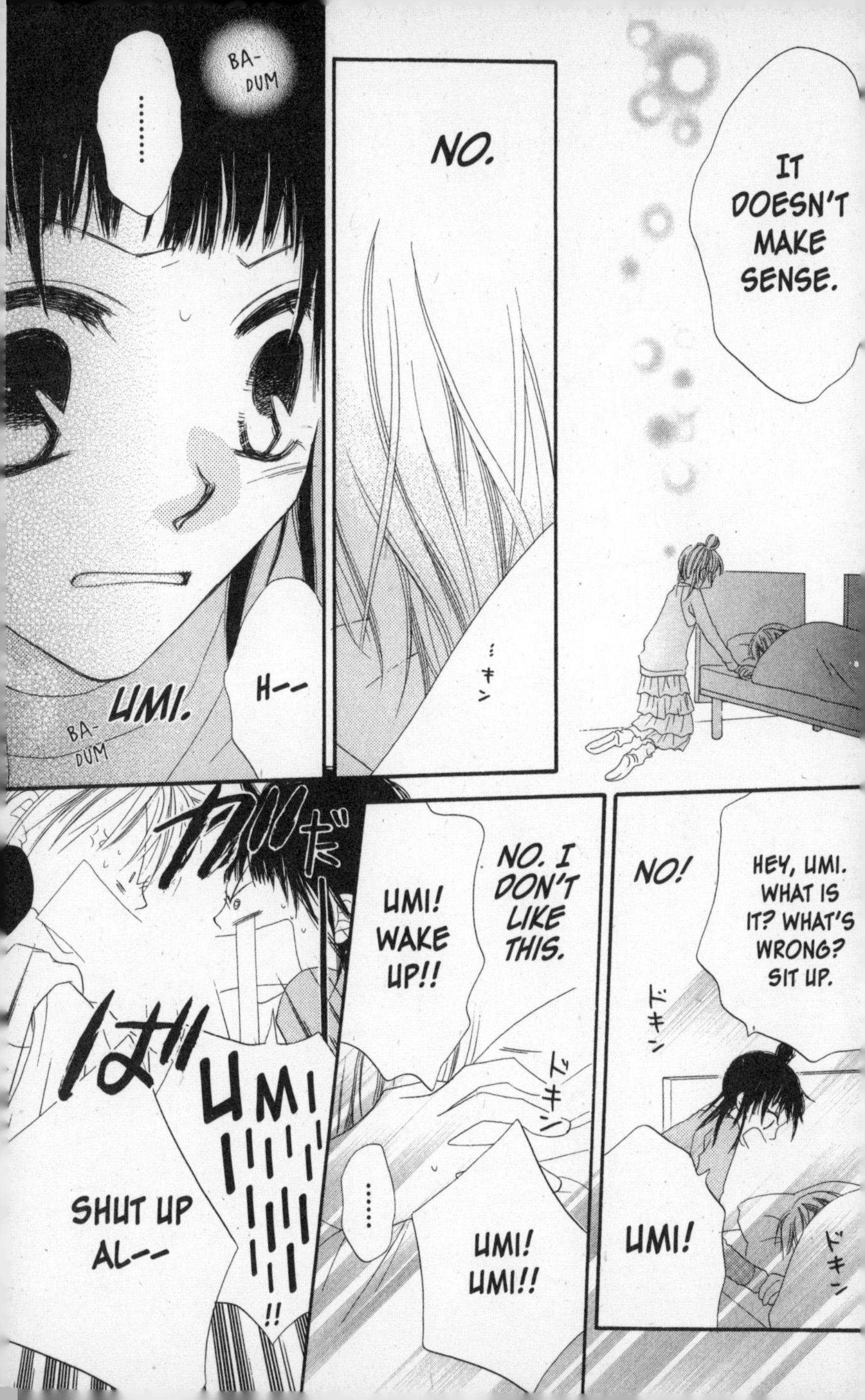
IT DOESN'T MAKE SENSE.
NO.
BA-DUM
......
H--
UMI.
BA-DUM
HEY, UMI. WHAT IS IT? WHAT'S WRONG? SIT UP.
NO!
ドキン
UMI!
ドキン
NO. I DON'T LIKE THIS.
UMI! WAKE UP!!
ドキン
......
UMI! UMI!!
UMI---!!
SHUT UP AL--

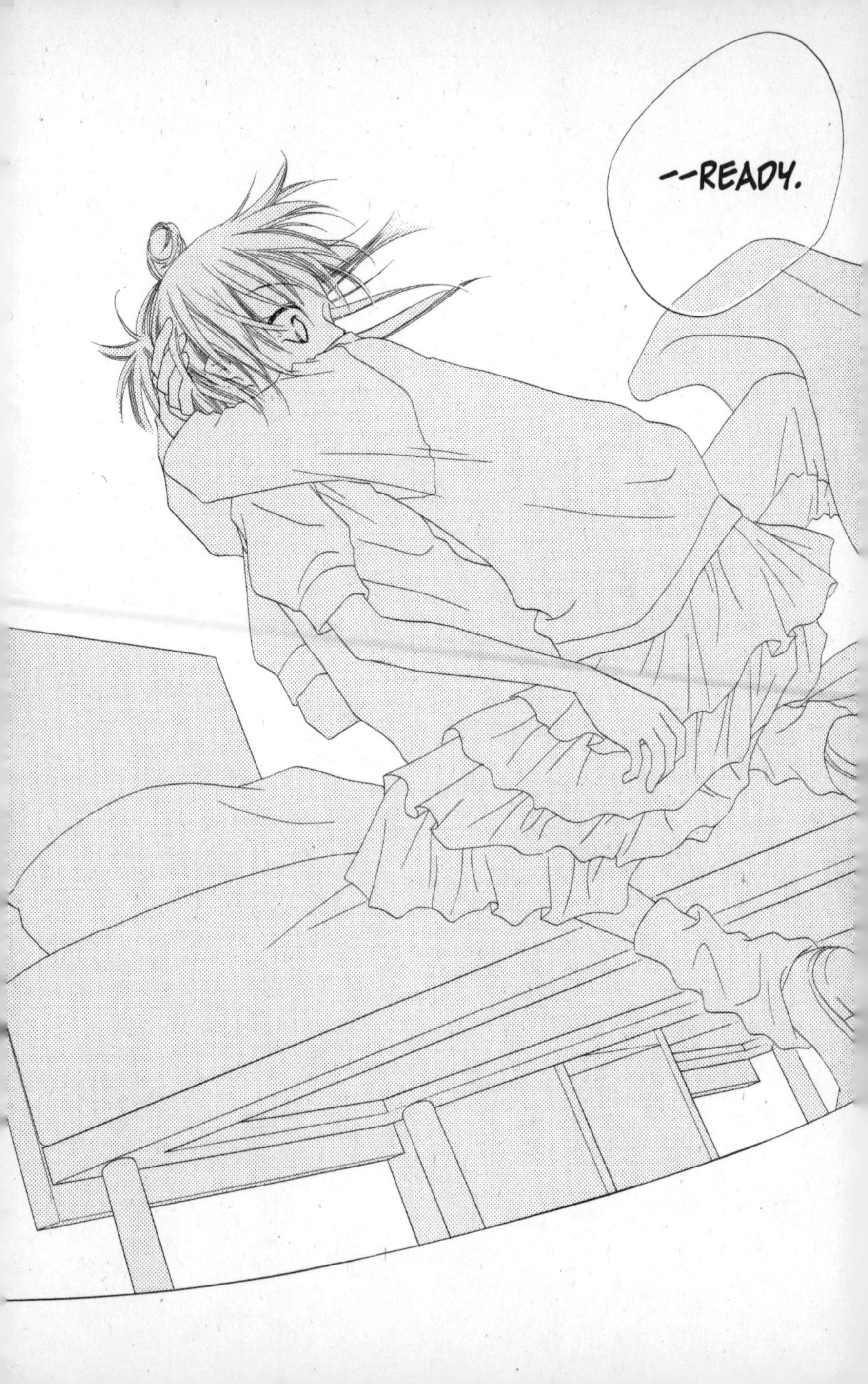
--READY.

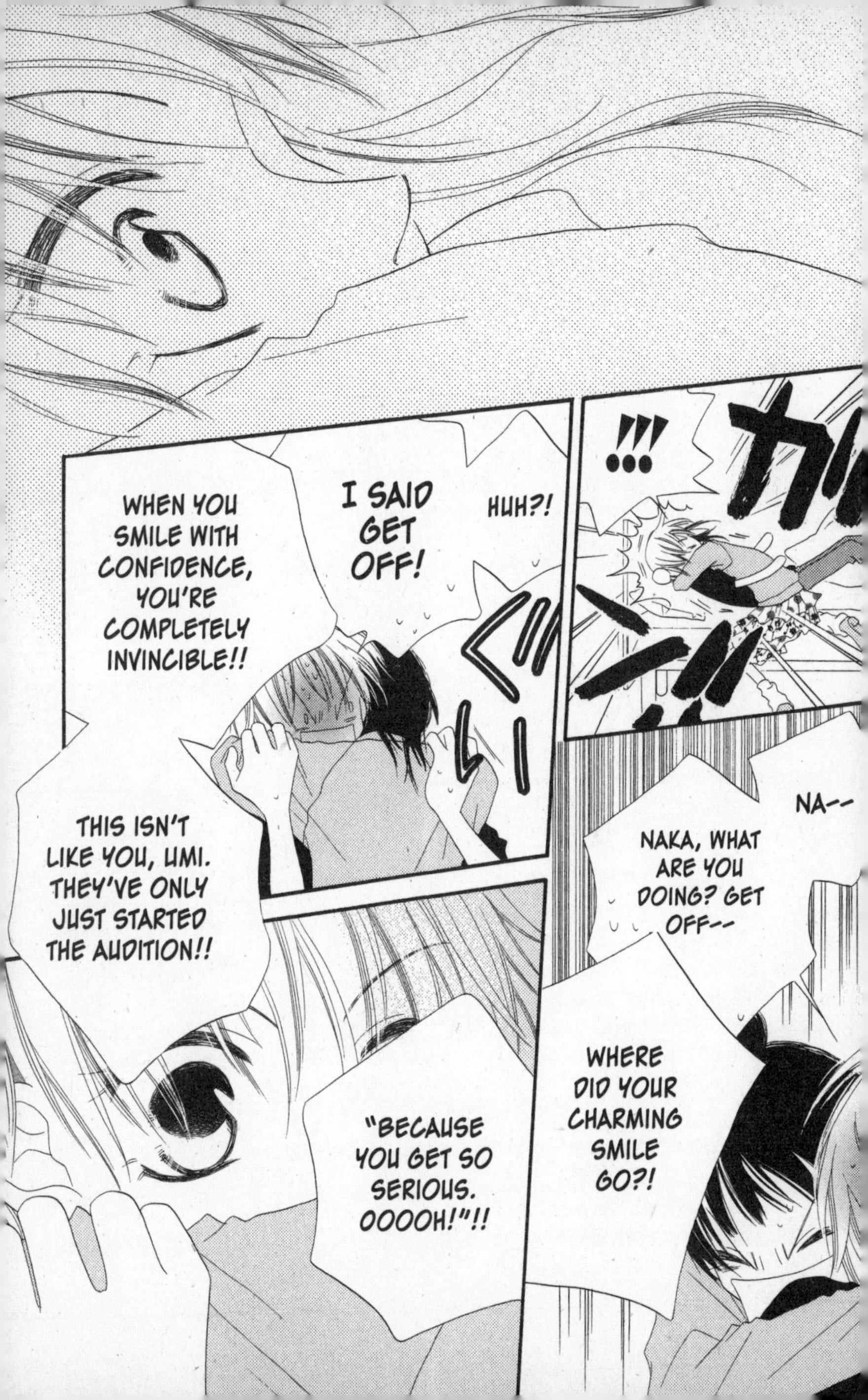
!!!
HUH?!
I SAID GET OFF!
WHEN YOU SMILE WITH CONFIDENCE, YOU'RE COMPLETELY INVINCIBLE!!
NA--
NAKA, WHAT ARE YOU DOING? GET OFF--
WHERE DID YOUR CHARMING SMILE GO?!
THIS ISN'T LIKE YOU, UMI. THEY'VE ONLY JUST STARTED THE AUDITION!!
"BECAUSE YOU GET SO SERIOUS. OOOOH!"!!

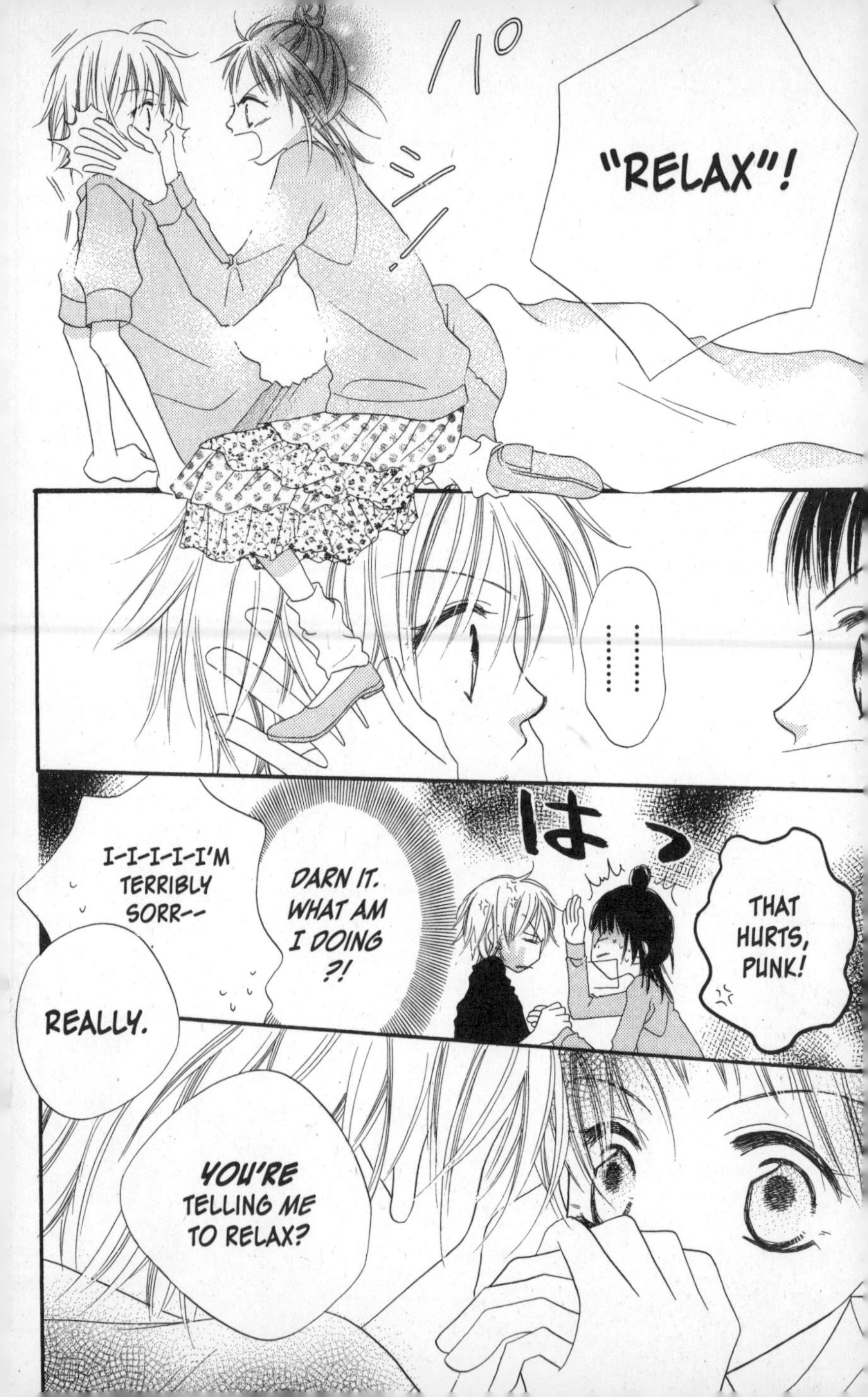
"RELAX"!
......
はっ
THAT HURTS, PUNK!
DARN IT. WHAT AM I DOING ?!
I-I-I-I-I'M TERRIBLY SORR--
REALLY.
YOU'RE TELLING ME TO RELAX?

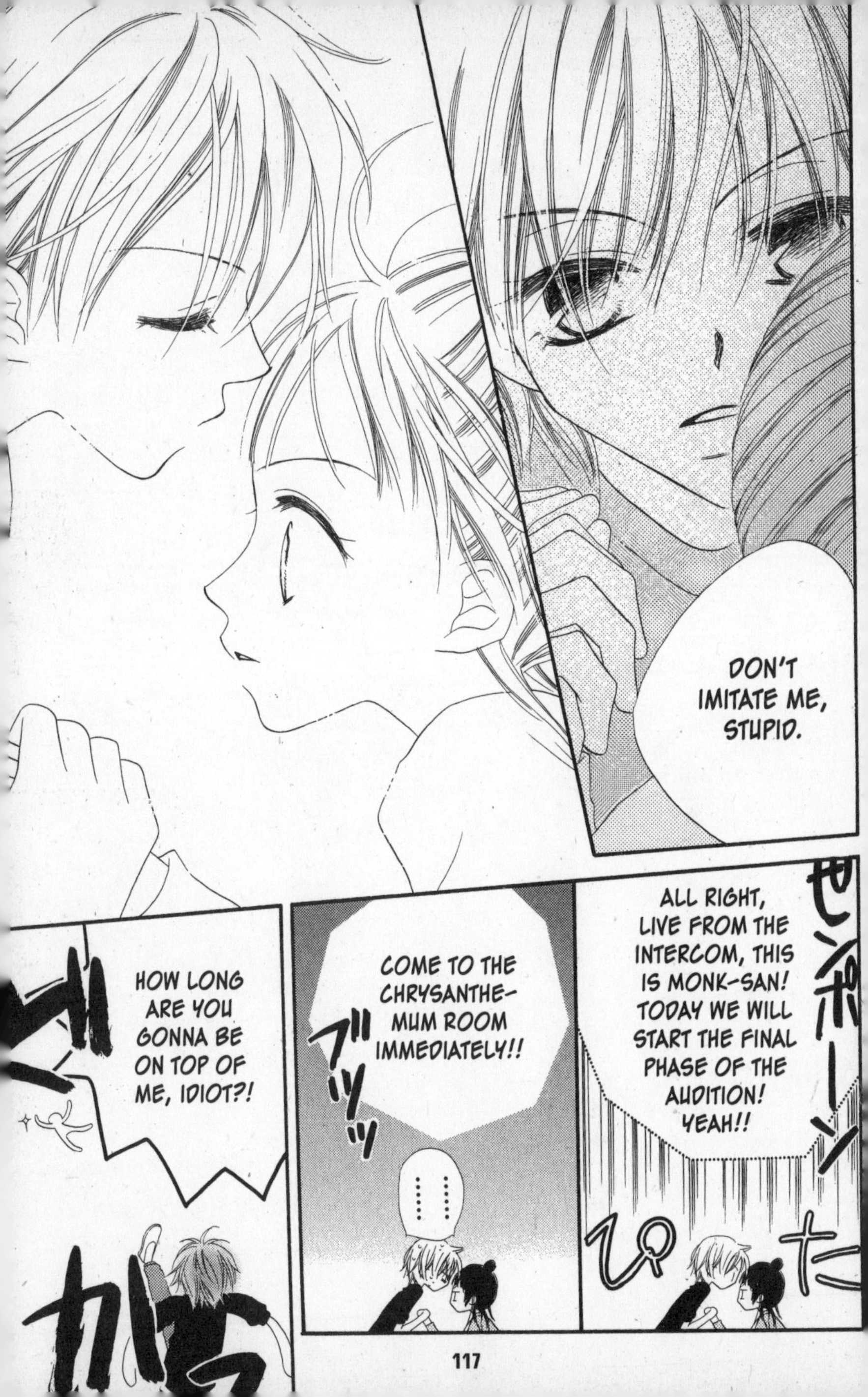
DON'T IMITATE ME, STUPID.
ピンポーン
ALL RIGHT, LIVE FROM THE INTERCOM, THIS IS MONK-SAN! TODAY WE WILL START THE FINAL PHASE OF THE AUDITION! YEAH!!
COME TO THE CHRYSANTHE-MUM ROOM IMMEDIATELY!!
ブツッ
......
HOW LONG ARE YOU GONNA BE ON TOP OF ME, IDIOT?!

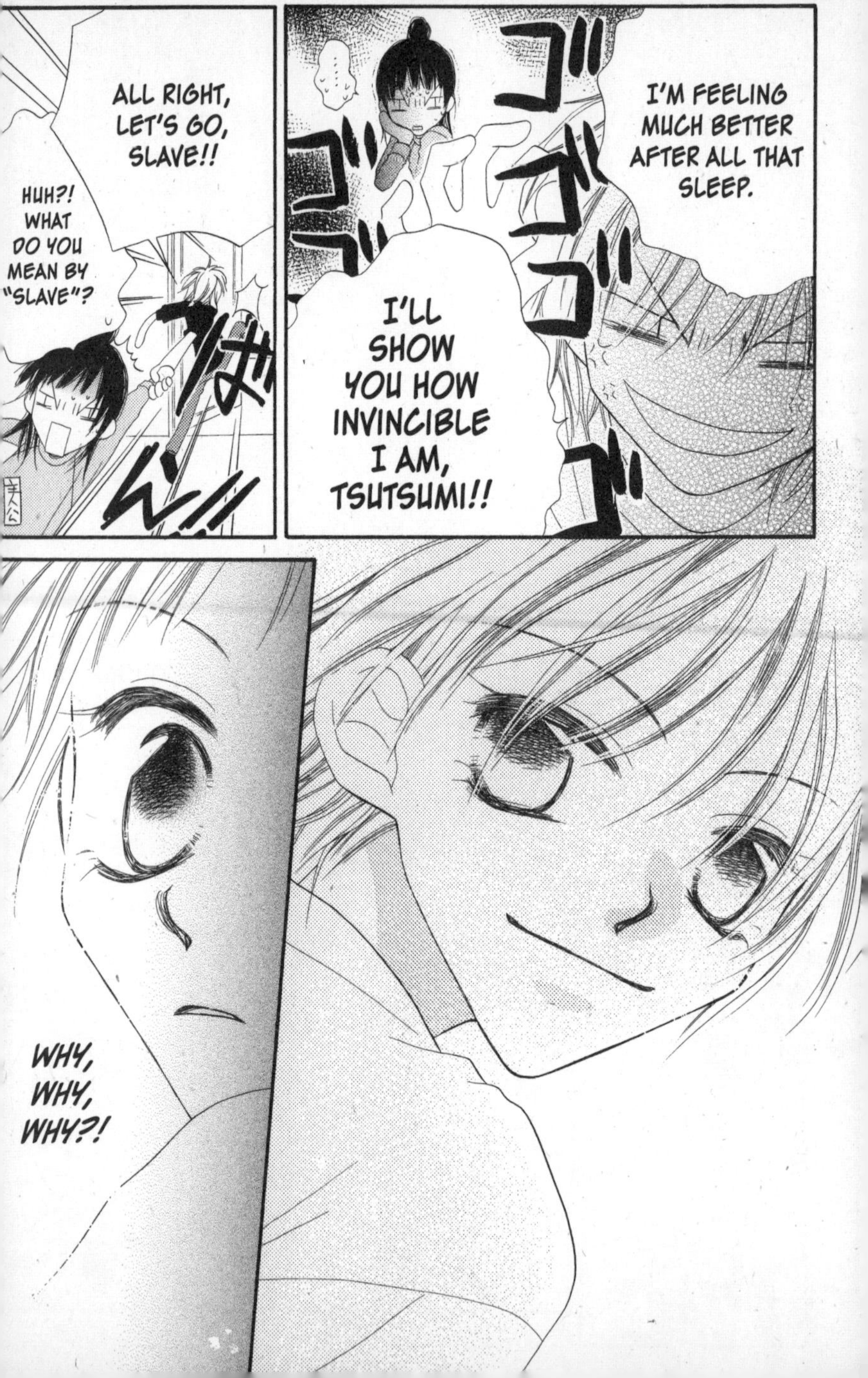
I'M FEELING MUCH BETTER AFTER ALL THAT SLEEP.
I'LL SHOW YOU HOW INVINCIBLE I AM, TSUTSUMI!!
ALL RIGHT, LET'S GO, SLAVE!!
HUH?! WHAT DO YOU MEAN BY "SLAVE"?
WHY, WHY, WHY?!

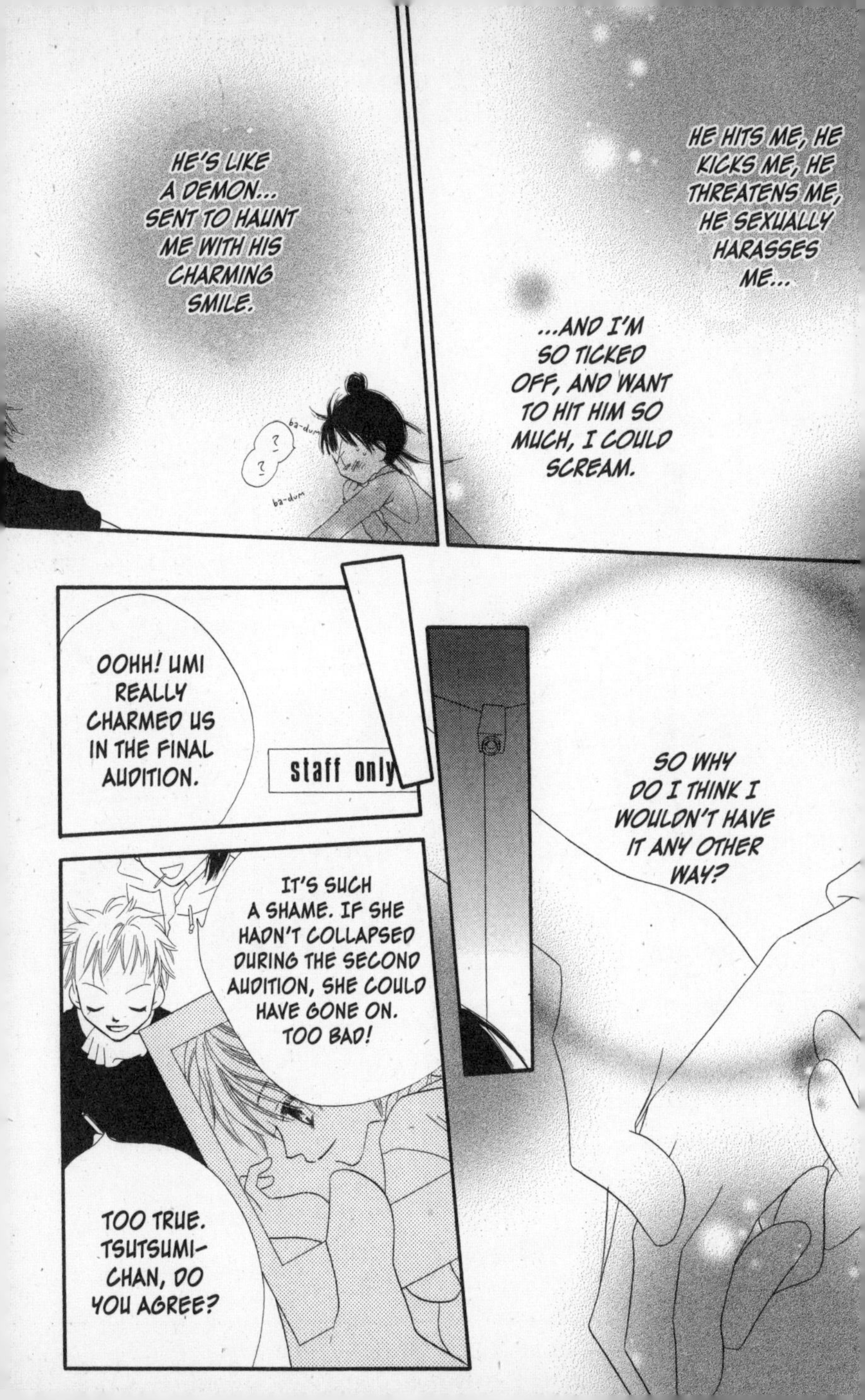
HE HITS ME, HE KICKS ME, HE THREATENS ME, HE SEXUALLY HARASSES ME...
...AND I'M SO TICKED OFF, AND WANT TO HIT HIM SO MUCH, I COULD SCREAM.
HE'S LIKE A DEMON... SENT TO HAUNT ME WITH HIS CHARMING SMILE.
ba-dum
? ?
ba-dum
SO WHY DO I THINK I WOULDN'T HAVE IT ANY OTHER WAY?
OOHH! UMI REALLY CHARMED US IN THE FINAL AUDITION.
staff only
IT'S SUCH A SHAME. IF SHE HADN'T COLLAPSED DURING THE SECOND AUDITION, SHE COULD HAVE GONE ON. TOO BAD!
TOO TRUE. TSUTSUMI-CHAN, DO YOU AGREE?

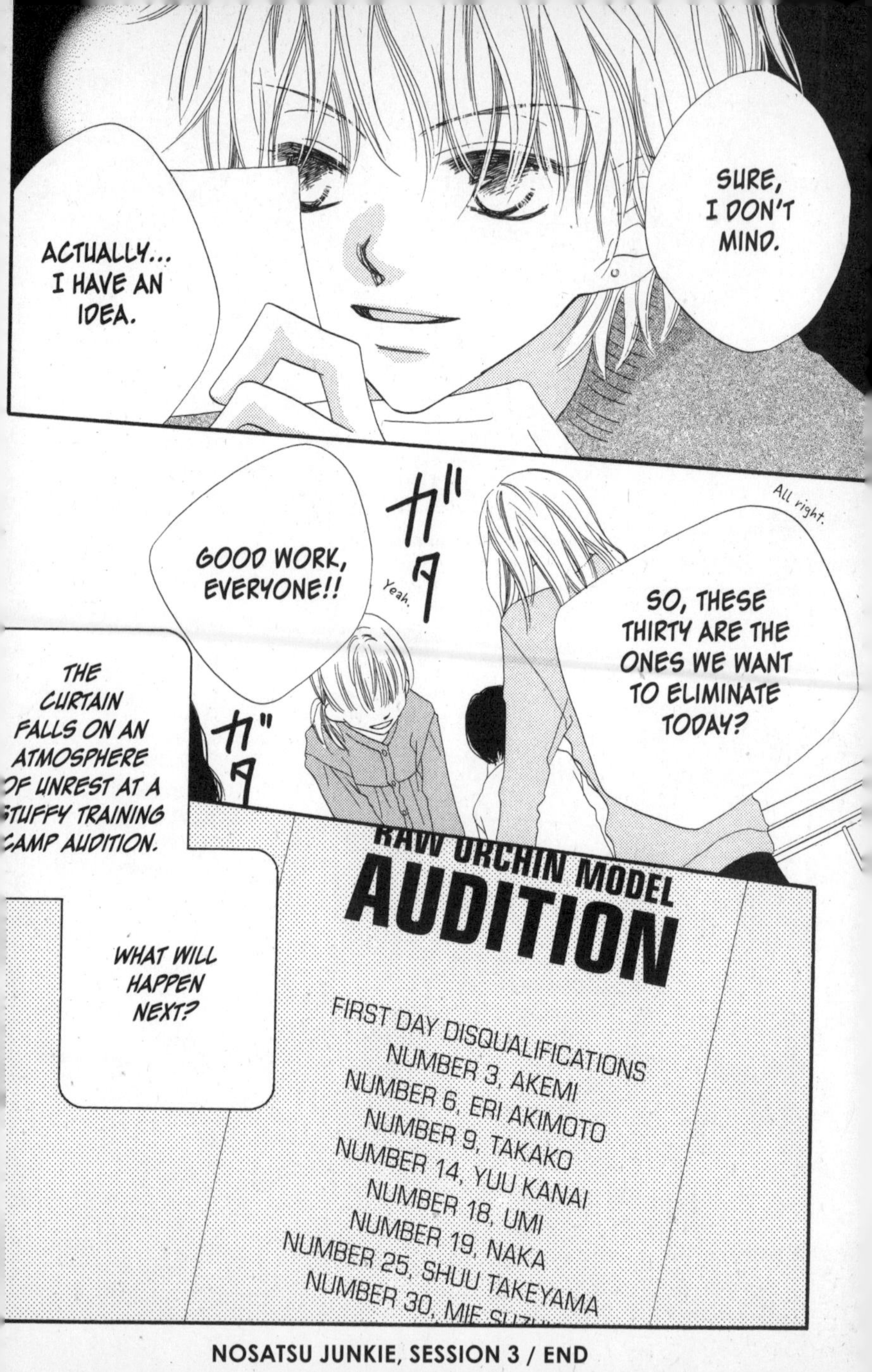
SURE, I DON'T MIND.
ACTUALLY... I HAVE AN IDEA.
All right.
SO, THESE THIRTY ARE THE ONES WE WANT TO ELIMINATE TODAY?
ガタ
Yeah.
GOOD WORK, EVERYONE!!
ガタ
RAW URCHIN MODEL
AUDITION
FIRST DAY DISQUALIFICATIONS
NUMBER 3, AKEMI
NUMBER 6, ERI AKIMOTO
NUMBER 9, TAKAKO
NUMBER 14, YUU KANAI
NUMBER 18, UMI
NUMBER 19, NAKA
NUMBER 25, SHUU TAKEYAMA
NUMBER 30, MIE
THE CURTAIN FALLS ON AN ATMOSPHERE OF UNREST AT A STUFFY TRAINING CAMP AUDITION.
WHAT WILL HAPPEN NEXT?

NOSATSU JUNKIE, SESSION 3 / END

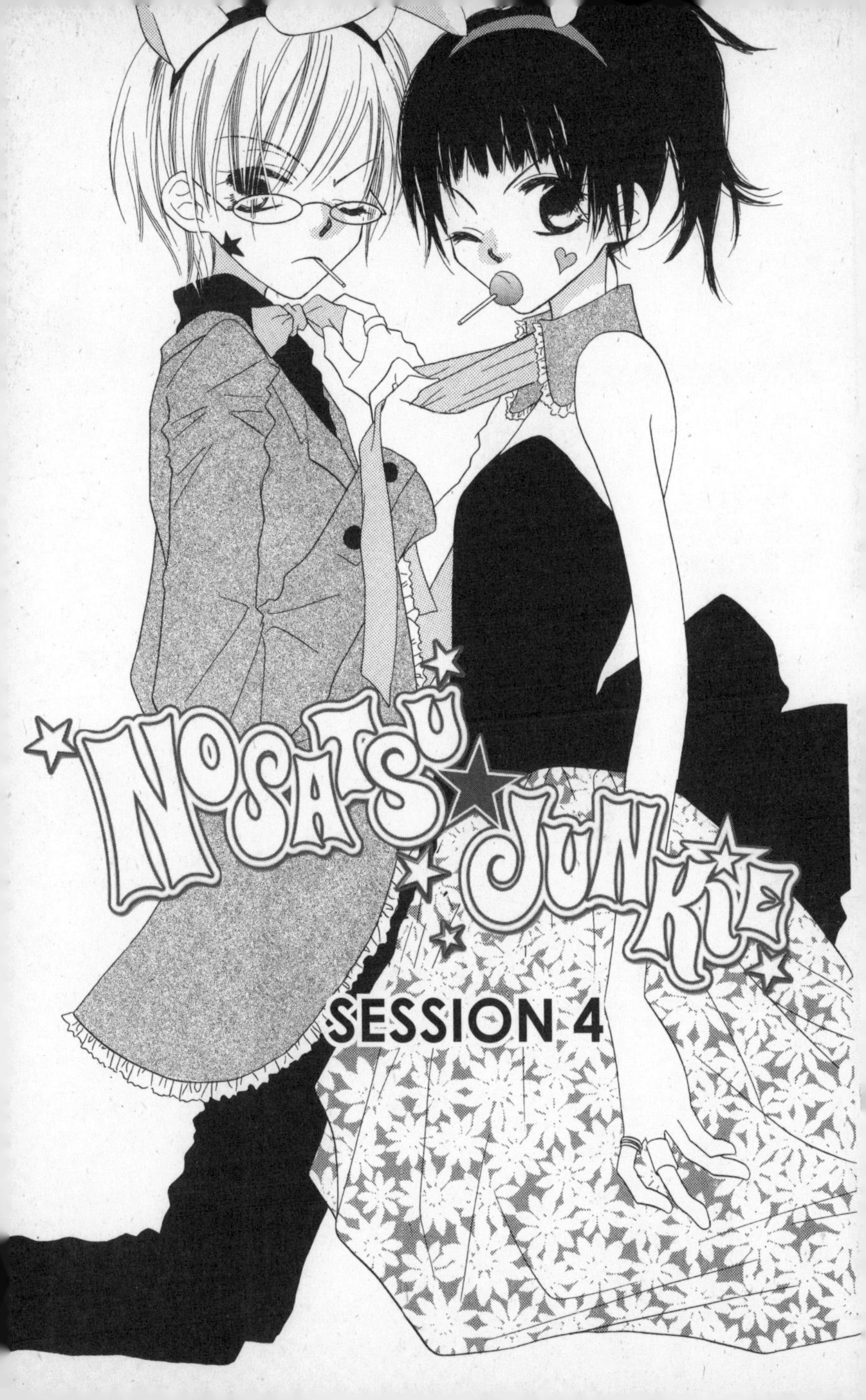
NOSATSU JUNKIE
SESSION 4

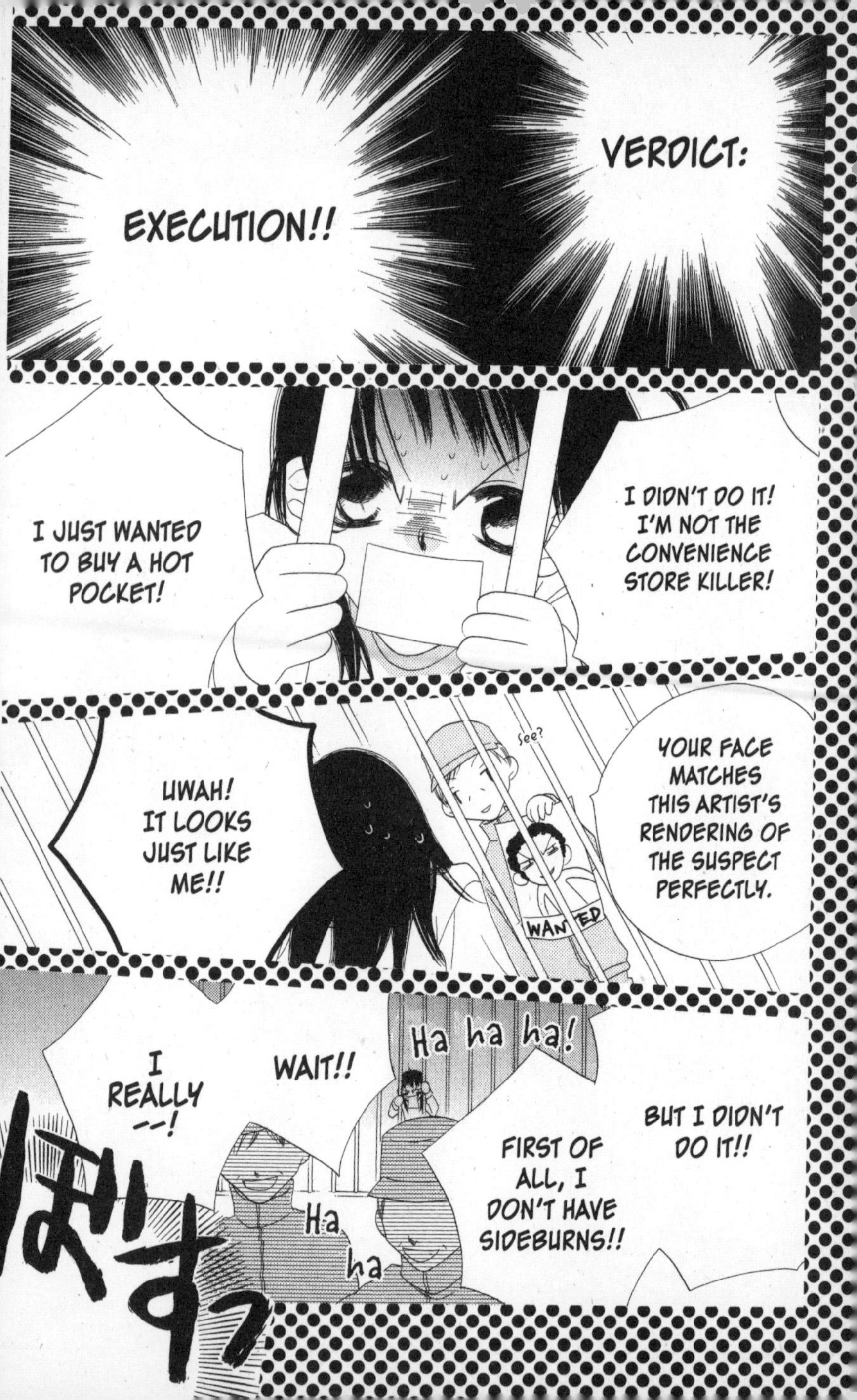
VERDICT:
EXECUTION!!
I DIDN'T DO IT! I'M NOT THE CONVENIENCE STORE KILLER!
I JUST WANTED TO BUY A HOT POCKET!
See?
YOUR FACE MATCHES THIS ARTIST'S RENDERING OF THE SUSPECT PERFECTLY.
WANTED
UWAH! IT LOOKS JUST LIKE ME!!
Ha ha ha!
BUT I DIDN'T DO IT!!
FIRST OF ALL, I DON'T HAVE SIDEBURNS!!
Ha
ha
WAIT!!
I REALLY --!
ぽすっ

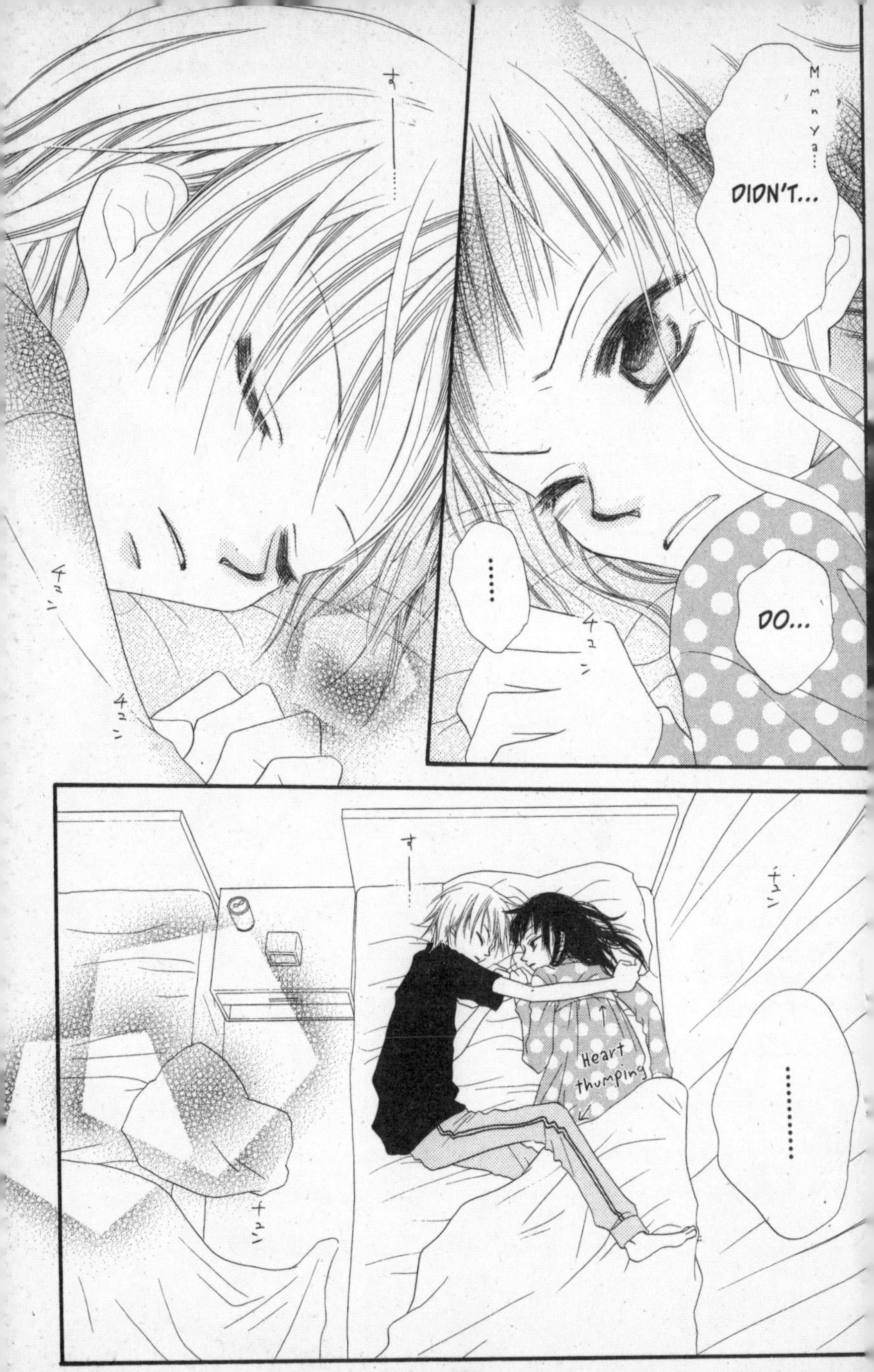
Mmn Ya...
DIDN'T...
......
DO...
キュン
すー……
キュン
キュン
キュン
....
Heart thumping
すー…
キュン

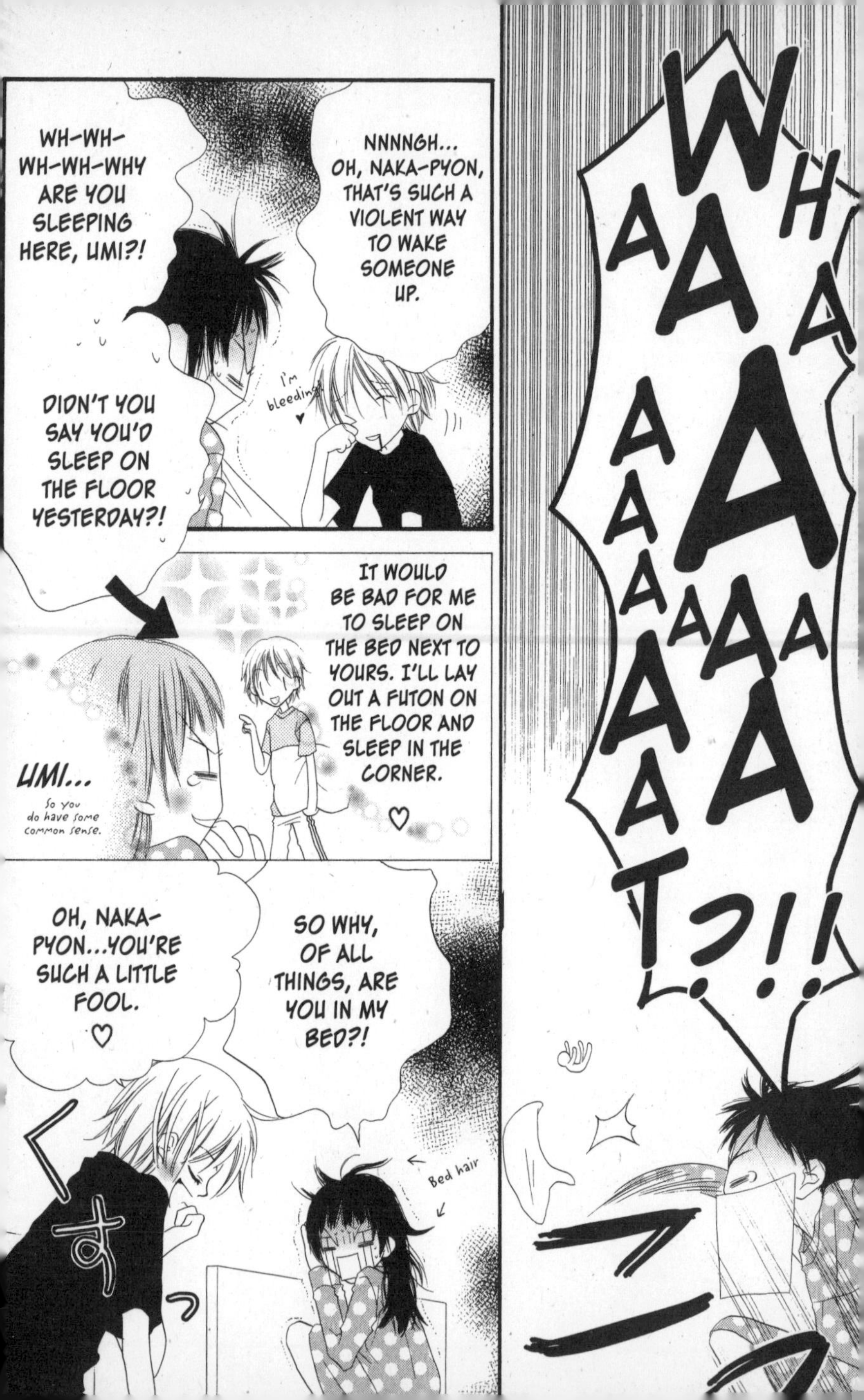
WHAAAAAAAAAAAAT?!!
NNNNGH... OH, NAKA-PYON, THAT'S SUCH A VIOLENT WAY TO WAKE SOMEONE UP.
WH-WH-WH-WH-WHY ARE YOU SLEEPING HERE, UMI?!
I'm bleeding
DIDN'T YOU SAY YOU'D SLEEP ON THE FLOOR YESTERDAY?!
IT WOULD BE BAD FOR ME TO SLEEP ON THE BED NEXT TO YOURS. I'LL LAY OUT A FUTON ON THE FLOOR AND SLEEP IN THE CORNER. ♡
UMI...
So you do have some common sense.
SO WHY, OF ALL THINGS, ARE YOU IN MY BED?!
OH, NAKA-PYON...YOU'RE SUCH A LITTLE FOOL. ♡
Bed hair
くすっ

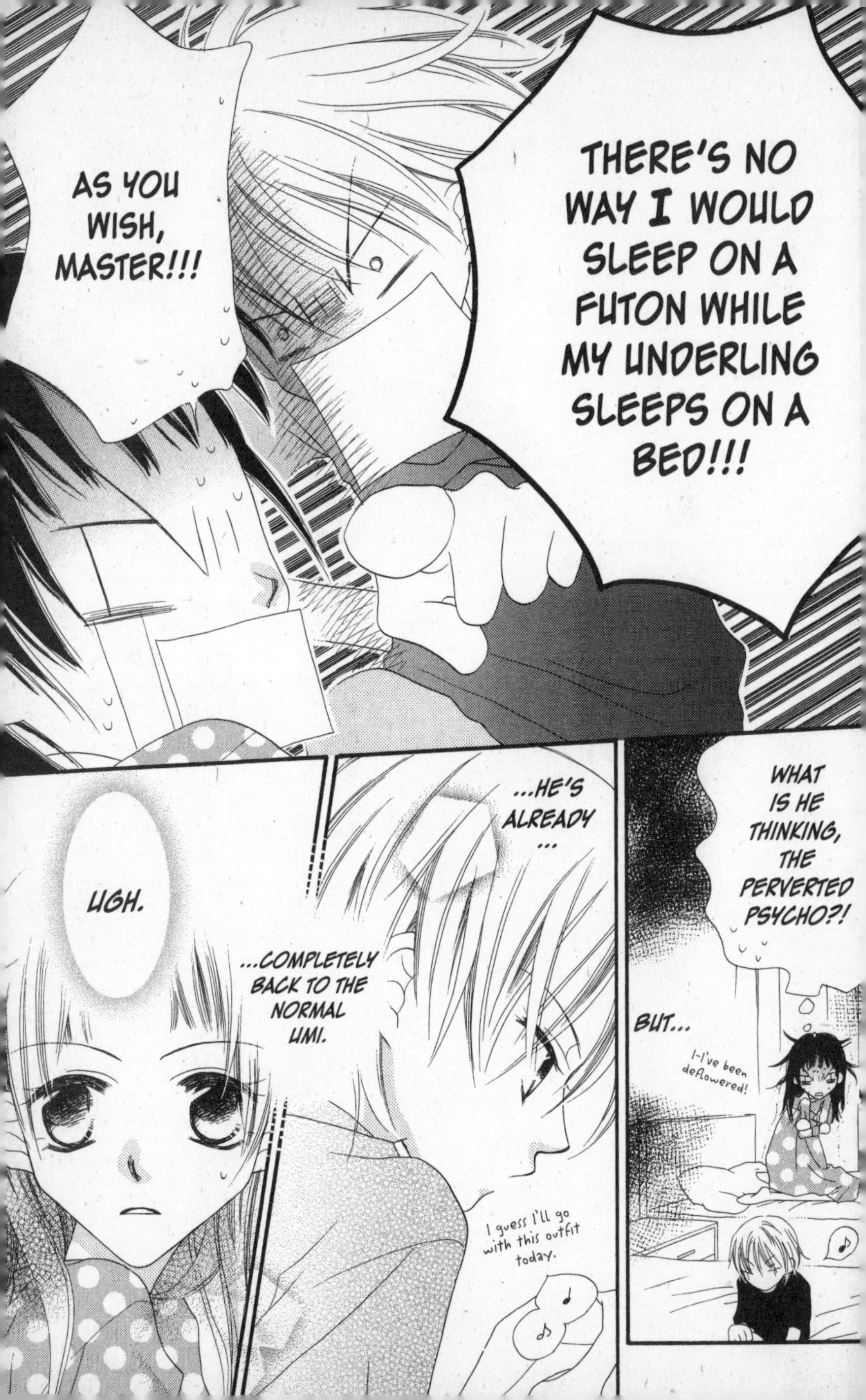
THERE'S NO WAY I WOULD SLEEP ON A FUTON WHILE MY UNDERLING SLEEPS ON A BED!!!
AS YOU WISH, MASTER!!!
WHAT IS HE THINKING, THE PERVERTED PSYCHO?!
I-I've been deflowered!
BUT...
...HE'S ALREADY ...
...COMPLETELY BACK TO THE NORMAL UMI.
I guess I'll go with this outfit today.
UGH.

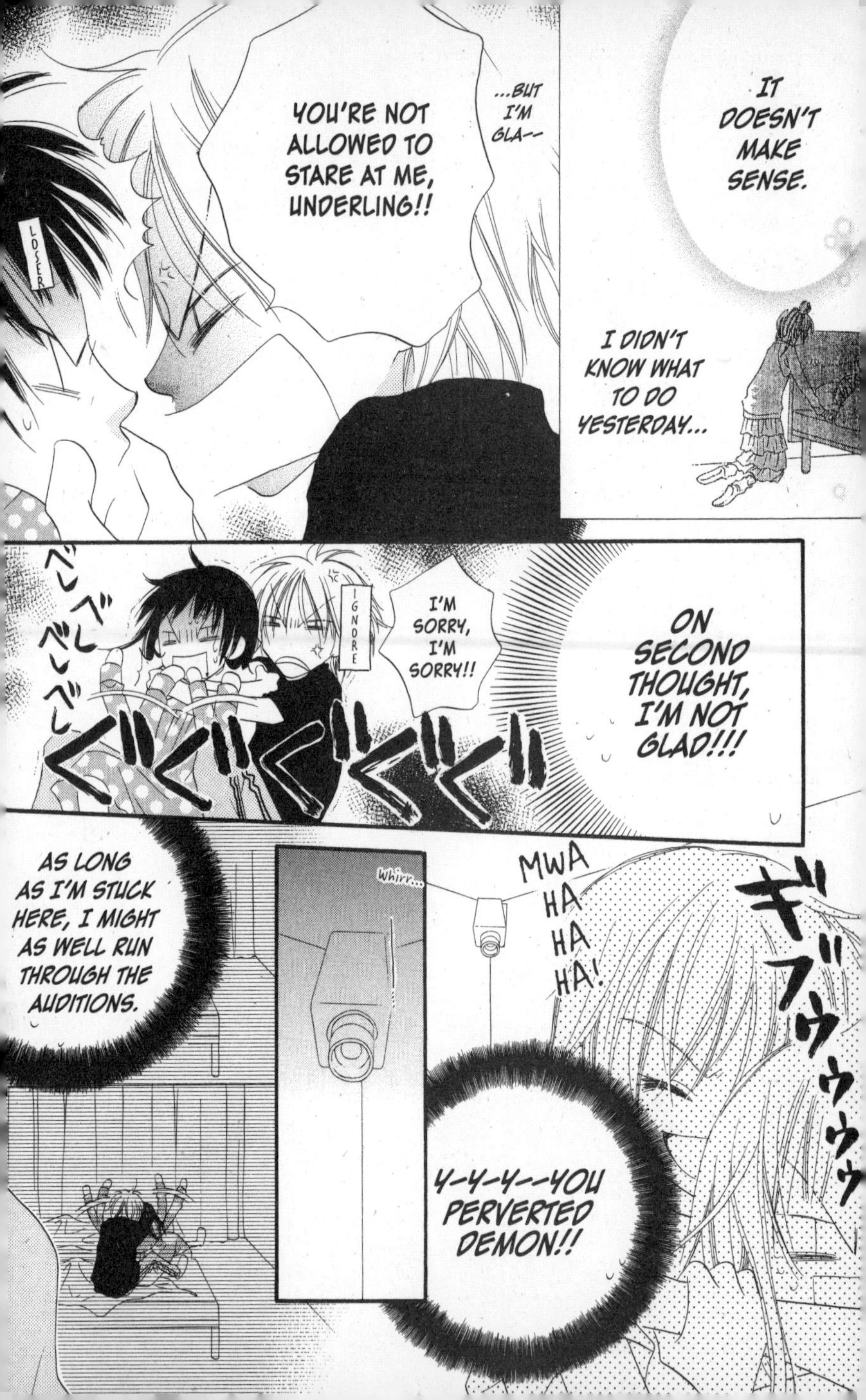
IT DOESN'T MAKE SENSE.
I DIDN'T KNOW WHAT TO DO YESTERDAY...
...BUT I'M GLA--
YOU'RE NOT ALLOWED TO STARE AT ME, UNDERLING!!
LOSER
ON SECOND THOUGHT, I'M NOT GLAD!!!
I'M SORRY, I'M SORRY!!
IGNORE
MWA HA HA HA!
Y-Y-Y--YOU PERVERTED DEMON!!
Whirr...
AS LONG AS I'M STUCK HERE, I MIGHT AS WELL RUN THROUGH THE AUDITIONS.

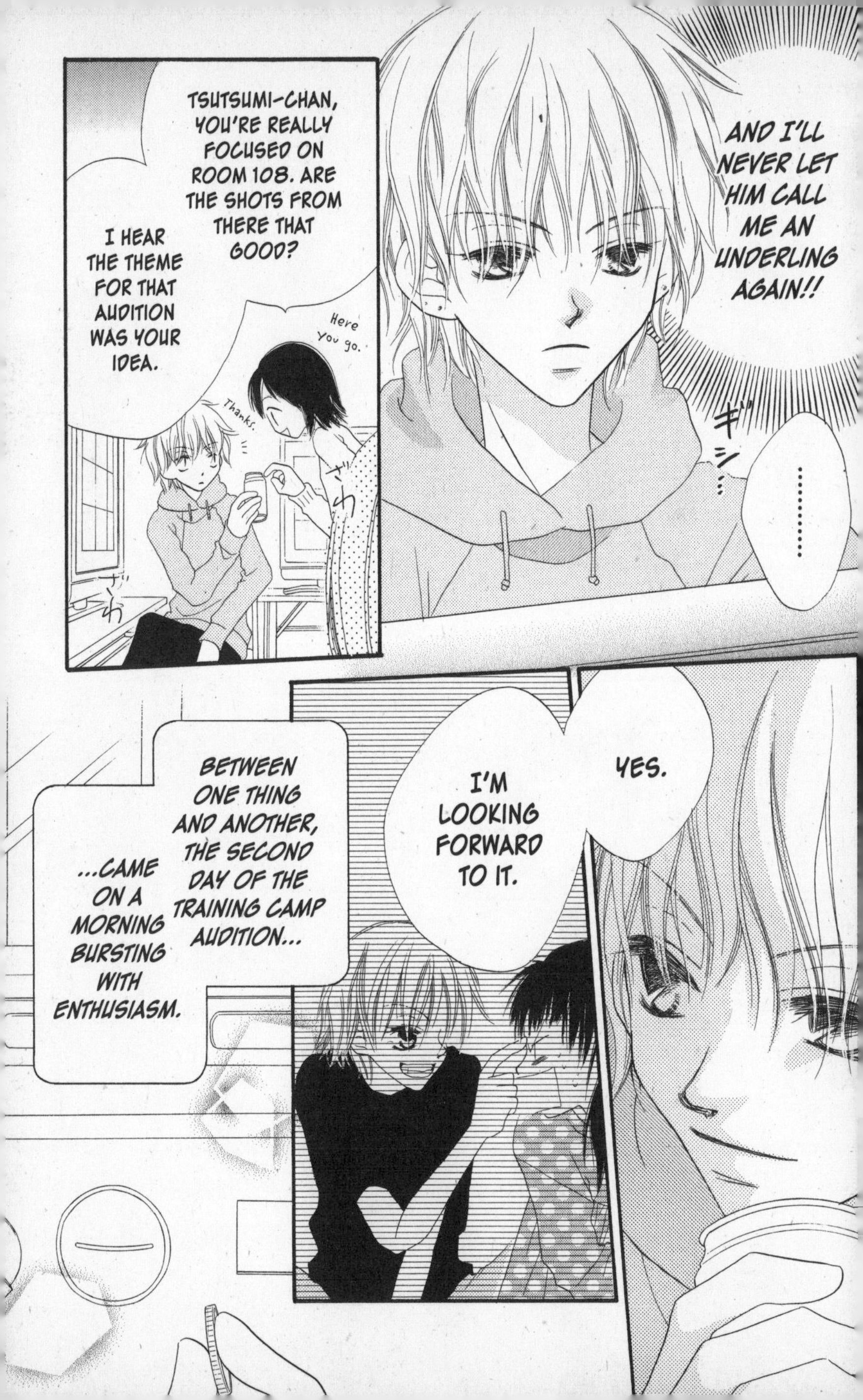
AND I'LL NEVER LET HIM CALL ME AN UNDERLING AGAIN!!
ギシ…
......
TSUTSUMI-CHAN, YOU'RE REALLY FOCUSED ON ROOM 108. ARE THE SHOTS FROM THERE THAT GOOD?
Here you go.
I HEAR THE THEME FOR THAT AUDITION WAS YOUR IDEA.
Thanks.
YES.
I'M LOOKING FORWARD TO IT.
BETWEEN ONE THING AND ANOTHER, THE SECOND DAY OF THE TRAINING CAMP AUDITION...
...CAME ON A MORNING BURSTING WITH ENTHUSIASM.

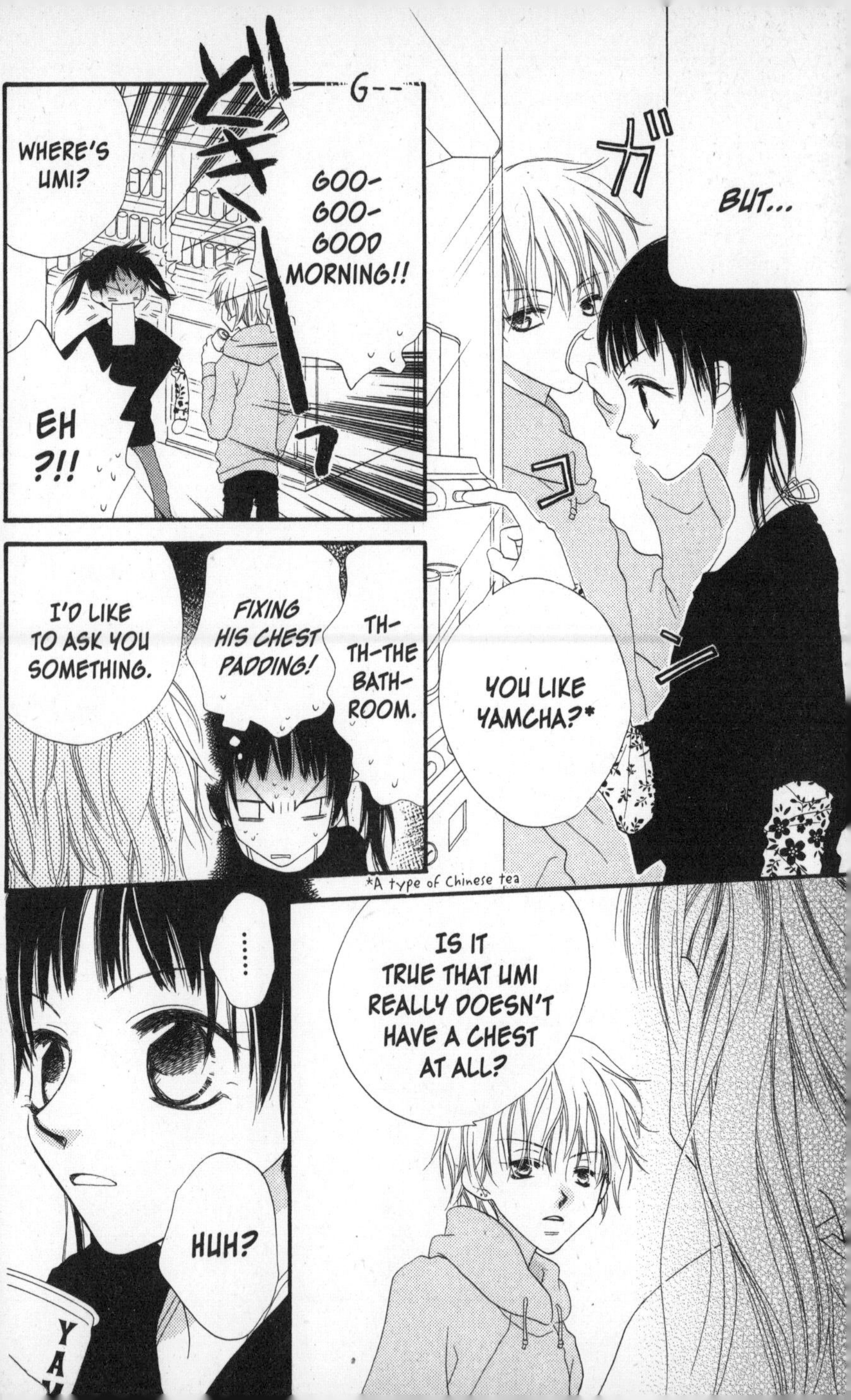
BUT...
YOU LIKE YAMCHA?*
*A type of Chinese tea
G--
GOO-GOO-GOOD MORNING!!
WHERE'S UMI?
EH?!!
TH-TH-THE BATHROOM.
FIXING HIS CHEST PADDING!
I'D LIKE TO ASK YOU SOMETHING.
IS IT TRUE THAT UMI REALLY DOESN'T HAVE A CHEST AT ALL?
......
HUH?

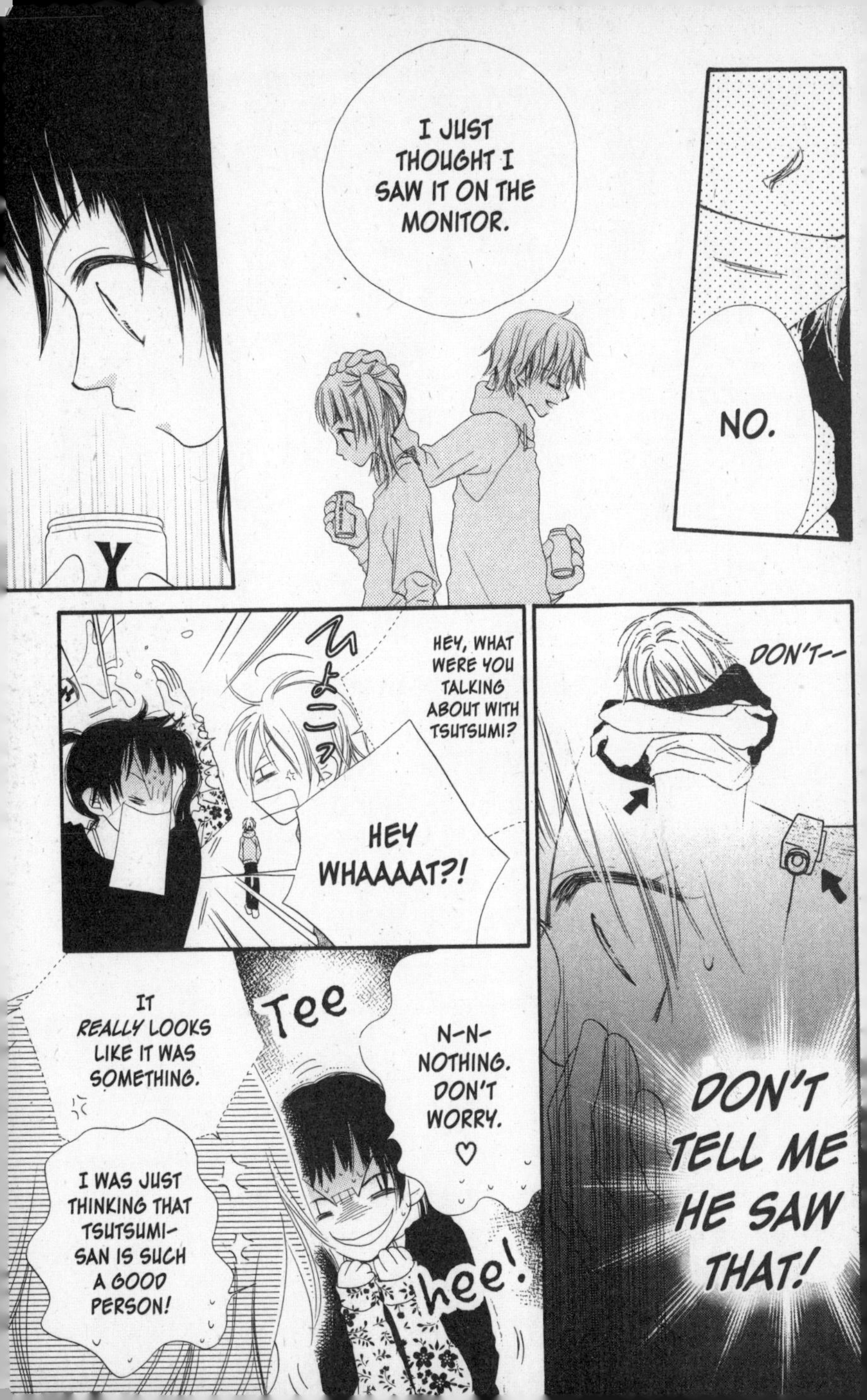
NO.
I JUST THOUGHT I SAW IT ON THE MONITOR.
DON'T--
DON'T TELL ME HE SAW THAT!
HEY, WHAT WERE YOU TALKING ABOUT WITH TSUTSUMI?
HEY WHAAAAT?!
N-N-NOTHING. DON'T WORRY. ♡
Tee hee!
IT REALLY LOOKS LIKE IT WAS SOMETHING.
I WAS JUST THINKING THAT TSUTSUMI-SAN IS SUCH A GOOD PERSON!

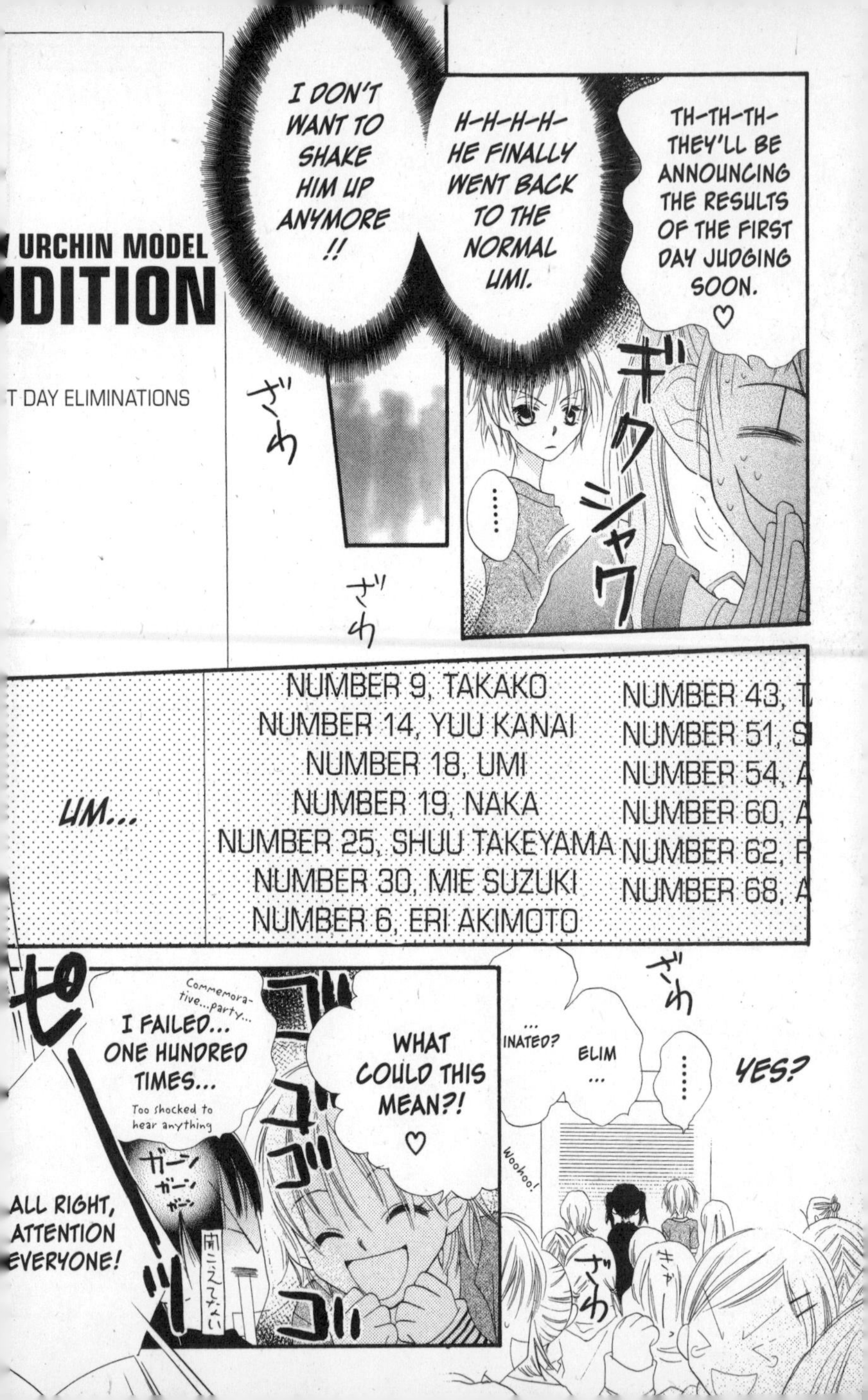
TH-TH-TH-THEY'LL BE ANNOUNCING THE RESULTS OF THE FIRST DAY JUDGING SOON. ♡
ギクシャク
H-H-H-H-HE FINALLY WENT BACK TO THE NORMAL UMI.
I DON'T WANT TO SHAKE HIM UP ANYMORE!!
......
ざわ
ざわ
URCHIN MODEL
DITION
T DAY ELIMINATIONS
NUMBER 9, TAKAKO
NUMBER 14, YUU KANAI
NUMBER 18, UMI
NUMBER 19, NAKA
NUMBER 25, SHUU TAKEYAMA
NUMBER 30, MIE SUZUKI
NUMBER 6, ERI AKIMOTO
NUMBER 43, T
NUMBER 51, S
NUMBER 54, A
NUMBER 60, A
NUMBER 62, R
NUMBER 68, A
UM...
ざわ
YES?
......
ELIM...
...INATED?
Woohoo!
キャー
ざわ
WHAT COULD THIS MEAN?! ♡
Commemorative...party...
I FAILED... ONE HUNDRED TIMES...
Too shocked to hear anything
ガーン ガーン ガーン
聞こえてない
ALL RIGHT, ATTENTION EVERYONE!

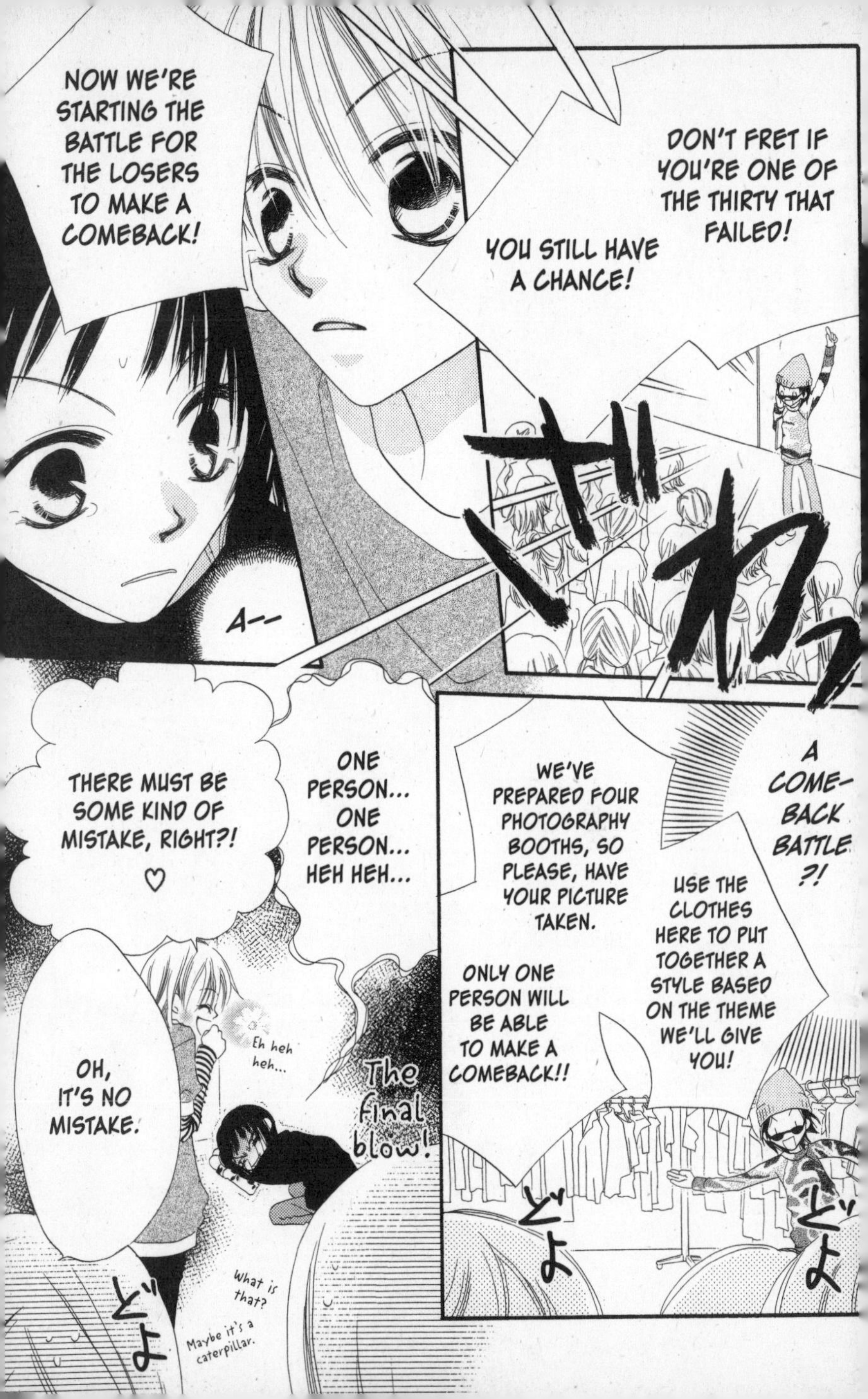
DON'T FRET IF YOU'RE ONE OF THE THIRTY THAT FAILED!
YOU STILL HAVE A CHANCE!
ざわっ
NOW WE'RE STARTING THE BATTLE FOR THE LOSERS TO MAKE A COMEBACK!
A--
A COMEBACK BATTLE?!
WE'VE PREPARED FOUR PHOTOGRAPHY BOOTHS, SO PLEASE, HAVE YOUR PICTURE TAKEN.
USE THE CLOTHES HERE TO PUT TOGETHER A STYLE BASED ON THE THEME WE'LL GIVE YOU!
ONLY ONE PERSON WILL BE ABLE TO MAKE A COMEBACK!!
どよ
どよ
ONE PERSON... ONE PERSON... HEH HEH...
THERE MUST BE SOME KIND OF MISTAKE, RIGHT?! ♡
Eh heh heh...
OH, IT'S NO MISTAKE.
The final blow!
What is that?
Maybe it's a caterpillar.
どよ

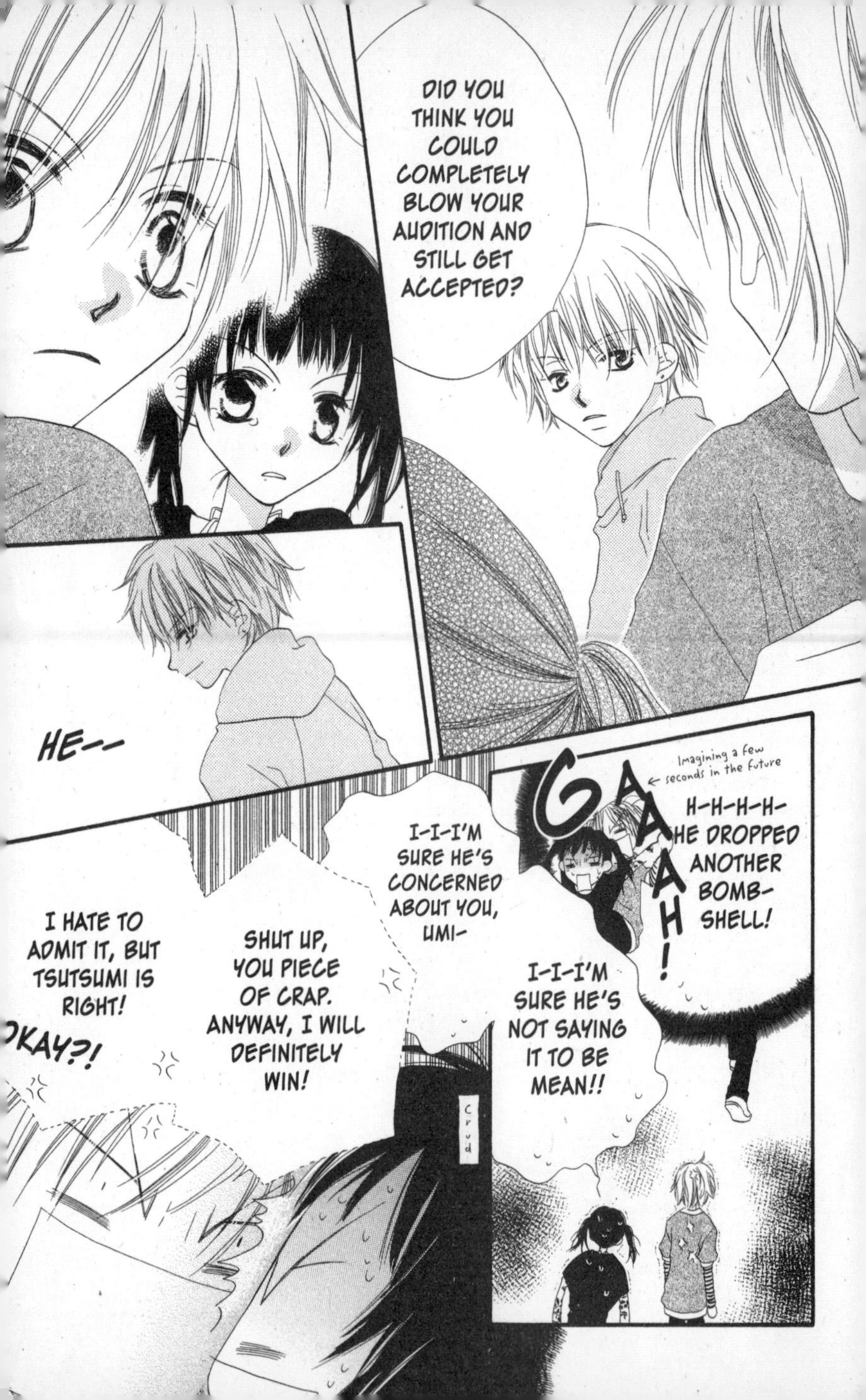
DID YOU THINK YOU COULD COMPLETELY BLOW YOUR AUDITION AND STILL GET ACCEPTED?
HE--
GAAAH!
Imagining a few seconds in the future
H-H-H-H-HE DROPPED ANOTHER BOMB-SHELL!
I-I-I'M SURE HE'S CONCERNED ABOUT YOU, UMI-
I-I-I'M SURE HE'S NOT SAYING IT TO BE MEAN!!
I HATE TO ADMIT IT, BUT TSUTSUMI IS RIGHT!
OKAY?!
SHUT UP, YOU PIECE OF CRAP. ANYWAY, I WILL DEFINITELY WIN!
Crud

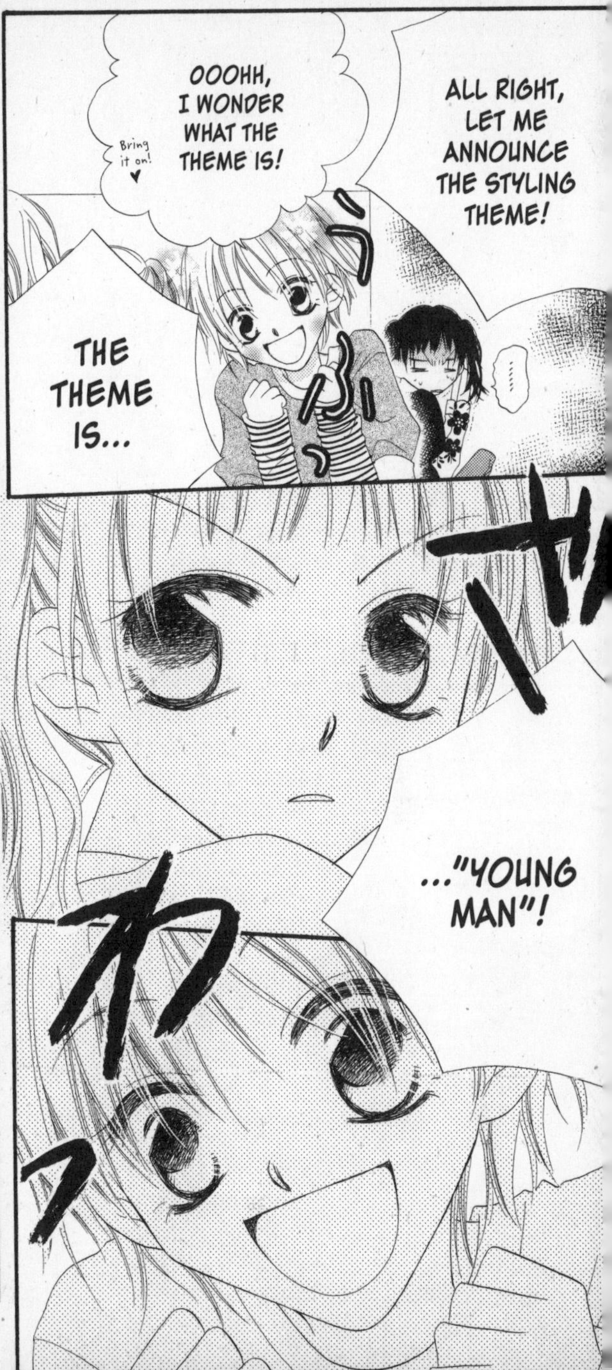
ALL RIGHT, LET ME ANNOUNCE THE STYLING THEME!
OOOHH, I WONDER WHAT THE THEME IS!
Bring it on! ♥
......
THE THEME IS...
..."YOUNG MAN"!

4

Thank you for all the letters and postcards. I reeeeeally love them. They're my treasures! Each and every word from you gives me strength. My only regret is that the replies are so late. I hope you'll wait patiently for them.

Not to change the subject suddenly, but I like models! I especially like Mariko Takahashi-chan and Ayumi Tanabe-chan. I saw Ayumi-chan live at show once, and her face was so small it was like, "Ugh, are you stupid?!" I wonder if that's true. Oh, I also like Imajuku and Emi Suzuki-chan. I've never really thought, "Let's draw them like this model!" when drawing Umi and Naka, but I would like to draw a serious model. I get the feeling I'm only drawing weirdo models.

And a weirdo photographer.

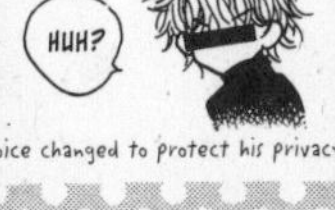
HUH?

Voice changed to protect his privacy.

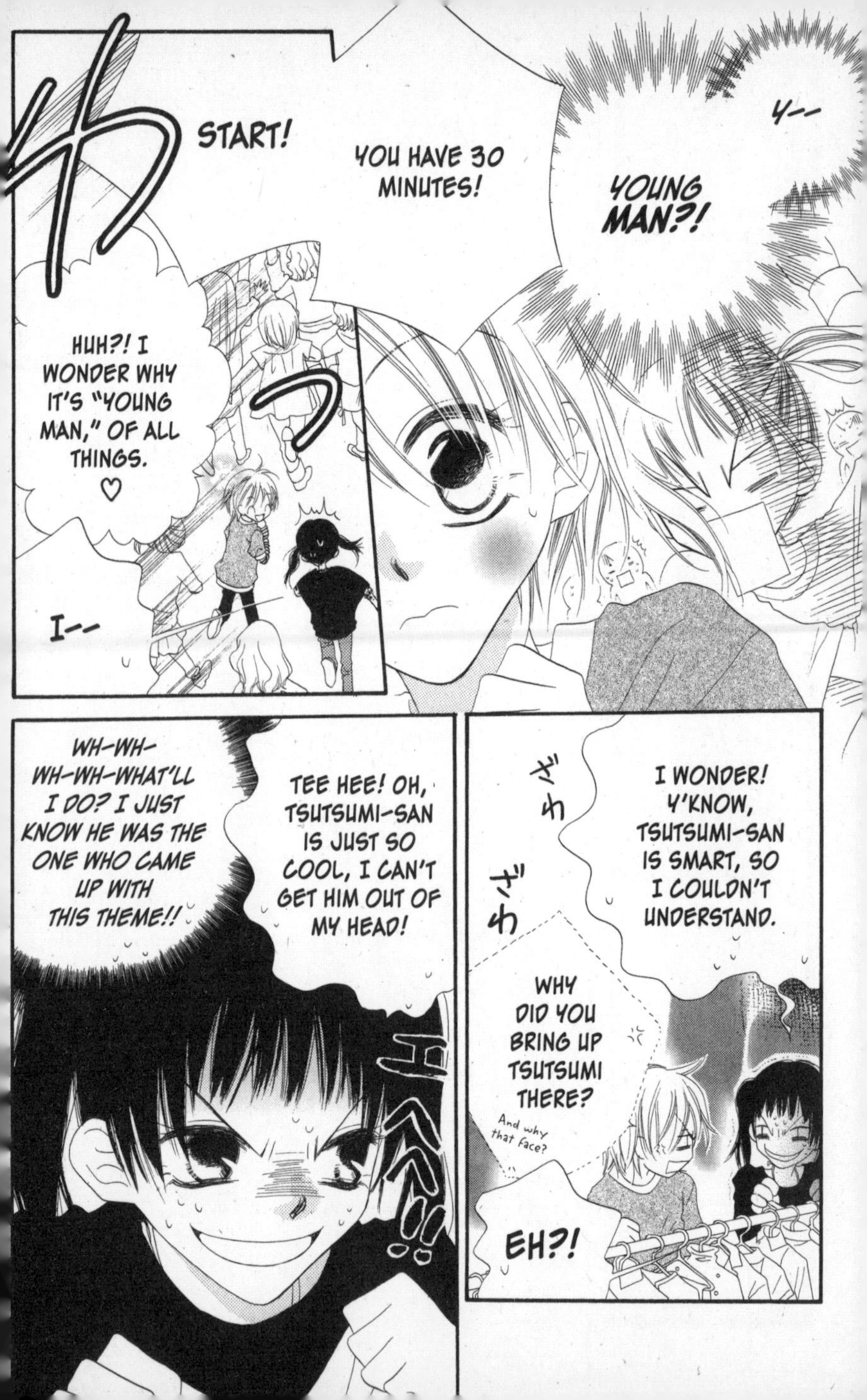

Y--
YOUNG MAN?!
YOU HAVE 30 MINUTES!
START!
HUH?! I WONDER WHY IT'S "YOUNG MAN," OF ALL THINGS. ♡
I--
ざわ
ざわ
I WONDER! Y'KNOW, TSUTSUMI-SAN IS SMART, SO I COULDN'T UNDERSTAND.
WHY DID YOU BRING UP TSUTSUMI THERE?
And why that face?
EH?!
TEE HEE! OH, TSUTSUMI-SAN IS JUST SO COOL, I CAN'T GET HIM OUT OF MY HEAD!
WH-WH-WH-WH-WHAT'LL I DO? I JUST KNOW HE WAS THE ONE WHO CAME UP WITH THIS THEME!!

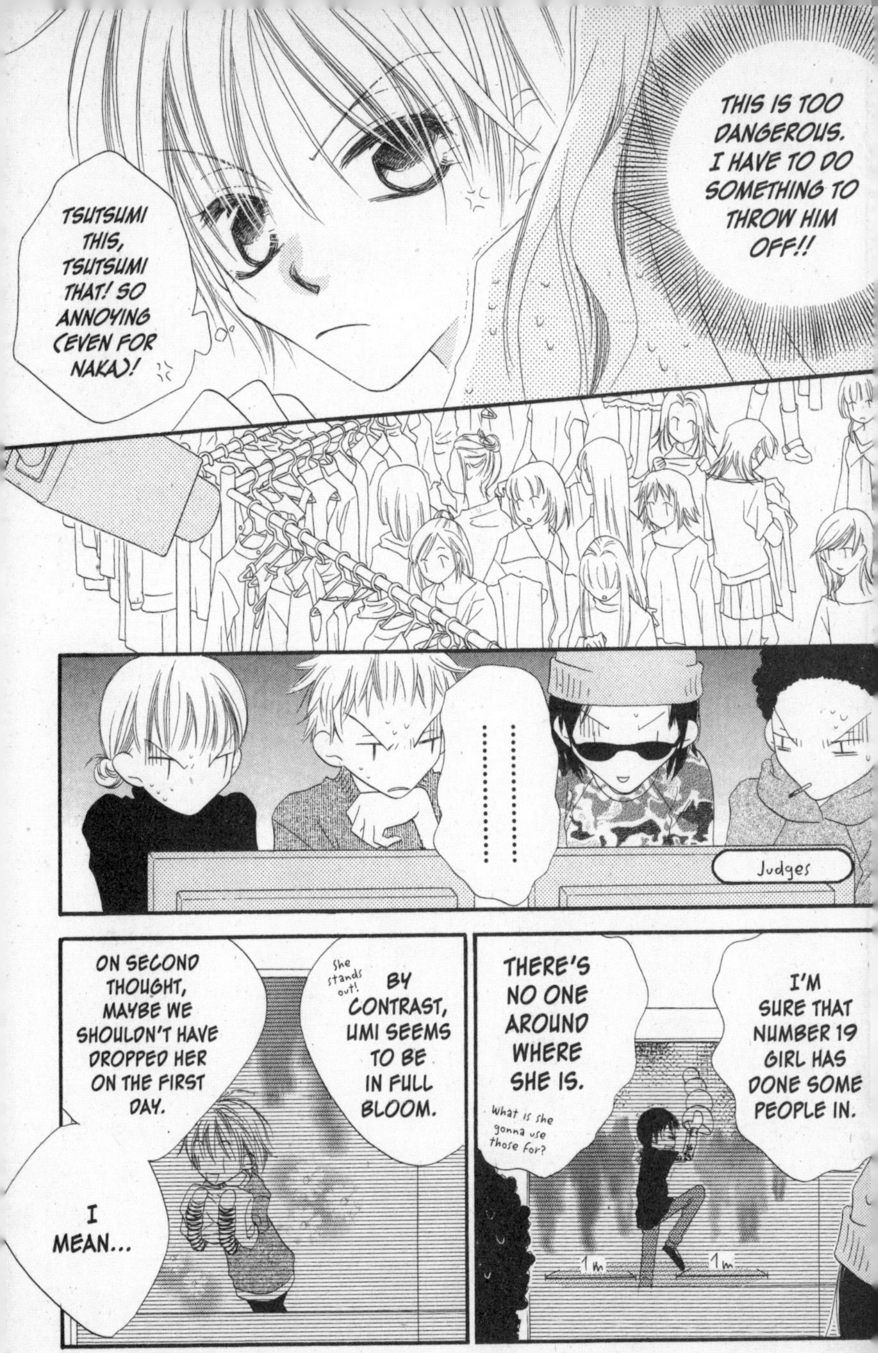
THIS IS TOO DANGEROUS. I HAVE TO DO SOMETHING TO THROW HIM OFF!!
TSUTSUMI THIS, TSUTSUMI THAT! SO ANNOYING (EVEN FOR NAKA)!
......
Judges
I'M SURE THAT NUMBER 19 GIRL HAS DONE SOME PEOPLE IN.
THERE'S NO ONE AROUND WHERE SHE IS.
What is she gonna use those for?
1m
1m
BY CONTRAST, UMI SEEMS TO BE IN FULL BLOOM.
She stands out!
ON SECOND THOUGHT, MAYBE WE SHOULDN'T HAVE DROPPED HER ON THE FIRST DAY.
I MEAN...

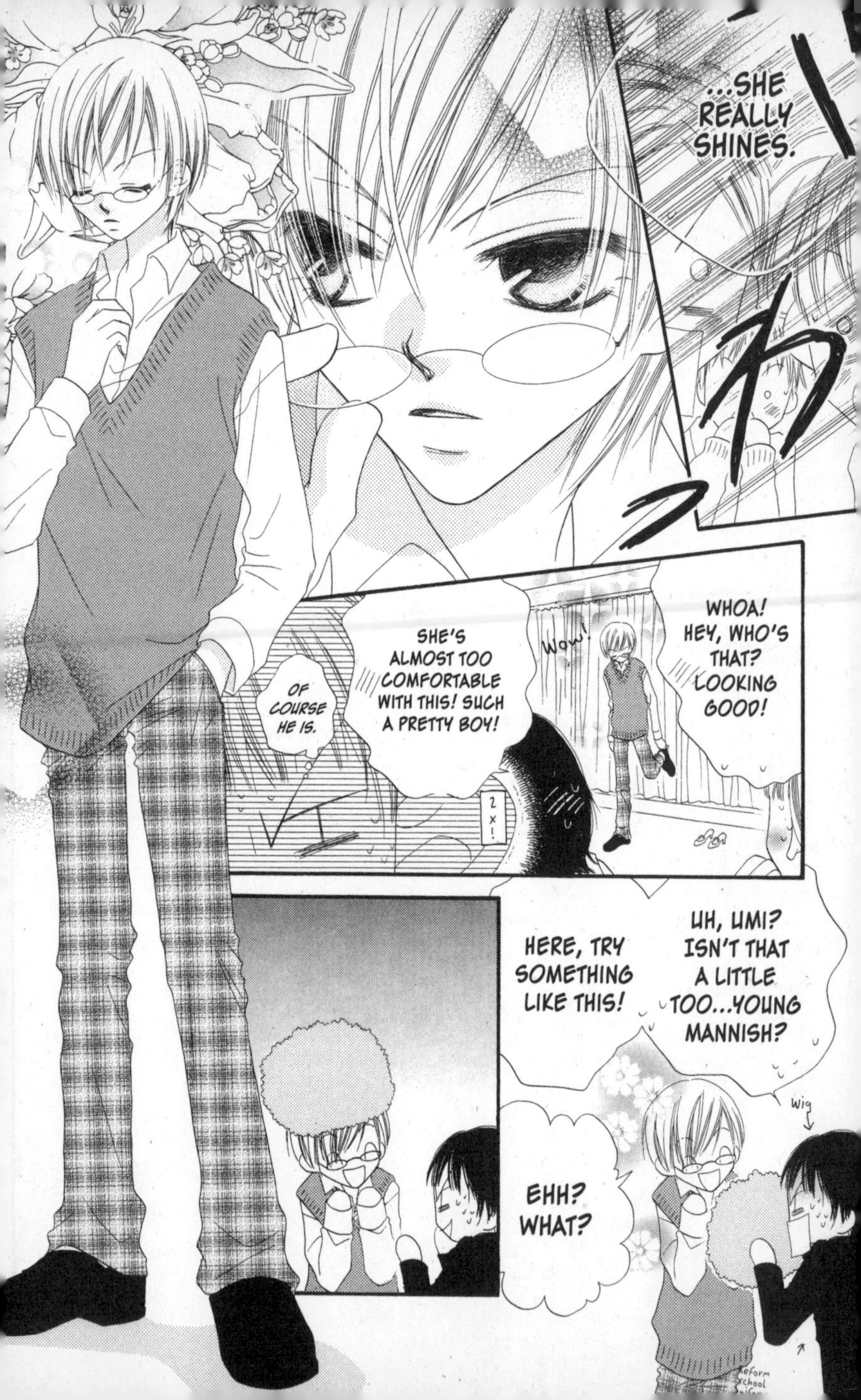
...SHE REALLY SHINES.
わっ
WHOA! HEY, WHO'S THAT? LOOKING GOOD!
Wow!
SHE'S ALMOST TOO COMFORTABLE WITH THIS! SUCH A PRETTY BOY!
2x!
OF COURSE HE IS.
UH, UMI? ISN'T THAT A LITTLE TOO...YOUNG MANNISH?
HERE, TRY SOMETHING LIKE THIS!
Wig
EHH? WHAT?

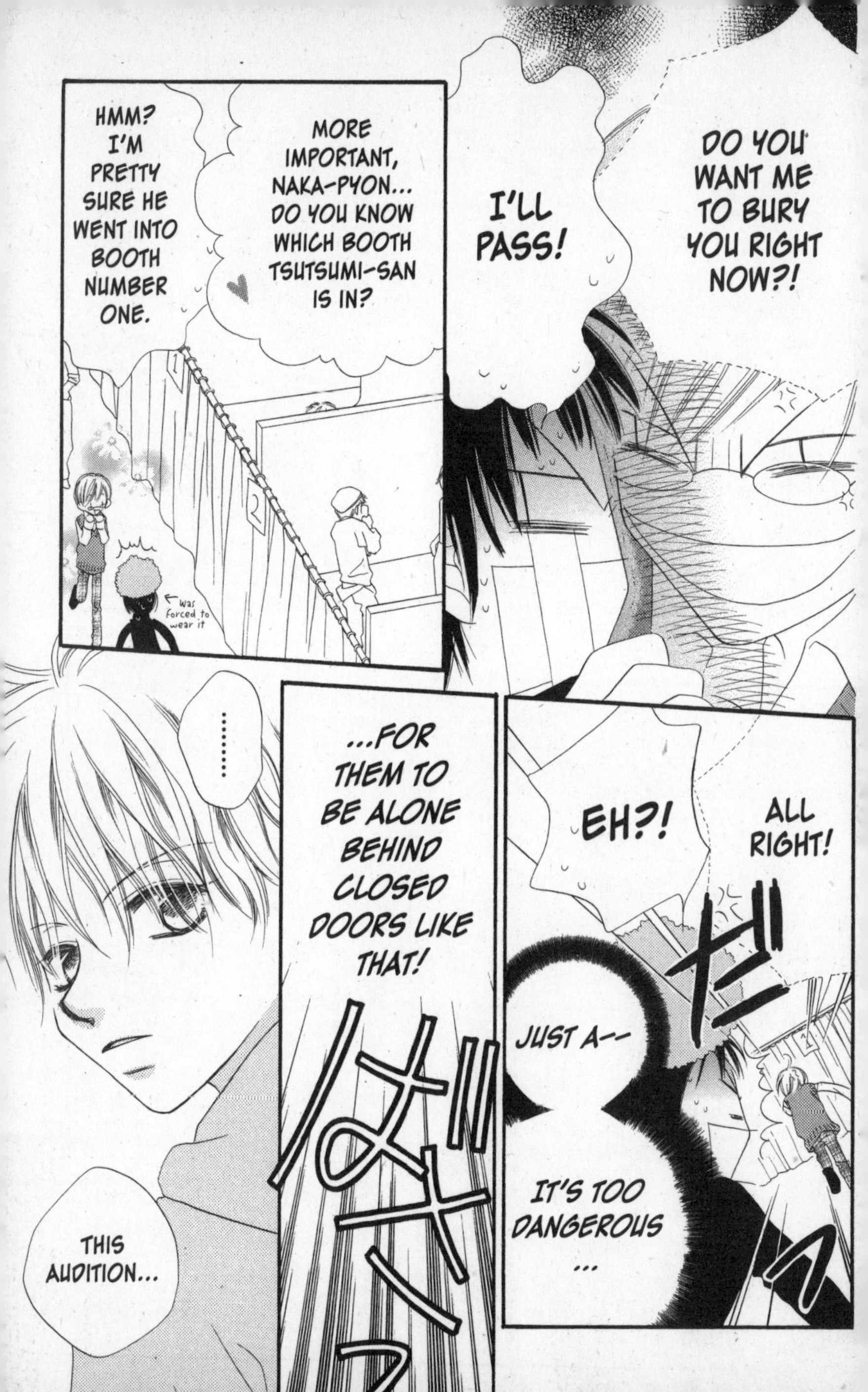
DO YOU WANT ME TO BURY YOU RIGHT NOW?!
I'LL PASS!
MORE IMPORTANT, NAKA-PYON... DO YOU KNOW WHICH BOOTH TSUTSUMI-SAN IS IN?
HMM? I'M PRETTY SURE HE WENT INTO BOOTH NUMBER ONE.
← was forced to wear it
ALL RIGHT!
EH?!
JUST A--
IT'S TOO DANGEROUS ...
...FOR THEM TO BE ALONE BEHIND CLOSED DOORS LIKE THAT!
......
THIS AUDITION...

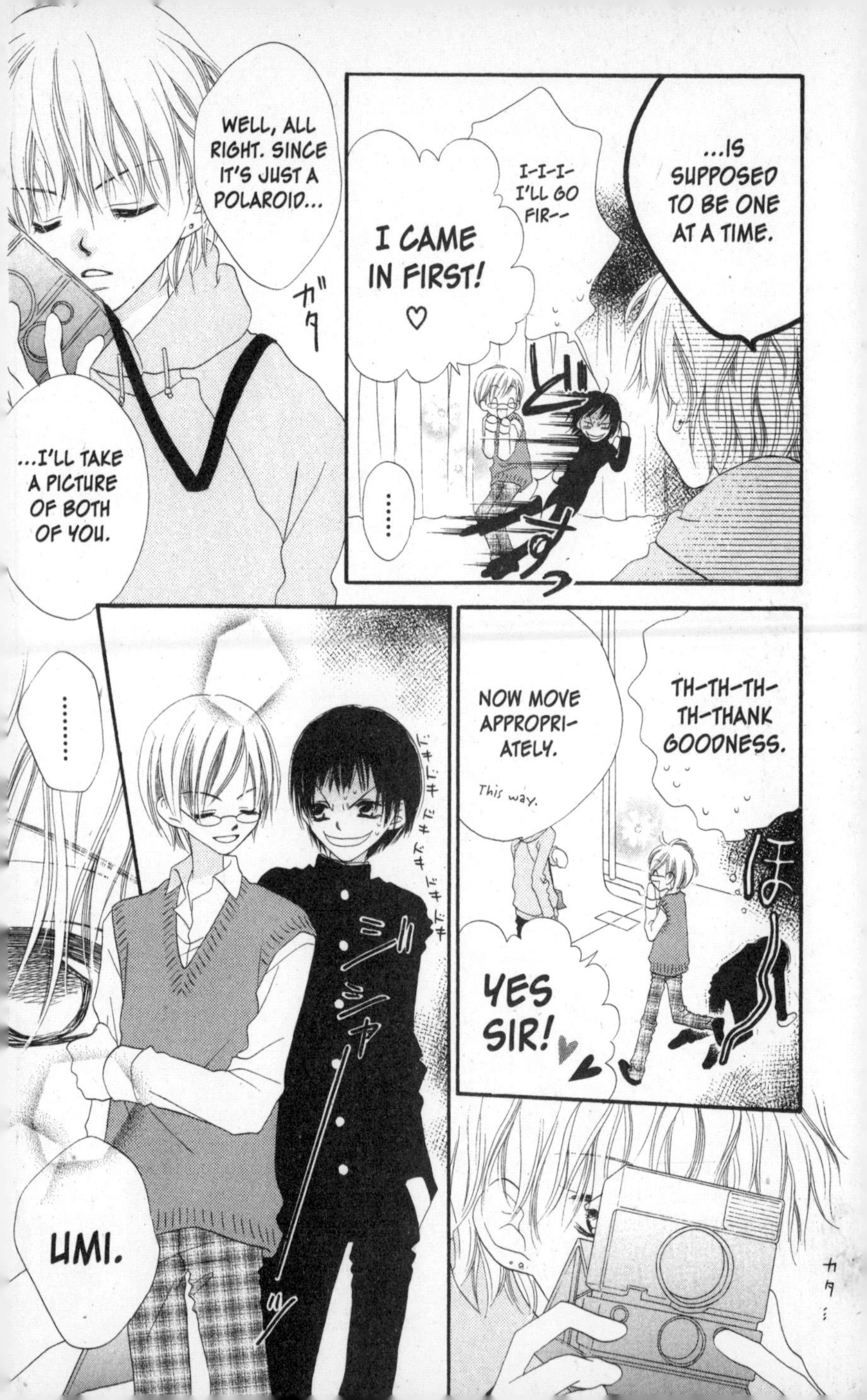
...IS SUPPOSED TO BE ONE AT A TIME.
I-I-I- I'LL GO FIR--
I CAME IN FIRST! ♡
......
WELL, ALL RIGHT. SINCE IT'S JUST A POLAROID...
ガタ
...I'LL TAKE A PICTURE OF BOTH OF YOU.
TH-TH-TH-TH-THANK GOODNESS.
NOW MOVE APPROPRI-ATELY.
This way.
YES SIR! ♥
カタ…
......
UMI.

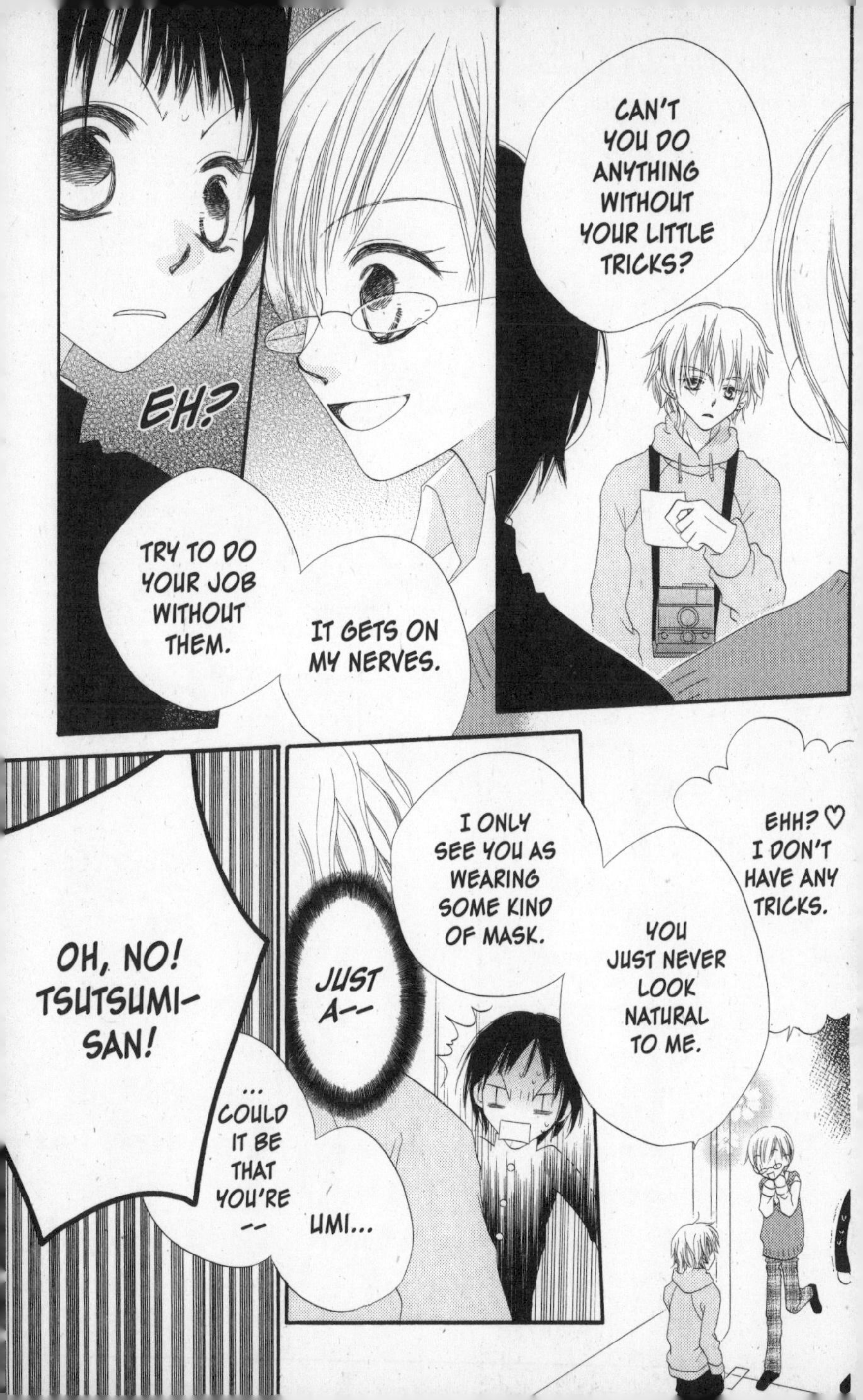

CAN'T YOU DO ANYTHING WITHOUT YOUR LITTLE TRICKS?
EH?
TRY TO DO YOUR JOB WITHOUT THEM.
IT GETS ON MY NERVES.
EHH? ♡ I DON'T HAVE ANY TRICKS.
I ONLY SEE YOU AS WEARING SOME KIND OF MASK.
YOU JUST NEVER LOOK NATURAL TO ME.
JUST A--
UMI...
OH, NO! TSUTSUMI-SAN!
...COULD IT BE THAT YOU'RE --

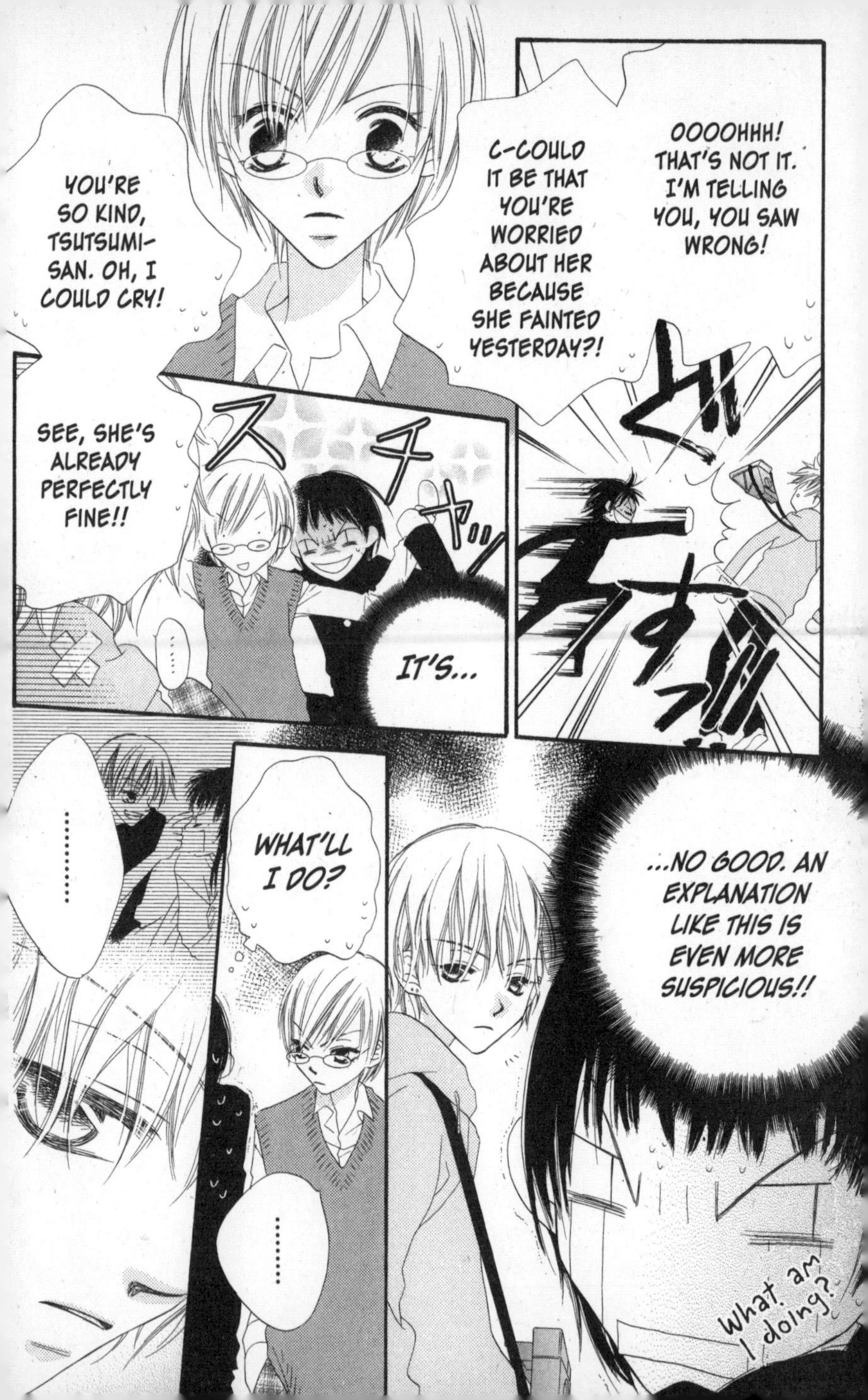

C-COULD IT BE THAT YOU'RE WORRIED ABOUT HER BECAUSE SHE FAINTED YESTERDAY?!
YOU'RE SO KIND, TSUTSUMI-SAN. OH, I COULD CRY!
OOOOHHH! THAT'S NOT IT. I'M TELLING YOU, YOU SAW WRONG!
スチャッ
SEE, SHE'S ALREADY PERFECTLY FINE!!
......
IT'S...
...NO GOOD. AN EXPLANATION LIKE THIS IS EVEN MORE SUSPICIOUS!!
What am I doing?
WHAT'LL I DO?
......
....

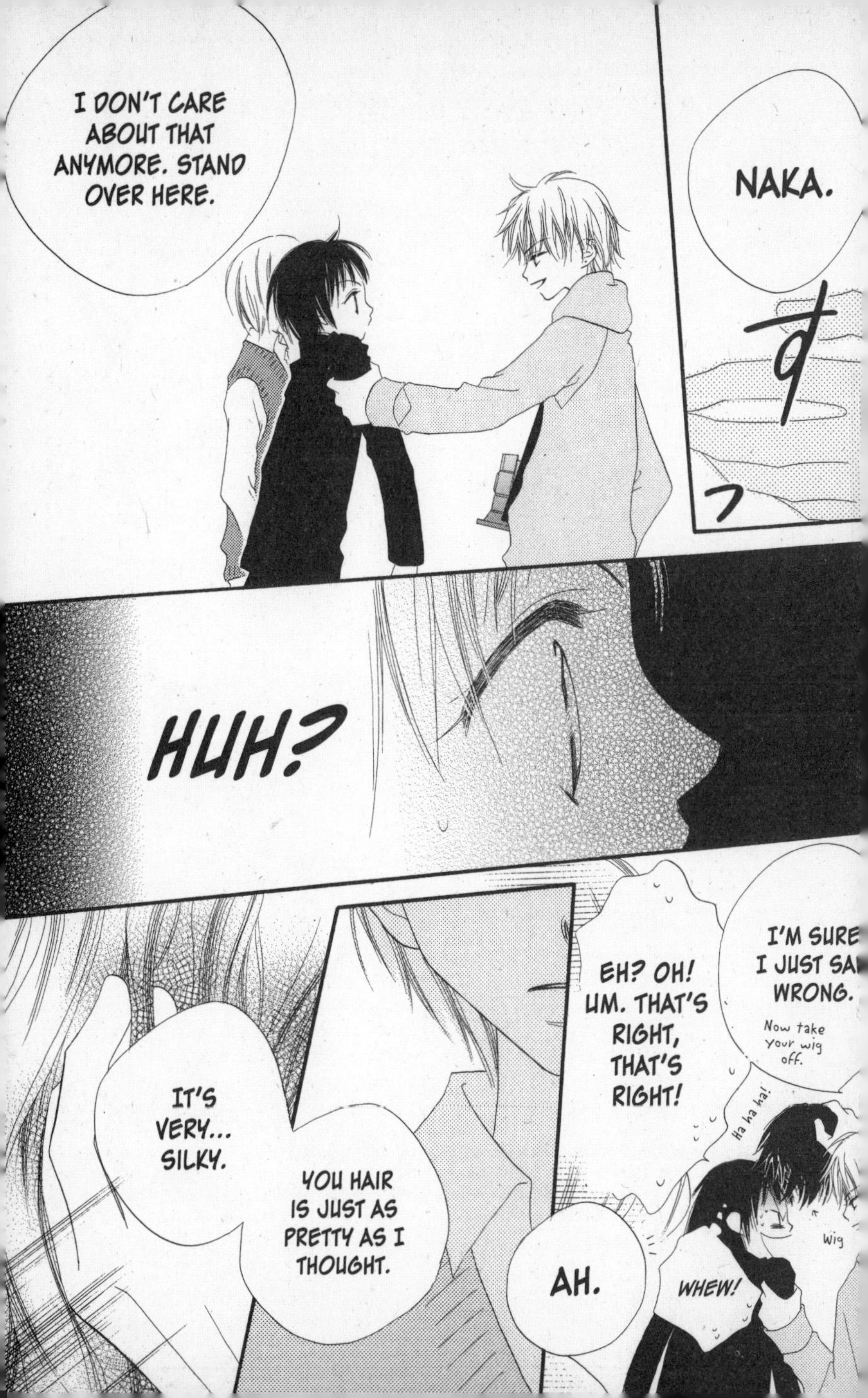
NAKA.
す
っ
I DON'T CARE ABOUT THAT ANYMORE. STAND OVER HERE.
HUH?
I'M SURE I JUST SA WRONG.
Now take your wig off.
EH? OH! UM. THAT'S RIGHT, THAT'S RIGHT!
Ha ha ha!
Wig
WHEW!
AH.
IT'S VERY... SILKY.
YOU HAIR IS JUST AS PRETTY AS I THOUGHT.

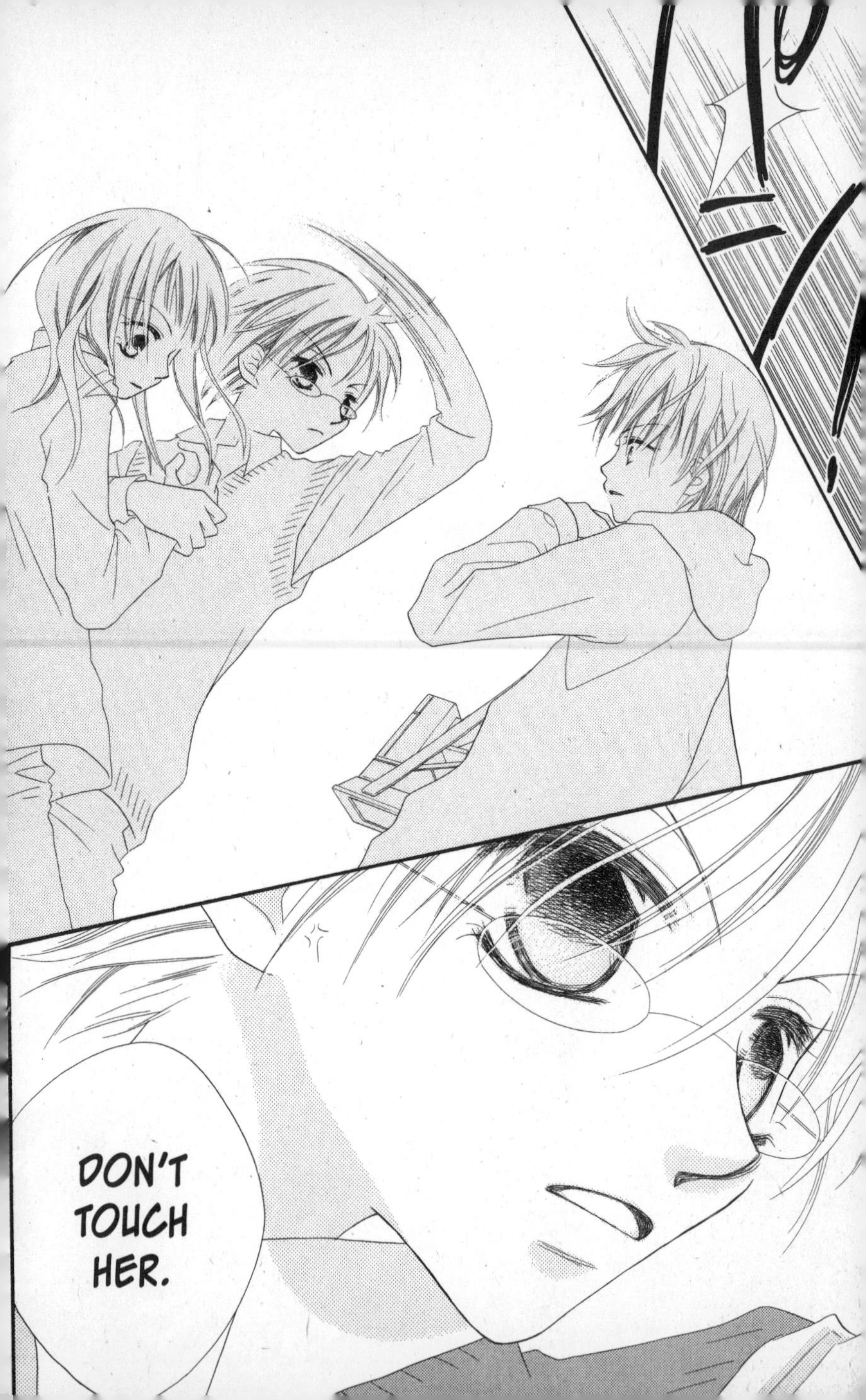
DON'T TOUCH HER.

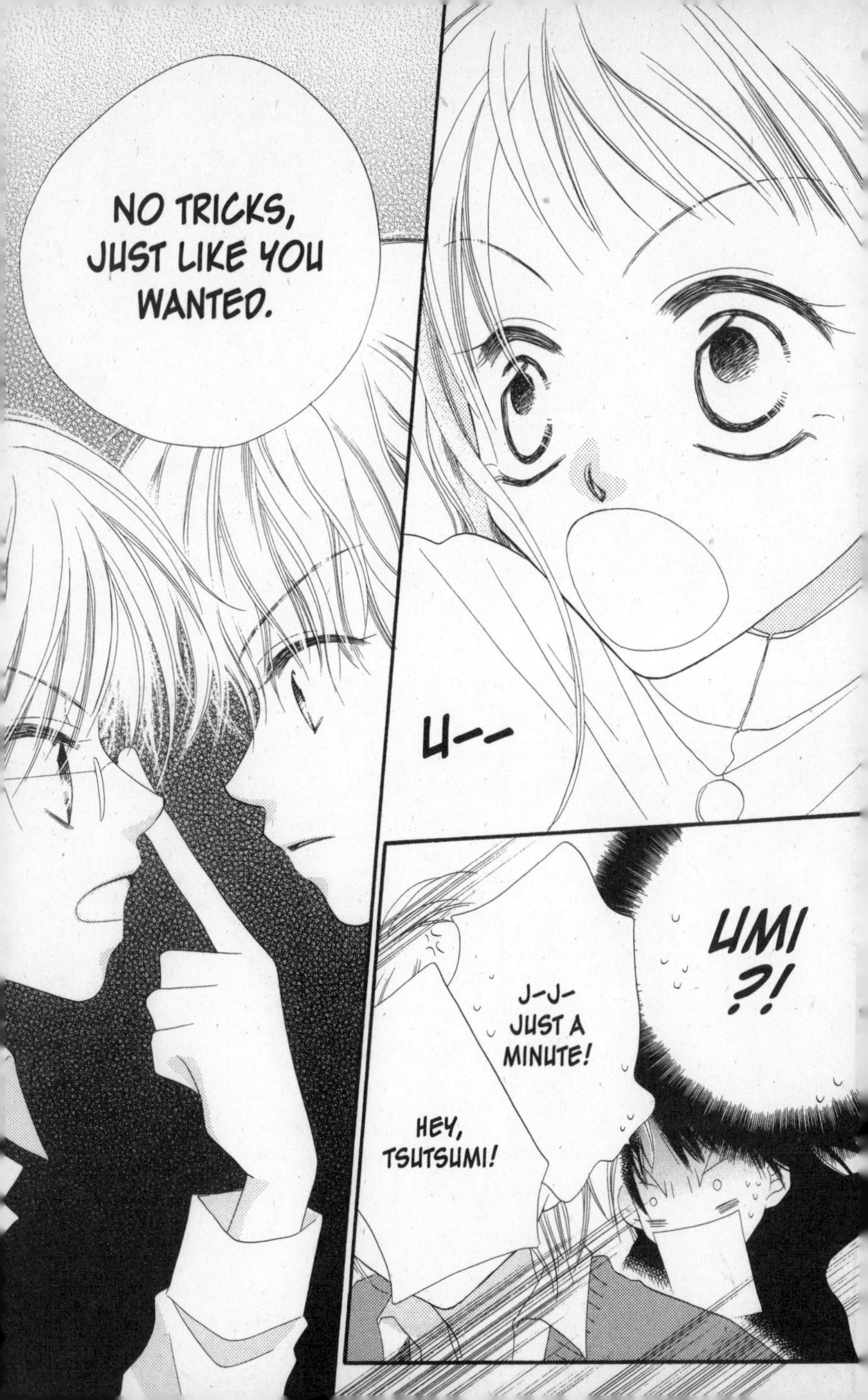
U--
UMI ?!
J-J- JUST A MINUTE!
HEY, TSUTSUMI!
NO TRICKS, JUST LIKE YOU WANTED.

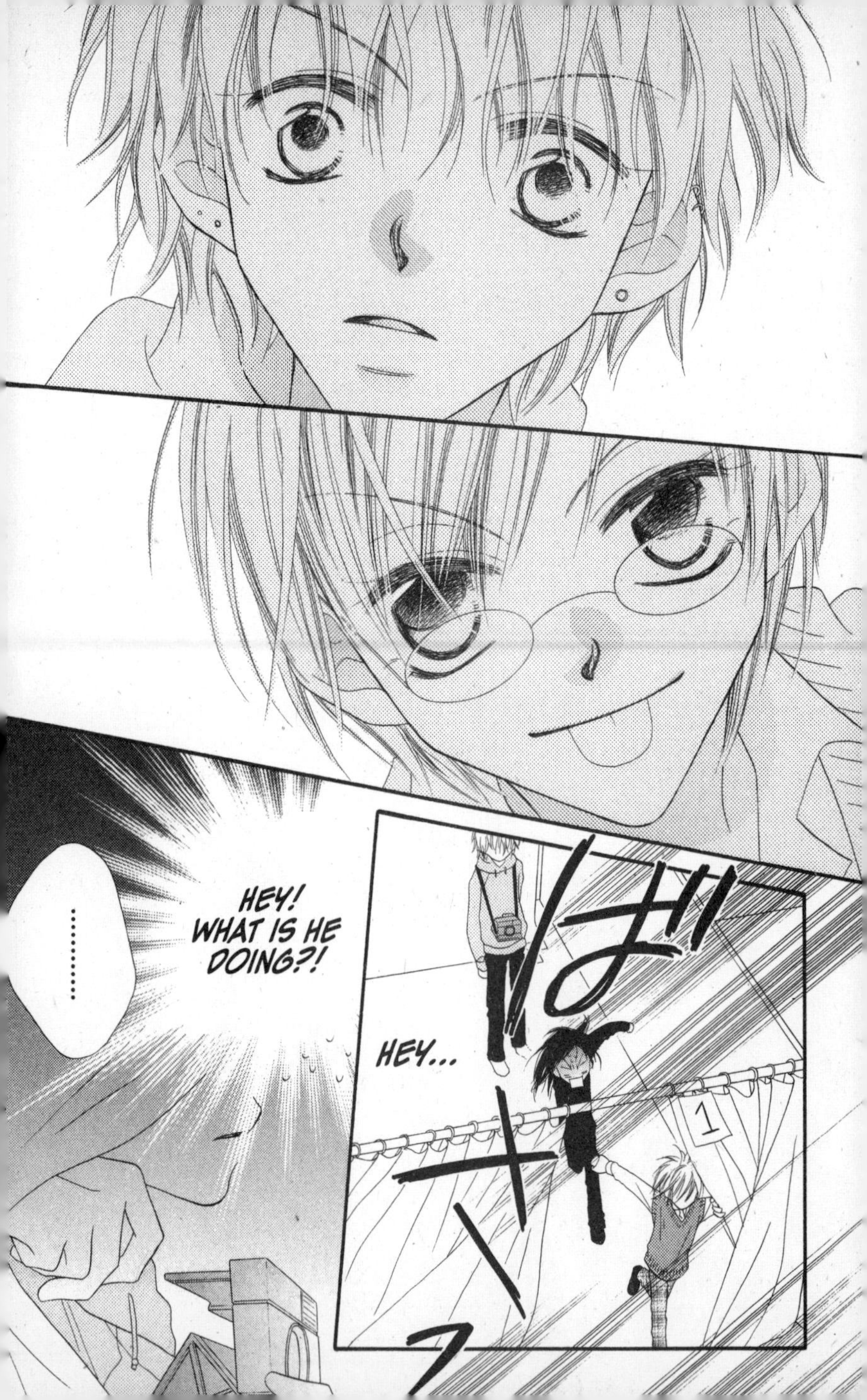
HEY...
HEY! WHAT IS HE DOING?!
......

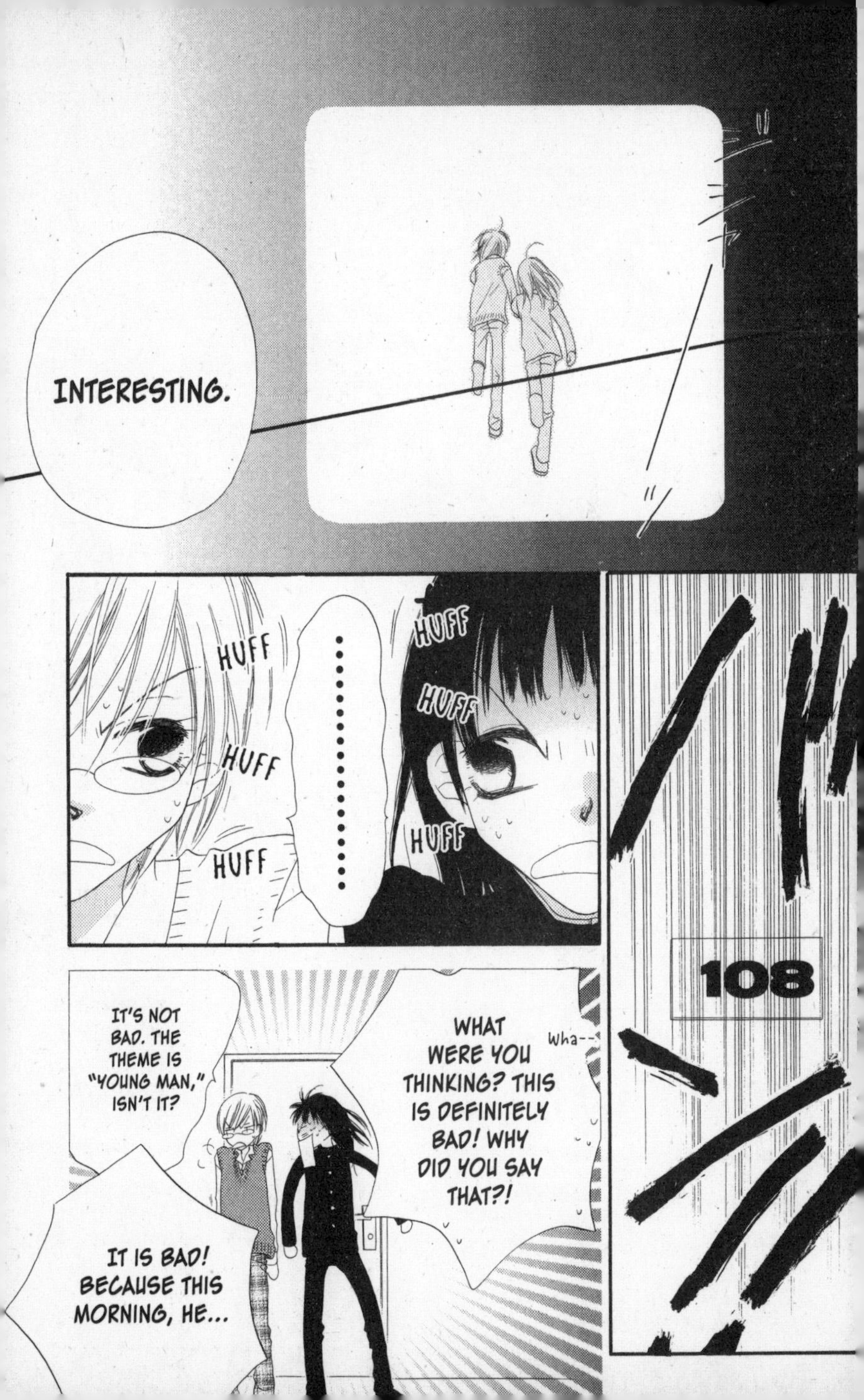
INTERESTING.
108
HUFF
HUFF
HUFF
......
HUFF
HUFF
HUFF
Wha--
WHAT WERE YOU THINKING? THIS IS DEFINITELY BAD! WHY DID YOU SAY THAT?!
IT'S NOT BAD. THE THEME IS "YOUNG MAN," ISN'T IT?
IT IS BAD! BECAUSE THIS MORNING, HE...

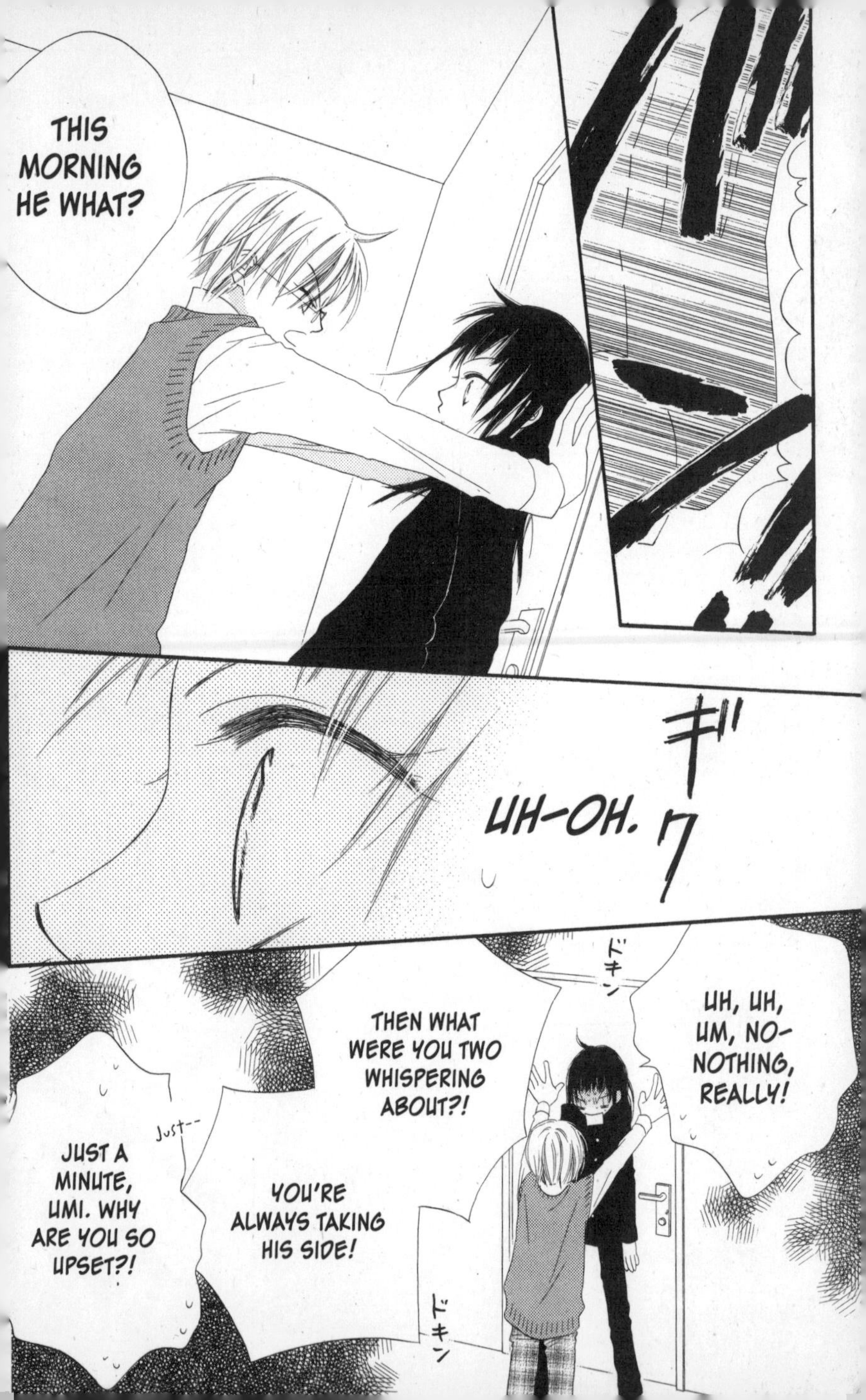
THIS MORNING HE WHAT?
ギク
UH-OH.
UH, UH, UM, NO-NOTHING, REALLY!
ドキン
THEN WHAT WERE YOU TWO WHISPERING ABOUT?!
YOU'RE ALWAYS TAKING HIS SIDE!
Just--
JUST A MINUTE, UMI. WHY ARE YOU SO UPSET?!
ドキン

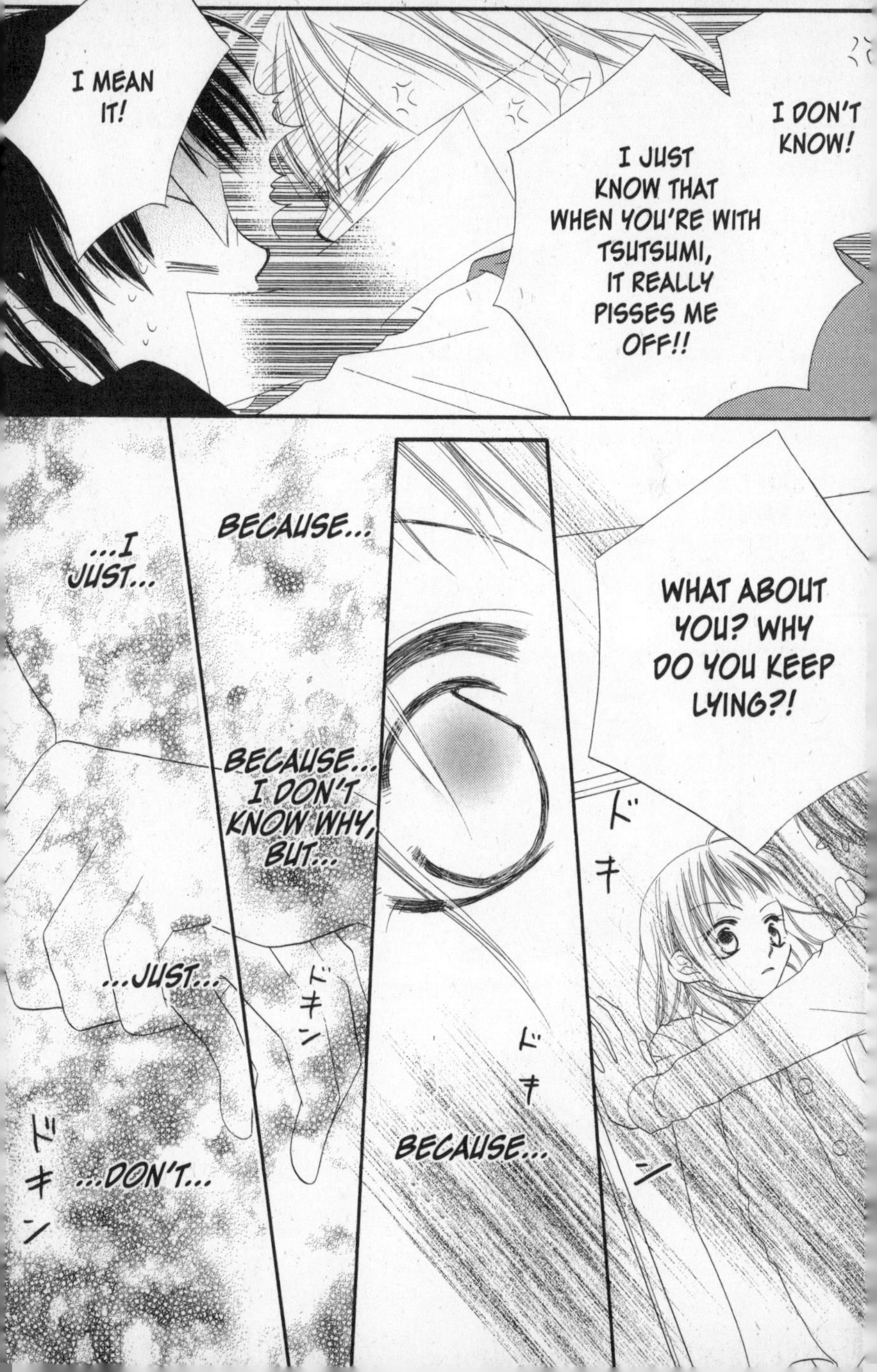
I DON'T KNOW!
I JUST KNOW THAT WHEN YOU'RE WITH TSUTSUMI, IT REALLY PISSES ME OFF!!
I MEAN IT!
WHAT ABOUT YOU? WHY DO YOU KEEP LYING?!
ドキン
ドキ
BECAUSE...
BECAUSE...
BECAUSE... I DON'T KNOW WHY, BUT...
ドキン
...I JUST...
...JUST...
...DON'T...
ドキン

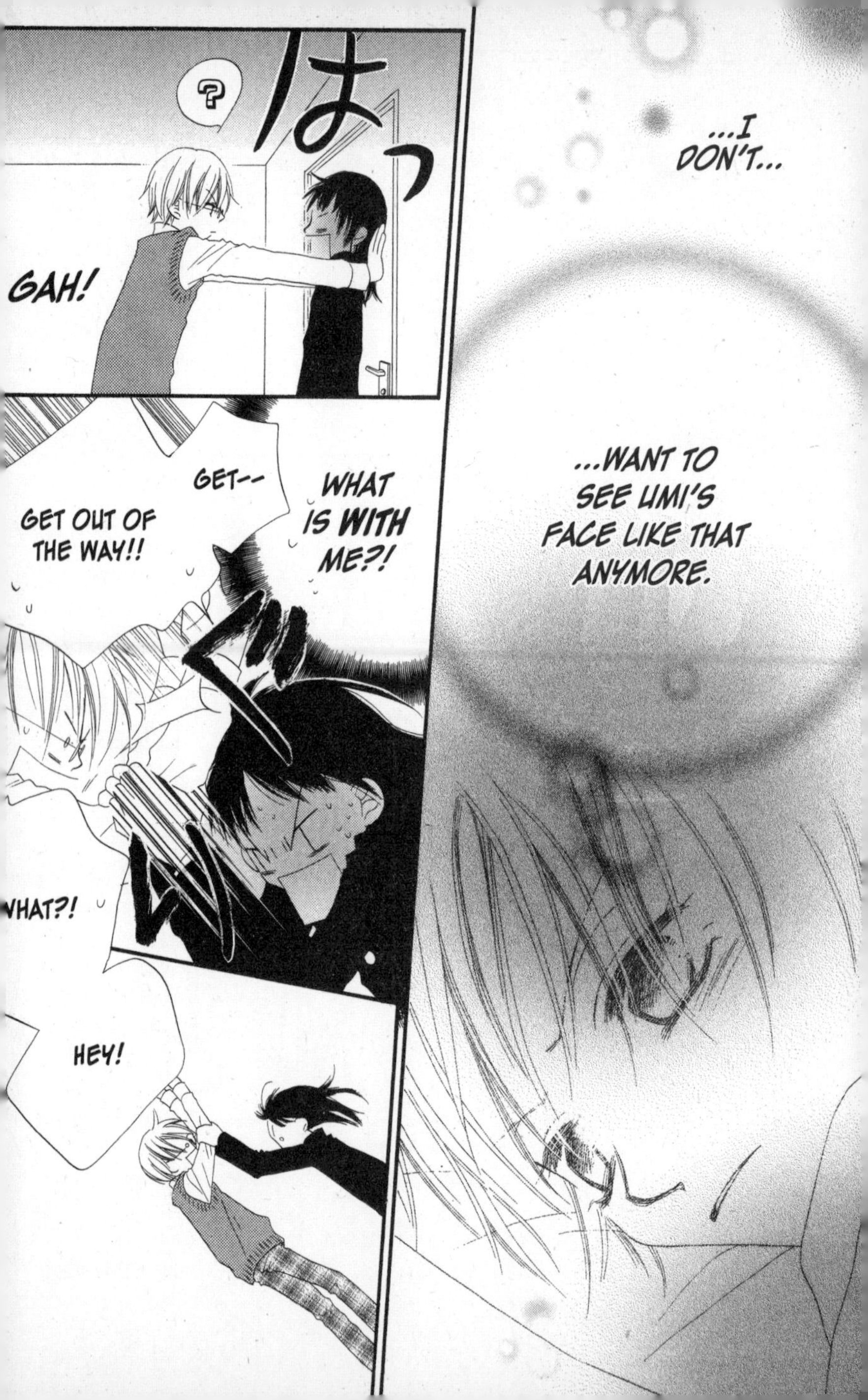
...I DON'T...
...WANT TO SEE UMI'S FACE LIKE THAT ANYMORE.
はっ
?
GAH!
WHAT IS WITH ME?!
GET--
GET OUT OF THE WAY!!
WHAT?!
HEY!

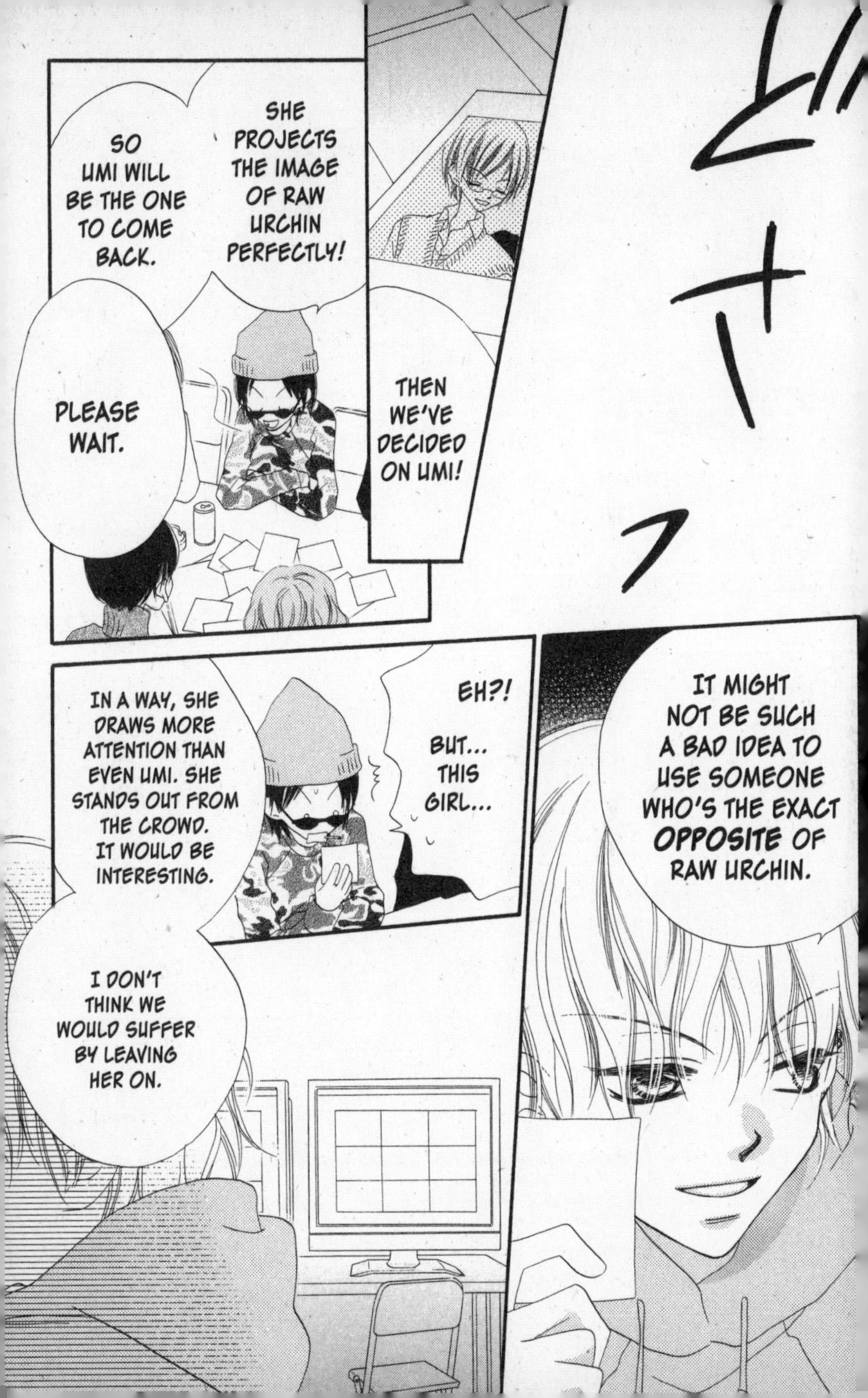
THEN WE'VE DECIDED ON UMI!
SHE PROJECTS THE IMAGE OF RAW URCHIN PERFECTLY!
SO UMI WILL BE THE ONE TO COME BACK.
PLEASE WAIT.
IT MIGHT NOT BE SUCH A BAD IDEA TO USE SOMEONE WHO'S THE EXACT **OPPOSITE** OF RAW URCHIN.
EH?!
BUT... THIS GIRL...
IN A WAY, SHE DRAWS MORE ATTENTION THAN EVEN UMI. SHE STANDS OUT FROM THE CROWD. IT WOULD BE INTERESTING.
I DON'T THINK WE WOULD SUFFER BY LEAVING HER ON.

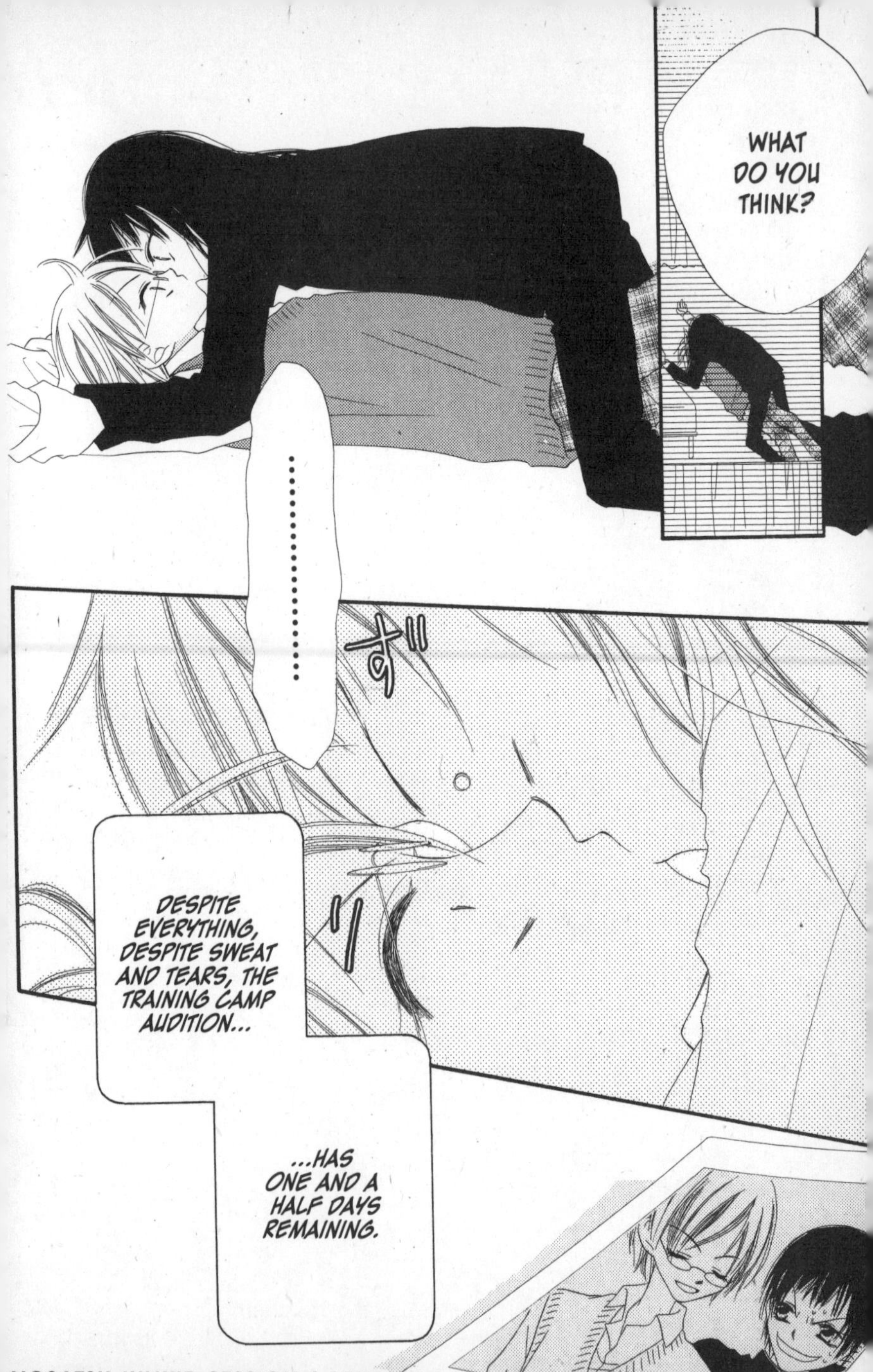
WHAT DO YOU THINK?
....
DESPITE EVERYTHING, DESPITE SWEAT AND TEARS, THE TRAINING CAMP AUDITION...
...HAS ONE AND A HALF DAYS REMAINING.

NOSATSU JUNKIE, SESSION 4 / END

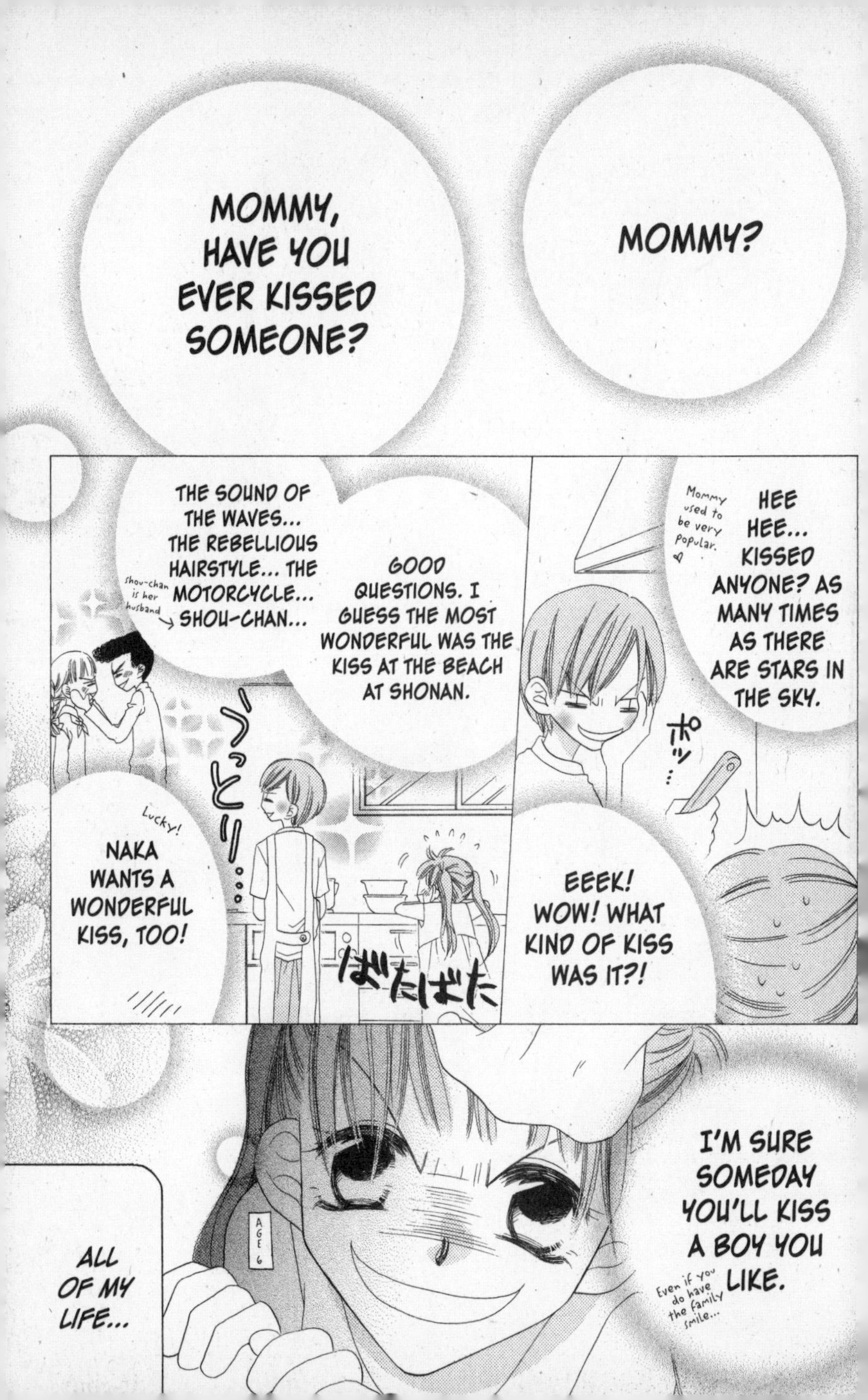
MOMMY?
MOMMY, HAVE YOU EVER KISSED SOMEONE?
HEE HEE... KISSED ANYONE? AS MANY TIMES AS THERE ARE STARS IN THE SKY.
Mommy used to be very popular. ♥
ポッ…
EEEK! WOW! WHAT KIND OF KISS WAS IT?!
GOOD QUESTIONS. I GUESS THE MOST WONDERFUL WAS THE KISS AT THE BEACH AT SHONAN.
THE SOUND OF THE WAVES... THE REBELLIOUS HAIRSTYLE... THE MOTORCYCLE... SHOU-CHAN...
Shou-chan is her husband
うっとり…
ばたばた
NAKA WANTS A WONDERFUL KISS, TOO!
Lucky!
I'M SURE SOMEDAY YOU'LL KISS A BOY YOU LIKE.
Even if you do have the family smile...
AGE 6
ALL OF MY LIFE...

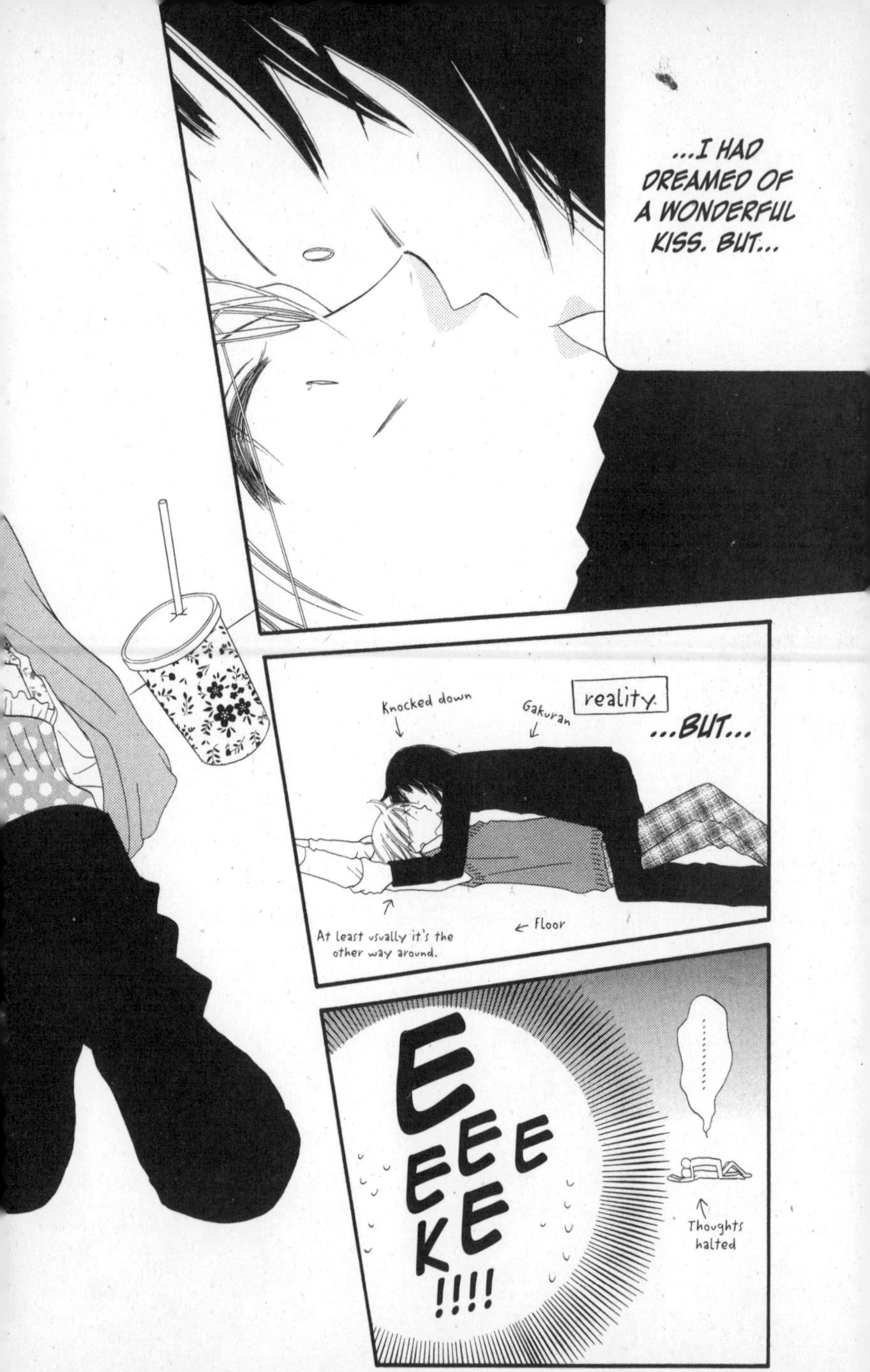
...I HAD DREAMED OF A WONDERFUL KISS. BUT...
reality
...BUT...
Gakuran
Knocked down
Floor
At least usually it's the other way around.
......
Thoughts halted
EEEEEK!!!!

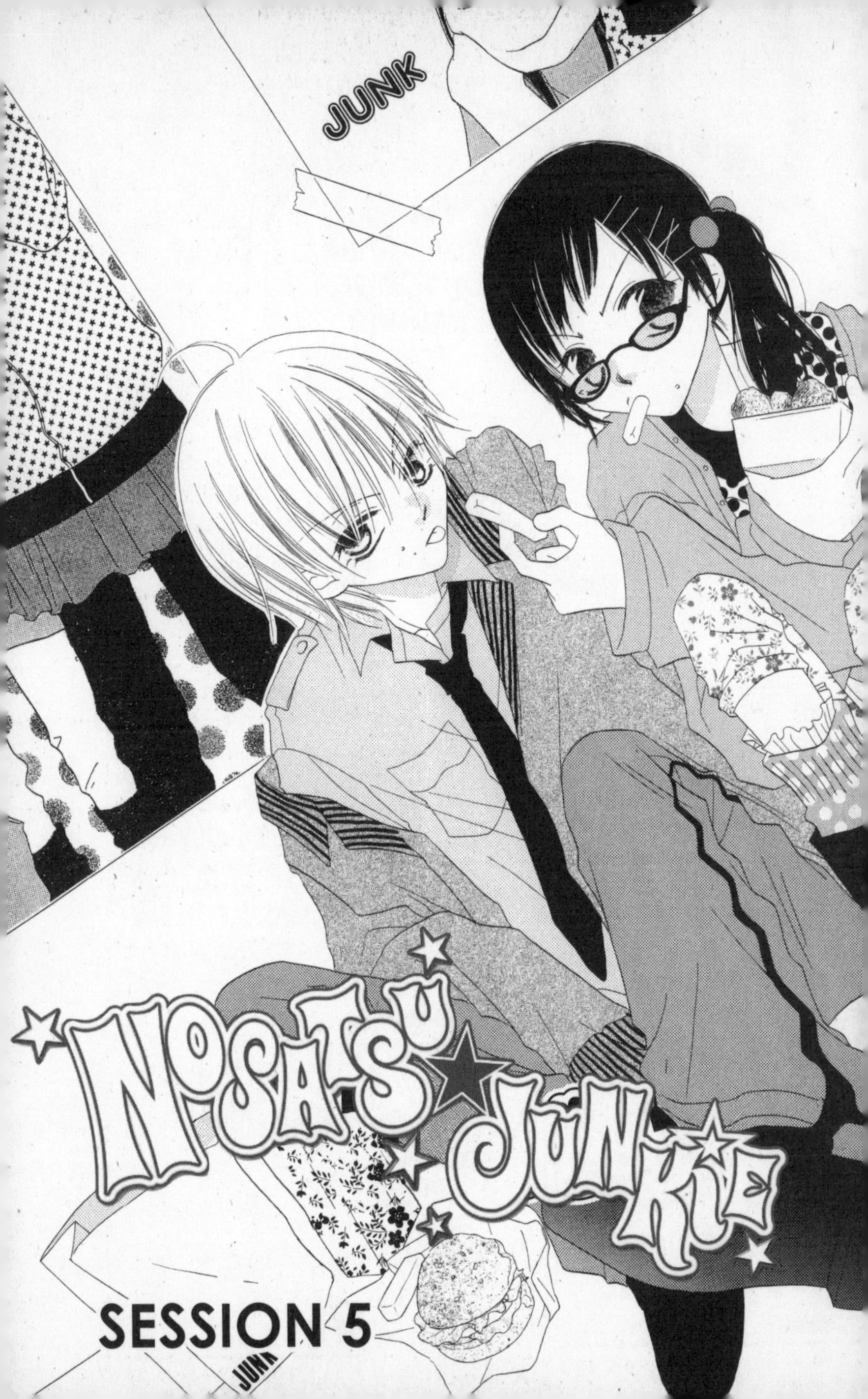
JUNK
NOSATSU JUNKIE
SESSION 5
JUNK

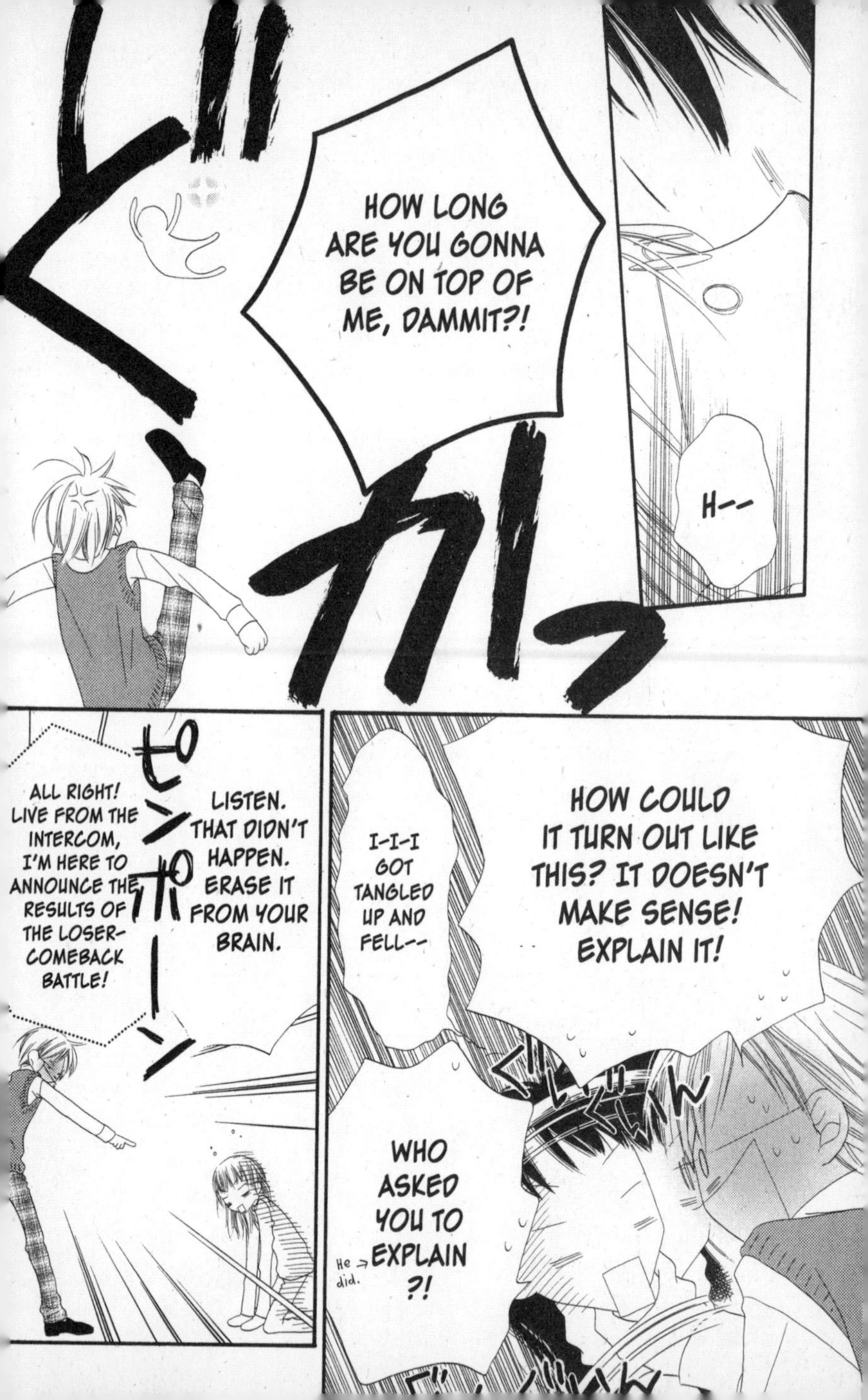
H--
HOW LONG ARE YOU GONNA BE ON TOP OF ME, DAMMIT?!
HOW COULD IT TURN OUT LIKE THIS? IT DOESN'T MAKE SENSE! EXPLAIN IT!
I-I-I GOT TANGLED UP AND FELL--
WHO ASKED YOU TO EXPLAIN?!
He → did.
LISTEN. THAT DIDN'T HAPPEN. ERASE IT FROM YOUR BRAIN.
ALL RIGHT! LIVE FROM THE INTERCOM, I'M HERE TO ANNOUNCE THE RESULTS OF THE LOSER-COMEBACK BATTLE!

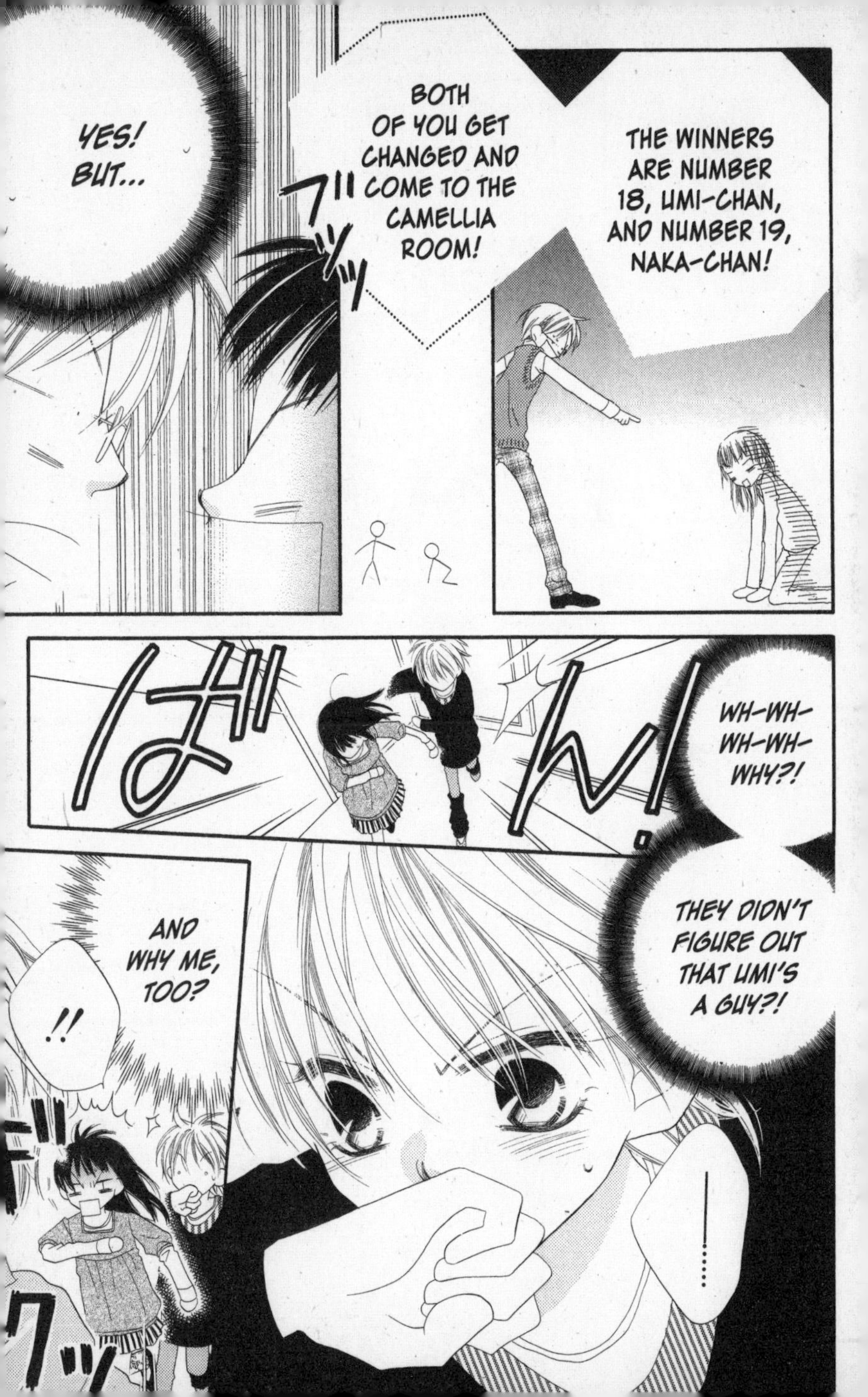
THE WINNERS ARE NUMBER 18, UMI-CHAN, AND NUMBER 19, NAKA-CHAN!
BOTH OF YOU GET CHANGED AND COME TO THE CAMELLIA ROOM!
YES! BUT...
ばん!
WH-WH-WH-WH-WHY?!
THEY DIDN'T FIGURE OUT THAT UMI'S A GUY?!
......
AND WHY ME, TOO?
!!

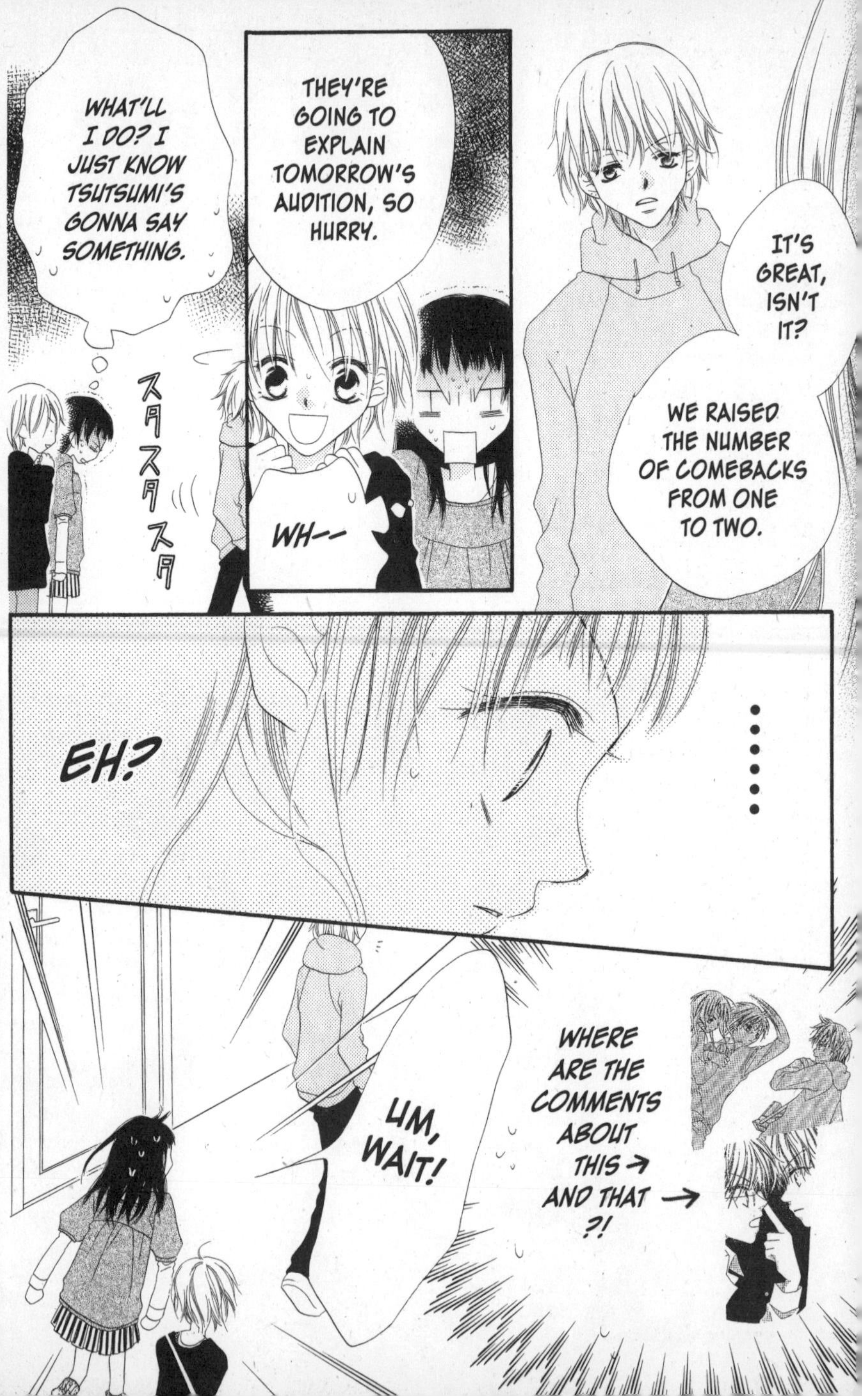
IT'S GREAT, ISN'T IT?
WE RAISED THE NUMBER OF COMEBACKS FROM ONE TO TWO.
THEY'RE GOING TO EXPLAIN TOMORROW'S AUDITION, SO HURRY.
WH--
WHAT'LL I DO? I JUST KNOW TSUTSUMI'S GONNA SAY SOMETHING.
スタスタスタ
......
EH?
WHERE ARE THE COMMENTS ABOUT THIS → AND THAT → ?!
UM, WAIT!

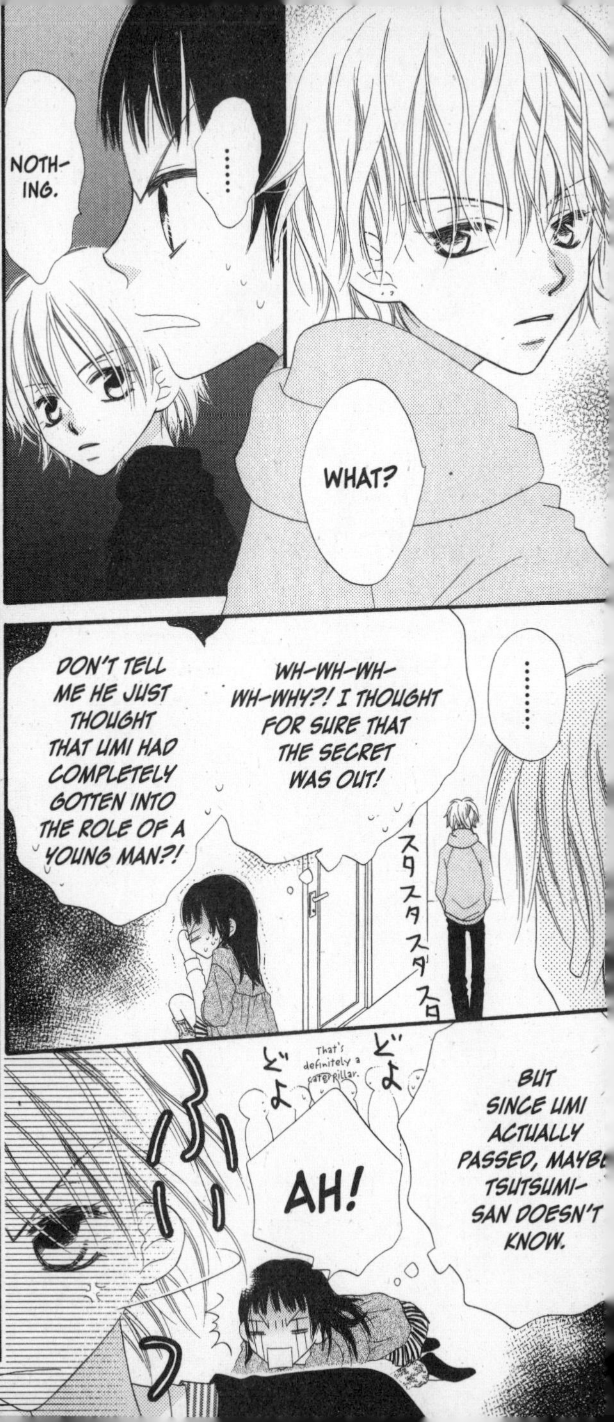
WHAT?
......
NOTH-ING.
......
WH-WH-WH-WH-WHY?! I THOUGHT FOR SURE THAT THE SECRET WAS OUT!
DON'T TELL ME HE JUST THOUGHT THAT UMI HAD COMPLETELY GOTTEN INTO THE ROLE OF A YOUNG MAN?!
スタスタスタスタ
BUT SINCE UMI ACTUALLY PASSED, MAYB TSUTSUMI-SAN DOESN'T KNOW.
どよ
どよ
That's definitely a caterpillar.
AH!

5

This is my last chat space. Thank you very much for reading my chat columns, even though they have no sense of unity. Sheesh, I'm so nervous...not only am I babbling, I'm revealing my true idiocy. Sorry!

I'm not very good, or experienced, and I am still learning...but please continue to read my work!

"Nosatsu" is published in Hana to Yume magazine, so if you like this, please check out the rest of the magazine, too!

And if you could write and let me know what you think of it, I would be so happy, I'd dance for joy! Though I'll probably get a lot of complaints that my handwriting is too sloppy. People always say they can't read it...which is truly heartbreaking.

Address:
Ryoko Fukuyama
Author, Nosatsu Junkie
c/o TOKYOPOP Editorial
5900 Wilshire Blvd., Suite 2000Los Angeles, CA 90036

Well, that's it for now. I'll do my best so we can meet again! See you soon, I hope!

With love,
Ryoko Fukuyama

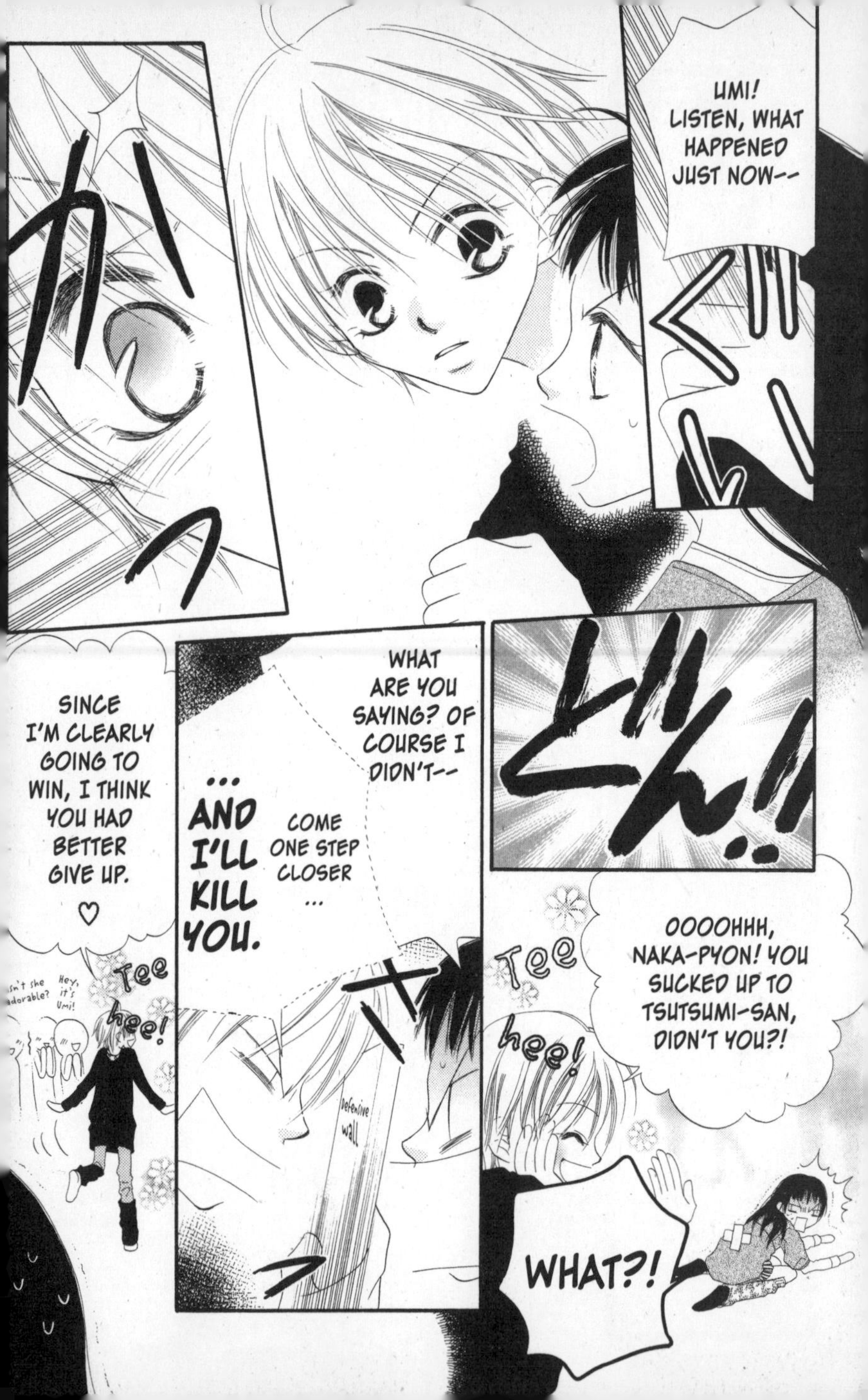
UMI! LISTEN, WHAT HAPPENED JUST NOW--
WHAT ARE YOU SAYING? OF COURSE I DIDN'T--
COME ONE STEP CLOSER ...
... AND I'LL KILL YOU.
defensive wall
OOOOHHH, NAKA-PYON! YOU SUCKED UP TO TSUTSUMI-SAN, DIDN'T YOU?!
Tee hee!
WHAT?!
SINCE I'M CLEARLY GOING TO WIN, I THINK YOU HAD BETTER GIVE UP. ♡
Tee hee!
Hey, it's Umi!
sn't she adorable?

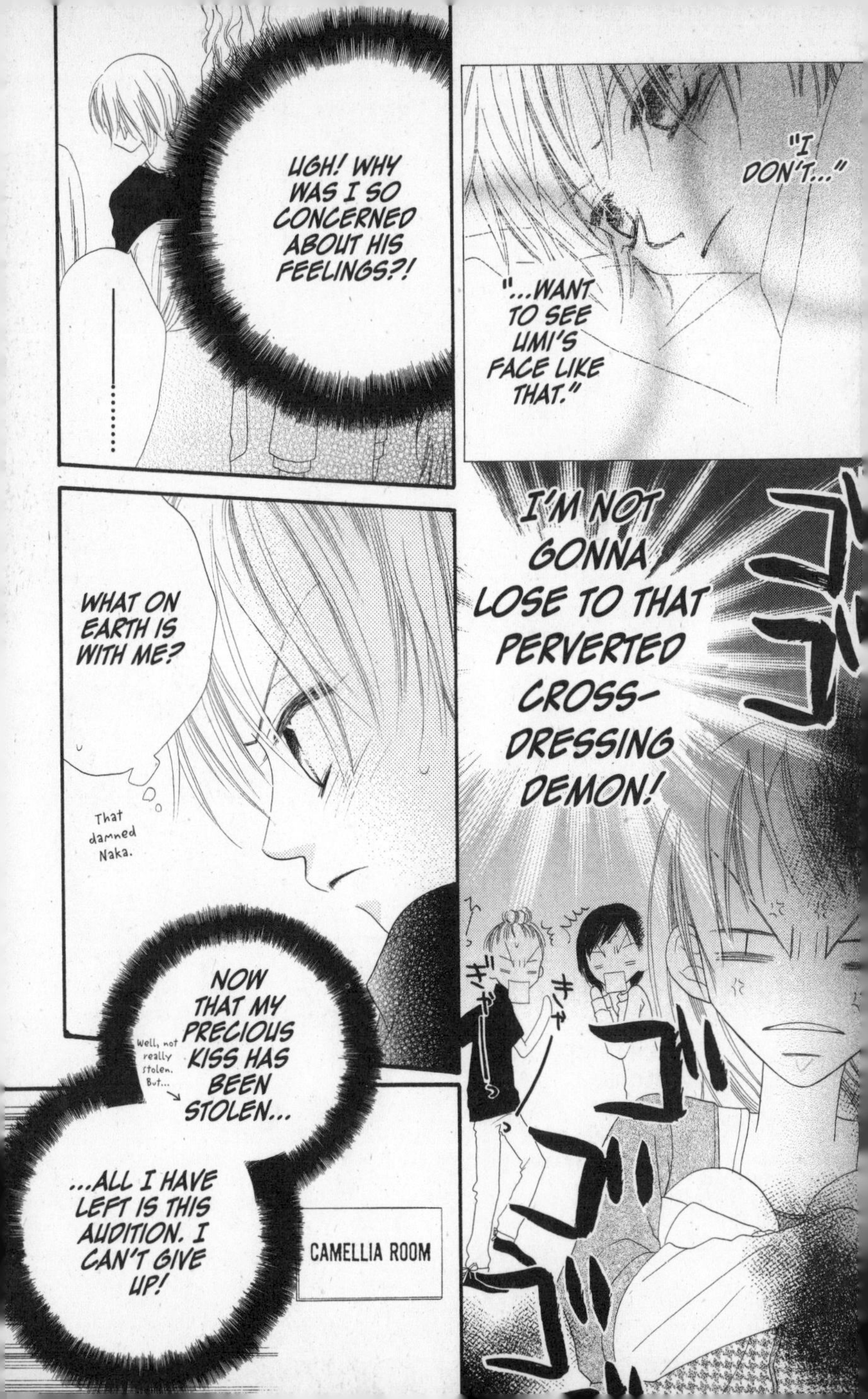
"I DON'T..."
"...WANT TO SEE UMI'S FACE LIKE THAT."
UGH! WHY WAS I SO CONCERNED ABOUT HIS FEELINGS?!
I'M NOT GONNA LOSE TO THAT PERVERTED CROSS-DRESSING DEMON!
WHAT ON EARTH IS WITH ME?
That damned Naka.
NOW THAT MY PRECIOUS KISS HAS BEEN STOLEN...
Well, not really stolen. But...
...ALL I HAVE LEFT IS THIS AUDITION. I CAN'T GIVE UP!
CAMELLIA ROOM

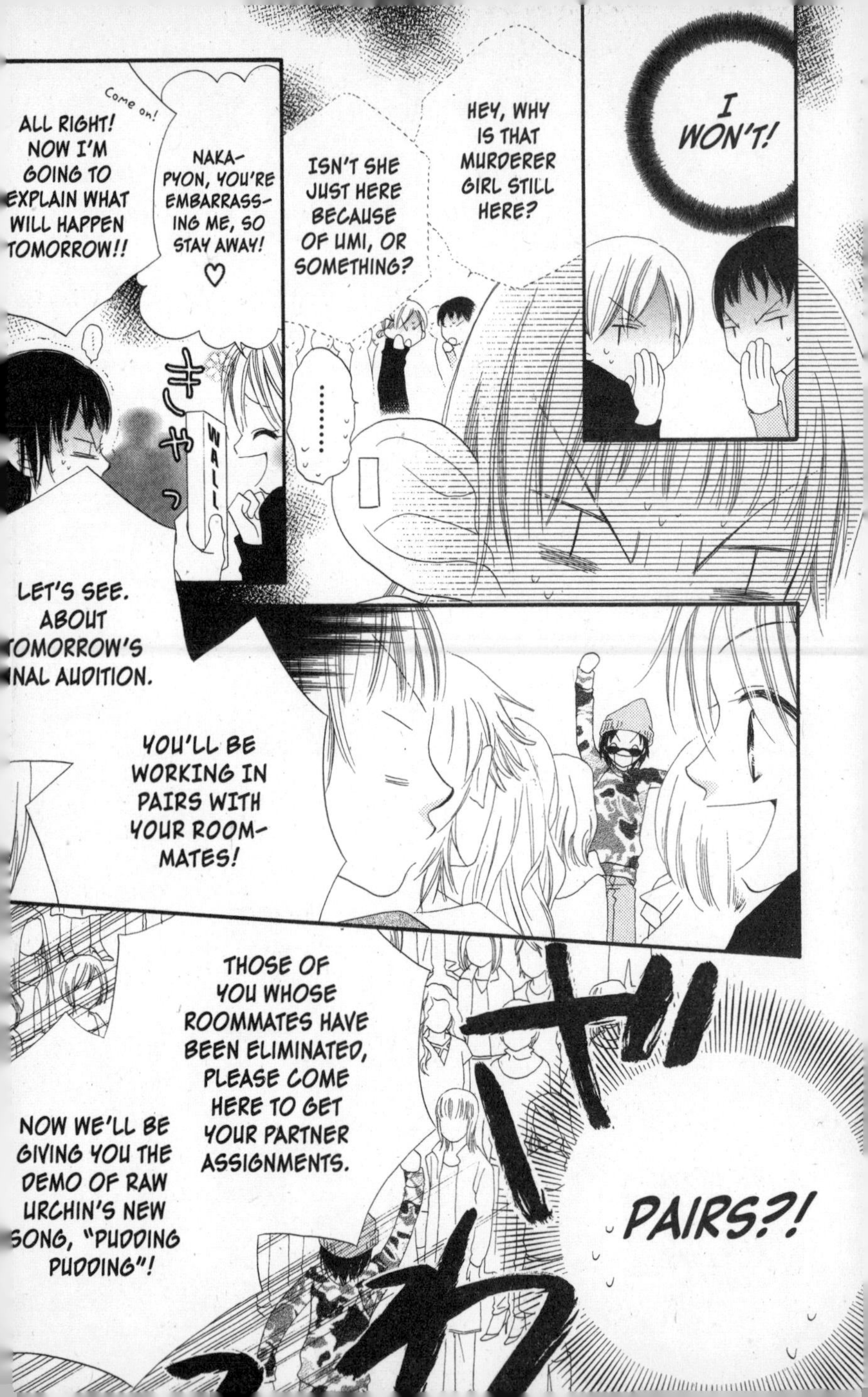
I WON'T!
HEY, WHY IS THAT MURDERER GIRL STILL HERE?
ISN'T SHE JUST HERE BECAUSE OF UMI, OR SOMETHING?
NAKA-PYON, YOU'RE EMBARRASSING ME, SO STAY AWAY! ♡
Come on!
ALL RIGHT! NOW I'M GOING TO EXPLAIN WHAT WILL HAPPEN TOMORROW!!
WALL
......
!
LET'S SEE. ABOUT TOMORROW'S NAL AUDITION.
YOU'LL BE WORKING IN PAIRS WITH YOUR ROOMMATES!
PAIRS?!
THOSE OF YOU WHOSE ROOMMATES HAVE BEEN ELIMINATED, PLEASE COME HERE TO GET YOUR PARTNER ASSIGNMENTS.
NOW WE'LL BE GIVING YOU THE DEMO OF RAW URCHIN'S NEW SONG, "PUDDING PUDDING"!

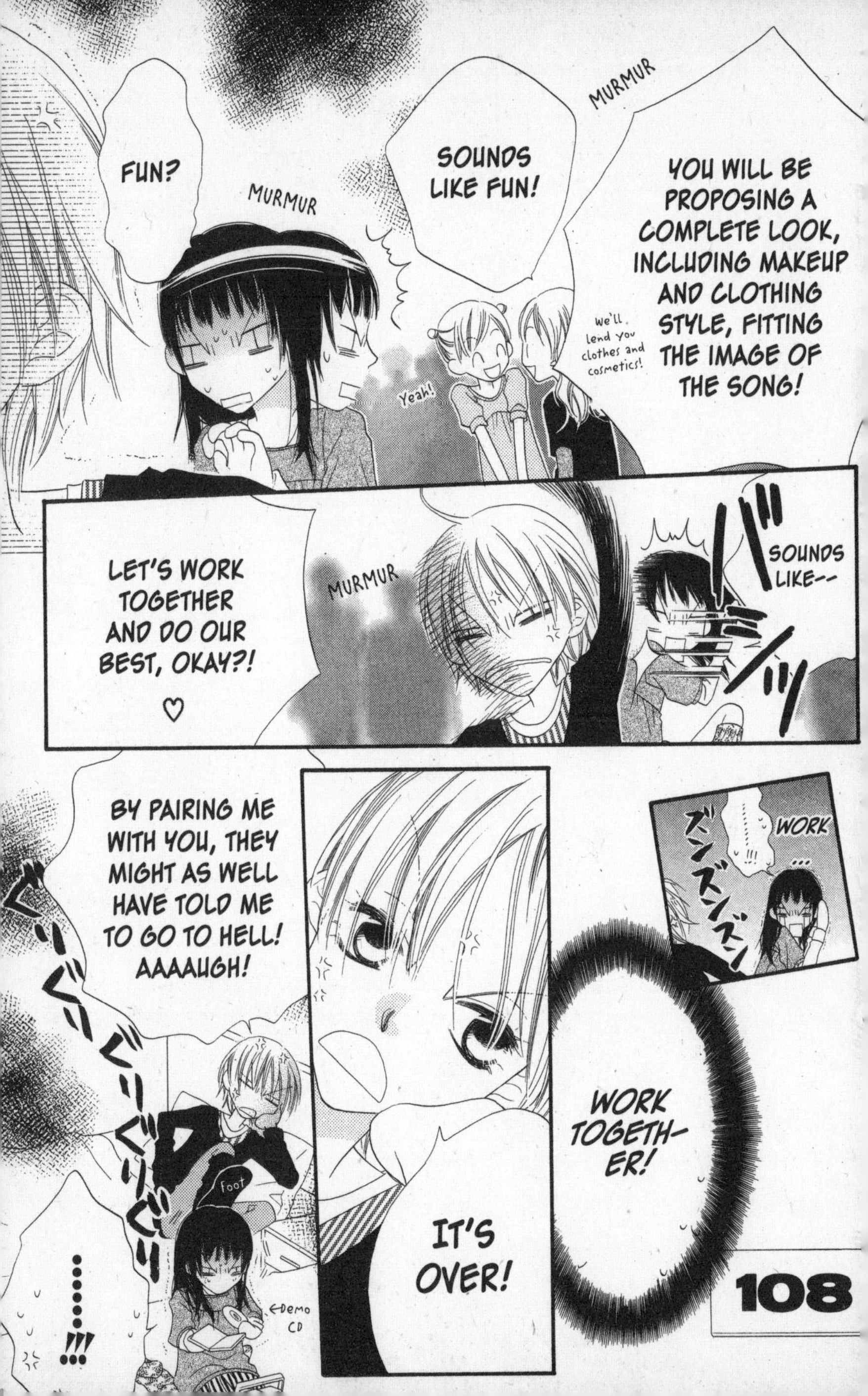
YOU WILL BE PROPOSING A COMPLETE LOOK, INCLUDING MAKEUP AND CLOTHING STYLE, FITTING THE IMAGE OF THE SONG!
We'll lend you clothes and cosmetics!
MURMUR
SOUNDS LIKE FUN!
Yeah!
MURMUR
FUN?
SOUNDS LIKE--
MURMUR
LET'S WORK TOGETHER AND DO OUR BEST, OKAY?! ♡
WORK...
!!!
WORK TOGETHER!
IT'S OVER!
BY PAIRING ME WITH YOU, THEY MIGHT AS WELL HAVE TOLD ME TO GO TO HELL! AAAAUGH!
Foot
←Demo CD
......!!!

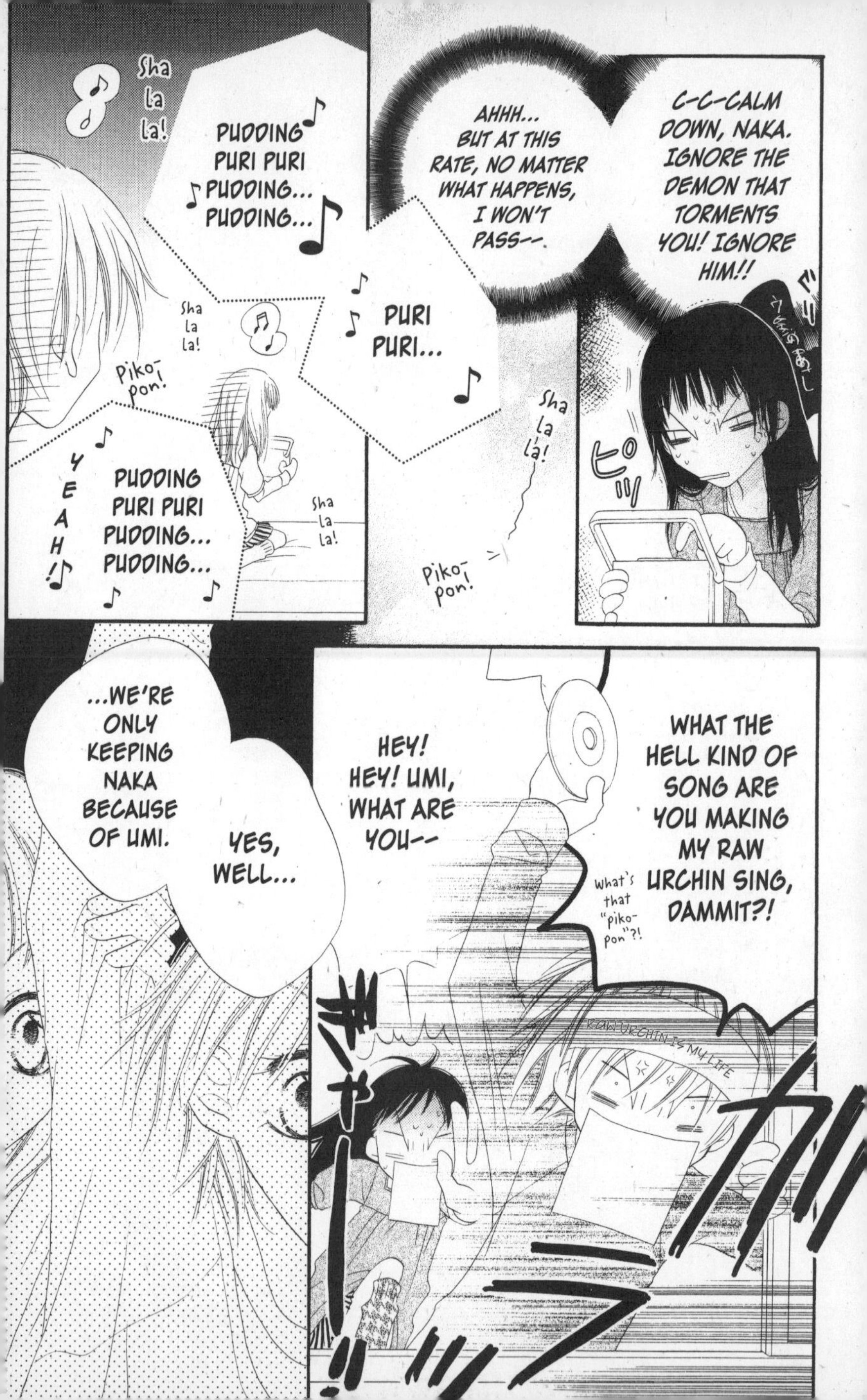
C-C-CALM DOWN, NAKA. IGNORE THE DEMON THAT TORMENTS YOU! IGNORE HIM!!
AHHH... BUT AT THIS RATE, NO MATTER WHAT HAPPENS, I WON'T PASS--.
Sha la la!
Piko-pon!
Sha la la!
PUDDING PURI PURI PUDDING... PUDDING...
PURI PURI...
Sha la la!
Piko-pon!
PUDDING PURI PURI PUDDING... PUDDING...
Sha la la!
YEAH!
WHAT THE HELL KIND OF SONG ARE YOU MAKING MY RAW URCHIN SING, DAMMIT?!
What's that "piko-pon"?!
HEY! HEY! UMI, WHAT ARE YOU--
RAW URCHIN IS MY LIFE
YES, WELL...
...WE'RE ONLY KEEPING NAKA BECAUSE OF UMI.

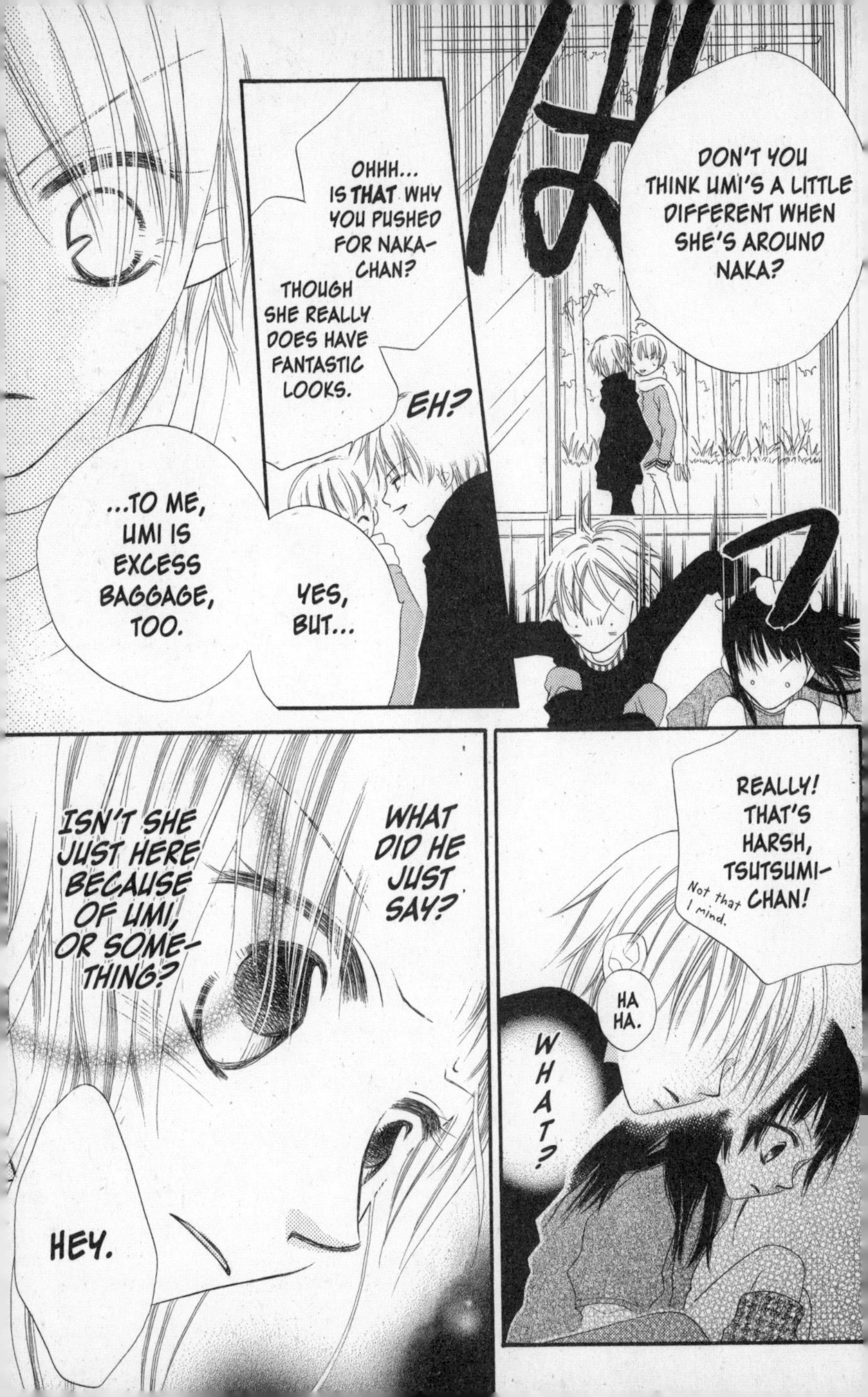
DON'T YOU THINK UMI'S A LITTLE DIFFERENT WHEN SHE'S AROUND NAKA?
OHHH... IS THAT WHY YOU PUSHED FOR NAKA-CHAN?
THOUGH SHE REALLY DOES HAVE FANTASTIC LOOKS.
EH?
YES, BUT...
...TO ME, UMI IS EXCESS BAGGAGE, TOO.
REALLY! THAT'S HARSH, TSUTSUMI-CHAN!
Not that I mind.
HA HA.
WHAT?
WHAT DID HE JUST SAY?
ISN'T SHE JUST HERE BECAUSE OF UMI, OR SOMETHING?
HEY.

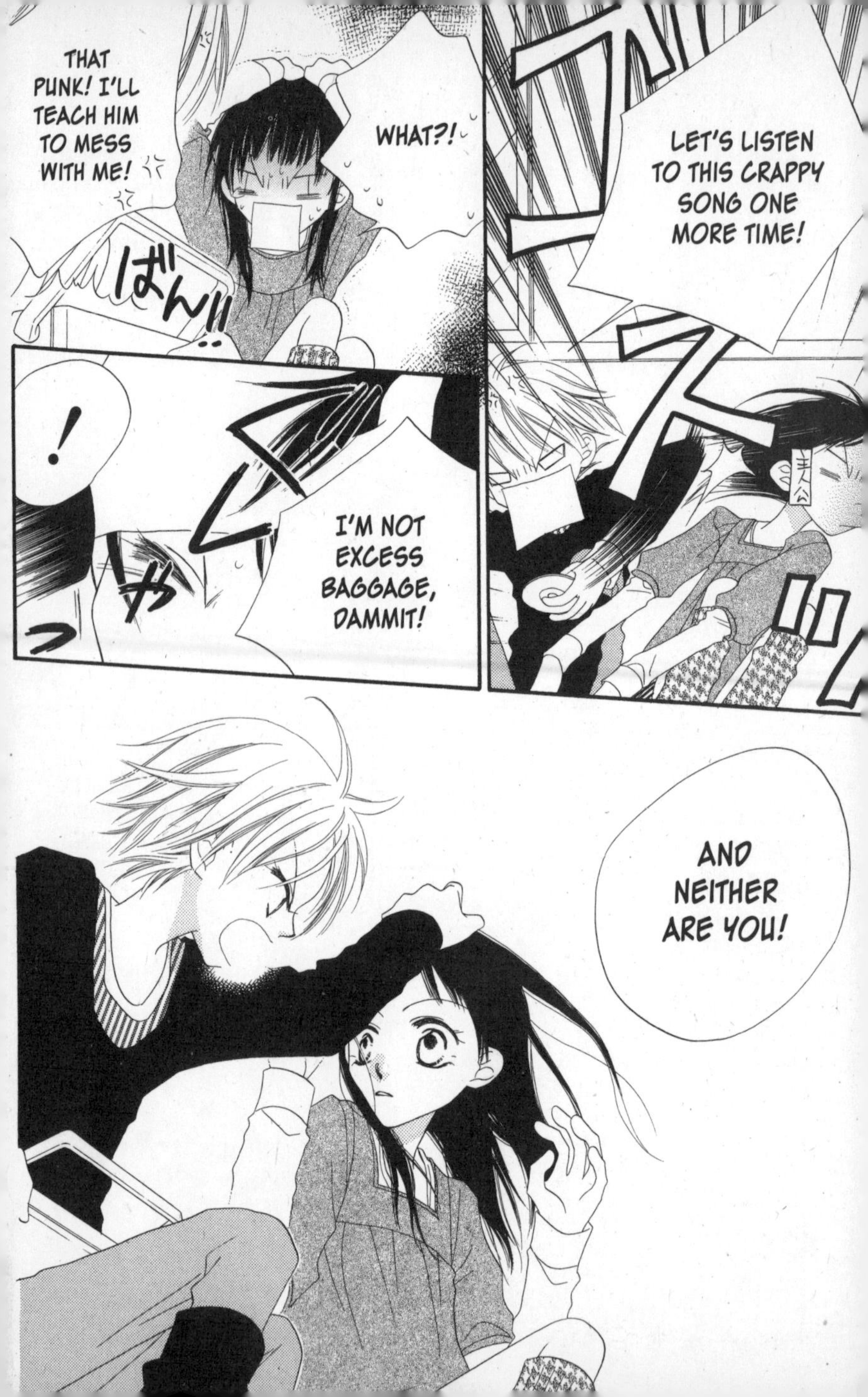
LET'S LISTEN TO THIS CRAPPY SONG ONE MORE TIME!
THAT PUNK! I'LL TEACH HIM TO MESS WITH ME!
WHAT?!
ばん!!
!
I'M NOT EXCESS BAGGAGE, DAMMIT!
AND NEITHER ARE YOU!

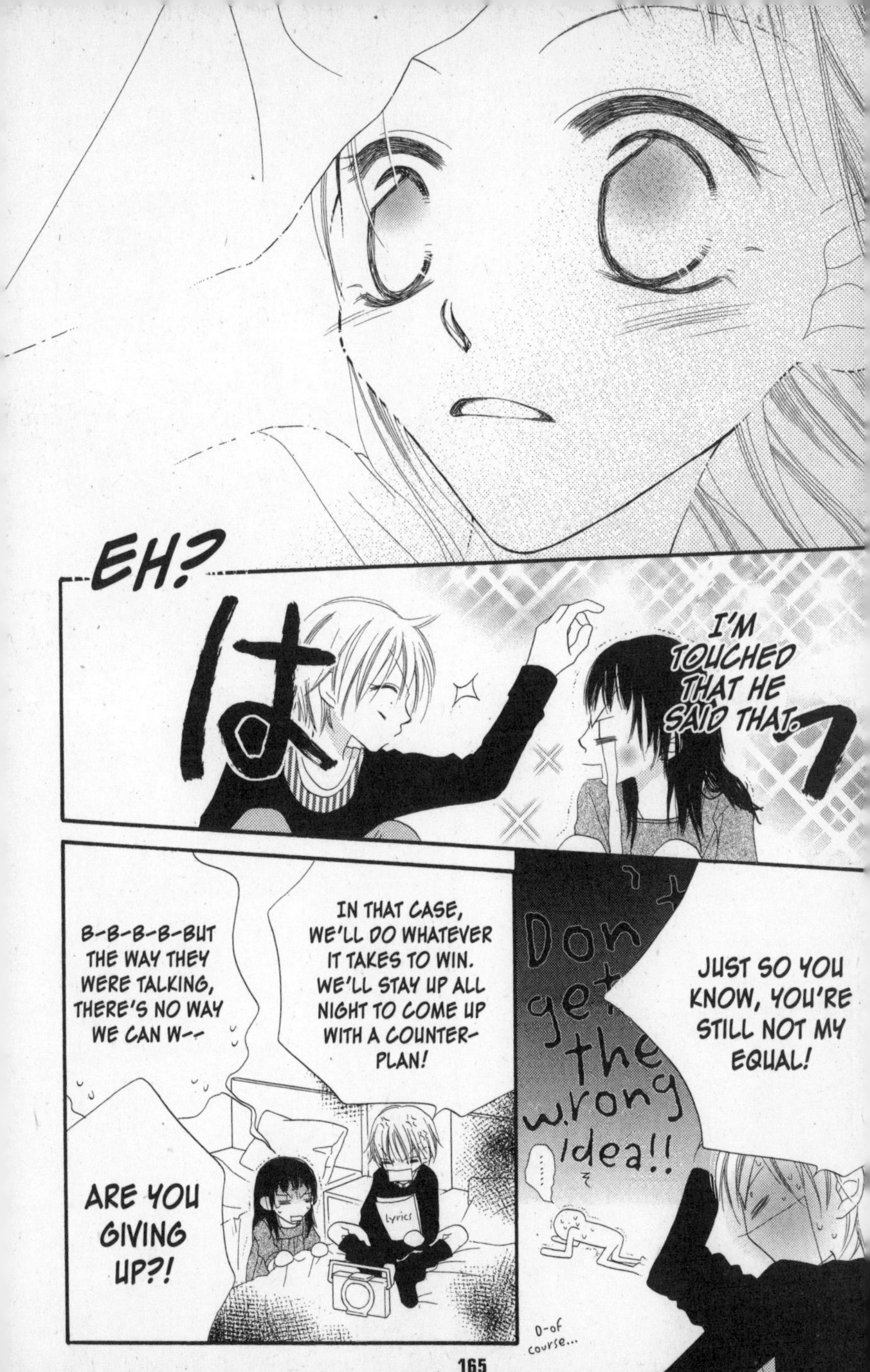
EH?
は
I'M TOUCHED THAT HE SAID THAT.
Don get the wrong idea!!
JUST SO YOU KNOW, YOU'RE STILL NOT MY EQUAL!
......
D-of course...
IN THAT CASE, WE'LL DO WHATEVER IT TAKES TO WIN. WE'LL STAY UP ALL NIGHT TO COME UP WITH A COUNTER-PLAN!
B-B-B-B-BUT THE WAY THEY WERE TALKING, THERE'S NO WAY WE CAN W--
ARE YOU GIVING UP?!
Lyrics

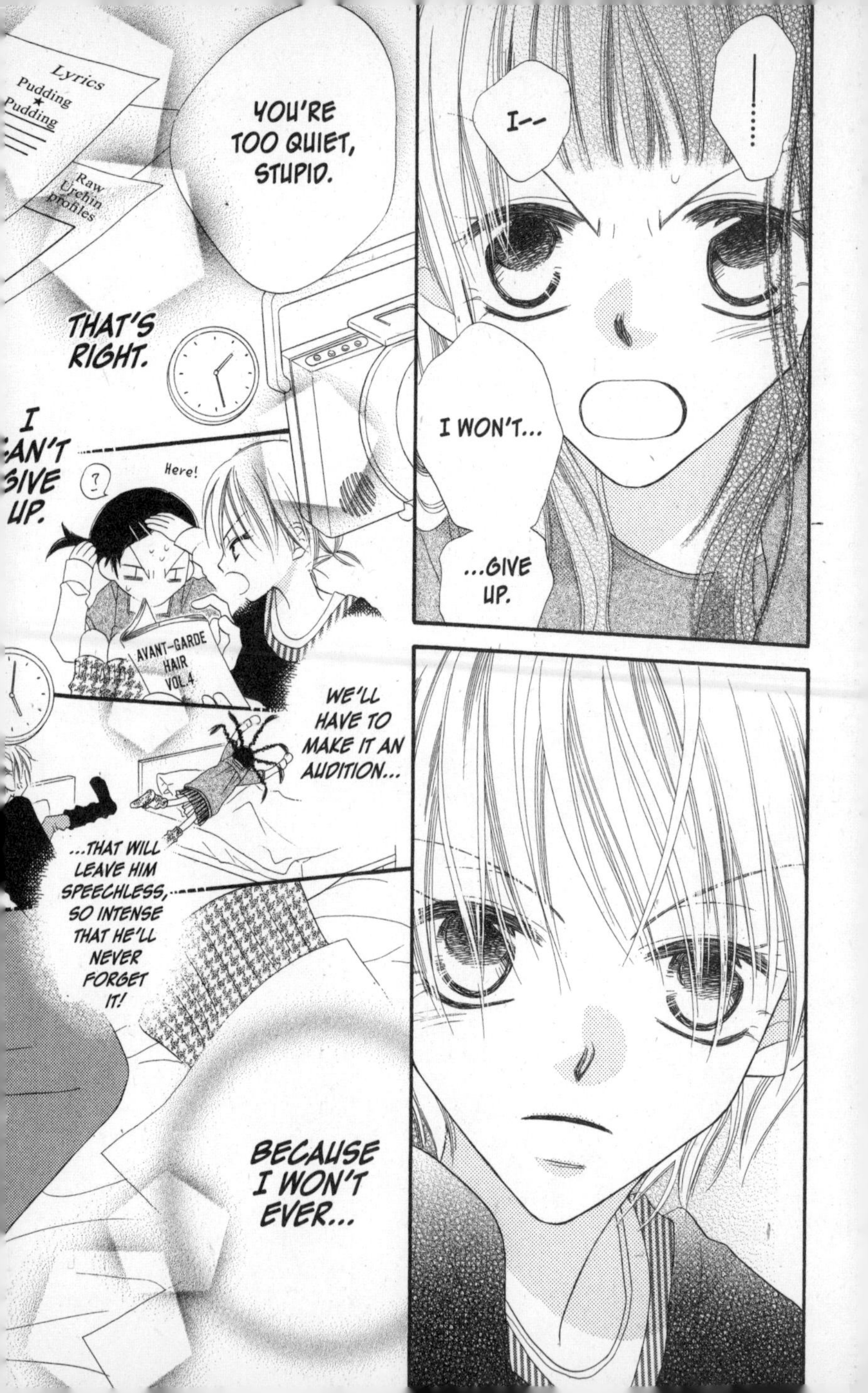
!......
I--
I WON'T...
...GIVE UP.
Lyrics
Pudding★Pudding
Raw Urchin profiles
YOU'RE TOO QUIET, STUPID.
THAT'S RIGHT.
I CAN'T GIVE UP.
Here!
?
AVANT-GARDE HAIR VOL.4
WE'LL HAVE TO MAKE IT AN AUDITION...
...THAT WILL LEAVE HIM SPEECHLESS, SO INTENSE THAT HE'LL NEVER FORGET IT!
BECAUSE I WON'T EVER...

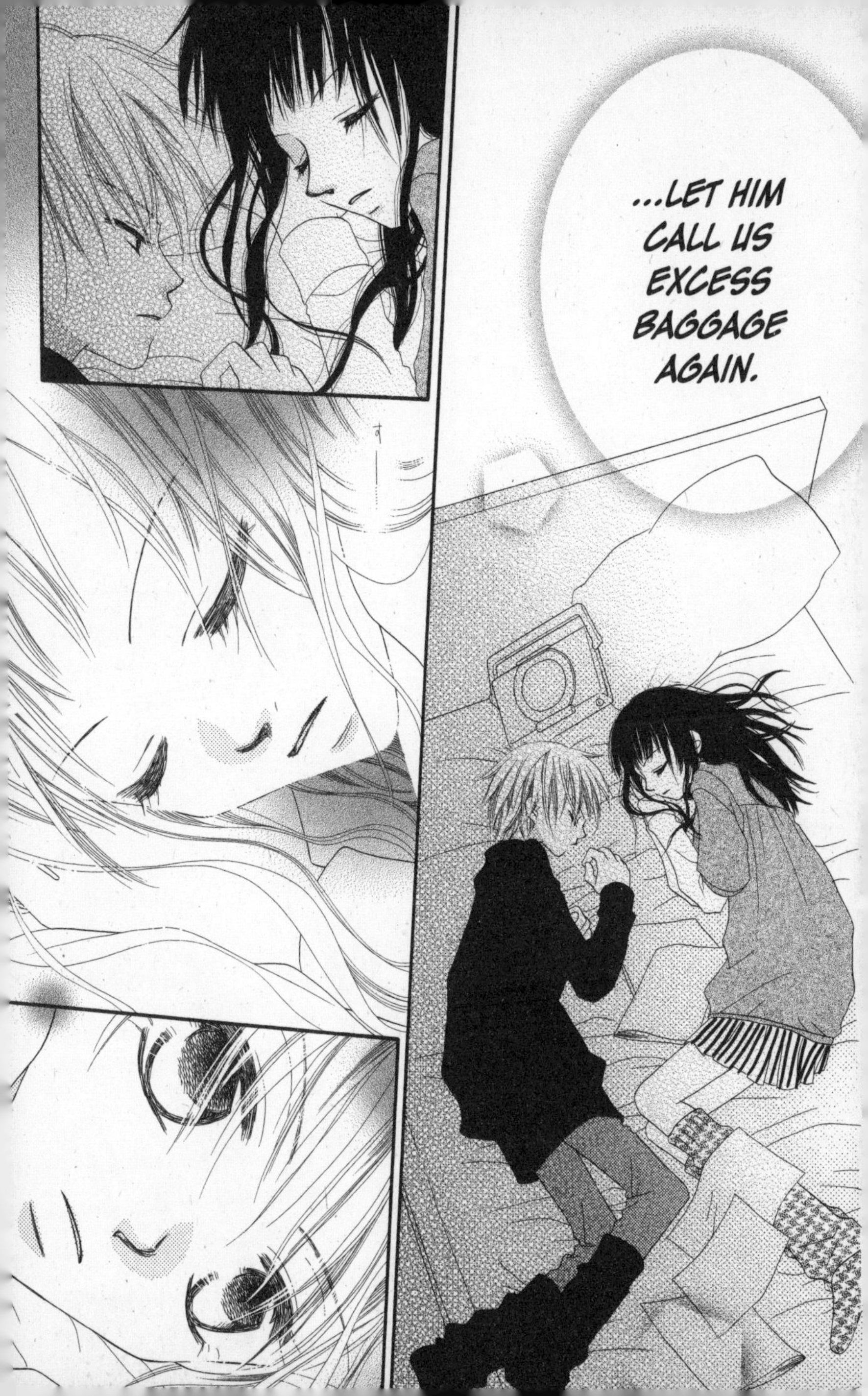
...LET HIM CALL US EXCESS BAGGAGE AGAIN.

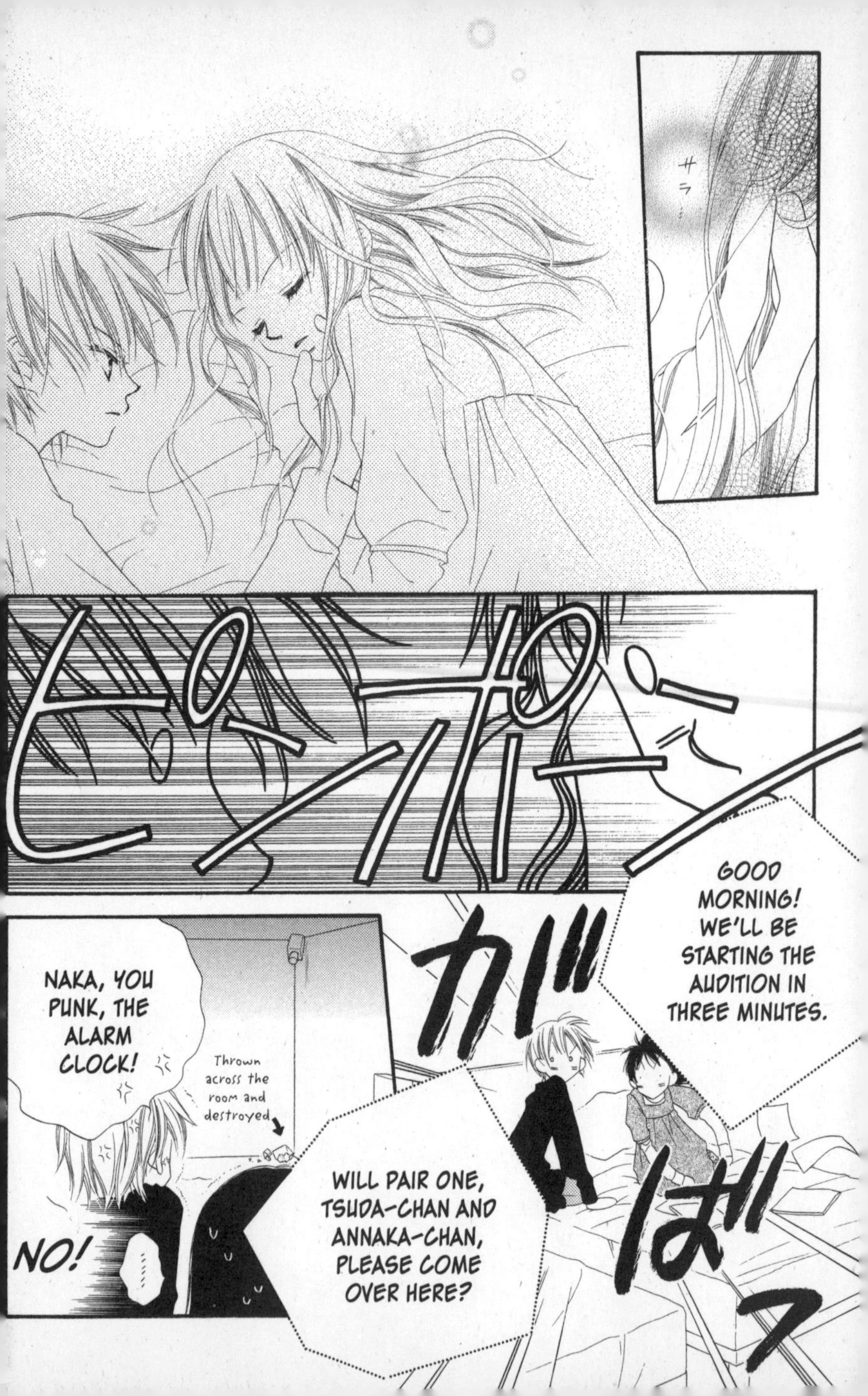
サラ…
ピンポーン
GOOD MORNING! WE'LL BE STARTING THE AUDITION IN THREE MINUTES.
WILL PAIR ONE, TSUDA-CHAN AND ANNAKA-CHAN, PLEASE COME OVER HERE?
ガバ
ばっ
NAKA, YOU PUNK, THE ALARM CLOCK!
Thrown across the room and destroyed
NO!
……

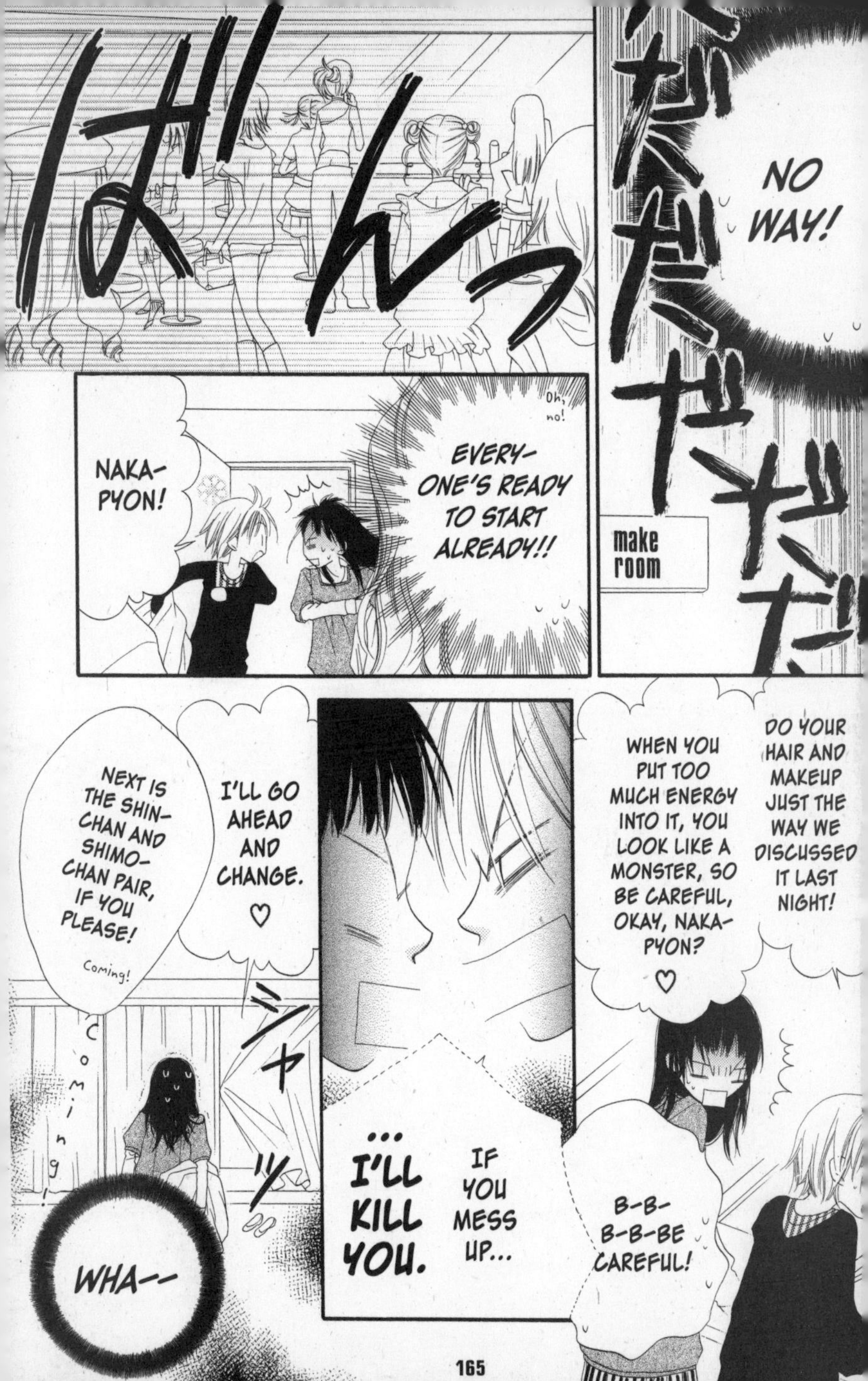

NO WAY!
make room
ぱんっ
Oh, no!
EVERY-ONE'S READY TO START ALREADY!!
NAKA-PYON!
DO YOUR HAIR AND MAKEUP JUST THE WAY WE DISCUSSED IT LAST NIGHT!
WHEN YOU PUT TOO MUCH ENERGY INTO IT, YOU LOOK LIKE A MONSTER, SO BE CAREFUL, OKAY, NAKA-PYON? ♡
B-B-B-B-BE CAREFUL!
IF YOU MESS UP...
... I'LL KILL YOU.
I'LL GO AHEAD AND CHANGE. ♡
シャッ
NEXT IS THE SHIN-CHAN AND SHIMO-CHAN PAIR, IF YOU PLEASE!
Coming!
Coming!
WHA--

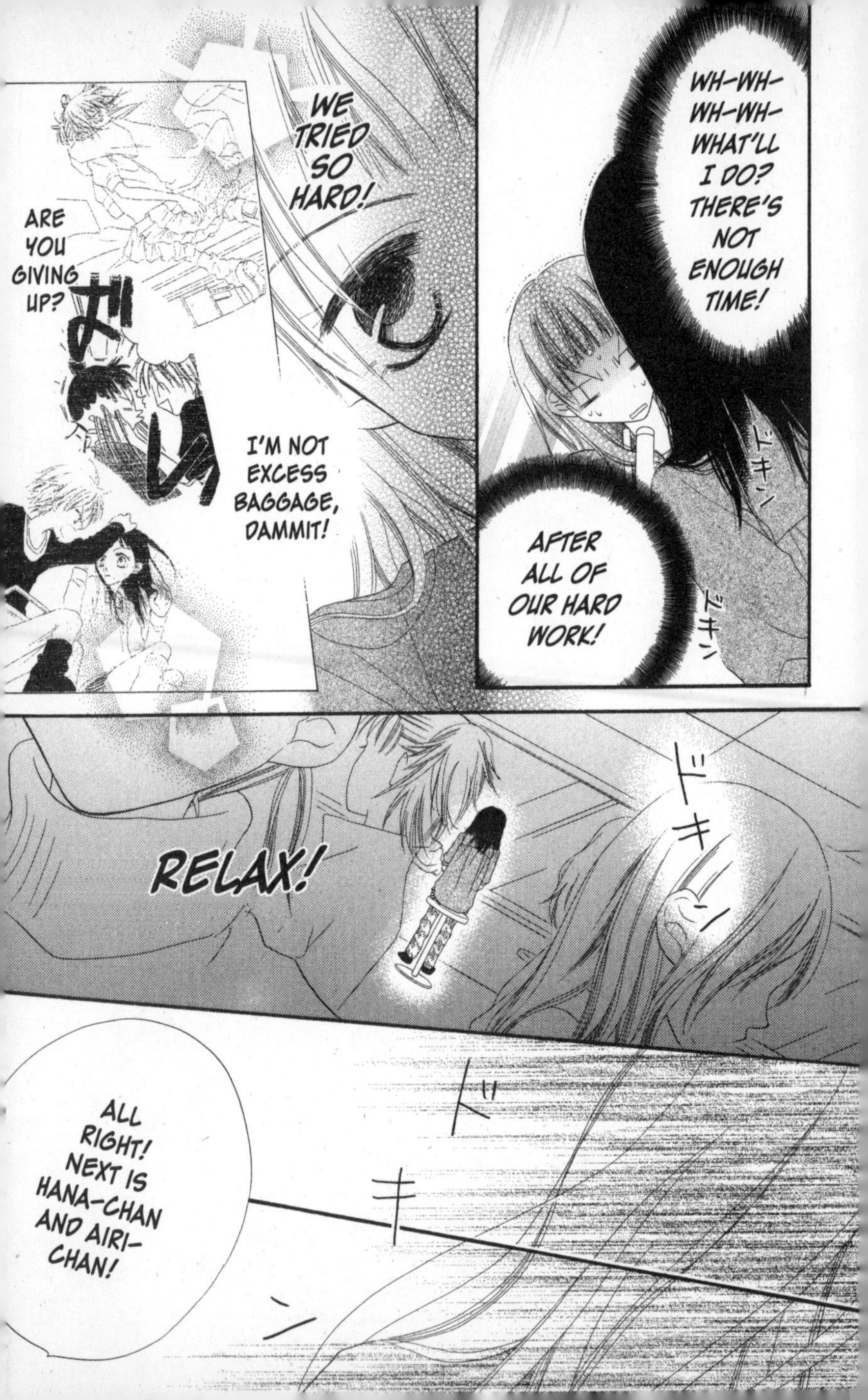
WH-WH-WH-WH-WHAT'LL I DO? THERE'S NOT ENOUGH TIME!
AFTER ALL OF OUR HARD WORK!
ドキン
ドキン
WE TRIED SO HARD!
I'M NOT EXCESS BAGGAGE, DAMMIT!
ARE YOU GIVING UP?
おい
ドキン
RELAX!
ドキン
ALL RIGHT! NEXT IS HANA-CHAN AND AIRI-CHAN!

I'M SORRY I'M LATE. I'M NUMBER 19, NAKA.

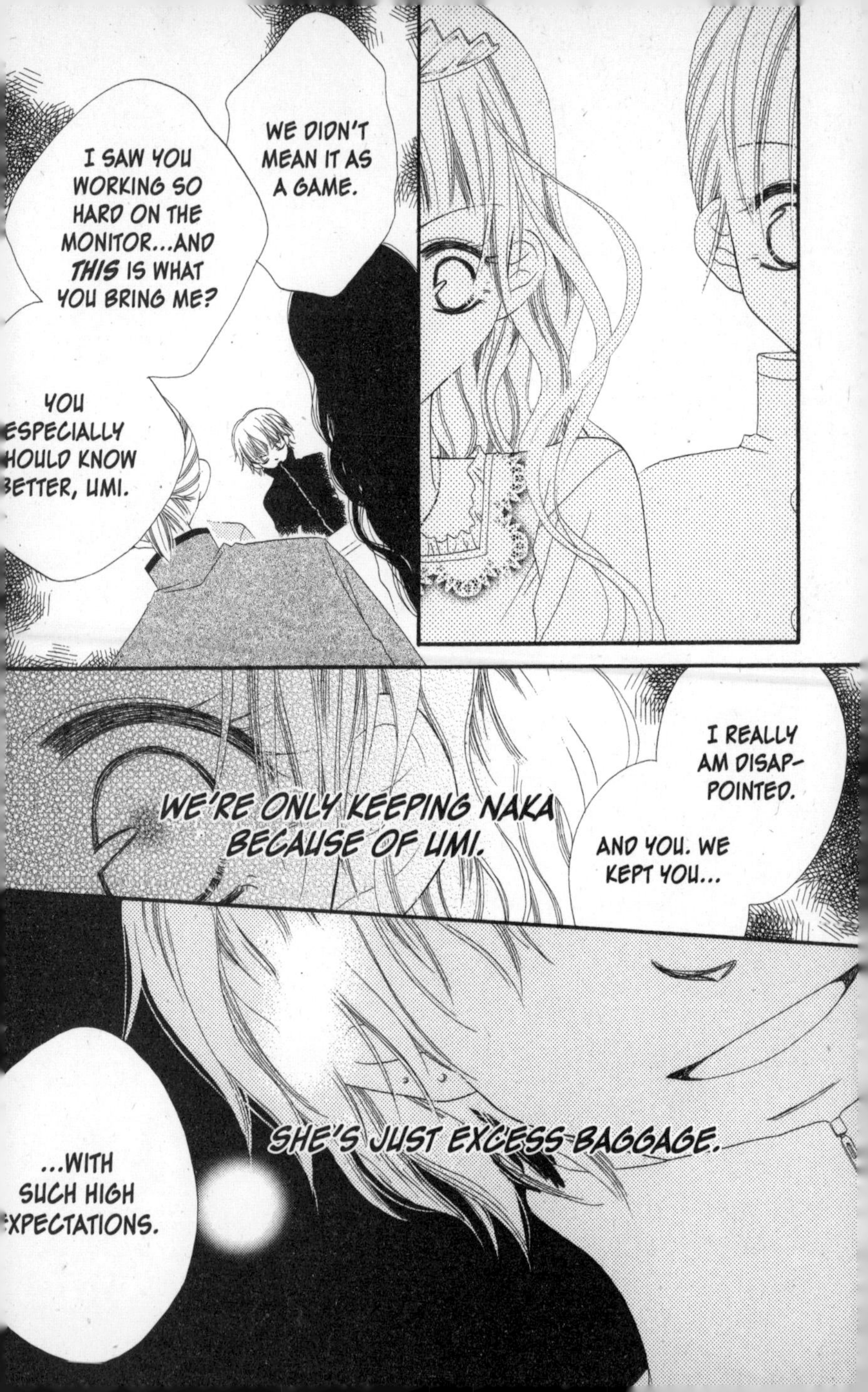
WE DIDN'T MEAN IT AS A GAME.
I SAW YOU WORKING SO HARD ON THE MONITOR...AND *THIS* IS WHAT YOU BRING ME?
YOU ESPECIALLY SHOULD KNOW BETTER, UMI.
I REALLY AM DISAPPOINTED.
AND YOU. WE KEPT YOU...
WE'RE ONLY KEEPING NAKA BECAUSE OF UMI.
...WITH SUCH HIGH EXPECTATIONS.
SHE'S JUST EXCESS BAGGAGE.

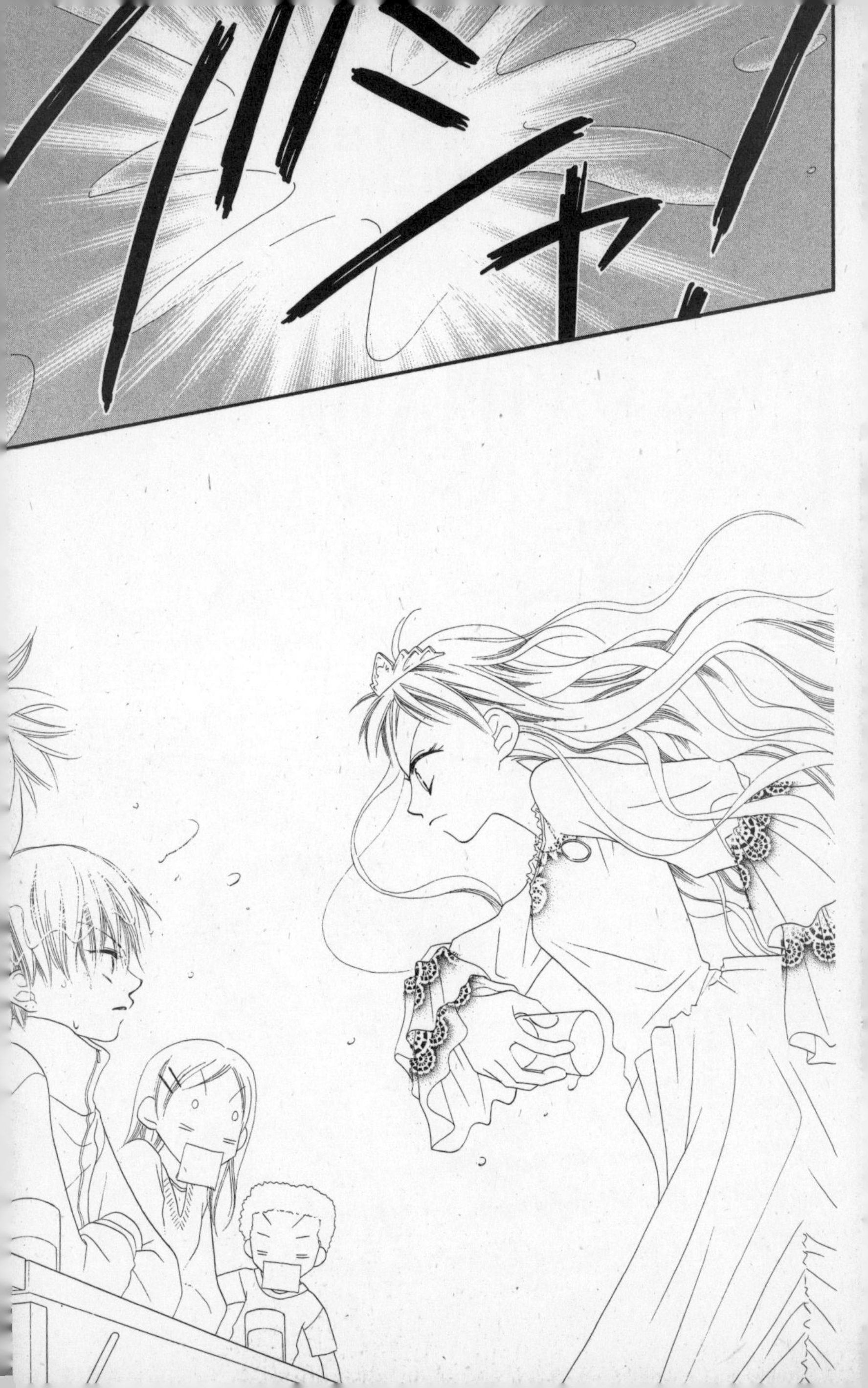

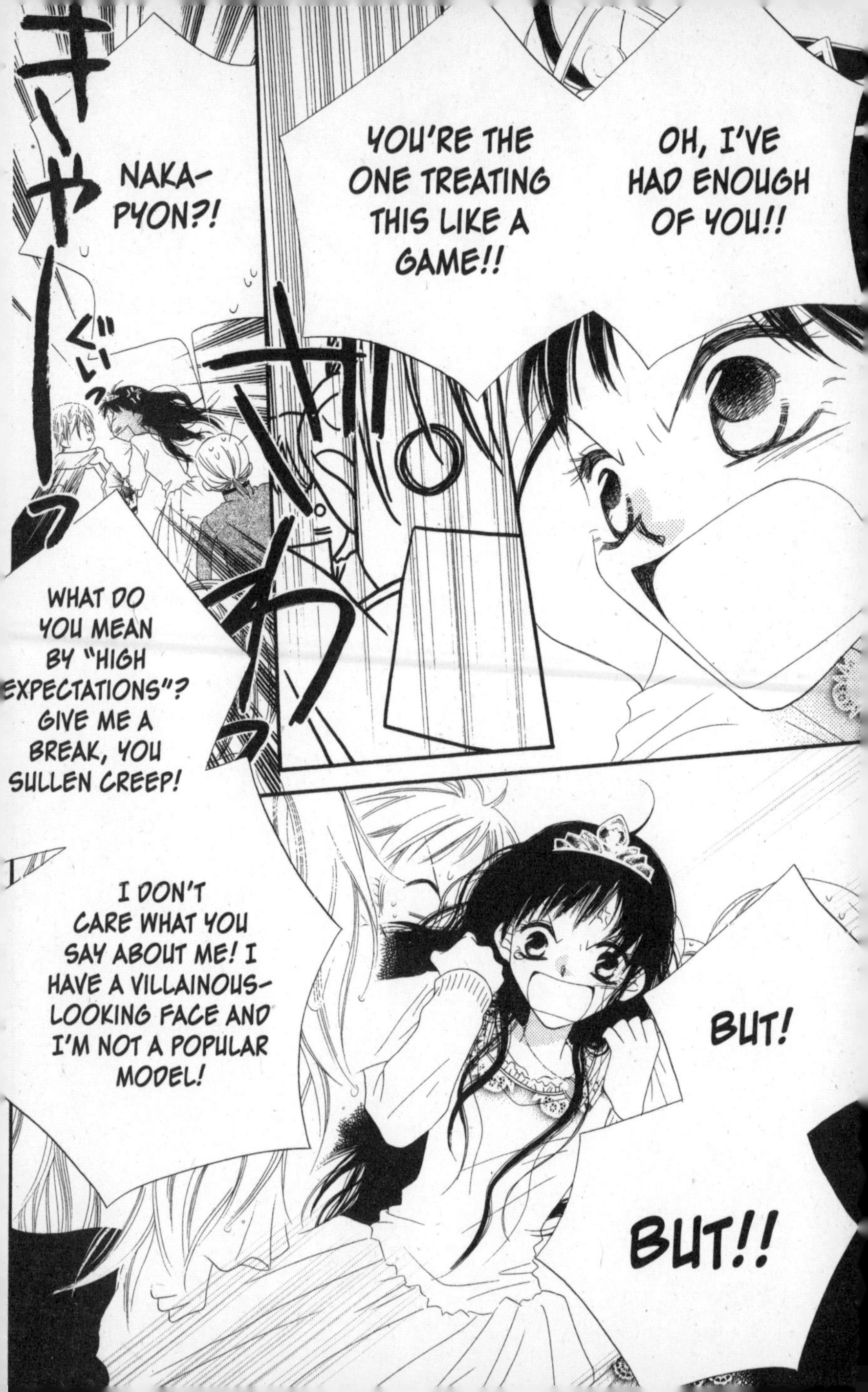
OH, I'VE HAD ENOUGH OF YOU!!
YOU'RE THE ONE TREATING THIS LIKE A GAME!!
NAKA-PYON?!
WHAT DO YOU MEAN BY "HIGH EXPECTATIONS"? GIVE ME A BREAK, YOU SULLEN CREEP!
I DON'T CARE WHAT YOU SAY ABOUT ME! I HAVE A VILLAINOUS-LOOKING FACE AND I'M NOT A POPULAR MODEL!
BUT!
BUT!!

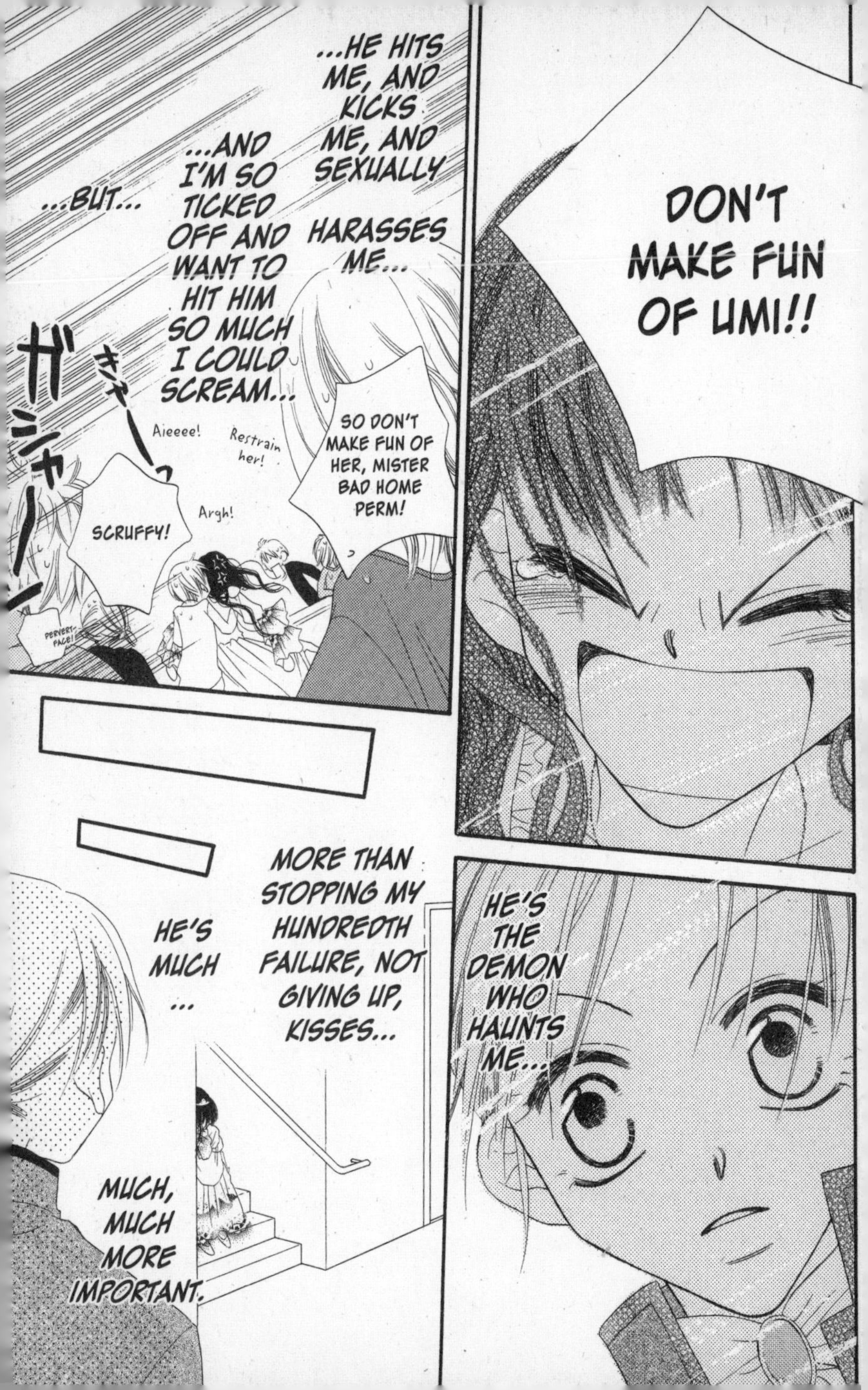
DON'T MAKE FUN OF UMI!!
...HE HITS ME, AND KICKS ME, AND SEXUALLY HARASSES ME...
...AND I'M SO TICKED OFF AND WANT TO HIT HIM SO MUCH I COULD SCREAM...
...BUT...
SO DON'T MAKE FUN OF HER, MISTER BAD HOME PERM!
Restrain her!
Aieeee!
キャー
ガシャーン
Argh!
SCRUFFY!
PERVERT-FACE!
HE'S THE DEMON WHO HAUNTS ME...
MORE THAN STOPPING MY HUNDREDTH FAILURE, NOT GIVING UP, KISSES...
HE'S MUCH ...
MUCH, MUCH MORE IMPORTANT.

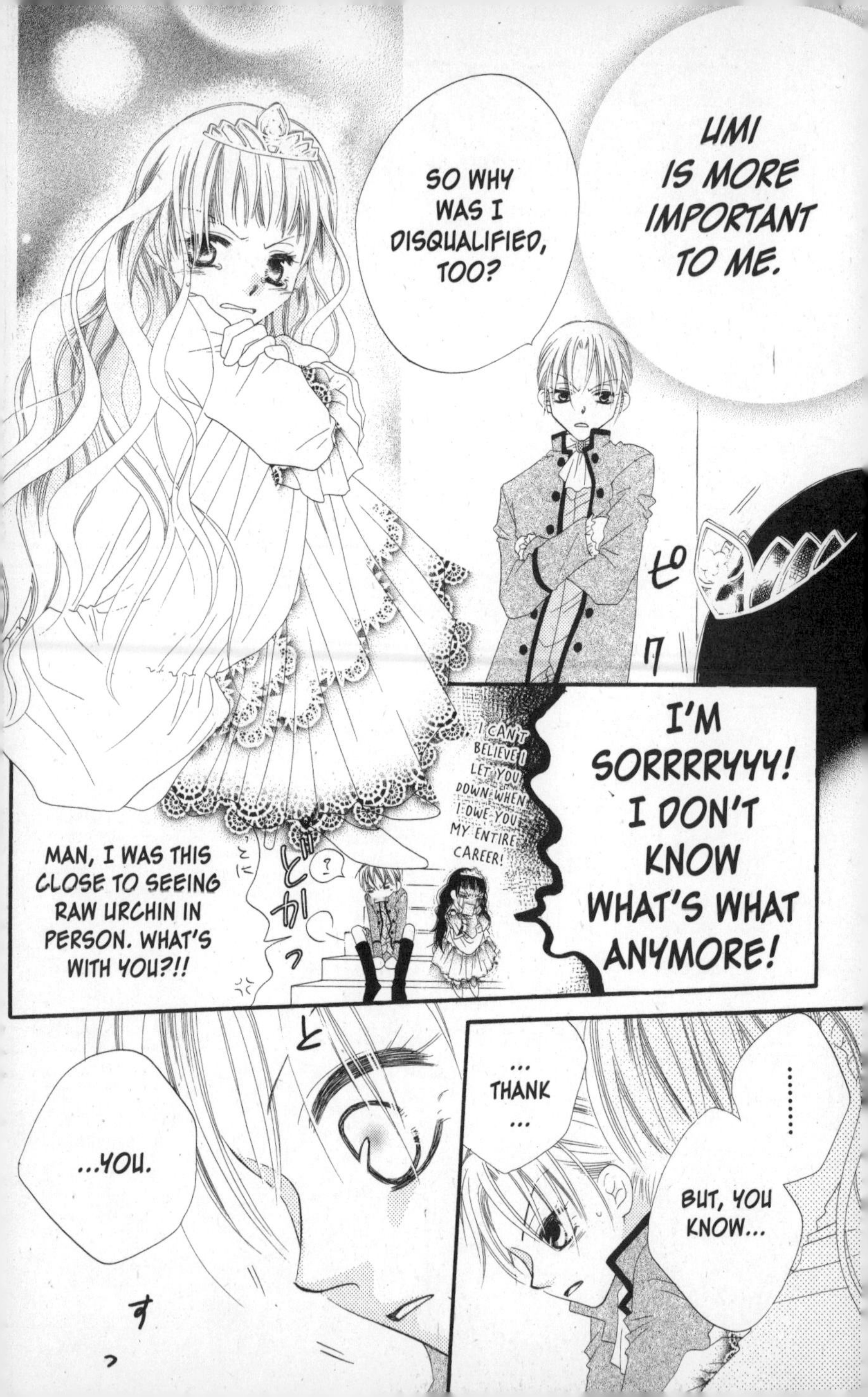
UMI IS MORE IMPORTANT TO ME.
SO WHY WAS I DISQUALIFIED, TOO?
ピク
I'M SORRRRYYY! I DON'T KNOW WHAT'S WHAT ANYMORE!
I CAN'T BELIEVE I LET YOU DOWN WHEN I OWE YOU MY ENTIRE CAREER!
?
どかっ
MAN, I WAS THIS CLOSE TO SEEING RAW URCHIN IN PERSON. WHAT'S WITH YOU?!!
......
BUT, YOU KNOW...
...THANK...
と
...YOU.
すっ

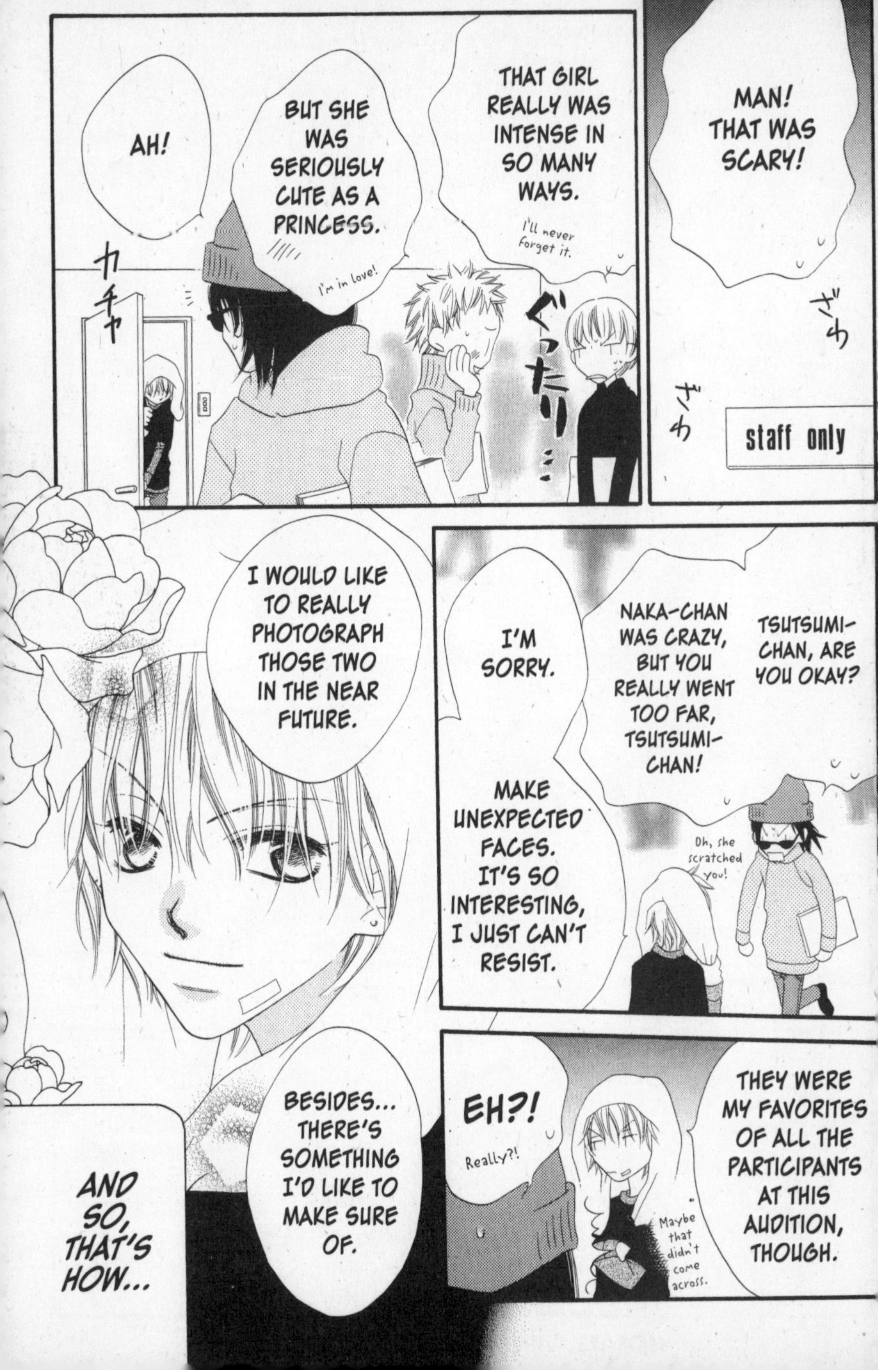
MAN! THAT WAS SCARY!
ざわ
ざわ
staff only
THAT GIRL REALLY WAS INTENSE IN SO MANY WAYS.
I'll never forget it.
ぐったり…
BUT SHE WAS SERIOUSLY CUTE AS A PRINCESS.
I'm in love!
AH!
カチャ
TSUTSUMI-CHAN, ARE YOU OKAY?
NAKA-CHAN WAS CRAZY, BUT YOU REALLY WENT TOO FAR, TSUTSUMI-CHAN!
I'M SORRY.
MAKE UNEXPECTED FACES. IT'S SO INTERESTING, I JUST CAN'T RESIST.
Oh, she scratched you!
THEY WERE MY FAVORITES OF ALL THE PARTICIPANTS AT THIS AUDITION, THOUGH.
EH?!
Really?!
Maybe that didn't come across.
I WOULD LIKE TO REALLY PHOTOGRAPH THOSE TWO IN THE NEAR FUTURE.
BESIDES... THERE'S SOMETHING I'D LIKE TO MAKE SURE OF.
AND SO, THAT'S HOW...

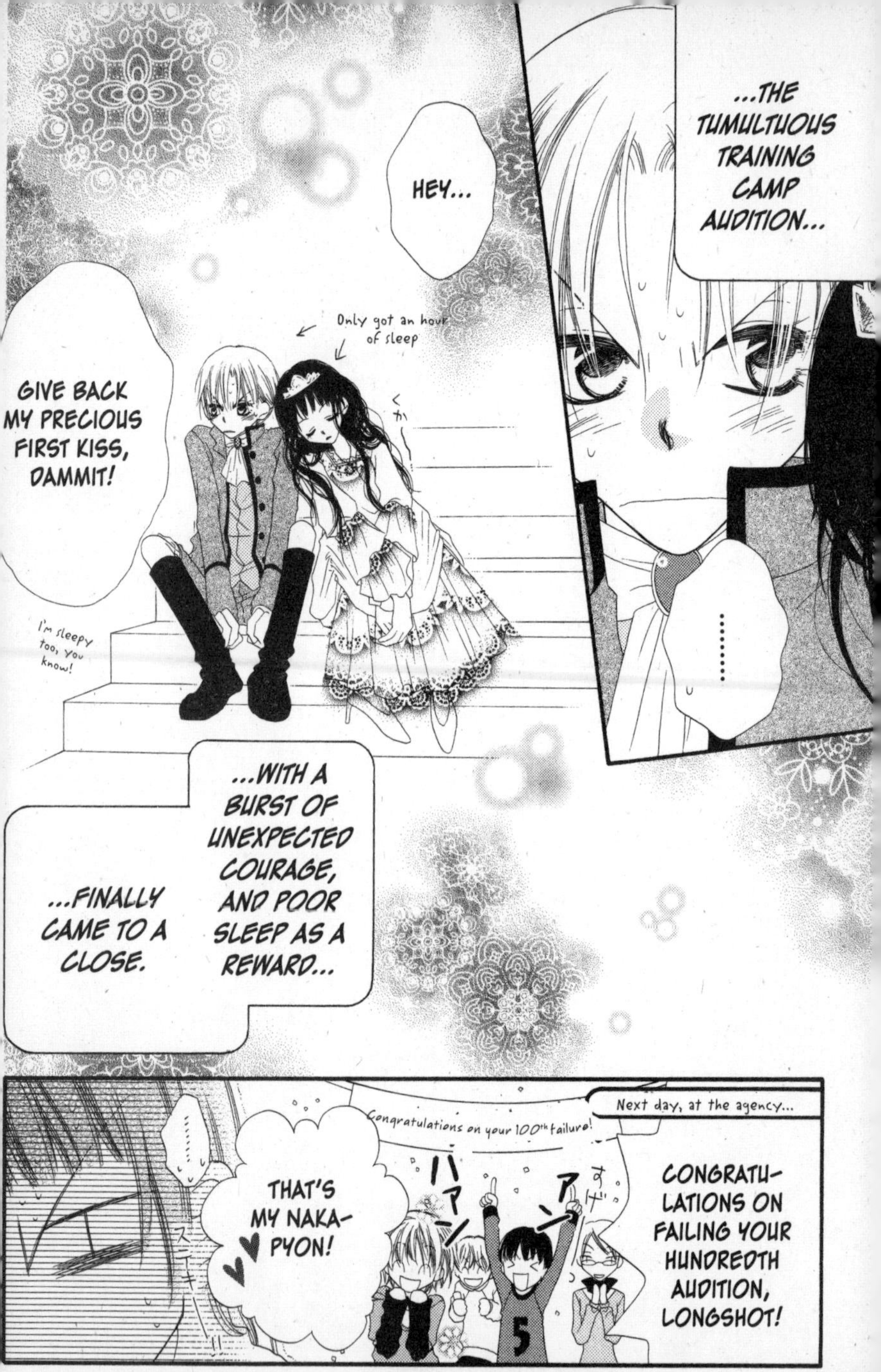
...THE TUMULTUOUS TRAINING CAMP AUDITION...
......
HEY...
GIVE BACK MY PRECIOUS FIRST KISS, DAMMIT!
Only got an hour of sleep
I'm sleepy too, you know!
...WITH A BURST OF UNEXPECTED COURAGE, AND POOR SLEEP AS A REWARD...
...FINALLY CAME TO A CLOSE.
Next day, at the agency...
CONGRATULATIONS ON FAILING YOUR HUNDREDTH AUDITION, LONGSHOT!
Congratulations on your 100th failure!
THAT'S MY NAKA-PYON!
......

NOSATSU JUNKIE, SESSION 5 / END

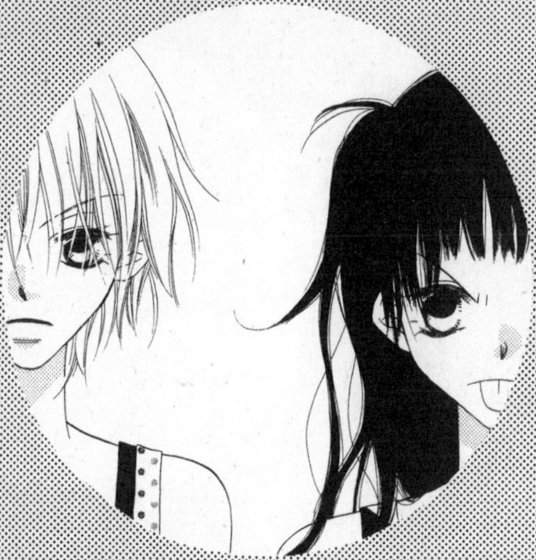

BONUS JUNKIE VOL.1

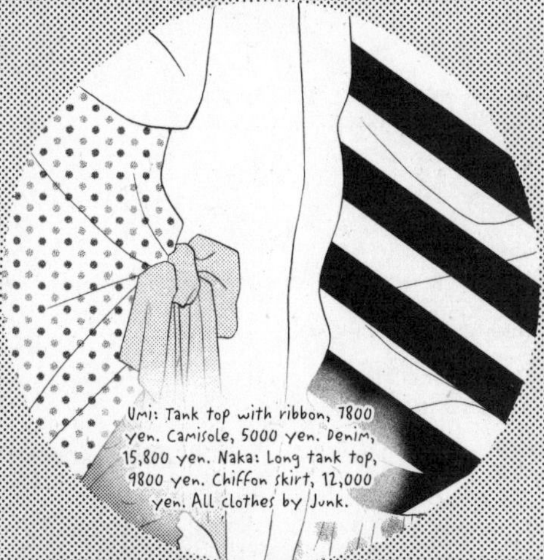
Umi: Tank top with ribbon, 7800 yen. Camisole, 5000 yen. Denim, 15,800 yen. Naka: Long tank top, 9800 yen. Chiffon skirt, 12,000 yen. All clothes by Junk.

BONUS JUNKIE

Session 1

This is a chapter that I'm attached to, where I regained my beginner's enthusiasm, emptied my head, and drew whatever I wanted, thinking, "Eh, maybe something like this." It was tough, but really fun. I got to draw lots and lots of clothes, models, photographs--all my favorite things! I loved it! Umi was more honest and open with Naka back then, wasn't he? Now that I think of it, we changed the title in a hurry after it was chosen to be serialized. I just remembered!

Session 2

I drew this chapter right after I heard that they wanted to continue the series, so I was insanely nervous. It was a much tougher battle than the first chapter, and up until the deadline, I was changing lines from this to that, and causing a lot of problems for my editor (sorry!). As for Yune-chan, she was more of a gal* in the "name" stage. It was really fun drawing Naka's crazy hairstyles and everyone's winter clothes. Umi really does harass Naka.

*"Gal" is Japanese slang for girls who wear outrageous clothes and makeup.

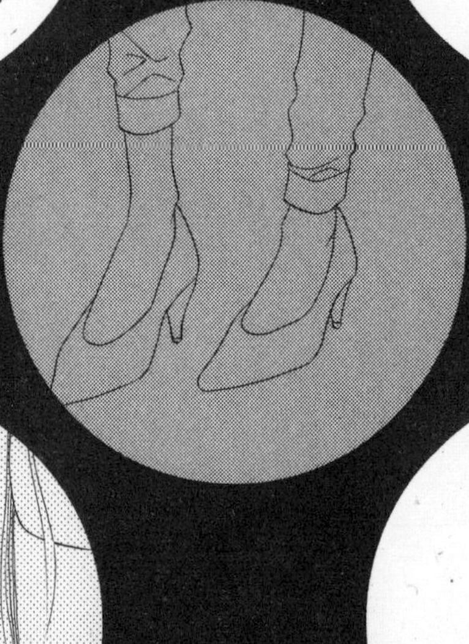

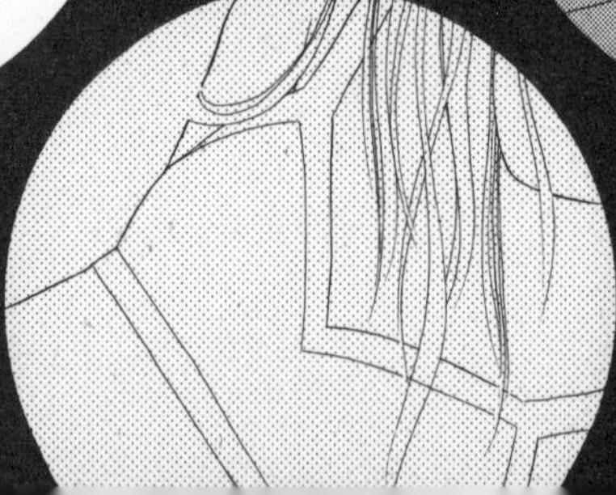

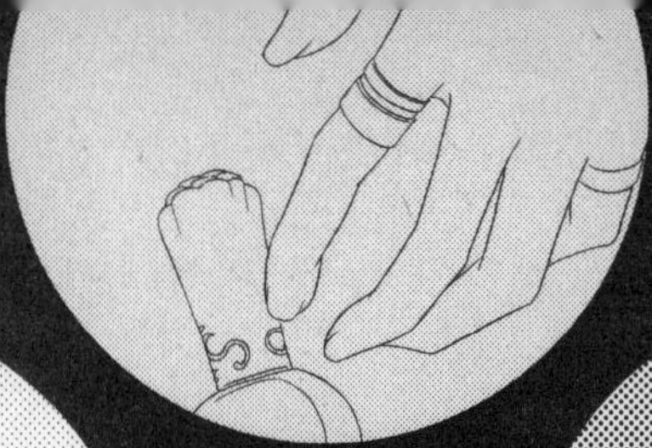

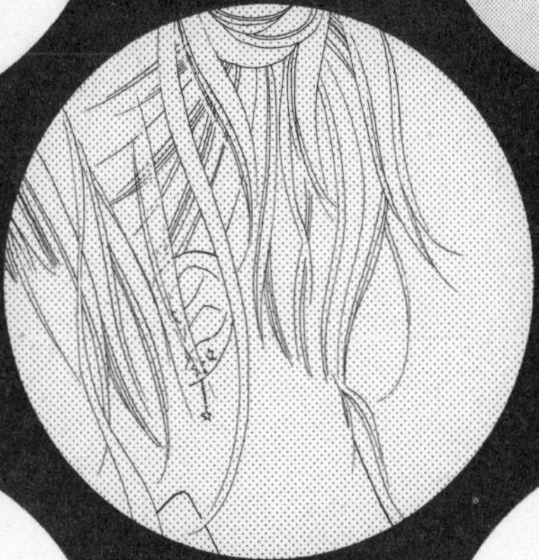

Sessions 3-5

My first story arc. When they asked me to do it, I was so happy, I cried like an idiot and was completely useless all day. Chapter three took a lot of time, but four and five weren't as much of a struggle because Tsutsumi-san made his first appearance in these chapters. Thanks to him, the story has now been moving quite easily! He's secretly my favorite character, though my editor doesn't understand (why?). This is a small thing, but...

...the "Raw Urchin" group that shows up in the story is based on the big family idol group, "Nama-Gaki." Just a little trivia tidbit. And the slight Lolita-ness in the cover picture for Chapter three, the princess, the prince--I got to do whatever I wanted on all of these, so they were all extremely fun. Oh yeah, it's mentioned early on (at least in my mind) that Tsutsumi-san is 17 years old--but because my drawing skills were a bit lacking, a lot of people were surprised to see in the next chapter that he's a high school student. But of course he's a high school student! He's 17!

BONUS JUNKIE

JUST WHAT SHOJO MANGA FANS CRAVE!

AFRO-SPLOSION!

PART 1

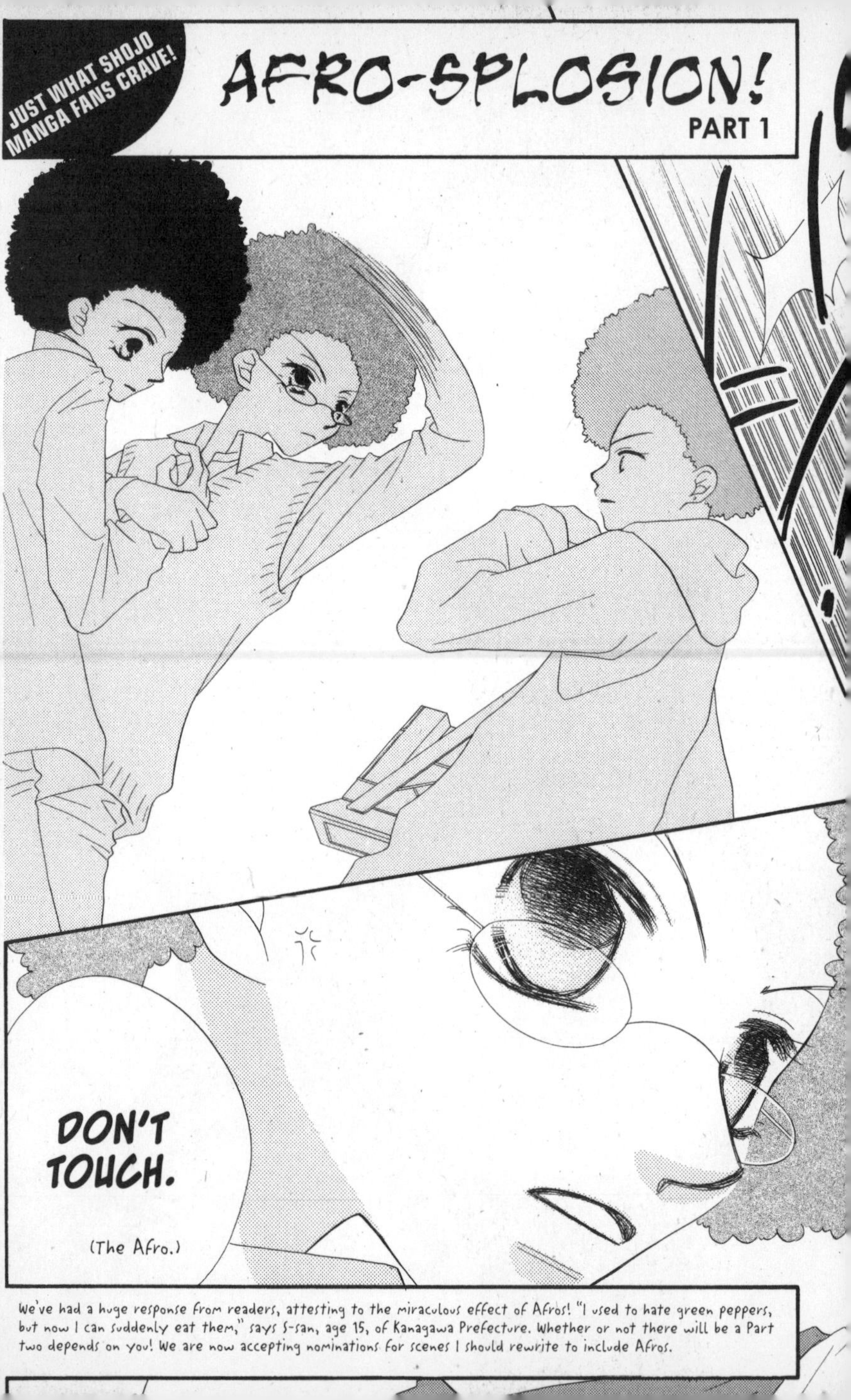
DON'T TOUCH.
(The Afro.)

We've had a huge response from readers, attesting to the miraculous effect of Afros! "I used to hate green peppers, but now I can suddenly eat them," says S-san, age 15, of Kanagawa Prefecture. Whether or not there will be a Part two depends on you! We are now accepting nominations for scenes I should rewrite to include Afros.

Er, aside from the page on
the right (was that okay?), this
is the end. Thank you very much for
staying with me this far. I was completely
nervous from start to finish, but I hope I was
able to convey even a little bit of how much
fun this was. Thanks to all of you, *Nosatsu* has
been published in book form. I truly, truly
thank you, very much! And I love you,
always. What with one thing and another,
I hope we can meet again in Volume 2.
See you later!

Ryoko Fukuyama

Special thanks to

Kyoko Inoue
Ayana Oguchi
Tsunami Minatsuki
Ui Hamure
Soyoko Igari
Hisamu Oto
Julietta Suzuki
Takumi Sugino

Book 1st Aobabai

Naoko Takeda
my friends
my family

and you

BONUS JUNKIE

BONUS JUNKIE / END

Next time in **NOSATSU JUNKIE**

Naka is pleasantly surprised to learn that she's landed another job...but not so pleasantly surprised to learn that Tsutsumi will be the photographer! Meanwhile, Ms. President notices that Umi is starting to look more and more manly, and warns him to be careful. Will everyone learn Umi's secret?

Find out in the next Nosatsu Junkie!

'TIL DEATH DO THEY START...
My Dead Girlfriend
Finney Bleak lives in a world of horror—literally. His family are ghosts, his classmates are monsters, and Finney is the most "normal" kid in school. Then along comes Jenny. Smart. Beautiful. And totally into Finney. Only problem is, she's kind of dead. As if romance wasn't awkward enough! Will Finney allow Death to stop him from being with his true love?
BY
ERIC WIGHT
THE "GHOST" ARTIST FOR
SETH COHEN ON THE O.C.
ROMANCE
T
TEEN AGE 13+
© Eric Wight and TOKYOPOP Inc.

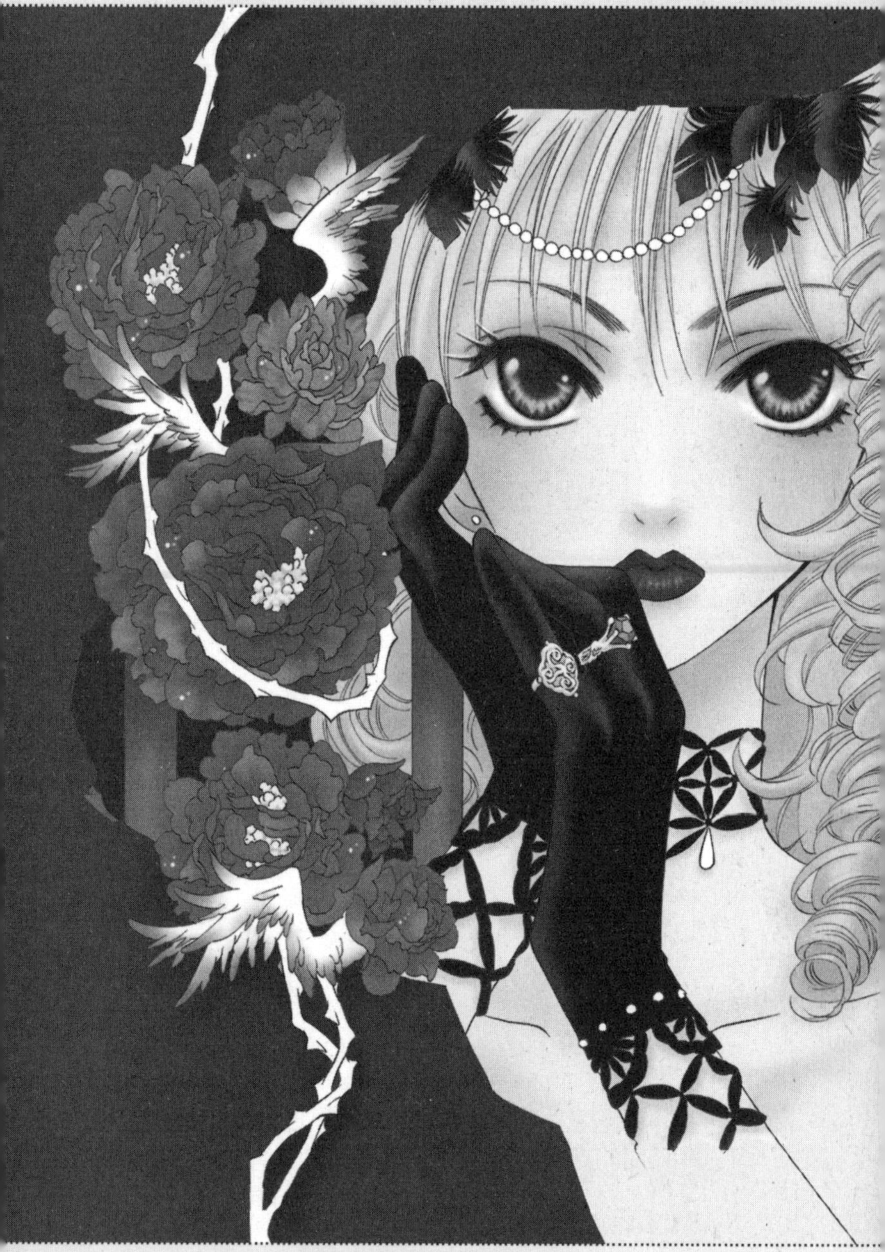

WWW.TOKYOPOP.COM

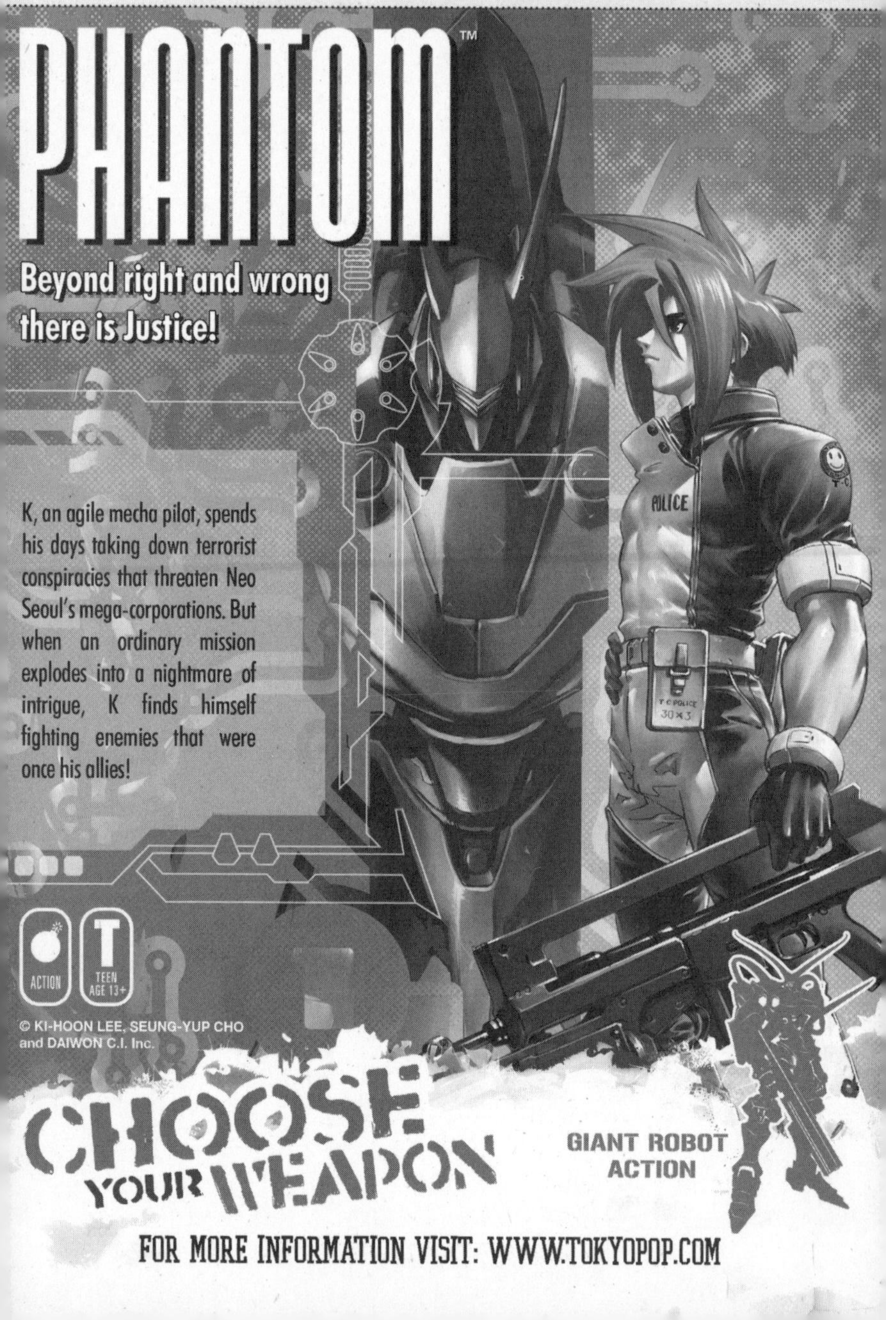
PHANTOM™
Beyond right and wrong there is Justice!
K, an agile mecha pilot, spends his days taking down terrorist conspiracies that threaten Neo Seoul's mega-corporations. But when an ordinary mission explodes into a nightmare of intrigue, K finds himself fighting enemies that were once his allies!
POLICE
ACTION
T
TEEN AGE 13+
© KI-HOON LEE, SEUNG-YUP CHO and DAIWON C.I. Inc.
CHOOSE YOUR WEAPON
GIANT ROBOT ACTION
FOR MORE INFORMATION VISIT: WWW.TOKYOPOP.COM

STOP!

This is the back of the book.
You wouldn't want to spoil a great ending!

This book is printed "manga-style," in the authentic Japanese right-to-left format. Since none of the artwork has been flipped or altered, readers get to experience the story just as the creator intended. You've been asking for it, so TOKYOPOP® delivered: authentic, hot-off-the-press, and far more fun!

DIRECTIONS

If this is your first time reading manga-style, here's a quick guide to help you understand how it works.

It's easy... just start in the top right panel and follow the numbers. Have fun, and look for more 100% authentic manga from TOKYOPOP®!

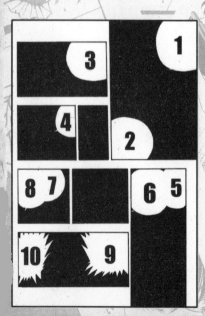